PLYMOUTH DISTRICT LIBRARY

Removed from
library collection

306.8743 R

Rebel moms : the
off-road map for the
off-road Mom /

33387004556736

Plymouth District Library
223 S. Main St.
Plymouth, MI 48170
Jan 2012

12/11

306.8743
R

12/11
SM

Rebellion Press.com
RP
Books For Rebels With A Cause

Rebel Moms

Rebel Moms

The Off-Road Map for the Off-Road Mom

Davina Rhine

iUniverse, Inc.
Bloomington

Additional copyline edit by Katy Krisak.
Rebellion Press logo designed by Juan Leon of Firelion Graphix.
This edition published by arrangement with Rebellion Press.

REBEL MOMS
THE OFF-ROAD MAP FOR THE OFF-ROAD MOM

Copyright © 2011 by Davina Rhine.

All rights reserved. No part of this book may be used or reproduced by any means, graphic, electronic, or mechanical, including photocopying, recording, taping or by any information storage retrieval system without the written permission of the publisher except in the case of brief quotations embodied in critical articles and reviews.

iUniverse books may be ordered through booksellers or by contacting:

iUniverse
1663 Liberty Drive
Bloomington, IN 47403
www.iuniverse.com
1-800-Authors (1-800-288-4677)

Because of the dynamic nature of the Internet, any web addresses or links contained in this book may have changed since publication and may no longer be valid. The views expressed in this work are solely those of the author and do not necessarily reflect the views of the publisher, and the publisher hereby disclaims any responsibility for them.

Any people depicted in stock imagery provided by Thinkstock are models, and such images are being used for illustrative purposes only.
Certain stock imagery © Thinkstock.

ISBN: 978-1-4620-2651-7 (sc)
ISBN: 978-1-4620-2653-1 (hc)
ISBN: 978-1-4620-2652-4 (ebk)

Printed in the United States of America

iUniverse rev. date: 11/15/2011

To the Mother-Woman-Hero's in my life:

For my own mom, Bertha Rhine, who stuck by us girls, even though she didn't have to; she was a married 60s mom, who was abandoned in a new state, Texas, with no family, battered and broke. She was left to raise three headstrong German-American girls in a violent, wild 'hood', all by herself. She (un)made it on minimum wage and a smile. Somehow we survived. I love you mom. Thank you.

For Sinead O' Connor whose bravery and music has helped save many young girls the world over, many times. With your *Universal Mother* album I knew that if you could do it, I could do it.

And for all the Rebel Moms in the world, who do what they do, each and every day!

To the Boys in my life:

For my partner, Jason Leon, who has helped me stay the course when all I really wanted to do was throw the damn book out the window and reclaim my life.

For my sweet baby Corben, my misfit and my muse.

Note to the Reader

The biographies of these amazing moms are told through my eyes with their consent. They have lived extraordinary lives and as such have extraordinary tales to tell. I trust their integrity and honesty completely; however, I have changed the names of their bedfellows to factious names, or omitted their names altogether, if their role in their lives or their children's, may have been negative, or less than stellar. This is simply to be journalistically fair, and considerate, since it's not the ex's stories being told from their perception and where they were in that stage of their lives, but the subjects.

My Red Airplane

He flies so high,
free in the unbound imagination
of a two-year-old
He soars

No limitations closing in on him
except for momma's lines of safety
His flight of fancy

Arms stretched out,
hands and fingers straight,
slicing the wind beneath him
He runs …

Blue eyes bright in frenzy
he's in a hurry to have fun

Our park is his landing strip,
he crashes on soft blades of green grass,
as the summer sun watches

His little engine is strong
He gets back up, and
takes off again

Corben,
my little red airplane
captured in time, still framed
in golden kissed black and white.

CONTENTS

Introduction

The idea for this book sprung forth from a need I had as a new mom. I was actively looking around for mentors in motherhood and not necessarily of the mini-van and cookie stereotype that is populated by commercial magazines. I had my share of them already in the two years of motherhood I had experienced thus far. There had to be more to it than selling me stuff, or exalting super-woman roles that were out of reach for most of us, including myself. Trust me, in my short twenty-four month tenure I tried. I tried hard. And I crashed and burned. You will hear this story repeated throughout this book as well. We were supposed to be happy, weren't we? That's what the image of motherhood kept telling us. So why wasn't I? Take it like a man, smile and stop complaining (for child support, good, caring, and safe day care, supportive work environments, the ability to be a primary care-giver in society and not be judged, the reality of trying to meet our children's needs while living in, or very close to, poverty, etc.).

As an activist, poet, essayist, and feminist-punk woman, I just knew there had to be communities and real stories out there. I just had to dig. This was in 2002. There was, and still is, a large *Hip Mama* audience and movement that's rich in parenting tales. In a matter of weeks, I consumed every available book and article on what I considered real-life motherhood. The bulk of it was mostly written, and very well-written, by Ariel Gore and the contributors of *Hip Mama Zine* and *Mamaphonic*. And a book, one-singular-book, that I could find on the subject (in 2002) was Adrienne Rich's *Of Woman Born*. This book was elemental in taking the lid off of Pandora's Box in 1976. But there seemed to be an overall dry run, or perhaps general silencing of mothers, between then and the emergence of the *Hip Mama* work.

I related to these few examples of printed literature and like a starving animal I engulfed them! I exhausted these shared moments of time captured and published by *Hip Mama*, and the intellectual probing and personal assessments of motherhood by one of my favorite poets. All before my son had his second birthday. I shook my head and it hung defeated. No way. No way, this is all of it … really? I was frustrated. I needed more. I needed to know who these women were as mothers themselves. I needed their stories, their biographies, their lessons and mantras, their shared wisdom, and I needed it urgently and collectively. And not just one or two personal accounts, but a tribes worth.

Who are they? How did they get to this point in their lives? What are they doing now? What defines their experiences? Are they ostracized and silenced, or having to censor themselves the majority of the time? Or are they having the time of their lives and there's just something wrong with me? Are they finding meaningful work? Or are they having to make-do? Are they struggling? Are they fighting for a better way? *What are they doing, why are they doing it, and how are they doing it?*

I needed an authentic, followable, off-road map for an off-road mom. Having a lack of one, I decided to help lay out that map. It was a natural fit, since I had been writing my whole life. The idea came as an epiphany at my son's second birthday party—literally! I didn't know yet what shape or form the book would take. (Nor did I ever suspect what a colossal amount of work I just carved out for myself, in addition to my day job, school, and everything else!) I just knew moms needed more, more of and from each other. A book about us, by us, and for us, loaded with viable tools of the trade. I recruited my first mom that day at the park after my son's party. You can read her story in the chapter *The Performers and Warriors*. Her name is Jenn and she is one hell of a woman and one hell of a mom. She's a great poet and actress too.

I searched high and low looking for women of merit. I sought out moms of varied achievements, moms the world ignores as average or abnormal, and moms who were still struggling to achieve and survive while raising their kids' right and with love. I have moms both well-known and obscure, moms from all walks of life: rockers, tattoo artists, Army and Navy veterans, writers, students, strippers, Ph.D.s, hair-stylists, designers, icons, fast food workers, gardeners, business owners, Buddhists, artists, hip mamas, activists, photographers, laborers, teachers, boxers, atheists, firefighters, office workers, servers, pin-ups, poets, preachers, librarians, herbalists, painters, lovers, life-livers, and more … Women with courage, attitude, conviction and love. And maybe a few tattoos. Women whose lives and the meanings of their lives were completely the antithesis of what motherhood was suppose to transform us into: quiet, obedient, hard working superwomen—an upper class deluxe edition model forced upon us all, yet ignoring our realities. Where are the children? Where are the communities? *Where are the women in that?*

The moms in this book (and I) have struggled to achieve the balance and happiness portrayed by successful moms whose voices have become diluted and softened by privilege and power, or perhaps heavily edited out. We quickly realized why our voices largely didn't exist in print, in the magazines, and in the news. We would break the myth! I looked for Amazonian lions and I found them.

Mothers who were so much more than just mothers. Women who had similar inner yearnings as I did: to achieve meaningful work, while providing for our families; nurturing our children perhaps in unconventional ways, but in ways that will lead to a better world, a better place for all kids. We want a real village, damn it!

Moms who had seemingly insurmountable odds stacked against them—but they had to find a way to make it, and with little support, and few, if any, real examples to lead them. Some of them even had to find a better way while faced with severe circumstances and struggles: discrimination, spiritual collapses, poverty and homelessness, the death of a child, disappointments, and addiction. These women share their stories of battle: overcoming depression, surviving sexual assaults and confronting the legal system and society that enables it, getting out of abusive relationships, the trials and tribulations of divorce, overcoming disabilities and stereotypes, and so much more. They also share their triumphs: in parenting (and all its varieties) from attachment, motivational, holistic, old-fashioned, to unschooling; and seeing their kids become wholesome and happy. They started bands, started businesses, got degrees, and created work that works for them.

We have endured heart-wrenching tragedies and overcame self-destructive habits, worked on our empathy and compassion, built up our skill-sets to be better people and better mothers. Some of us came from broken homes, or abusive/neglectful ones. We needed to figure out a better way to do this right, and with love and respect. Some of us were fortunate and came from great, loving, supportive homes, but chose a different path and felt isolated, alone. But we found as moms, we also have much to celebrate too: making ends meet, seeing justice served, annoying our politicians with their condescending lip service, putting out records, launching indie start-ups with a lot of heart and a few pennies, getting promotions, writing books, doing something we love well, making our bodies and identities our own, standing up for ourselves, our kids, and others, creating holistic support systems and community groups in our neighborhoods, having our children emerge as caring leaders to their peers, and redefining overall our successes and our values—and on our own terms.

Overall, are there others out there like us? The answer is yes. I suspect we are the majority, not the minority, contrary to mainstream media and images/stereotypes. My findings are based on the fact that many moms, including ones who appear "normal, extremely successful or mainstream" on the outside, have had significant interest in this project as well. (The book I was published in, *If Women Ruled the World*, in 2004, supports this too.) I have found we are all asking the same questions on the inside, and all paths lead here.

We're redefining ourselves in the face of the challenges of the mom stereotype being pushed upon us from seemingly everywhere, but instead of it transforming us into the Betty Crocker CEOs of tomorrow, we become the Amazons of today. We fight for our right to self-perseverance much like the infamous women at Troy and the Black Sea Region. We fight to protect our children, our world, our communities and our dreams—even in the midst of backlash from a society that is owned by Big Business. Big Business that needs moms that buy, and moms that behave as workers, women and mothers. The idea of us, Rebel Moms, as teachers, activists, veterans, feminists, rockers, business women, etc., rocks the boat. But ladies and gentlemen, the mother lionesses are out of their dens. We have children and a world to truly protect and invest in. I learned from all the women I reached out to about this project that they too were looking for a mentor, a map. If at the least, to help them know that there are other women and mothers raising the same questions, battling the same issues, and living, or trying to, with the same passion and gusto; all the while having to do it in a world that misunderstands us at best, mistreats us at worst.

My vision for the book is that it will serve as a point of reference for mothers seeking new modern role-models and mentors while providing an essential insight for hope and a reference of experience, and a cursory look into the lives of marginalized Amazon Warrior Moms. I know it will encourage mothers feeling locked into, or out of, the Betty-CEO stereotype, or being put down as the Worthless-Welfare mom, a way of seeking freedom and the tools to fight for it … whatever her battle may be. It begins with a feeling of something is wrong: *I'm not content though the world tells me I should be.* Many of the mothers in this book had to do heavy soul-searching to define what the best way is for them to parent and articulate this with my help in order to share their stories of hope, salvation, and endurance. They provide you with options, ideas, solutions, brainstorming, philosophies, and works in progress. Real Mothering, Real Womanhood, Real Rebel Moms!

Sincerely,
Davina Rhine

The Activists and Feminists

In this chapter you will meet strong, amazing women who fight the current. They stand up and battle for what's right.

If you ever needed help finding your way to courage, or how to securely stand on your own two feet while squaring off, the stories you are about to read will help you find and shape your voice.

These mothers have fought for victims of the international child and sex slave system. They have spoken up for exploited animals that have no voice in the meat, fur, and 'science' lab industries. They have helped women find their voice after being isolated in both bouts of depression and personal attacks. They believe women should have more say and control not only of their bodies, but the birthing experience. They bend the ear of big business while being a pain in their ass. They make their own medicines and encourage others to become enlightened, focusing on natural sustainability, team work and sharing. They march on D.C., for women's rights and children's rights. They have reached out for help when dads became dead-beats, and when they were coldly turned away—they started their own activist community and family support groups, specifically supporting women of color and mothers who are marginalized. They give a hand and a helping heart to teen moms, refusing to kick anyone when they're down. They have fought for their Ph.D.s, and they have fought and fallen for our country. They fight everyday for our children and a better world for all of us …

Welcome to the bold world of the Activists and Feminists.

"Fuck the System makes for a bad-ass patch, but is even more bad-ass as a child rearing ideology."

Carol
Activist Galore
Columnist
Glamour Girl
Assertive Peace Maker
Vegetarian
Washington, D.C.

Carol is a fully engaged activist and writer. Some of her favorite bands are X, Agnostic Front, and The Briefs. She uses cloth diapers and obsessively recycles. She loves crosswords and books. She and her husband Dave love going to punk and drag queen shows. Some of her favorite authors are Margaret Artwood, John Irving and Marion Zimmer Bradley.

Carol is currently a mom who works at home raising her son, Acie. She thinks the whole "stay-at-home" mom/dad thing is very misleading. It implies one isn't working, when you are.

She hates hearing men say about their wife's occupation, "She doesn't work. She's a stay-at-home mom ..." Women she has talked to say it almost the same way, as if they are unsure of what they do is work or not. This doubt comes from the fact that child-rearing work is simply undervalued in our society. Mothering is not valued as a contributing and valued role in our society. She vividly remembers a conversation with some guy:

Guy: "So what are you doing now?"
Carol: "Oh, I had a baby."
Guy: "Yeah, I know, but what are you DOING now?"
Carol: "I HAD A BABY."

There's a book called *The Fifth Sacred Thing* by Starhawk. Carol loves this work of fiction because what the author does is create this ideal society that functions within and outside the current society. Motherhood and mothering is equally as important and critical to the society as the jobs of plumber, or doctor. Carol hopes someday mothering will be as important and considered as integral to the future of our society as a businessman is to the future of our country, and not just in lip service.

Carol's other job is activism. Her entire family is engaged in it. Her son has been to several protests, including a Pro-Choice Rally, and one opposing the War in Iraq. Their home life is activist and ethically driven. They are a vegetarian, animal rights, and human rights family, and environmentalists as well.

The Pro-Choice Rally she took Acie to, was in D.C. Carol isn't sure if everyone understood it was a baby in her sling or not. The fellow marchers however, were very positive and responsive to Acie's presence there among them. Carol described it as, "A big love-in." She has never been so catered to and looked out for. She got smiles, and people stopped to take pictures. One woman there who had an older toddler even stopped and chatted with her. It was a beautiful moment between women and families. They were both there for the protest and had signs that read, "Thank you for supporting my RIGHT to CHOOSE," and "FUCK PATRICARCHY."

A counter-protestor shocked her into silence by saying, "Thank you for not killing your baby." Carol regrets not "shocking" him back by whipping out her breast to breastfeed right then and there. Many people who are passionate about deciding for a woman if she should have child or not, are also so anti-child. She feels the same people who are opposed to choice, are also opposed to breastfeeding in public, and support cutting welfare, jobs, and are pro-war. As far as Acie is concerned, Carol hopes … "I don't expect to raise a famous revolutionary, but a thoughtful, caring, vocal citizen in the world. I think the impact of one person trying their best is radical."

Carol has protested the circus, and fur shows too. She also has marched for the homeless and has worked in soup kitchens. Once Acie is older she plans on them both going together to work in soup kitchens and to become more involved in the Food Not Bombs movement.

"I don't expect to raise a famous revolutionary, but a thoughtful, caring, vocal citizen in the world. I think the impact of one person trying their best is radical."

Food Not Bombs is an anarchist collective that believes in decentralization and is open to involvement by everyone. Their stance is that government and corporate policies are designed to cause hunger and poverty in amidst of literal wealth and abundance. The basic principle (or irony) the group points out is: if the government spent the money they allocate for bomb-making on food instead, no one would starve, or go without. They need volunteers to help collect food, cook and distribute, and there are chapters everywhere; get more involved, just sign up at: FoodNotBombs.net.

Her activism started years ago. The early defining moment in her life was in junior high. She was raised Presbyterian, and went to Kenya on a mission to build a school there. In Kenya, she spent many nights staring up at the stars under the night sky. It was here she realized there was no god, just vast nature. She has been an atheist ever since.

Shortly thereafter, the Oliver North scandal came out. She was shocked at all the blatant lies. She was pissed and disappointed with government contradiction, and realized everything she had been raised to believe in were lies. Out of her growing frustration she started listening to bands like Black Flag and the Dead Kennedys.

She went to her first punk show at the age of fifteen. It was a band called Government Issue. It was followed by more shows like Inquisition, Wardance Orange, and Action Patrol. She also went to a PETA (People for the Ethical Treatment of Animals) benefit show at the mall. These events, moments, and movements gave her the tools for creating positive change. Shortly thereafter, she did some canvassing for Earth Day 1990 too … "It was an improvement on my teenage angst rebel-without-a-cause middle finger."

She went to work professionally in fields that built up community. She has worked as a day care teacher, and for non-profit agencies. For seven years she worked as a special needs care giver. It was an after school program (through her local district) for autistic, disabled, and handicapped kids. She also worked with children in the psychiatric ward, as well, at a local hospital. She later worked for a teenage shelter and a home for abused women. A principle she lives by is:

> "I think holding true to your beliefs and applying them to your life is a revolution in itself. Recycling, being a vegetarian, and being aware of the companies you support with your dollar. Of course the most mutinous act: treating others like humans. Dignity … how wild!"

One thing she doesn't do is TELL people things. She prefers to make information available and let people make their own choices and decisions. After dedicating ten years of her life as a full-time activist, she needed a break and became a massage therapist briefly. It was a better paying and less stressful way of working while still giving back to the community. This was her profession before becoming a mother.

She also writes a successful and loved column in the *Punky Moms Zine* (PunkyMoms.com). She developed a philosophy that she articulated in her first column: *Practical Applied Punk Philosophy*. Here's what that column said:

"Fuck the system makes for a bad-ass patch, but is even more bad-ass as a child rearing ideology. It's typical for a woman to feel a loss of identity in the abundance of mothering; and for a punk momma forgoing the scene hub of shows for bath-time and lullabies; it is quite easy to feel alienated from her community and herself. But don't look as this time as an absence or retirement from the scene, instead, consider this your chance for **Practical Applied Punk Philosophy**.

From the moment that wee egg is fertilized you have the opportunity to question authority like never before. Today's conventional wisdom can be the antithesis of intuition and instinct, and is often market driven. Gleaning sound advice from utter crap takes research and insight, and that skeptical punk brain of yours is the perfect tool for the job, and that middle finger rather practical.

My punk eye for the momma life led me to midwifes, attachment parenting, and cloth diapers. The list is huge and grows as my son transitions from a big baby to a small boy.

Books have always been my favorite resource, but I also tapped into my mother and grandmother—two exceptional and practical mothers, very willing to use hindsight to evaluate the choices they made and how they were influenced by the times in which they lived. Grandmother feels she has seen a full circle with me. My parenting and lifestyle is very similar to her mother's, just more deliberately so. My layette was minus some typically key items; if a cavewoman hadn't had an equivalent, I question what its purpose for me was. Not that I am living an austere life, just not a life taken out of a *Parents Magazine* photo shoot or a Gerber ad.

Your Punk eye may lead to a different way from mine. What's important is that you trample out your own path; that you remain true to yourself, and, as always, Punk-as-Fuck!"

As she notes in her column, she practices attachment parenting. The one thing she really likes about it is the life balance it promotes. Attachment parenting is a child-rearing philosophy that focuses on the relationship between the parent and the child. It is, however, not too overly focused on the child or too withdrawn from

Rebel Mom Carol practices attachment parenting. The one thing she really likes about it is the life balance it promotes.

the child. It truly focuses on the relationship that is being built. It enables trust between the child and parent, not overt isolation, nor complete submissive dependence. It's empowering for both parent and child alike.

Carol feels as Acie grows, their relationship will have a balance of: trust, respect and love; which will allow his personality to grow and create open communication between them. She considers this aspect critical for her to be successful in parenting. She wants Acie to be confident, and secure enough in his relationship with his parents, to be able to find his authentic self; including his strengths and weaknesses without it being based on what her or her husband's beliefs are.

She also feels that children are often used as a sick marketing tool in the United States—a way to sell you everything and anything. Be it your kids screaming for McDonalds, or the newest gadget, or newest nuisance product that is designed to keep your child as far away from you as possible. She cites that many marketed items like bouncers, baby gyms, mats, yards, entertainers, bottles instead of breast, are counter-productive to attachment parenting and frankly unnecessary. She is shocked at all the marketing both parents and kids are getting bombarded with everyday, ranging from: baby-milk warmers, bottle-warmer chargers, baby-wipe warmers, breakfast cereals, T.V. dinners, fast food, clothing fashion, videos and music, electronics, toys, toys, and more toys, all aggressively marketed towards kids and parents. She feels having a few indulgent items here and there is okay, but right now it's extremely excessive in our current society.

Carol cites the marketing wars for example, which start before your child is even born, and she concludes that if you buy into it, you lose your self-esteem and your integrity as a parent and a human being. [It also compromises your decision making position as a parent. Also, if children are exposed to *all this stuff*, they lack the skills to decipher it and believe this product defines them and is somehow crucial to their existence.] It's been established that materialism (or our modern way of living/consuming) is linked to depression and depression is dangerous.

When Carol was a child she suffered severely from depression. She is not exactly sure why or whether or not if Post WWII materialism had anything to do with it, but she feels she did not have the best life to start with because of this depression. Her childhood per se was good. When she was twenty-two years of age she had to face it, "The tendency once your depressed is to speak it. You get kind of satisfied once your feet are in it, but for me, no more."

One thing she figured out when she was younger is just because someone treats you a certain way doesn't mean that is how you should be treated for the rest of your life.

She manages her physiological tendency towards depression with strength and determination. She doesn't soak her feet in it anymore or dwell on it. She takes action to counter it. She will do things that motivate her and help her get past the 'feeling.' Her life is good, and will continue to be good, because she forces it to be that way and keeps that line of thinking going. It's a frequent inner dialogue that works for her and has helped her manage her depression successfully for over ten years now.

Carol met her husband Dave through mutual friends when she lived outside of Washington D.C. They have been together for over eight years, of which they have been married for five. They have traveled extensively together on tour with numerous bands they are friends with. Her husband works for an independent record store which allows them to stay current in the music scene. At the time of this writing, she is thirty-three-years old and Acie is three-years-old.

They had been talking about having a baby and planning on it when she got pregnant with Acie. They kept it quiet for a while, but the news came out to friends at a late night diner after the September 11th 2001 attack. A friend of theirs expressed grief over the world climate and decided she would not have kids. Their friend did not want to bring a child into a world like this. Carol assured her with humor, not to worry, because they were having one and their child would fix everything.

One of the hardest aspects of parenting that Carol has had to deal with is the decrease of contact with other adults. She has worked hard to maintain a strong network of support amongst friends and family. She speaks to her mom daily. (As she is relaying this, I suddenly see Carol hunched over cream and speckled countertops with her mix of blonde and lipstick red hair pulled away from her face—as she becomes animated in conversation and fueled by coffee; much like when we initially interviewed. The only distraction I could foresee is an incoming call, or Acie demanding attention.)

Her best friend from Los Angeles calls daily for long talks. She also watches a friend's son and has long and frequent hang-outs with her. Her local friends have also been great about staying in touch with them. The 'family and friends' hang-outs and BBQs are becoming more frequent as their friends become new parents, thus rounding out the social circle.

The Punky Moms message board online has been a great resource for her. She has an entire crew of mommas from all over the country that she can count on and lean on, and vice versa. The forum helps develop personal support through friendships, as well as parental discussions and debates.

When she is out, Carol gets her share of raised eyebrows, but no one says a word to her. At least it has not happened yet. She's not sure if this because she looks happy, and Acie looks happy, or because she is substantially taller than the average woman and is covered in tattoos, "GRRRRRR! Fear me!" She did however prefect the "back-down stare," when she was working with disabled children. She took the kids out for community outings and after seven years of staring off strangers who would dare to stare rudely at the children, she's got it down.

She attributes parenting to improving her health. Before becoming a mom she normally had to hold down two jobs and was broke. She also went out every night and can't do that anymore either,

> "I have never been better rested, better fed, and most importantly, more focused on the finer details of my own life as in motherhood. I love seeing all the tiny moments of my son's life and I love that we know each other as well as we do. I love that my life's work is palpable. I love that it is ALL MINE ..."

She laughs when she shares that she is happy they have created this awesome family, but also that "Dave loves strong and stubborn women." Once Acie is older, Carol plans on doing more direct activism again … "Anything would be great. When Bush Sr. was inaugurated, I just happened to find a street protest and picked up a sign. I feel I must continue to, so that the next generation can continue to have the right to dissent."

**Since this interview: Carol's family has happily grown by two additional children and she has become the Queen of Cool Cakes and Bakes with her own pastry catering line: Hausfrau Cakes.*

"The blood of the street runs through my veins. I am a champion of the people, and what concerns my people concerns me. I am a catalyst for change."

Dr. Taj Anwar
Street FTP Hip-Hop Activist
Trend-setter
Smokin' Skateboarder
Model
Vegetarian
M.O.B.B—Founder
NYC, New York.

Taj Anwar is a divorced New Yorker whose occupation is that of activist and whose personal goals are to fight for freedom, justice and equality. She is the founder of M.O.B.B. (Mother of

Black/Brown Babies), and recently completed her doctorate studies in philosophy and sociology and earned her Ph.D.

She loves Range Rovers, getting tattooed, and skateboards. She skates every where she can and enjoys doing it with her oldest son Dub, who skateboards too. I imagine them freestylin' on stickered up boards in empty parking lots, with graffiti art as their backdrop, as well as trying to navigate through the crowded streets of NYC. She also enjoys community work and hanging out with her children.

Her other two favorite hobbies would be sleeping and sex, though she doesn't necessarily get enough of either, she chuckles. She lives her life with fire, passion, and conviction. Her friends call her Red, for a number of reasons that include: her intensity, and the fact that she is a hard-core street activist who believes in the right to bear arms—for defense, but who is also a dedicated peace activist who longs for a society free of violence, that is safe for women, children, and people of color. She acknowledges that there is no one like her, and she's okay with that.

Taj Anwar approaches activism with a winning, successful combination of achieving a serious minded goal with a fun approach. You will constantly find her mixing DJ events and parties with activism legwork aimed to help feed people, increase knowledge, sign petitions, and engage people to commit to the FTP movement. (For the People, Free the Prisoners, Fuck the Police, etc.)

Music plays a huge role in her life and some of her favorite artists are Andre 3000 from Outkast, Viva Fidel, and Good Charlotte. She enjoys almost all dancehall artists and dub artists too. For Taj, music and activism go hand-in-hand. When she is working, she is also having fun.

Taj Anwar has three children ages two, four, and seven. They are nicknamed Dub (the oldest), Amon, and her daughter Peaches (who is the youngest). But Taj was mothering before becoming a birth mother.

"I have always been a mother. Even before I had natural children, I took care of my friends just like I was their mother. In all of the schools I have worked in, many students have told me I am like their mother. I treat all children just like they belonged to me. I'm a Cancer—which is the mother sign of astrology. So it's no surprise that's how I am."

Taj's activist and support group M.O.B.B. was born after becoming a single mom and she wasn't getting child support from her ex-husband, and was denied any assistance from the government while she was working. Taj found herself suddenly single and on her own to take care of her family. She worked a variety of jobs, and was going to school, but couldn't make ends meet sufficiently, so she applied for food assistance.

The government/county told her if she could afford to buy her schoolbooks then she could afford to feed her children, and that basically she had to make a choice: feed her kids, or go to school. Meanwhile, her ex suffered no serious legal or social consequence for failure to provide child support. This enraged her:

"They said since I had the money for books and other school expenses that I should have money for food. Literally, that was it. And I didn't argue. I wasn't going to quit school for that. I'd rather just hustle in other ways to get the money for food for my kids, and me go without than to quit school. School was my ticket."

In regards to suddenly being a single parent she adds:

"My reality is WOW. I am responsible for someone else other than myself. Being a single parent has been rough. I have been off and on again as a single parent, because their father and I would break up, get back together and break up again. In 2006, we finally divorced.

My reality is that I am the sole provider for my children. The financial help is not there and the physical support is few and far in between. My reality is not to be angry because I cannot make their father do anything. My reality is that every day I have to hustle between two jobs and multiple small businesses, as well as care for my children. My reality is that my children will not want for anything. Whatever they have earned is what they will receive. My reality is that I will never tell my children that they cannot get something they have worked extra hard for in school and at home to get. My reality is that, short of prostitution, I will do ANYTHING to make sure my children eat."

When the New York State Department of Family Assistance told her she had to choose between feeding her kids, or going to school, in order to get their help—it motivated her to not only do both, but to create her own options and self-support system. She knew many families in the same, or similar, circumstances as her own. She built a network that helps sustain families despite the backlash from government and lack of aid, and to do it defiantly with integrity; hence the birth of M.O.B.B, which has become an ideal model for community building, that spread to cities all over the U.S.

M.O.B.B. is strictly a community funded grassroots organization that specializes in street activism, and providing a place where mothers of color and multi-racial families can safely turn to for love, help, and understanding; which is generally absent in mainstream organizations that tend to treat women and mothers in a patronizing fashion. Such as how Taj was treated, when faced with the obstacles of trying to manage as a suddenly divorced working student and mother of three. M.O.B.B. is not only specific to the needs of their community, but for women of color, simply because there lacks such an organization.

Do you need a support network of moms that are open-minded, loving, and that look more like you? Check out Mothers of Black & Brown Babies at: Mobbb.org! What does hip-hop, activism, and motherhood have in common? Everything!

M.O.B.B. is an online community too, with each local area having momma crews for street development, activism, and welcoming new members and moms-in-need. Several things make M.O.B.B. very unique: they turn down government funding which gives them complete control over what they do, and they foster relationships building a sustaining supportive network for mothers. Collectively, they address problems mothers face, and collaborate for creative solutions to those problems. This is in complete contrast to mainstream organizations that tend to stereotype based on a variety of factors (but not limited to) like race, and social class; which leaves a lot of women unwilling to turn to mainstream outlets for help in parenting, or life, because the assistance is condescending.

M.O.B.B. also has annual conferences, educational whole-being workshops, community drives and events, a sharing network for helping moms meet each other's needs, and an intern volunteer program for college students focusing in the areas of psychology and social work. M.O.B.B's self defined description is, *"Pro-Choice, Pro-Children, Anti-Hate, Anti-War, Anti-Hunger, Anti-Police Brutality, Anti-Racism, Anti-Sexism, Anti-Domestic Violence, Pro-Love, Pro-Life, Pro-Peace, Pro-Hip-Hop."* Taj's plans are to grow the group more and develop it into a driving force that champions for the rights of mothers and the rights of families in the economy, housing sector, the workplace, and for moms and children caught up in the penal system. M.O.B.B. is a sister organization under the FTP Movement umbrella and you can learn more about the group at: Mobbb.org.

The FTP movement is an urban movement similar to the original Blank Panther Party Movement focusing on self-empowerment and liberation. It shares similarities as well to the Anarcho Punk Movements. FTP seeks to meet the needs of the urban community in a way that is helpful and provides long term solutions without the patronizing handouts from a government that perpetrates the problems of exploitation, oppression, sexism, motherism, political persecution and racism. It's a movement for building unity, self-determination and self-sustaining growth while challenging the system that allows things like police brutality, racial profiling, and exploitation to occur. You can learn more about the movement and how to get involved at: FTPMovement.com.

Taj's community activism and parenting are both hands-on. She doesn't expect schools or television to raise her children, although a lot of parents rely heavily on the two. She does expect, however, help from the community and believes that it takes a village to raise a child and all children—it should be a shared responsibility and commitment if we all want to live happily and safely together. She openly embraces other children and helps out in many ways, direct and indirectly through other-mothering locally and her activism, and expects the same. Through her own example she hopes her children will be leaders and not followers:

"I hope that my boys see that a head-strong and focused woman can lead and that they look for strong characteristics in their chosen mates and will feel adequate. I want my daughter to know that she comes from a long line of strong women and that she shouldn't expect anything less from herself; so when she goes into a relationship or chosen career, she has a strong foundation that will make her less susceptible to insecurities. I instill this by being a positive role model to my children."

Taj wants her children to grow up happy, healthy, educated, and well-rounded. She hopes their experiences will enable them to grow, and that, "They don't fall like a stumbling block and stay down, that they get up and hit the ground running." That is how she was raised and how she is. She tries her best to instill the same philosophy into her children, and tries to develop their self-esteem by assuring them that they are priceless, and their morals, principles and beliefs can't be bought. She wants them to think very highly of themselves and be comfortable in being who they are, and not desiring to be someone else—which is something Taj struggled with growing up.

Taj is very concerned about the type of society our kids are growing up in, which contradicts the positive messages that most parents are aiming for.

"I think society has sexualized children. They are growing up too fast. I think the hormones in the food have our children developing at a rapid speed—and it's unnatural. I think that the toys like Bratz that are geared towards small children are dangerous, because it promotes materialism. I think today's society has made shows like Sesame Street lame to children by today's standards. I think society promotes bigotry and non-tolerance amongst our youth. I think that society has not properly reprimanded our children, or taught our children to respect their elders. You have children fighting children, and teachers—what the hell?"

Although Taj loves mothering, she feels she must always be on guard, especially concerning the world her children are growing up in:

"When people who think like Bush are in power [President Bush was in power at the time of this interview.], world relations will continue to suffer. You do not lead by hitting people over the head. That is assault, not leadership (A quote from Eisenhower.). I think the world is a different place from which it was when I was growing up, particularly for children. I must stay safe, smart, and sharp."

Taj believes that if enough people care we can turn this situation around and protect ourselves and our children, from violent messages without creating the false and dangerous delusions that violence doesn't exist. It is a balancing act, but she handles it an honest and forthcoming manner with her children. She explains to them the danger in guns, why an adult may need one, and the responsibility one must shoulder …

"The key is to be involved. If we as parents are involved as to what our kids are exposed to, I think that can deter the violence. For example, my son drew a handgun on a box the other day and was planning to cut it out to use for a toy. The gun was very detailed. No one could say I promote violence because I have a gun strapped to my back on a tattoo, or that I have been known to get training on guns. I explain to my son that for one I am an adult. For two, I am trained to use a gun. Third, they have no idea where I keep my gun. My gun is to protect myself and my family. If you are not grown, if you are not trained to use a gun, or if you are not responsible enough to keep your gun in a safe place, then you have no business with a gun, period.

We have to be real with our kids. I am not a sugar-coating kind of mother. I don't use cute nicknames for things, nor do I dress things up and put a bow on them to make it look better than what it is. That is how I was raised and I always appreciated the sense of reality that I had."

Her children are already demonstrating that they are independent and self-assured kids. Her oldest son recently learned what the word achieve means, and was asked by his school what he wanted to be when he grew up. He replied, "A scientist." Dub is only seven, but he already knows that in order to find cures for people suffering from disease and sicknesses that he would need to become a scientist, and to become a scientist, he would need to go to college and earn honors. Her children have also seen their mom lead by example by hitting the textbooks almost every night, working on college projects, earning and graduating with multiple degrees. They have seen her overcome obstacles, including two areas she has struggled with since she was a child, which is dyslexia and having a horrible memory. It was her greatest challenge in school and to this day she still occasionally says some words backwards, but now she just laughs at herself and tries again. As a child, she was teased without mercy by the neighborhood kids, and it motivated her to finally become a doctorate; to prove to herself that she could do it.

> "The Ph.D. was really for me. I am none of those mean things that I was called growing up. I am not stupid, slow, or retarded. I was diagnosed as dyslexic in elementary school, and they really did not think I would even finish high school, so they tried to steer me in a vocational direction. But I knew that when I graduated from high school with a vocational degree-—as well as a college prep degree—that I had the drive to succeed in college. It was a way of thanking my mother for her support. I care about my ability to reach that goal, not so much as being called Dr. I really don't give a damn about that. It was a way of showing myself that I could do it."

It was exhausting for Taj to complete her college plans for her Ph.D. when she became a parent, but even more so when she became a single one permanently. Her children didn't know any different, she would just stay up late and work on schoolwork at the end of the day. On average she slept 3.5 hours a night until she was done with school, which was excruciating. Although she does have the academic credentials to teach college right now, she plans on waiting until her forties, when she feels she has had more life experience to offer. Her ultimate plan is to teach a sociology course that focuses on economics, along with demographics, and how society's exploitations (like racism, and classism) *infects* both society and capital.

Her divorce was painful and she had a hard time getting over that, more than the mean childish teasing she endured when she was younger. Her ex-husband initiated the final divorce, but Taj realizes now it was for the best. During the transition she struggled because she felt physically free, but emotionally trapped. Once it was officially and legally completed, she felt relived. For anyone going through a divorce this is her advice:

"Only time heals. There is nothing I can say to make it better or to heal faster. It hurts like a muthafucka, literally. I really felt that I was going to die from heartbreak. I was that hurt. Once I pulled myself together, I made it through. The kids were actually my saving grace. I pulled it together for them and because of them. Really, they helped me. They had no idea what had happened, they just knew that all of a sudden Mommy and Daddy weren't together anymore. But they had the undying love from me. I'm sure they still wonder what's up with their dad, and they are happy when he comes around, but they know no matter what, I got them."

She doesn't regret the marriage since it yielded her three amazing children. In fact, her and her ex-husband were using birth control when they had their first two children, but like many things in her life, Taj believes it was fate and they were placed in her path, "Motherhood is a divine appointment, and I am honored to be chosen." She may not look like the other moms you see on T.V., mainstream magazine covers, or even her own P.T.A. (Parent Teacher Association) board, but that doesn't stop her from being a world renowned activist and a devoted kick-ass mom.

"Society would like to judge a book by its cover. By looking at me you cannot tell what I know, what I have accomplished, who I am. When people are told of my accolades and what I have done in my short life, some people seem surprised. But I was always taught to be an individual, and that my works and actions will speak for themselves. I do not fit society's look of a mom. I wear tight pants and timberlands. I have tattoos on fifty percent of my body. I am a vegetarian. I skateboard. Instead of wearing an apron, I wipe my hands on my ripped jeans when I am cooking. And I'll wear sneakers and jeans to every P.T.A. meeting. But no one can ever say that I am not a good mother."

Even though she is covered in tattoo's, has a nose ring, and has long dreadlocks that sway against the back of her knees, she feels at ease even with mainstream moms, mostly because they all share a common interest, their children. That ground makes it easier for her to talk other moms, and once they get past the outward appearance, and get to know one another, they discover they have more in common than they previously thought. One thing that helps keep her open minded is the activist, hip-hop, rap, blues, punk and art moms she hangs out with on a regular intimate basis. They are all into culture, openness, helping their children explore the world, and not being confined to one philosophy or surroundings. Nonetheless though, she does assert with a bit of humor, "Mainstream means you are typical, not original. So I enjoy being a remix."

She approaches life with a pro-peace and pro-love stance, hence why she can be anti-mainstream and stand up for what's right, but embrace those that seem to fit right into the mold of society's preferred lifestyles which are generally anti-humanitarian, anti-animal, and anti-earth. She is true to herself and her lioness heart, and to live any differently would be living a lie. Taj has numerous tattoos, but two of her favorite are:

> "One is of my mother on my back by an artist named Animal of Infamous Tattoos. He knew that it was a very important tat and he made sure it was right. My other one is a pic of me with my children on my lower left leg by an artist named Tuki of City of Ink. He drew it at like four in the morning while I was at his house. I was fast asleep and he had just finished a tat. He drew it, not knowing what my kids looked like or their sexes. He drew them perfectly. He knew how important it is to me to protect my children and it's a pic of me walking behind them with an M-16 strapped to my back. But the tender look on my face, and the content look on their faces, is priceless. My eyes fill with tears every time I look at it."

Taj's future plans do include more tattoos, and teaching college, but she also hopes to open a collective community day care center where there won't be any cost ... just parents working together and doing the general clean up. What's her secret to a hectic life? She paces herself since there aren't enough hours in the day, and what doesn't get done by a certain time will have to wait to be worked on the next day. Her best suggestion for balancing it all is simply to just live, "Life is short, lean. Live [and] love."

**Since this interview: Taj has remarried and started an activist fueled merch line, Dopest Babies Mama, and a very cool educational and philanthropic catering line called: Feed the People. You can check out both at TajAnwar.com.*

"My focus is on the human slave trade and my plans are to move to Thailand to help women and children who have been sold/ coerced into the sex slave trade. There is definitely not enough being done about it in this world."

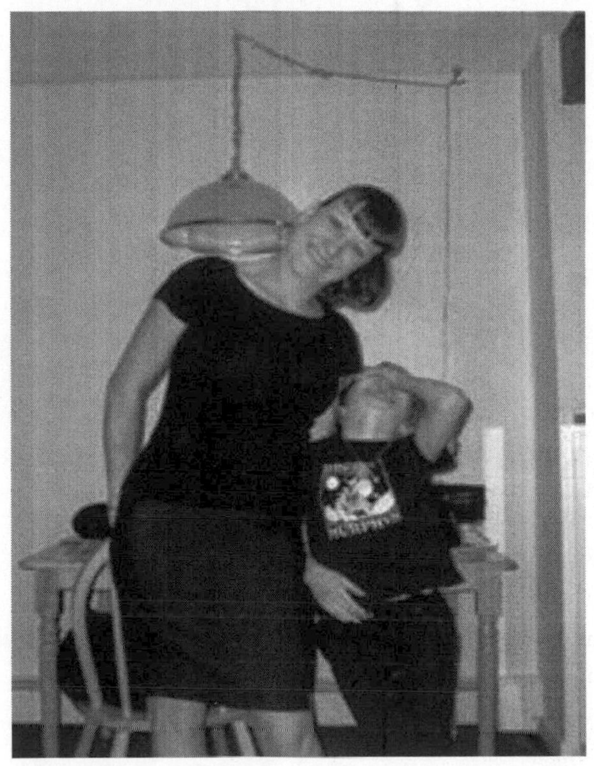

Natasha
Military and Iraq War Veteran
Human Rights Activist
International Law Student
666 Pin-up
Austin, Texas.

Natasha is a full-time student, an Iraq War Veteran, and a mother for peace. She has a lot of passion and her main drive is to help others who are being exploited. She believes one person can make a difference.

As a political activist she is tired of living in a bumper sticker society and feels bumper stickers are the literal beginning and end of most Americans involvement with politics or activism. She thinks most Americans are apathetic and that the direction our country is going in is scary. Her opinion of the posthumous Bush Jr. administration is indignant—that they dropped the ball on taking care of veterans and soldiers. Previously, she protested the Iraq War on Capitol Hill.

Putting her money where her mouth is, Natasha worked heavily on Kinky Friedman's Campaign for Governor of Texas in 2006 (sadly, he lost) and she is working on the Texas Coalition Reform System right now. She feels the police in Texas are very corrupt and racist and this needs to be widely exposed and not tolerated by authority. Activism and helping people are what she is all about.

She is currently pursuing her Ph.D. in International Law in Austin, Texas, and plans on creating laws in the United States that will persecute westerners for sexual crimes they commit while on '*vacation*' overseas. There is a huge sex slave 'market' overseas (There is also one here in the U.S. that preys heavily on illegal immigrants, especially teenagers and children.) that involves child-sex acts, as well as sell and trade of sex slaves, of all ages. It is particularly dominate in third world countries and Westerners (including Europeans and Greeks) are the biggest buyers according to official sources.

As we are talking, knowing that these men who wear designer pinstripe suits, that are predominantly Anglo, corporate types are hurting these children and getting away it, literally makes me hurl green and yellow chunks in my nearby toilet. Natasha further explains (in her nasal-yet-southern drawl) what we all know: they can't sleep with five-year-olds here, but they can go overseas and legally participate in and pay for such acts. She adds, "As a survivor of childhood sexual abuse, I know firsthand the damage it can cause and how it shapes the rest of your life. I cannot, however, imagine what it must be like to be sold into slavery on top of that."

In addition [to changing the legal system here] she is also working on a counseling program for children and female victims of the illegal sex-slave trade. Most women and children are either violently forced into the "ring," or are coerced. Natasha recoils in repulsion as she describes the pedophilic '*travel groups*' of westerners that go to Cambodia to pay for sexual acts from children. It's a huge black market and an underground travel system that is well organized and funded by almost exclusively rich and powerful men, the kind of men that are respected in our society and have high profile careers. Natasha hopes through legislation and work (here and abroad) that this network of pedophiles with buying power will be eradicated and fully criminalized, while building a support and recovery network for its victims. There are two books she cites as great sources to learn more: *The Natasha's* by Victor Malarek, and *Woman, Child for Sale* by Gilbert King.

She recently traveled to Thailand and worked with victims there. She also visited Cambodia with her husband Jon, and they helped provide over 100 books, plus supplies, for the young children. She was shocked that most of the students didn't have shoes because of how impoverished they were. The teachers however were some of the most inspiring and dedicated women she has ever met.

> **"As a survivor of childhood sexual abuse,
> I know firsthand the damage it can cause and how it shapes the rest of your life.
> I cannot, however, imagine what it must be like to be sold into slavery on top of that."**

She met her husband years ago while working as a stripper, connecting over a lap dance. They have been married a decade and he embraces and supports her activism by being directly involved with it. What initially led her into a life of first stripping, and then activism, was her own childhood sexual abuse and a later sexual assault.

"Incest and sexual abuse is denial and betrayals by those who are suppose to protect you. My family was a military family, and my dad was an abusive alcoholic who was Army and never there. All of my brothers were molested by Catholic Priests, and my oldest brother molested me until I was thirteen-years-old.

When I lived in St. Louis, one night on the way home from school I was waiting at the bus stop after finals, and two men raped me. I had to get an abortion and religious freaks were banging on my car and yelling at me. After all of this, I dropped out of college and started stripping. My mom was in denial of everything and said I was just trying to get attention."

It was after she started dating her husband Jon, that she left the world of striping, and started working through her problems related to the neglect and abuse from her family as well as the rape. Her husband understood and was her advocate.

Natasha has a heightened sense of awareness and is very protective of her elementary school-aged daughter Nadia. (At a grocery store once, there was a guy desperately trying to get Nadia's attention, and the entire situation was creepy. He didn't even address Natasha; he kept just trying to talk to Nadia. I had a similar encounter at a grocer. A stranger kept following us around and he was paying me numerous compliments on Corben's beauty—while attempting to touch my son's face and hair.) Natasha knows a large part of society chooses to be blind to these dangers, but they are everywhere, and you leave your child vulnerable if you are not on guard. She is saddened by a recent kidnapping that occurred in a San Diego cul-de-sac ... the little girl was later found dead.

Natasha is thirty-eight now, and practices what is called *Radical Forgiveness*. It is a literal movement of self-empowerment enabling victims to heal, confront, and forgive (see RadicalForgiveness.com). Natasha recommends an amateur filmmaker named Angela Shelton. She made a cross-country documentary about abuse and at the end visits her dad who had abused her as a child.

Natasha and her husband didn't think she could have kids because of a prior medical diagnosis. When they learned she was pregnant, it was happily unplanned. They knew they had to start thinking about their future and for them that meant college. There was no way they could afford it, so they decided to go after the G.I. Bill which meant joining the Navy. They were in the Navy for four years and had joined when Nadia was three-months-old. Natasha started her first period after pregnancy (and breast feeding) on the first day of boot camp. She worked weird shifts and had a hard time finding day care. The military had a six-month waiting list for their day care, which is known to be the best in the United States, excelling and exceeding all legal requirements and standards for public day care. Ultimately, her sister became Nadia's nanny which was critical when she was later deployed.

The military took its toll on Nadia. After the September 11th Attacks Natasha was in a lockdown for three days on a military base and could not leave. In addition, her shifts were over twenty-four hours each. Nadia frequently expressed fear that her parents may not come back. If there were any emergencies declared Natasha had to spend the night on base, even if she had already worked a full shift. She recalls the difficulty of being a parent in the military:

Want to learn more about the sex slave trade and what you can do to help? Check out these books: *The Natasha's* by Victor Malarek, and *Woman, Child for Sale* by Gilbert King. And if you have been hurt and want to fight back, but also want to move on, check out: RadicalForgiveness.com.

> "A famous quote from higher officers was, 'Children weren't issued with your sea-bag.' If a single parent goes into the military, they have to sign over custody to a family member when in training, and permanently if you are going to have a military career. It's even harder and more complicated if your spouse becomes deceased, or you go through a military divorce. How do you afford day care on a military salary? We spent 500.00 a month for Nadia and she still had severe separation anxiety because her dad was stationed in Norfolk, Virginia, and I would be gone for duty twenty-four hours at a time [excluding the deployment and lockdown periods]."

Natasha's experience was horrible, especially when she developed a nervous system disorder due to her military duty—mustard gas exposure and a separate fall injuring her back and hips. Her condition was worsened by military medical indifference. She was a Navy runner and had to undergo surgery and tendons were worn. She developed a virus in her central nervous system; which was later diagnosed as both Fibromyalgia and Gulf War Syndrome (shared symptoms)—both are disabling and chronically painful muscular and skeletal diseases and syndromes.

Before being formerly diagnosed the military sent her to "head" doctors who insisted she was making it all up. They were convinced it was an emotional sickness, not a physical sickness. This denial went on for over a year and a half. During this confusing period, she still had to work as a Navy electrician in excruciating pain, and was denied health care for her sickness by the military. It was finally her female civilian gynecologist that properly diagnosed her disorders. She now receives military disability, in addition to her G.I. Bill for college.

Natasha has to walk with a cane and is limited physically to what she can (and can't do) however, she lives every day to the fullest and refuses to let her disability get her down. She frequently turns to acupuncture and massage therapy to help ease the pain. She believes a positive attitude is the best medicine around. Her overall opinion on the military (and the government that runs it) is bleak:

> "I remember a poor little girl from Alabama in a bunk above me; she came to boot camp with just the clothes on her back. It is the poor who serve their country and it always will be. These 'officials' who are running our country and making decisions don't have a clue about anything and don't care to."

Growing up in the Army, Natasha has lived almost everywhere. She spent her formative years in Germany and France. Her father is a Texan, and her mother Ukrainian and French. Natasha's grandmother died in a Nazi camp during WWII. Her grandfather defected from Ukraine and was assassinated in Kiev. The only reason her mother made it out of the Nazi camp was due to forged SS documents.

Natasha's family moved to the United States when she was fifteen-years-old. She has lived in Louisiana, Texas, and Missouri, but has made the city of Austin, Texas her home. Natasha considers herself simply, an American.

Over the years, she has worked as a: waitress, airline employee, travel agent, sailor, pan-handler, recovering addict, and student. Her job now is as a mother and a mentor to her daughter Nadia. As a family they make frequent trips to the library, and read every night. Their parenting philosophy is to include Nadia in everything they do, and to incorporate learning into daily activities. For example, Nadia wants to be a Bat Girl so they have all studied Bats so Nadia can perfect her Bat Girl-Superhero craft.

Natasha feels blessed because Nadia is a natural leader and they have helped cultivate this personality aspect by encouraging her in everything she has wanted to do and learn about. Nadia now takes her place at the protests with her signs and opinions, and is very empathetic to those who are being hurt. She was deeply troubled by the mass killings in Darfur and participated in a protest against the genocide.

Natasha knows firsthand that kids in our culture are suffering from lack of P.E. in schools and too much Ritalin. Natasha herself used to be medicated with prescribed anti-depressive drugs,

> "I wear my emotions fairly close to the surface and have always struggled with ways to deal with it. I did the same self-medication that most of us have, but as of late, I have just decided to embrace it. The same levels of emotions that allow me to experience great sorrow are the same ones that allow me to experience tremendous joy. I am learning to love myself more and more each day and allowing myself to fall occasionally along the way. I make mistakes, but I try to learn from them. Like I tell my daughter, it's not a mistake if you learn something from it. It's a lesson."

She feels that our culture's tendency to over medicate itself (and our children) is killing our creativity, as well as severely damaging our nation's mental and emotional health. There is nothing healthy about zombie children, and plastic adults. For children who are hyper, she feels all they need is a positive redirection of their energy, and to let that energy out through physical activity. She concludes that mental focus will follow and as the parent or teacher, just keep repeating the above as needed. She speculates that the majority of kids on

Ritalin shouldn't be. The combination of documented forced administration of Ritalin in schools and the poor academic performance of many schools, has her considering pulling her daughter out.

Natasha also fears what the American diet is doing to our kids. Since lower middle and lower class families can't afford Whole Foods or to buy organic exclusively, if at all, the options are more limiting and she thinks the weird science of modern American food is killing us. She feeds Nadia a very healthy diet, and buys organic when she can, but she is limited to what is affordable (like most of us). She believes our food is poisoning us. Natasha is a concerned global citizen who literally tosses and turns at night, if she doesn't keep her frustration in check.

It was frustration with preppy school kids that initially attracted her to the subculture scene. She hung out with them at school, and "they just talked shit about everyone," and she didn't like that. She just woke up one morning (at fifteen years-of-age) and shaved her head. She went to school and most of her friends dropped her, because she no longer looked the same. She developed some new ones that understood her teenage angst. It was a fragile age for her, but she finally felt good to hang out with others who didn't need to talk down to other people in order to make themselves feel better.

Her newly formed band of misfits became political activists without even knowing it per se. They launched a petition against a waste injection nuclear plant that was being proposed in their town of Corpus Christi. She grew her hair into a mohawk and has been a political activist ever since. She loves the music that also happened to come along with her newly formed identity: Punk Rock. It was political and satirical. Bad Religion and Swinging Utters are two of her favorite bands. She also likes classical music and old country. She remembers the old days fondly, "Back then you had to do your own piercings and make your own clothes. There weren't shops or places to buy your stuff. It was defining because it was anti-culture and not something you could just buy to be."

When she isn't holding a protest sign, this six-foot tall queenie is striking a pose as a vixen in mini-skirts and fishnets.

She has blood red hair that vampires would die for and pouty lips. As a self-proclaimed fallen Catholic, it makes sense that she would model for 666 Photography in Austin. They specialize in vintage influenced pin-up photography of obscure and beautiful women. You can check out more of their amazing pin-ups, and Natasha herself at: 666Photography.com.

She can't wait to finish school and start working with the United Nations and the United States to pursue legal changes to insure persecution of westerners who violate children and/or buy slaves abroad. It won't be too much longer before she starts helping to radically change the rest of the world and her closing wishes for mothers is …

"It is up to us to teach our daughters how to expect to be treated by example. If we allow our husbands and boyfriends to treat us badly, then we teach our daughters to learn they are worthless. On the other side, we have to teach our sons how to treat women."

**Since this interview: Natasha is recently divorced, but is happily pursuing life in Africa, and writing a book about the deceptions of the Military.*

"I think the counterculture mommas are the fiercest ones out there. We are not afraid to love our children and protect them at all costs. There is a certain lack of self-consciousness amongst these moms."

Kristin
Military Wife
Feminist Mentor
Stay-at-Home Working Mom
Lovely Law Student
Fort Worth, Texas.

Kristin is a married Air Force mom who has two children. However, she doesn't fit the picture of the traditional military wife with her nose and nipple piercings, broken rose and flaming heart tattoos. Most military wives are expected to obey their husbands, as they themselves obey military command. She steps out of this chain-of-command. She expects respect and equality within her relationships, both inside and outside of marriage.

She is an educated and opinionated feminist. She wears the feminist badge proudly now, but before she really knew what it was, she was being called one simply for speaking her truth.

Growing up Kristin never felt like she had a purpose, and she didn't fit in anywhere. It never occurred to her that she could do anything great. Her fate has changed. All it took was life making it happen, and suddenly she was inspired to help others who have gone down a similar path to her own. She is currently working on getting a degree in legal sociology, with the intent of earning a Ph.D. Her husband is her biggest fan, and her two children her muses. However, it is her own experience of being a teenage mom who made all the wrong choices (except for having for her son) which inspires her to reach out and mentor other teenage mothers.

Once she is done with college and her doctorate studies, she plans on raising funding that will allow her to open a home for teenage moms that will serve to empower, educate, help and support them while teaching them the skills they need to live on their own successfully as (young) single parents. She wants to show them that not everyone is disappointed in them. She does not promote teen pregnancy, but she wants them to know that they, "Aren't just a statistic and they don't have to be a high school dropout and a 'drain' on society." Her attitude is what's done is done, so we (society) need to quit kicking them and start helping them.

She brings her own experience to the table for this nonprofit plan for a group home and teen mom mentoring. By the time she had become a teenage mom, she had already been disowned by her family for suicide attempts, and she had no one to turn to for support. She lived back and forth between her grandmother, friends, and boyfriends. She found herself pregnant at nineteen. It was like walking around in the dark having to feel your way out by touch and smell alone, but with a baby on your hip.

She eventually found the *Hip Mama* zine and the books by writer Ariel Gore, which helped give her some sense of normalcy and parental insight. However, as a teenage mom she needed more than just material to read. She needed human contact that was sincere, loving, helpful and encouraging. We all need people we can look up to. Growing up she didn't have a role model, and ironically, it is the obstacles and joys of teenage motherhood that created the woman she is today. She is now a role model for others who seek her help or friendship. She's not sure exactly how she will get the funding for her home, but knows when she gets closer to graduating with her Ph.D. it will all work out with a little luck, lots of hard work and passion. In the meantime, her door and heart is open to anyone who needs her. She has helped young moms that have turned to her for advice about life, choices, obstacles, finding resources, careers, school, as well as parenting. Her mentoring process has already begun with the most radical social approach: human compassion, understanding and love.

Many women suffer from the sexual exploitations of adults that occur to them in their teenage years, and this is another key to where strong non-sexually objectified female mentors are critical, as well as the understanding of, and the empowerment of teenage girls to ward off exploitations by having a strong adult network. Some Riot Grrrl enrichment would go a long way too.

She now has a strong sense of self and purpose, and feels she became a woman after becoming a mother. She doesn't have to be the black sheep anymore. She exclaims with gratitude and humor that finally, "The gods were good to me when they gave me my son Gabriel thereby opening this door for me." This was her transitional period of hanging out with the wrong crowd and the wrong man. She was putting up with all kinds of "shit from men that should have warning labels." [Many women suffer from the sexual exploitations of adults that occur to them in their teenage years, and this is another key to where strong non-sexually objectified female mentors are critical, as well as the understanding of, and the empowerment of teenage girls to ward off exploitations by having a strong adult network. Some Riot Grrrl enrichment would go a long way too.]

During this time it never occurred to her (nor had she been taught) that having unprotected sex could get you pregnant. She was shocked to find herself a brand new mother at the age of twenty. She had no job, and before her affair she had just left an abusive relationship, which her parents denied ever happened. They underestimated the impact their denial had on her; in addition to the suffering and damage the relationship caused her. Her mother thought she was "stupid" for not having an abortion, but Kristin was young, hopeful, and certain it would all work out.

Her relationship with her parents had never been strong, or intimate. Her mother was very liberal and let her and her three sisters do whatever they wanted. She moved in with her dad as a teenager and went through an environmental shock. Her father and his second wife were very strict and they had a tight grip on their kids. She felt she was suffocating with the lack of trust they had in her which lead to her becoming manic depressive. She developed an obsessive compulsive disorder and ultimately attempted suicide twice before turning eighteen. She had been cutting herself with razors before the suicide attempts started.

> "I tried to commit suicide twice in six weeks and the second time I came very close to succeeding. I was asleep in a hospital for a couple of days and when I woke up, my dad was there. The first thing he said to me was that he was very angry with me and I couldn't come home to his house. This broke my heart. I always wanted to be like my daddy. I had only lived with him for three years. I moved in with his mom, and have tried and tried to talk to him, but he isn't interested. I've only recently been able to deal with this."

Even though Kristin has rebuilt her life, and now has a great second marriage (Her first marriage was to Gabriel's father after he left his wife), two beautiful children, and is a grown woman now, her father still refuses to have any contact with her. She mourns the loss of this relationship daily. She feels she made many mistakes as a teenager—but he as a parent made many mistakes too. She has been able to forgive herself (and her father), she just wishes her father could understand and maybe, just maybe, could have been there for her on a more emotional level—or start being there now.

With her first son Gabriel, she had hoped his father wouldn't ignore him like he did his sons from his first marriage. He left his other family to start theirs. She hoped he would somehow be different. She wanted him to, "to want to get a better job, and a better apartment." She wanted all the things he didn't. [A lot of girls and young women tend to date bad/undeveloped/lazy/unmotivated or abusive/controlling men and then try to change them and mold them into what they want them to be: typically, better suitors, or more or less equals to themselves.]

Her dream of having a house with a big yard for her son came crashing down when shortly after a year of marriage, she came home one evening to find he had packed her stuff and told her he no longer wanted to try, it wasn't working out. He kicked her and their son out of the apartment, and he kept their only car. She had literally no belongings or money, and little direction to go by. This is when she started developing a true sense of self and inner strength. Looking back, she was incredibly hurt at the time and feels it was the gods clearing the way for her to find herself, and for her second husband to find her. Next to having her son, she knows it was the best thing that could have ever happened to her.

She turned to the world of art, literature and music to help her develop her inner voice and round out her true sense of purpose. She discovered an abundance of articulated social and political opinions that she could suddenly relate to and understand.

"I like Ani Di Franco. Her lyrics are empowering and she is very strong, and listening to her music makes me feel very strong. They talk to me. I like a lot of 'chick singers,' because they are empowering. Gina B. Nahai is the best author I have ever read. Her books are about women staying strong and living their lives for themselves within the tribulations of being a woman in Tehran, Iran. Ariel Gore is a strong and smart woman, that is a gifted writer and I'm glad I discovered her books."

During this stage, she learned some things about herself including the love of cooking, which to her is an art form. She started writing and keeping a journal. She now collects song lyrics and scrapbooks them to keep a collage of meaningful words for inspiration during hard times. And she fell in love with tattooing and piercing:

"I had wanted my nose pierced since I was fourteen and now was the time. I don't think there was any symbolism to it besides aesthetics. I felt like a bad-ass when I got it pierced. I feel like that every time I get a tattoo or a piercing. I love to go to the tattoo place, because I can face big scary tattooed guys all by myself. I must be bad! Right after I get one done, I start thinking of what I want next and where I want it."

Kristin met her second husband and during this time and they fell deeply in love. When she met him, the spark felt right and she knew he was the one. She suddenly found her place in the world and she had the epiphany that she could do anything she wanted. She has temporarily put school on hold as they have had their second child together. (He has now become the legal father of Gabriel as well.) As a military family they get moved around about every three months. Once they are stationed somewhere longer she plans on resuming her schooling and working towards her dream of opening the home.

She believes that motherhood is the most important role and all too often people take it lightly. She has encountered a lot of people who seem to have kids because it is the socially prescribed next step following the career, the marriage, and buying a house. Somehow it falls into a social status checklist.

Kristin thinks people, spiritually, are either good or bad at their core, and that parents don't necessarily make them that way. She feels that all we can do is instill our morals into our children and allow them to spread their wings; they will become whoever they will be. She does draw the line though at shoving our beliefs down our children's throats, which is a mistake she thinks many parents make. She feels it's critical that we give children enough space and room for independent thinking within our boundaries of guidance.

She feels "unimportant" in society as a stay-at-home working mother. She thinks there are two sides in society, which are those that have kids and those that don't:

> "Some people with kids, and most without, expect young children to act like small adults. This just isn't realistic. I don't think society makes any allowances for children. There aren't a lot of kid friendly places for day-to-day errands, or even places to go. Where do you take a two-year-old for entertainment? It is odd that society isn't very kid friendly considering it isn't rare to have kids. Everybody raises their kids differently, but very few people think that there may be techniques that vary from their own that could work also, unless of course if Dr. Phil suggests it. Every kid is different and society needs to realize they can't all be treated the same. Public schools should tap into this."

She expects her children to grow up happy, smart and open-minded. If she raises them to be self-sufficient, do what they want, and to treat everyone with respect, then she asserts that she will be successful as a mother. She hopes her children never feel worthless like she did as a child and teen. A value she plans on instilling in her children is to stand up for what's right and for what they believe in. She will support them 100% as well, even if her opinion differs. She knows this self-confidence and self-trust is the cornerstone of a healthy self-esteem. Though both of her children are very young right now, both are under five-years-of-age, she is instilling this by example already.

She is very vocal when strangers or outsiders start judging her or imposing their views, uninvited, on to her and her family,

> "If a woman decides to get an abortion, somewhere in the world, if she is okay with it, then why should it bother me? If two men want to get married, it has no effect on me. Let them have their love and marital benefits. Who I am hurting if I decide to practice paganism? Let me go to hell. I think too many people are in too many other

people's business. Everyone needs to step back and take care of their own business, before they start telling everyone else ... who is going to hell and who isn't. I want to live as I want to live. I just want the truth to be told, my feelings on certain situations, and my intentions. So often it seems I am misunderstood. I don't mind that I have slept around. I have tats and a couple of piercings. I am very open-minded, and I am a pagan. But I am still a good mom, and I don't rob liquor stores."

She feels that similar to children, there are different types of moms in the world. There are some that are her age (she is now twenty-five) that feel the need "to follow the standards set by society," and other moms more like herself, that she can identify with. She relates to moms who have a shared common background of living through similar situations and they aren't afraid to talk about it. This is evident from the ease of her conversation amongst a room of mothers from all different walks of life. Kristin is very soft-spoken, but very articulate and comfortable in her own skin. In fact, she will securely lock her penetrating Atlantic blue eyes onto yours and her stare forces your attention. The conversation is not over until she releases that intense gaze. Beyond just the obvious differences in appearance from mainstream mothers and counter/subculture mothers, Kristin feels the ability to talk candidly about real experiences both about mothering and beyond it, is what truly makes us counter/sub culture moms, different. [Mainstream moms are starting to articulate their experiences, struggles, and suffering more vocally, thanks to the feminist subtext of the alternative parenting cultures, but the mainstream media inclusion of these voices is still vague and fails to address the complex challenges affecting and concerning parents—while completely ignoring working class parents.] Many people are unhappy with the way the world is being run, and run down, by both big business and the government (which legalizes it). This exploitation directly impacts families and local economies. Most people don't say anything for fear it will make them unpopular by defying and challenging the norm—which can also be threatening to ones livelihood. Kristin thinks this fear of speaking up and out, is even worse for mainstream moms who may feel disempowered and scrutinized more so than they did before having kids. This scrutiny encompasses every part of their lives: their image, career/work, their children's behavior, their time and financial limitations, activities outside of mothering, their political life, etc; anything can label them un-motherly and thus a failure—even if it's simply not being able to do it all, with or without resources. She detests the popular advertised mother who seems to have to been re-virginized through laundry soap, mini-vans and popular entertaining. This is not who we are, we are more than taxi's, baby-sitters, and cake bakers. Even mainstreams moms are belittled by this popular myth and stereotype. Kristin crisply adds, "We are smart enough to know that we don't have to lose our identity when we become mothers."

Kristin fell naturally into a subculture way of life, since that is where society places her belief systems. She is very comfortable there though, since there is so much open-mindedness. She likes being who she is and not being judged for it. It's her opinion that most subculture moms kind of fell into motherhood and found themselves pretty damn good at it.

> "We use our instincts (with a little help from Ariel Gore) rather than Dr. Babywise to raise our children. I think a lot of mainstream moms have their kids because they got married and that is the next step, therefore they never really get close to their kids. They are usually older and probably settled down. At least in my case, we move and see different ways of life. I feel as if I am educating my son so that he knows not everyone lives like he does. Counterculture living is a hell of a lot more open-minded than the mainstream. There is a lot more freedom to be who you are. I also think the subculture or counterculture mommas are the fiercest ones out there. We are not afraid to love our children and protect them at all costs. There is a certain lack of self-consciousness amongst these moms."

Kristin does believe that mainstream moms and subculture moms could exchange great ideas and significantly open up the path of communication, if a dialogue between the two began, and revolutionize parenting and the perception of mothers in society. She doesn't necessarily buy into the popular stereotype that is being peddled that tells the mainstream mom who she is (while making it clear who subculture and working class moms aren't), and thinks most mainstream moms will reject it after a while, especially as we all work towards making the world not only a cooler place, but a much better one.

As she works on school, raising her children, and developing her project for the home for teenage moms, her voice quivers in anticipation … "I want to help young mothers and girls find their voice. Helping these girls avoid what I went through as a teenager and a new mom gets me excited enough to make my hands and voice shake."

"Back when I was 'becoming' who I am today, I was yelled at for looking the way did. I was told I was 'going to hell' simply for my hair, clothes and make-up. I heard so much that made no sense to me."

Jenn Bats
Death Rocker
Manager and Co-Founder of the Release the Bats Club in L.A.
Vegetarian
Animal Rights Activist
Rockin' Retail Worker
Los Angeles, California.

Jenn is a thirty-something, hard-working, fun-loving girl. She wears black all the time and her hair is dyed bright red and deep black. She has over twelve tattoos and adorns herself in dark make-up. She is a "free" person, who doesn't let "little things", like the daily grind, child-rearing stresses, or other people's stereotypes and attitudes, get her down. She's very honest, "perhaps too honest sometimes with others." It's important to her to make those that she cares about happy.

Jenn has been a vegetarian and an environmentalist for over six years. She loves animals and just couldn't eat them anymore. She wishes people would think about animals and stop torturing them, eating them, and killing the endangered. She is adamant about recycling and keeping the earth in tip-top shape. She wishes that "people would stop throwing their trash on the ground for Christ's-sake!"

One of her favorite books is *And I Don't Want to Live This Life* ... It's written by Deborah Spungen and is about her daughter Nancy, who was killed by her boyfriend Sid Vicious in a drug-induced nightmare. Jenn mostly likes to read historical biographies. She shares her love of reading (in addition to green living views and animal rights) with her teenage daughter Akasha and recently passed this book onto her.

Jenn likes 70s punk, 80s goth, new wave, and metal. Some of her favorite musicians/bands are: Siouxsie (of Siouxsie and the Banshees), Bauhaus, Sisters of Mercy, Anton Lavey, the Cure, Guns-N-Roses, the Clash, the Sex Pistols and David Bowie. Her absolute favorite artist though is Rozz Williams (solo artist, sadly deceased, and the founder of Christian Death). His music really affects her deeply, because it is "amazing, interesting, dark and tormented."

Even though the death rock scene and punk scenes are polar opposites from each other (yet closely related) they both define her and her reality. One thing she loves about the death rock scene specifically though is that, "It is full of really creative, talented, and open-minded people," which Jenn feels this is how the world should be, but it isn't. She feels religion and bigotry are closely related and that's why world at large isn't the world it could be—a world without violence. She is an atheist and had this to say:

> "I believe in reality. I believe in myself and the people in my life. I do not believe in 'god'. I think that had there been science 2000 plus years ago, religion would have never happened. I also don't think it makes any sense to deprive yourself of things because a book tells you too. The bible is irrelevant in today's world. I'm not saying it's wrong to believe in God, go ahead, but don't judge me for not believing. Being fanatical doesn't help any religion look good."

Jenn formed her atheist opinions in early youth after negative encounters with Christians (whom she witnessed yelling at people and judging people), and as an adult after experiencing how government uses religion to manipulate and control the masses [think of how our former President Bush Jr. had used '*God & Democracy*' as a rallying cry to invade Iraq, while handing out huge war profiteering contracts to his Secretary of Defense and Vice President, Dick Cheney and his companies.]

She distrusts the government and disapproves of the laws that make it okay to kill animals (legalization of unnecessary animal experiments for corporations that serve as liability waivers, vanity killing for furs, and corporate torture farming). She also feels that the government has failed (at large and in general) to enforce laws that prosecute or prevent rape. *[The social indoctrination of sexism supports rape and the sexual objectification of women, girls, and gay individuals. These attitudes persist despite any formal laws on the books to the contrary, because of the lack of legal (therefore, lack of social) enforcement. The second rape occurs when victims are blamed for the violent crimes of their attackers. The blame-the-victim legal attitude in courts is a prime example of making the laws ineffective—which is the judicial intent—so that we as a society can continue to excuse rape and other violent crimes.]* The reaction that Jenn frequently receives is that, "It's weird or perverse to not eat animals, or for women to stand up for themselves."

The blame-the-victim legal attitude in courts is a prime example of making the laws ineffective—which is the judicial intent—so that we as a society can continue to excuse rape and other violent crimes.

Jenn has been running the Release the Bats! club at the Que Sera Bar in Los Angeles, California, for almost a decade now. It is a notorious club known throughout the world. Some of the great bands and artists that have performed there are: Gitane Demone, Kommunity FK, Element, Cinema Strange,

Frankenstein, Frank the Baptist, and Dinah Cancer with Penis Flytrap & the Graverobbers.

Hollywood in the early eighties had an abundance of death rock clubs that faded as make-up metal dominated the L.A. scene. Jenn and her boyfriend Dave yearned for a club like the ones that were around when they were teenagers. They had always thrown parties, loved decorating, and having a good time to awesome tunes. They had been going to the Que Sera Bar for quite some time and discussed the idea of throwing a gothic rock party for Halloween in 1998 with the owner Benz. They wanted to bring back the aesthetic that was once that scene. They held the first Release the Bats! party that year. It had such a strong turn out that they have been doing it every month ever since, for over ten years now. They deejay, book the bands, and handle all of the events for it. Release the Bats! occurs monthly, so there is no burn-out for either event-throwers or party-goers. You can learn more about the club at ReleasetheBats.com.

Dave and Jenn have been in a relationship for over eleven years now and were friends before that. They have mutual respect for each other and trust each other completely. They have never doubted their love, because it is so strong. They are best friends which has enabled their relationship to be long-lasting. The fact that they knew each other so well before dating helped a lot too. They view their relationship as an accomplishment of love. He makes it "okay" for Jenn to be herself and accepts her for everything she is including "Crazy, moody, bitchy, and silly."

Dave is a cyclist and a musician. He is also a vegetarian. They have several cats, of which one is diabetic, and another one which suffers from a hyperthyroid. Dave is a wonderful stepfather to Akasha, and she spends her winter and summer breaks annually with Jenn & him.

Akasha has been living with her biological father during school terms since she was four years old—which is when he ran off with her.

Jenn was only nineteen when she started dating Akasha's dad. They seemed to be similar people, both gothic and atheist.

She wasn't thinking of her future (as most teenagers aren't) and they had an unplanned pregnancy. The first pregnancy was aborted; she was not ready to have kid. A year later, they had another unplanned pregnancy and she decided to carry this pregnancy to term.

"I was going to have an abortion again, but after that one, I just couldn't do it again. I'm glad we as women have that choice, but it's not a good time. I talked to my mom, who had me around the same age, and asked her how she did it with no money or a real home. She told me it was all about the love and that if you're ready, it will work. I felt like I was ready this time.

I was with this guy for over a year now and believed I was ready to settle down and be a mom. I made the right choice for the most part. I got a great kid out of it. I may have made a mistake as far as the guy goes, but without him, I wouldn't have her.

I had hoped and planned to have a happy family like you see on TV, like the Munsters or the Addams Family. But that's not how it worked out. I didn't really know Akasha's dad like I thought I had. We ended up having nothing in common. He wasn't what he seemed. I was a death-rock-atheist-chic. He turned normal on me and began listening to country music and watching sports. And soon he became engulfed in Christianity. The fights began."

Since Jenn was not in a happy relationship, her marriage to Akasha's dad was over in a year. Akasha was almost two-years-old when they split up. They were apartment managers at the time and when the split up occurred, she had to move out since she couldn't take care of all the duties on her own. She was temporality forced by circumstances to let her ex have physical custody of Akasha, since she now had no job or a home suddenly. She never intended on not having her daughter with her full-time. She thought there was a mutual understanding that this was temporary until she got on her feet and got her life back together.

During this time that Dave reentered her life as a friend and they started dating shortly thereafter. She knew her life was going somewhere, she just didn't know where. She also knew she loved her girl and her little girl loved her too.

"After days of trying to get in touch with Akasha (She and her dad had been living with his mom at this time.), I received a message on my answering machine from my ex saying that he moved to Minnesota with my daughter. I freaked out and felt totally alone and helpless. I should've sent the cops after him, but was concerned about how that would affect my then four-year-old kid, and I didn't. The ONLY regret I have in my life is that I didn't get her back, that I didn't put up a big enough fight. If I had only done something then, she would be living with us right now. Akasha and I have since discussed this and she knows the whole story."

The first few years after this, Jenn did the best she could to get along with her ex for Akasha's sake and make the best of the situation, while sharing custody. Akasha frequently lived back and forth between them, during school terms she lived in Minnesota, and during the summer she lived with Jenn in California.

In 2001, her ex remarried and sued her for full custody. All parties, including the new stepmom, had to be interviewed by a Guardian Ad Litem. (A court appointed guardian, normally a legal volunteer who works for the courts, who has no relation or social relationships to the family members. They are appointed normally for the duration of the court hearings to act in the single interest of the child as defined by: law, conservative family culture, and the judge.) The Guardian concluded from all the interviews that there was no reason that Jenn should not have as many parental rights as her ex. Then they went to court. Jenn had to be on speaker phone for the court hearing since it was being held in Minnesota. The judge concluded there was nothing wrong with Jenn as a mother (or a person) in spite of the personality allegations being brought against her by her ex: devil-worshiper, atheist, and radical.

The ex and his new wife tried to use her "lack of religion" and the "way she looks" against her. They failed to make any valid points or arguments. Jenn's advice for anyone going through a custody battle is:

"Be honest. Courts can see though most nonsense. I went in real honest, real and smart, and all that shows. I don't play games, and I don't mess around. I'm very upfront."

They finally settled on sharing custody with Jenn having Akasha winter and summer breaks. She did this partially for her daughter who had been in the same small community and school since she was four and Jenn didn't want to disrupt that. Akasha expressed fear of starting over at another school and leaving her friends behind, even though she did want to move to be with her mom and Dave. (Jenn was completely supportive and understanding and didn't want to force Akasha to do anything she was not ready for, or comfortable with.) Jenn has assured Akasha time and time again all she has to do is say the word and she will come get her.

They talk everyday online and over the phone, and they are very close despite their long distance relationship during the school year. They make their situation work for them. Jenn firmly believes Akasha will be with them full-time once she is ready. Until then, they will maintain their current relationship which is strong and thriving.

Akasha is now thirteen-years-old, and Jenn is thirty-four-years-old. However, Jenn's maturity doesn't mean that dealing with her ex has been a walk in the park. In fact, it has been anything but …

"Her dad and stepmom are fanatical Born Again Christians who live in a small town. They have tried to turn my daughter against me from the start. They tell her because of my hair, tattoos and lack of 'GOD', that I'll be going to hell. It's been a tough trip. Especially, since I had to contend with a man that hated me and wanted my daughter to hate me too. It's very hard to deal with them. They take things way too serious and it causes issues with my daughter, which in turn makes me upset.

But my daughter understands I am different, but in a good way. She has chosen to follow in our footsteps rather than her dads. By that I mean she has chosen to believe in herself, rather than a religion and she has also chosen to become vegetarian. For this she gets tons of grief from her dad and stepmom, but she sticks to her choices and beliefs. They often make her sad and push her to the edge, especially when they won't give her credit for having a mind of her own, and when they push their beliefs down her throat.

The bottom line is that I've always been real with her and in return I have an open-minded, intelligent, thoughtful daughter. I'm very proud of her."

Jenn loves photography, and she makes photo albums of life, capturing moments both when Akasha is away at school, and while she is there on vacations. This enables them to document and share their time together and apart. She takes photos of all occasions and keeps them in chronological order. The photo albums chronicle all their times with family, friends, pets, and all the changes everyone goes through. Jenn also keeps journals as well. It's a story of their lives that go all the way back to 1990, even before Akasha.

Akasha was named after one of Jenn's favorite characters, the elder queen vampire in Anne Rice's novel *Queen of the Damned.* The movie came out a few years later, but at the time the name was virtually unknown.

One thing Akasha loves about her breaks with her mom and stepfather is that she gets to pick out tons of cool clothes from the Hot Topic store her mom manages. As far as parenting goes, Jenn had this to say:

> "I think I had a natural instinct for mummy-hood. I always loved kids, even as a kid. I never had any big goals for 'becoming' something, or someone. I thought that being a mom and staying-at-home doing mom things was the coolest. To raise a little person was an awesome experience. Even if my time was cut short with my girl, due to my divorce, I know I did a great job with the time I had her with me. I've realized also that it gets easier, as well as harder, as kids grow up. It's easier because they can take care of themselves in so many ways. But then dealing with pre-teens is terrifying! I know what's going on in her little head, because I remember what was going on in my head at her age! There's a lot of drama in there, the boys, the peer pressure, plus the completely different parents. I never forget what it's like to be a kid. I can't understand how 'adults' forget so quickly. Once you've forgotten you lose all sense of what your kid is going through, and that's not fair to the kids."

"I never forget what it's like to be a kid. I can't understand how 'adults' forget so quickly. Once you've forgotten you lose all sense of what your kid is going through, and that's not fair to the kids."

Jenn knows there's a lot of unchartered parenting in her future as a parent of a teen, but she knows that the qualities she and her daughter share [being: loving, honest, open-minded, real and tolerant] will help carry them through the teenage years. Jenn leads by example, and is not one of those parents that say, "Do as I say, not as I do …" Jenn always listens to her daughter and is always fair. She admits sometimes this is a challenge, but she keeps this in the front of her mind at all times so that she can practice what she preaches—even in the heat of the moment.

Her ex continuously throws obstacles at her and her relationship with Akasha, but she never lets him succeed, since her will is stronger than his. She also has the ability in general to look beyond the bad things and make good out of them. Jenn does have many concerns about the state of the world which she summarizes as …

> "The world is so fucked up and complicated right now. I make things as happy as they can be in such a scary place. Honestly, I think the world is way too wrapped up in organized religion. No one can think for themselves anymore. Living in fear is not living at all. I think our [former] President Bush is a moron who led the herd to destruction. I chose not to follow. I wish people would just stop and think more often, rather than act so fast.
>
> Sometimes I feel there are so many good people, fighting the good fight. Then I realize that there are so many more that aren't. In many ways, society is more open to 'alternative' lifestyles now. I feel, we as 'alternative' people, are becoming more abundant. As we get older we are having our own children, who follow in our footsteps and are out there doing good things. We are all trying to make the world a better place, but there are evil religious freaks that are trying to take over and strip us of our freedoms.
>
> I do however have hope for the kids. There are so many people breeding, being wasteful and thoughtless of their actions, and their kids are products of their environments. All I can hope for is that they see more and learn more than their parents have to offer them. Some parents are just clueless."

In spite of everything being mainstream nowadays including punk and gothic, Jenn still gets looked down upon for being a death rock mom. It is okay as a fad sold to kids and teenagers through commercialization and marketing, but it's not okay for it to be a way of life, dress, and values—for the long run.

She does know some moms now that are similar to her, and they share a common objective: to teach their children not to be afraid of what other kids might consider scary, that there are good things in the dark. They also are firm believers in teaching tolerance of all people, "Just because someone is different doesn't make them bad." A basic family rule of theirs is:

> "Live and let live, unless someone oversteps their bounds. Don't get in my face, don't push your beliefs on me, or my family, and don't mess with us and we will all live happily ever after."

Jenn was always attracted to darker things, like Halloween, spiders, skulls and spikes. She has loved boys in make-up ever since she can remember. She remembers being ten-years-old and driving down Hollywood Boulevard with her beloved Grammy & Papa and seeing a punk dude for the first time. He had a huge blue mohawk and a leather jacket on. She thought he was the coolest person she had ever seen. She knew she wanted to look like that way, and be that.

Her parents were hippies. They both dressed different from all the other parents. Her dad had long hair and biker tattoos. Her mom was a lot like Stevie Nicks, in the sense that she dressed like a gypsy and was a free thinker. Jenn grew up listening to the Beatles, Janis Joplin, Rolling Stones, the Doors, and Pink Floyd. They lived in the Valley, which is the dominant agricultural area of central California. The area was made famous by the popular eighties movie *Valley Girl*, that stared a very young [and cute] Nicholas Cage as a punk rocker.

Her parents didn't really get the whole "goth" thing, which back then was real obscure. Once they realized she hadn't lost her mind in the "depths of darkness" they dealt with it pretty well. They could relate to her because they got the same stares, yells from strangers, and misunderstandings that she did.

She went to her first goth club at age seventeen, and from the moment she walked in, she knew this was where she belonged. She didn't go to college; she went to Helter Skelter (a death rock club in L.A.). A decade and a half later, everyone she knows she met there. Times have changed since she was a teenager …

> "I don't get yelled at in the streets or attacked by religious people as often. It still happens, but not like it was when I was a teenager. But it was kind of nice being 'different,' now everybody is goth or punk, or so it seems."

However, once mainstream moms get to know her they like her. In fact, she was a nanny for six years for some wealthy and affluent mothers—with her dark make-up, bright hair, lace and spikes. Jenn knows that counterculture moms generally teach their kids to be themselves despite what others may think. She adds that, "But if you're a good, smart person that's not a 'counterculture' mom that's okay too. I've known plenty of 'normal' moms who are great moms and great people."

For the future Jenn is eagerly waiting for the day Akasha will want to come live with Dave and her permanently. Jenn is also working on making stories out of the events of her life and hoping to get them published. Other than that, they are working on opening Release the Bats! at various clubs throughout the world.

Awesome!

"We need to redefine mainstream. We are the mainstream, and what people are drawn too. We aren't underground, we are ABOVE ground."

Kimberly
Fierce Momma
Style Queen
Hip-Hop Organizer Extraordinaire
Warrior Mammas Productions Creator
Heal from Depression (Blogspot.com) Founder
M.O.B.B. Activist
Atlanta, Georgia.

Kimberly is a Warrior Mamma who works at home raising her son, and taking care of her family, while doing unpaid work through local direct-action activism and global internet community action building and developing critical community cohesiveness. Both jobs are very time consuming, exhausting, demanding and the most rewarding work she has done yet.

She recently graduated from Georgia State University, earning her degree in journalism and African-American studies, after attending both part-time and full-time for a span of eleven years.

She is a Libra who is always seeking balance, clarity and completion. She recharges herself through spiritualism and listening to good tunes. Some of her favorite bands and singers are Lizz Wright, Nina Simone, and Nirvana.

Kimberly has several tattoos of which her most recent is an Amazonian warrior who is visibly pregnant and in her last term. Her warrior is armed with swords in each hand, and is covered in earned (periods of tribulation and trial) tribal tattoos. The tattoo is symbolic to Kimberly, who is a strong woman, and a fierce, protective mother. She's an intense modern urban warrior.

She views motherhood and activism as two jobs that go hand-in-hand; to have an interest in the success and development of your child, in turn means having an interest in the success and development of all people in your community and surrounding communities. This is the motivation that keeps her up at night working when her body would rather be sleeping.

Motherhood led to her forming a media productions group and an online community called Warrior Mammas. She views motherhood not as a fragile, delicate, and docile state of being—a popular myth of generations past—nor as a corporate glossy photo shoot for the super rich—the current popular myth—but as an active human state that fully engages, confronts and challenges all parts of living, functions, formalities and society; both within the home and extending outside of the home. She feels the goals of the business world at large tend to be rather counterproductive to the needs of the community and of mothers. [Oil spills and environmental destruction, unpaid maternity/paternity leave, no benefits, low wages and excessive hours; companies like Coca Cola using the only water wells for making Coke in India causing deadly drinking water shortages according to the IRC (India Resource Center—IndiaResource.org), Nestle promoting *bottle is best* in third world countries causing infant mortalities (The campaign against Nestle started in 1977 in the U.S., and has been maintained by the international non-profit Save the Children

(.net) activist group, etc.] Kimberly wirily concludes that motherhood in and of itself is activism. Shortly after becoming a mother, Kimberly had started the online community board which recently celebrated its 200th member, and produced the *Best of the Warrior Mamma Board.* The best topics were reposted for viewer participation: Wonderful Birth Stories, Preparing for Natural Childbirth, Cesarean Art, Thoughts on Your Vagina, How A Warrior Mamma Makes It Through, Circumcision or Not, Orgasmic Birth, and Vaccinations. You can visit the online community at: Groups.Myspace.com/NaturalBirth.

She created the group after having an unplanned, unassisted home birth (this was very literal—she planned on having the baby at the hospital—but didn't make it in time) to support what our bodies naturally know how to do. She wanted to encourage women to learn to trust their own instincts, while providing support, sharing resources and experiences. She has seen how this online dialogue truly makes a difference in the lives of women who find little public support elsewhere. Her partner Kenyatta and she had planned on having a natural birth in a controlled setting in the hospital with a living birth plan. They prepared themselves with taking local doula classes called *Birthing in Awareness.* (The class is based on the book *Birthing from Within* by Pam England.) Kimberly feels these two things were critical to their successful home birth.

> "I am 99.9% certain that this six-week course prepared us for the amazing birth we were to experience. This class was greatly a reminder that if we 'let our bodies give birth', and truly listen to our intuition, we could have the natural childbirth we desired. We had to create a living birth plan, as opposed to just a written one, for the hospital file. The living birth plan is a collage on poster board, filled with words and images of the things we desired for our birth. This way, regardless who would be on staff at the hospital, from the doctors and nurses to the housekeeping personnel, anyone that walked into my room would be able to see what I did want and what I did not want for my birth."

The day their son Solomon was born, was also the same day her partner celebrated his tattoo studio's sixth anniversary. They were at the shops celebration party which consisted of clients, friends and family. Kimberly had enjoyed a two hour massage prior to the party and started to have minor cramps, she didn't realize she would shortly be in active labor. A friend of hers suggested she just dance and not get caught up in the timing of her contractions. She swayed back and forth to the music, in a trance, as the contractions got stronger. She wanted to rest for a while at home after the party, before heading to the hospital, and she soaked in a lavender filled bath.

According to Kimberly, lavender slows contractions in early labor, but speeds them in active labor (which she didn't know she was in). [Both the American Pregnancy Association (.org) and the super-cool Holistic Diva at Wordpress.com confirm this.] In less than ten minutes, she was on the bed pushing. They focused on doing their co-chanting and Kenyatta raced off to wake Kimberly's mother to let her know that her grandson was about to be born. Her mother was distressed over Kimberly having a home birth and Kimberly reassured her by calmly telling her:

> "Just let it flow mommy. Just let it flow. My mother left to call the paramedics, but Solomon and I were in no mood to wait. From lying on my side, I instinctively got on all fours and begun to push. Three or four good pushes did the trick. Kenyatta was on the phone with Solomon's godmother and yelled, 'I see the head!' Then I yelled, 'Get the camera!' I took hold of Solomon's head and with one final push guided him out."

If you want an awesome, organic homebirth like the one Kimberly and her partner had, check out the book they recommend: *Birthing from Within* by Pam England. Then make your living birth plan, get your groove on, and chill!

Kimberly's positive birth experience is completely opposite of what most of us experience in a controlled hospital environment, but it is what we hope for. It is this desire for what families really want and what women really know how to do, but aren't confident nor supported in doing, that led to the Warrior Mamma's group and explain its success. It's an organic moving blueprint that makes birth the magical, surreal, spiritual, safe, and private experience it should/could be. Currently, they are also planning on home birthing their second child this upcoming March.

The Warrior Mamma's group is a non-profit media productions and public relations company. They put out a free quarterly newsletter called *Being Resourceful*, which features profiles of local Atlanta independent businesses, healthcare tips, a poetry column, and has rotating columns that focus on the city's visual arts, music and literature scenes, as well as a reader's column. It has an on-line collective that hopes to influence local community by having the businesses support the community and vice-versa.

Kimberly is currently working on a second Women's Health Conference to be held at Georgia State University. It's part of a Health and Healing Series. The set subjects/agendas they plan to explore are: *Sexuality and Sensuality*, *Forgiveness for Yourself and Others*, *Being at Peace with the Essence of Who You Really Are*, and *the Balancing Act of being a Woman, Spouse, Worker, Lover, Activist and Anything Else without Losing It!* Three very important questions that Kimberly is asking women and also wants to include in the forum are:

> "How do you peacefully achieve being a mother, community activist, a sensual being, and a partner all at the same time? Sensuality and sex is a big part of our lives and affects women, even though they may not think it does. How do generational patterns affect women and mothering? Talking about generational patterns, stuff to keep and stuff to get rid of. Women, why don't we get along with each other, and why can't we put our own insecurities behind us?"

They plan to address other important concerns such as breast and ovarian cancers, S.T.D's, diabetes and depression. The first symposium was held in 2005 and was titled Uterine Fibroids: The Silent Epidemic, and was extremely successful with over two hundred attendees and vendors.

She has numerous other community/activist projects including Healing from Depression.Blogspot.com, which is an online resource or one-stop directory of resources to heal from depression and other mental illnesses for women of color. She created the site when she went through a severe depression and didn't have a safe place to turn to, and specifically a group that was inclusive of women of color, that she could relate to on multiple levels. She started suffering from depression in 2001, a few years before Solomon's birth. She had suffered from spiritual, emotional, and physical distress from an abortion from a prior relationship. She lost her job due to downsizing a few months later. As the days passed, she felt weaker and didn't want to get out of bed. She kept telling herself, "Get it together! You're a black woman and you're stronger than this!" Every time she thought she was out of it, it would go away for awhile, then come creeping back. She realized it was because she never addressed the underlying causes of her depression, nor did she address the lack of communication between herself and (her) god,

> "I 'hit the wall' in October of 2002, feeling overwhelmed by life, angry at everyone and myself, and unsure about my desire to live. I did begin talk therapy, but I was not honest in the process. The female psychologist I saw prescribed a small dosage of an anti-depressant. In taking that prescription to my former holistic ob/gyn, I was denied the medication and given a cold shoulder by this doctor—a very disappointing experience. Here I am at my wit's end, exposing all my vulnerabilities and crying out for help. What I received was no warmth and no support from this highly sought after physician and I was told by her to control my depression by taking birth control pills!"

Heal from Depression. Blogspot.com is an online resource for women of color. Rebel Mom Kimberly created the site when she went through a severe depression and didn't have a safe place to turn to, and specifically a group that was inclusive of women of color, that she could relate to on multiple levels.

After a short, but needed, stay at a psychiatric hospital, she managed her depression through medication, on-and-off-again as needed, mediation, and reconnecting to her spiritual roots. She dealt with the hurts from her past, and she started to close the wounds, leaving finally just scars. It was during 2003 that she and Kenyatta, who had been her tattoo artist since 1997, developed a deeper romantic relationship (after light, casual dating since 2001) and she started to feel more positive about the overall direction of her life. Thereafter she learned she was pregnant with Solomon, not a planned conception, but "a timely part of her journey." Just shortly after having Solomon, she experienced what is called the Super Woman complex that many mothers suffer through and it trigged another bout with depression:

> "There is so much to the transition into motherhood! After having my son, I became so busy and plunged myself into several business and community projects, trying to prove that I could handle everything, AND be a mother of a newborn. I soon realized I took on too much, and my inner spirit screamed, 'STOP!' In March of 2004, I began to pull back from a lot of things I was involved with and began an active process of self-discovery that unfolds everyday (really, as it always has). Much of my therapy calls for me to answer the questions I've never asked myself. I'm discovering what is fulfilling and depleting in my life and I am now looking at who I am (my absolute ingredients) and not what I do. I'm defining the terms in my life that I always just went along with, and I speak and give thanks to God more openly than before."

Part of that journey was to understand her past and the generational patterns of her family and changing those habits, or dispositions. As a mother, she is re-examining her childhood and how that affects her today … and understanding how that "kept her from doing work she feels like she should be doing." She has a very loving family that has always been there for her, but like every family they have their own unique signatures, or parental impressions. Her father was the one who was the joker or the clown, which lightened the stress or tense moments in the house, especially when her mother was sulky.

> "My momma would come home moody and stuff and we never knew how to please her, she was not emotionally available. She was the judge of the house, and daddy was the peacekeeper and comedian."

Kimberly in retrospect understands more now about both of her parent's behavior. Her mother was generally mad at her father for his behavior which included flirtations and nights out, but directed her anger towards her children instead of confronting or addressing him, the source or cause of her anger. Her father was well aware of her mother's anger and the causes, but instead of addressing it, he let Kimberly's mother re-direct it onto their children. He tried to deflect the anger by being comedic, and the situation just frequently repeated itself. It's generational patterns like this that Kimberly is becoming conscious of and changing …

"I will be damned if Kenyatta makes me mad and I take it out on Solomon. Did our parents have the tools, or not have the tools to handle these situations? We're they aware of them? Did they know how it affected everything? What leads to that behavior? Be it alcoholism, food, self-destructive behavior … It's that stuff that's gets learned that we have to get to the root of. That stuff that leads to us, that crazy stuff. Don't dwell on the past, but it's the past that leads us to the present; we need to look and understand it. What did I do? I didn't take a quick fix, or unlearn, or revise the past. I am breaking co-dependent behaviors, patterns, and generational curses because some stuff is just getting old."

It's this ongoing engagement with depression (both its insights and frustrations) that inspired her to start the Heal from Depression site. More specifically, she saw a community need that she felt compelled to address and help fill.

"Many have asked, 'Why is your website only targeting women of color?' First and foremost, it is understood that depression does not discriminate. Women, men and children of all ethnicities are subject to mental illness. Unfortunately, a large percentage of people of color suffer from depression, and are not seeking help to heal from their illness; those that are in search of help may not have access to all the resources that are available. Heal from Depression seeks to (1) eliminate the shame of dealing with depression and other mental illnesses, and (2) to connect people in need of assistance to the multitude of resources within the mental health and wellness sector. Complete wellness—a healthy mental, emotional, physical, and spiritual existence is the goal!"

Another part of her journey has been to analyze the imposed "Super Woman" complex, and she has realized it is unrealistic and damaging to women and mothers. Trying to live up to the Super Woman ideal is one of the issues that led to the post-partum depression occurring. She frequently found herself battling with the "balancing act" questions:

"I'm staying at home; does that make me a bad mom? I'm looking at a *Working Mother* magazine cover of a CNN Anchor with three kids, and really the real story was kind of left out. I was trying to read in between the lines, going through her day ... and obviously she has money, but it never got to the root and how she did it, and not that we need to know her business, but if you're telling a story that is suppose to encourage mothers to go back to the paid workforce we need to know all of it. The story and cover just kind of imply it magically happens, the positions, the pay, the ease, the great childcare and schooling, the perfection. There's no talking about the nights of crying, not knowing what's going to happen, it's promoting this image (of Super Woman/Mother), but it keeps women at bay from the reality or truth of it all. I mean I don't like cooking; I do it now that I have a family, but does she do it (Super Woman) when she is doing everything else too?

Children shouldn't be the sole concern of one person, but the whole community. If we have happy, healthy, and loved kids, we will have healthy, productive, moral and motivated adults. The problem with the Super Woman/ Mother complex is that it makes both children and the community itself our sole responsibility: socially, culturally, and monetarily, but only in accordance to the manufactured image.

I have worked since I was fourteen and the past three years I haven't had a job, (except the one of managing a home and raising a child) but it's been a really humbling position, because I have always attached my self-worth to financials. I still battle with myself when I can't pay a bill or buy groceries, what does that mean to me as a capable woman? But also, not to say I don't care about the well-being of my family, but for some people it's what they eat and breathe. I don't understand that. I am not that kind of mother either. Now that I am a mom, am I supposed to just suppress those things that make me who I am or that I live and strive for? But how do you balance both (Super Woman and the Self) in a positive and healthy way?"

Kimberly and I talk in depth over the phone about the media's obsession with presenting us with these images and stories that women keep trying to live up to, and we can't. Kimberly's soothing and smooth voice erupts into robust laughter, as I tell her, comically, my story of going crazy trying to do it all. We see the humor in our initial naiveté. It took looking deeper, for both of us, and almost having a physical and mental breakdown from exhaustion, to figure out that we can't be this *Working Mother* magazine hero—not without getting a lot of help, help that isn't there.

Our voices turn solemn when we move the conversation from us to our children. Children shouldn't be the sole concern of one person, but the whole community. If we have happy, healthy, and loved kids, we will have healthy, productive, moral and motivated adults. The problem with the Super Woman/Mother complex is that it makes both children and the community itself our sole responsibility—socially, culturally, and monetarily, but only in accordance to the manufactured image. If we empower it, we are disemboweled as part of the bad mother complex. However, the glossy image of Super Mom sells, and sells well, even though she is ironically vague, and her story lacks details and depth.

We (all moms) are motivated to just keep trying, until we get it right, according to this image, but we do not understand why we don't have all the opportunities and resources that Super Mom has. It is implied that it should just come naturally. Then why aren't we getting the jobs, the promotions, the affordable and great schools for our kids that these marketing stories are promising? We are getting stressed out when we try to be these super-moms, and we know deep down it's not working, and these expectations that we are trying to measure up to is at the expense of both ourselves and our family/children. The perks like great schooling and promotions aren't available to the majority either, no matter how hard people work and the promotions are wanted or needed. Kimberly recognizes this as well and still finds herself trying to live up to both of these expectations: Super Woman, and Super Mom. She is aware of the cultural pull, and that helps to keep her focused and balanced when it gets overwhelming with too many expectations—or when it gets frustrating from the limited, or lack of resources, and support in general for mothers. She knows that to be a mother doesn't mean you're not a woman, or a person, and vice versa and the whole person needs to happy and fulfilled in order to be whole. This makes for a kick-ass woman, and a kick-ass mom. Kimberly lives by the philosophy of:

> "If mothers are happy, the world is happy. Not to say that it's women's responsibility—but if momma is not happy, no one's happy. Think about that on a global scale, and women are setting the tone. If we are happy and healthy, so is everyone else. We can have an enterprise ourselves, if we can just pull together."

Kimberly was inspired by an *Essence Magazine* conference she attended that had a similar proposal called: *Peace of the World is Equal to the Peace of Women.* The conference looked at the peace process both starting in the home, and how outside factors impedes on the peace process by having anti-women practices, that hurt women, which hurts children, and finally hurts society. It impacts everyone globally. The goal of the conference is to start a pro-woman, pro-child, pro-community dialogue. Maybe we can make changes and have a peaceful world. Kimberly knows this can be achieved, but in the meantime we have a very anti-child, anti-woman, anti-people-of-color, kind of world—and there are immediate needs that have to be addressed. She is disappointed by how much those who benefit economically from families and women do little to give back to them; from employers, to businesses, to government. She looks around her community and knows there are huge companies in Atlanta like Coca-Cola and Home Depot that could give, or donate to life-sustaining programs and help build needed schools, but they don't …

> "The way it is, this idea that: if it's not making us more money, why change it? Their big business picture doesn't make any sense, if your communities don't thrive, how will your businesses?"

When Kimberly was recruited by the founder of M.O.B.B. (Mothers of Black/Brown Babies), Rebel Mom Dr. Taj Anwar, to help meet the needs of families/children/mothers—she knew this was something she could do now, to help make peace and activism a way of life for her community. She is also their Natural Birth Consultant, "I'm not a health care professional, but when you experience something like that, you earn an honorary badge when you're pulling your own stuff out." M.O.B.B. is a great outlet for Kimberly since it allows her to stay in contact with other moms who have had similar experiences, and share personal and local goals. The group focuses on anti-system self-sustaining activism that takes a bite out of capitalism and the ineffective, self-esteem depleting welfare and social aid system.

Kimberly also joined the group to meet her own personal needs too. She found that being a mother was a demanding, lonely, and stressful job. She needed a support network of women to help her, and who could understand the unique obstacles she faces as a mother of color in the Southern United States. This helped her through her depression, because there were others she could relate to. The M.O.B.B. group also values creativity as sources of necessary spiritual life, and welcomed Kimberly lovingly: tattoos, dreadlocks and all.

Kimberly and M.O.B.B., in conjunction with her partner's tattoo shop, recently sponsored a twenty-eight family fund drive for their community. It was a huge block party event where you could hear live music, get tattooed, and eat great food. They were able to raise funds to assist these families with food, baby items, and toiletries. They have an ongoing effort online with a continuous family sponsorship program that people can donate to. In general, Kimberly has this to say about M.O.B.B:

> "The whole point of M.O.B.B. is to take care of women in urban areas and black and brown mothers in these areas ... and there are a lot of mothers who aren't getting support at all. There is a group street movement to protect the community, food drives out in the street every week, displaced homeless, FTP (Fuck the Police/ Free the Prisoner/For the People Movement), and we are trying to do something on

$$$$$$$ KMART COUPON $$$$$$$

5% OFF YOUR NEXT PURCHASE OF A SINGLE SPORTING GOODS ITEM AT KMART

EXCLUDES CLEARANCE ITEMS, POOLS, TRAMPOLINES, SWING SETS AND ITEMS NOT SOLD IN SPORTING GOODS DEPT. VALID IN-STORE AND ONLINE.

9700054767297438

OFFER ID 9851 OFFER VALID 09/17/15 THRU 09/24/15
Excludes clearance items
See reverse of coupon/receipt for details.

Shop online at Kmart.com

STORE COUPON TERMS AND CONDITIONS

Member offers: Valid for original member only; Use of this coupon constitutes your acceptance of the SYW terms and conditions available at www.shopyourway.com/terms; Points earned from this coupon are typically valid for 90 days but may sometimes be longer. Check your account for details.

All offers:

- Redemption limited to either digital or in-store printed version of this coupon.
- Cannot combine with other coupon for same item(s) and cannot double.
- Limit (1) per transaction. Requirement before taxes and after discounts.
- Void if transferred, copied, obtained via unapproved means or where prohibited.
- Other use constitutes fraud.
- Coupon value pro-rated across all qualifying items; including qualifying items purchased in addition to minimum requirements or limits and will be deducted from any refund.

Not valid on clearance; non-merchandise; concessions; gift card; federal or state regulated items; alcohol; tobacco; fuel; items behind pharmacy counter; prescriptions; prior purchases **& online** purchases unless otherwise indicated; partial-paid special order items; Lands' End; Scrubology; Sears merchandise; Nicki Minaj and Adam Levine collections. If front of coupon indicates that offer is valid online, additional exclusions may apply and can be found at online checkout. Cash value 1/20¢; Valid in US and Puerto Rico unless otherwise noted on front of coupon.

kmart SM

all levels to help people. We want to feed our kids every day, make a decent living, many of the activists are just a step away from being there themselves."

Kimberly knows all too well why we need groups like FTP and M.O.B.B. to do the work both not being done, and undone by our corporations, churches/institutions, and governments:

"I was always the rebel of the class, if it's not Jesus, it's not right. And they (churches/institutions) won't let go of that. Some people are closed-minded and can't be challenged. The things with priests and politicians, the things they do, like molesting kids or taking bribes in order to pass laws that hurt the public, the lying, not to say they all are doing this, but a lot. We know the Catholic Church covers it up, and secret organizations like Skull and Bones are for politicians in the making. When you look at the government or someone who is suppose to be taking care of you or keeping the peace, you don't want to think the system you are suppose to be living in, is corrupt.

The FTP Movement and M.OB.B, is very hands on. We are going to take care of it and were not going to ask anyone else to do it. Even if we can't give money we have at least time. We needed M.O.B.B. If ... an organization that looks

like ... and it has to be one you

c... t helpful, but they don't

a... have a need to help, and

b...

$$$$$$$ KMART COUPON $$$$$$$
40% OFF
$30
FOOTWEAR
VALID IN-STORE AND ONLINE

9700054767297445
OFFER ID 10145 OFFER VALID 09/17/15 THRU 09/24/15
Excludes clearance items
See reverse of coupon/receipt for details.

...mmunity, have a ne... She advises the to... in dialogue with ot... and promoting; ha... fine it, as well as ev... n to ask for help. Fo... munity, most of the... n Thanksgiving, but... done during the holi... You can look at a va... ary movements for... , and what to do, ... s that most of us a... from government to the workforce, to the lack of sharing resources, and the few that vocalize this dissent are ostracized; leading many to fear stepping out of line, but when people see courage over and over, that compels others to act on their beliefs and seek freedom. She doesn't understand how people can't act on their conscious.

> "I have spurts where I write, when I can't sleep. I was awake and watching an Iraq situation, a little girl got shot in the ear … caught in the crossfire. What is the progress of that? You can't say that's freedom. The whole philosophy of where they came from, and what they have committed to do … even Condoleezza Rice … does she ever look at herself in the eyes? How can they stand to look at themselves in the mirror?"

Kimberly knows that if corporations really listened to mothers, and if they ran their businesses like their own homes, everything could be different, from health care to the way we work and live. We could achieve holistic balance, and that's helpful for everyone. Now that she is a mother, she is redefining what she will and will not do. As a parent, the concept of time has more meaning and impact especially over the course of a lifetime. She will no longer do solely clerical or administrative work. She wants employment with substance:

> "If you could create more open-schedules, flexibility, you want that purposeful work you feel you are meant to do. I just can't believe I have to give up my interest and passions just to make some money right now. That is my prayer right now that the creator is going to give me a job that is meant for me …"

She is considering becoming a doula (a doula is similar to a midwife who helps with the pregnancy and birthing process in a non-medical fashion) because she feels it's an intimate way to touch the lives of women and children positively, while helping create a more natural world for us to live in. As an activist and a naturalist, she firmly believes that if we did everything together as a tight network, and did the best we could, we can do that on a larger scale for change. She cites a friend's career as an ideal model:

"One example of a very cohesive team is my friend Kristy. She is the administrator at a private school. She created a program of extra curriculum, and eventually it became its own job. She created her own job essentially. Her program is successful because they work together as a group, and if something needs to be done, they all do it. Their foundation is strong because everyone gives input, the people working there love children, doing new things with them and creating. Everyone has a specific kind of responsibility. Even when there is work that needs to be done outside their job description they do it, because they all take pride in their work and are all committed. There is a respect factor and they are all valued, and not just in lip-service, but how they are treated and are involved. Kristy is an exceptional leader."

Her ideal career would include event planning for concerts, and forums focused on health and women's needs. She recently completed a huge event for a national DJ Competition called, Needle to the Record. She was asked to organize and promote the event. It attracted national and well known talents in the world of battle turntablism, like DJ Beverly Skillz, DJ Wick-It, and DJ SPS. Special guests included KRS One, Drop Bombz, Intellekt and the Dirty Digits, and Dres Tha Beatnik. Special judges even included DJ Lord from Public Enemy, DJ Synthesis from Psyche Origami, DJ Klever from Crate Bullies and DJ Machete-X from Arrested Development. Needle to the Record was so successful she been asked to do next year's event and to help coordinate an effort to bring it to every major city nationally. You can learn more about the annual DJ competition at: Myspace.com/NeedletotheRecord.

For all her triumphs, hardships, successes, and the path of discovery she is on, Kimberly feels that:

"I just want to be stronger in myself and my career goals. Feeling good about myself will trickle down to my parenting. The more secure I feel about myself, the more secure I am about my career. I'm learning about my background and self-esteem. I have built my self-esteem on pleasing others, and now I am realizing I have to break that.

Turning thirty meant going through another decade of my life and reviewing everything. In my twenties a lot of great things happened. I was in the experimental stage and yet strict in my roots, but it is what has helped me become stronger and helped me do what I have done so far. I feel great about what I do, and I don't have to look at anyone else for approval, but I also don't feel like I have done that on a lot of scales, but looking at the philosophy of life, I typically live as honestly as I can. I have to be true to myself and I really want to live that. I have never felt a true connection to it, not to say I have lived a fake life or anything, but I want to be more true to who I am … really. Creating and flowing throughout the day, fulfilling my spirit."

After having Solomon, Kimberly didn't plan on having anymore children. Now that she is expecting her second child Sarah in a few months, it is redefining her as a woman and her relationship with Kenyatta. She is compelled to figuring out new options for herself and her daughter too.

Her main parenting philosophy is: following your child's lead and being in tune with your family, yourself and your children. The more Kimberly learns about herself, her childhood, what works and what doesn't, and how that applies to her children, the more rounded she is in her approach. She feels if you observe children it will bring you to the essence, or art of living, "Children's spirits are so close to the source, why should we suppress that?" She gets frustrated when she sees people and parents being hostile or inpatient towards children's natural tendencies or curiosities.

Children tend to be creative, and adults destructive. Kimberly thinks that schools, despite their intentions, with their authoritarian structure contribute to this polar dynamic. That is why she has chosen a friend's school that is a family school co-op for Solomon. It is a supportive and open environment and there are no issues with policy, regulation, and test-score driven education.

"Part of my job is taking care of him, and watching him. I didn't really look into day care, even the outside of the day cares doesn't sit well with my spirit. It's too close to the street, and some of these school's are owned by companies with billions of dollars that aren't taking care of their teachers, or students. Each school could be improved upon. That's why when this family home school co-op opportunity presented itself it was the right program for us."

Solomon is being raised in a healthy, nurturing and warm environment. His life is enriched with meeting a variety of people and diverse cultures through art storefronts, his father's tattoo shop (Solomon had an in-house nursery there) and activist gatherings. Kimberly adds, "Solomon picks up on this creative energy from people from all different walks of life. He is very sociable, open and accepting." When she sees Solomon creating and building with his toys all over the floor, she doesn't even want to keep him from doing it. He's into his creativity; the toys can be all over the floor for the time being. Letting go, relaxing, and prioritizing is a learning process she experiences daily.

Maintaining her relationship with Kenyatta takes effort too. Just like any commitment, it takes a lot of understanding, compromise, and faith which provides stability for the moments when bad judgments happen, misunderstandings, or clashes of anger. They have very different communication styles. He is very quiet and she is very expressive, but they are a good team when it comes to taking care of business, and holding each other up as well, when things are stressful or hard. Being in a committed relationship takes work and dedication just like being married.

> "A lot of people presume the work ends when you get married, and the work doesn't stop, and it should start before marriage. We had planned on a beach wedding, but my father had a stroke so we postponed it. Other things have happened and we aren't going to stress ourselves out about it right now. I dig my family and the way we are, and what we are creating here and now.
>
> There are times I wonder what it (life, love and living) would be like if this or that happened, but this is what I asked for, and he gets the job done and he is responsible. It may not have all the confetti and sparkles all the time, like I expected, but that (romance, sparkles, infatuation, love) may come from me as I grow stronger. Marriage doesn't have to be our parent's marriage, or other people's concepts of marriage. Go against ideas. You have to make up your own concept of what it is. For the most part we make it work together, but that's not necessarily together forever."

Kimberly is observant of the cycles of life, and she knows not everything is forever and many things go through organic cycles; including love and relationships. However, the one thing she is certain in is her future with her family, career, and with herself. She feels her rounded belly swollen with life and looks down at the Warrior Marks she has earned that stretch across it, and knows that she is …

"Unshakeable. I don't care what happens or is happening around me. I know, without a shadow of a doubt who I am. And nothing is going to faze me. I am an emotional being, but that's who I am and I am secure in myself."

Freakin' a!

**Since this interview: Kimberly and Kenyatta have their second child, a beautiful little girl named Sarah.*

"Society expects me to do this, as a mother, with little to no resources and no back-up, as sweetly and prettily as possible, and to conform to a set standard of living, or else face even more struggle and condemnation. Forget it!"

Crystal
Herbalist
Lovely Landscaper
Community Visionary
Retailer
Music-Maker
Sculptor
Teacher
Viridita
Austin, Texas.

Crystal is an amazing practicing herbalist and botany teacher in her mid-thirties who helps people heal, mend, and prepares them to take better care of themselves. She dreams of owning her own business, which she is building now … one client, and one handmade organic body product, tonic and salve at a time.

Plants, family, friends, art, and music are the foundation of her inspiring story of strength and ordeal.

When she isn't making medicine or music, teaching or attending class, she is spending time with her seventeen-year-old daughter London, her six-year-old son Robby, and her domestic partner. As a family they enjoy seeing bands play, attending politically minded social events, shopping at the farmers market, and digging around town for urban-archeological artifacts and wildcrafting. Wildcrafting is the practice of finding and harvesting wild edibles and herbs. She is developing an action plan to build a community center while building her business simultaneously.

She is frequently inspired by her favorite artists and writers such as Clarissa Pinkola Estes, Nina Simone, Jane Goodall, Susie Bright, Hildegard de Bingen, Emma Goldman, Georgia O'Keefe, and Stephen Buhner. Their lives have spoken to her courage and grief, giving her hope. Their works have awakened her imagination intellectually.

She couldn't afford medical insurance for London (or for herself), and out of necessity started studying holistic medicine, and treatments that she could make. Now she is able to keep her family healthy with good nutrition, supplementation as needed, and herbal medicine.

She's from Waxahachie, Texas, but moved to the city of Austin, when she was in her mid-twenties, as a single mom to make a better life for London and herself. Austin has helped Crystal build a strong, solid foundation for their lives. It's where she met her life-partner and had her second child. The city's vibrant culture and emphasis on whole living and green values led to Crystal's disciplined and advanced study of plants and medicine. It was fate that it would become her profession.

She couldn't afford medical insurance for London (or for herself), and out of necessity started studying holistic medicine and treatments that she could make. Now she is able to keep her family healthy with good nutrition, supplementation as needed and herbal medicine. She learned that many common conditions were easily treatable with gentle herbs and dietary modifications. She's concluded that the conflict of interest between a patient's health and the need to push pharmaceuticals make most doctors treatments suspect. She prefers to go to a holistic medical doctor when it's warranted [which curiously isn't covered by most insurance companies] so that she knows there's a better balance.

Considering I have an interest in holistic medicine and I'm a failed organic gardener (I tried really hard—nothing lived!), I was captivated and wanted to know how we, as moms, could empower ourselves. Crystal shared some basic starting steps:

> "I think at its most basic level, an interest and connection with plants is the important thing involved, and incorporating them into your daily life. People have been using herbs as food and medicine for thousands of years. It takes time and training to gain experience. Be aware of your own bioregional plants first and foremost. What surrounds you is going to be your best plant allies. Take plant walks with knowledgeable people; get as many field guides as possible. Practice ethically, and never harvest endangered or at-risk plants. Care for the places you visit and gather from, have fun and experiment! Read as much as you can from reliable sources."

For additional and/or professional development, she suggests:

> "You want to gather knowledge in every way you can, mainly from the plants themselves. Keep your personal anecdotes and historical usage written down. Study with as many teachers as you can, and attend workshops. Get involved with other herbalists and form a network with them. Become a member of an herbal community and help educate others as you do so. There are no state certifications; however there is the American Herbalist Guild, which is a highly respected organization of professional herbalists who are dedicated to promoting a high level of professionalism in the therapeutic usage of herbal medicine. You can become a member of, and at a certain level you may apply to become a professional member—which takes an incredible amount of documentation and experience.

There are many well respected herb schools and herbalists out there. Try to find one in your own area, or as near as possible, in order to gain a greater understanding of what medicine is most available to you and how to use it properly. There are online courses too. I personally give plant walks, as well as more one-on-one apprenticeship, educational opportunities, and mentoring. I have recently begun teaching at the Wildflower School of Austin."

Crystal places emphasis on freshly handmade products. She uses as much locally sourced and organic products as possible. She has clients that come to her with a variety of needs and ailments and she tailor makes teas, decoctions, tinctures, syrups, oils, salves, creams, herbal vinegars, and various other treatments, depending on the condition of the client. She also has a retail line for general conditions and remedies too. But it's not all work and no play, and serious conditions! She recently launched a line of body products consisting of facial serums, body creams, scrubs, toners, salves, masks, bath bombs, cleansers, belly balms for expectant moms, and "tons of other goodies!"

You can reach out to Rebel Mom Crystal for info on her custom herbal treatments at: ViriditasBotanicals@gmail.com. Don't forget to check out the American Herbalist Guild too!

Her practice has grown by word-of-mouth and the fruits of her hard work. She's doing it with a lot of heart, little capital, and one treatment at a time. She has always wanted to run her own show and to be able to provide for her family, while doing something great and good for the world. You can reach out to her to get info on her products and herbal insight at: ViriditasBotanicals@gmail.com.

It has taken years of work for Crystal to be a successful herbalist with a thriving small business. She's had an avalanche of struggles, obstacles, cyclical growth, let-downs and achievements, over the last seventeen years. It's only through relentless effort and dedication that she has made it to where she is now. It certainly wasn't a smooth straight line, more like a cross-country run with some Category 5 storms and a few pit stops. Her introduction to motherhood and womanhood is bittersweet.

"I realized that I had become pregnant within a couple of weeks of my little brother committing suicide. He was my closest friend and I loved him so very much. It was incredibly devastating. I turned seventeen eleven days after he died. I was shocked to find that I was pregnant. It was like a jolt of reality into this nightmare I was in the midst of. I decided to continue with the pregnancy. I felt it was really meant to be and the timing too coincidental. There was really no question in my heart as to what I was going to do, and there was absolutely no logic to my decision."

Teenage Crystal was under acute stress with the horrific loss of her brother and couldn't think clearly about the future. What she does recall thinking though is that, yes … she would lose some parts of her life, including personal freedom, but would be growing something so full of potential, and life—a child—and that is exactly what her heart needed. She knew she would soon be responsible for another human being that she would love, tend to, and worry over.

She is saddened by the reality of how many people are left behind to suffer when someone makes the choice to kill themselves. The only condolences she can offer if you ever face this nightmare is that time really does help soften the blow …

"Things will get better, but really will never be the same. You're a different person forever and that changes the entire way you exist. I personally believe my brother is still around, just in another form. I can say that for me, I probably should have gotten some counseling or something of that nature; art and music therapy perhaps? I think that's what I did in my own way. Survivors of suicide should know that they are not alone. It's such a tragic thing to try to cope with, and everyone deals with it in a different way, in their own time. Give yourself time, space, and outlets to express your grief."

She feels that steadfast, thoughtful, and loving parenting is crucial to kids and their emotional states. She holds her parents accountable for the outcome of her brother's life. I can relate. [Crystal's childhood in some ways mirrored my own, and the first time I tried to kill myself was in the third grade. My mom, after discovering the empty pill bottle of Aspirin (I was in third grade after all!), made me drink coffee all night and walk around. The last serious attempt I had made was at seventeen years of age. I did some serious bodily damage with a more potent bottle of then legal and over the counter mini-thins, but I survived it. I am so glad I did. I love the life I have built brick-by-brick, the family I have made, and the woman I have become. I'm also proud of the many generational patterns I have broken, freeing my son up for a safe, loving, and healthy home environment free of abuse.] Crystal tells us what growing up was like:

"My parents fought a lot. They were very young and divorced when I was five and remarried other people. Then they fought a lot with their new partners. There was bitterness and animosity between all concerned. There was bad talking about each other and not working together in any way to promote the best environment for us to grow in. They were too caught up in themselves to really be effective parents most of the time. I think now, that in their own way, they did try. There was drug and alcohol addictions, and unstable, abusive behavior. Each set had their own brand of insanity. I think that although my dad's house was more stable, and there was no drug addicted personalities to deal with, it was just as difficult to deal with the mental health issues my stepmom had/has. It was very oppressive and frustrating to say the least.

My mom and stepfather were out of it most of the time—particularly—my stepfather. He was a raging alcoholic, and very abusive in many ways, undoubtedly to us, but more so to my mother. He had an abusive childhood and it carried over onto us in certain ways. They both had issues with drugs and alcohol, in a serious way, there was cocaine, alcohol, and pill combos. The parenting and lifestyles that resulted were truly unfortunate to say the least, and the friends that those things brought around, ugh. The stories I could tell.

My brother and I moved back-and-forth between homes. When one became too much to deal with we packed up and would go to the other's place, numerous times. Dealing with these kinds of issues every waking minute with no reprieve was hard, more just like surviving; not growing into well-rounded cultured people with experiences and opportunities. We were more like objects that existed in their worlds or something, not people to nurture and grow. Although it's easy to judge, I have to say they tried the best that they knew how, I guess. Some did better than others. After my brother died certain people did mellow out. Others absolutely did not."

When she became a very young mom, she had little confidence and lacked critical familial nurturing skills. Life was taken on a more day-to-day basis. She was just trying to deal with the "family insanity" and trying to figure out how to get out of her parents crazy lives, while learning what the world was about and who she was. She lived with her then-boyfriend and London's biological father and it was a brief, but tormenting, couple of years. He was a "total jack-ass, habitual liar, and a thief." She was isolated and he was mentally abusive. She found that her only hope to get away from him was to move back home. It took a couple of years for her to transition and become grounded, as well as financially stable. But her trials and tribulations were not over yet.

She escaped the two homes of varying hell's to end up in a third. London was around the age of three, or four, when she met her next boyfriend and Crystal was in her early twenties. She was certain this one was the real deal since their courtship was wonderful and profound in the beginning—and the transition to their committed relationship seemed to be positive and wholesome. He was a feminist thinking man who believed in the values of utopian anarchy, animal rights, and a vegetarian lifestyle, while fighting against injustice and jamming out to politically minded bands and playing in one. He introduced her to the works of Emma Goldman and other activist philosophers. They had a wonderful time, and most importantly he adored her daughter. They seemed the perfect couple when they moved in together and became a small family within a bigger community one. Then his behavior gradually became poisoned and she became entangled in a web of manipulation and escalating abuse.

"This was really difficult as I really didn't see what was happening at first, exactly. Things lead up to the situation it became. I had a lot of self-esteem issues and was still working through my brother's death, and trying to be a good mom and to support her the best way I knew how. I was still growing up. He was a supposed anarchist when I met him, so how things progressed was really confusing to me. Physically, he got more threatening over time and finally it escalated to full-on-violence.

When I realized that I needed out of the situation, I had been dealing with his control issues and his incessant grinding down of my self-worth. It made it rather difficult to just up and say, 'All right I'm out of here.' Especially, when I did he was really threatening and insanely jealous, and just wouldn't let go. There were a lot of guilt trips. It was difficult to escape for several reasons. There was this assumption that this 'couldn't happen,' and when it did I was really ashamed I had 'let' it happen. Though that's not how I felt exactly, but there was this confusing contradictory reality that I was trying to understand, make sense of and deal with.

I probably could have handled it better. I never wanted to involve the police in any of my affairs if I didn't have to. I have a deep mistrust of the cops. But I should have filed charges, got a restraining order immediately, and been done with it."

She was dismayed at the acceptance of his behavior by her peer group of like-minded individuals:

"The community in which I closely associated myself with was always supposedly against this kind of behavior. Yet when it came down to it those politics weren't nearly as important to certain groups of people—though definitely not everyone. Political ideology was simply in regards to other things, like foreign policy or whatever, not the reality of interpersonal relations right in their face. There was disenchantment with that, and in my own self, and it was hard to just eliminate this person as I had always insisted would be such an obvious and easy decision for anyone in an abusive relationship to do. Things are complex, you know?

After I recovered from that experience, which was so messy, I tried to be amicable enough with that person and just work on never letting anything like that happen to me or anyone else again. It certainly raises some of the same kind of issues within the sub/countercultures that mainstream culture also hasn't dealt very well with like domestic violence, rape, and the abuse of women. These kinds of issues have been more successfully dealt with at times in Austin.

There was a badass momma who did get out of an abusive relationship here and just got completely away from him, kids included, but the community was divided over it. Particularly, the men who really weren't prepared to call this man out as he was really popular. However, there was also a very strong group of people who were committed to supporting her and the kids while that transition was made. Another instance here was a situation involving another group of people, still within some of the same community in a way, but who were more specifically anarchists. There had been a couple of situations where women had been sexually taken advantage of and even raped. The community of people rallied behind those women—even though some of the guys were friends of the perpetrators—and confronted them outright together as a group. In one case the guy got ran out of town. In the other case, the situation was a little vaguer, but he was totally called out in group sessions of the community, and he had to deal with the situation directly. The women ended up feeling at least in some way that the situations were effectively dealt with. It was awesome."

Crystal was able to seek safe shelter with close friends while her daughter spent the summer with her grandparents. This gave her an opportunity to rebuild her life, work and save money, and sever physical ties with the abuser. By fall, she had secured a very cute duplex that was finally just London's and hers. Her advice for anyone in an abusive relationship is:

"Get a restraining order, file charges, and get completely away from him. Do not give it a second thought—ever! No friendly talks, no compassion, no kid visitation, no nothing—at least until you are well established in your own life and that person has shown a clear and long standing reconciliation of behavior, as in years. I was a total mess then and just having a hard time mentally, emotionally, and financially. Thankfully, I got my own thing going … but I still had to deal with him for a very long time since it wasn't a very clean break, and he kept coming around. I would try to be friends; he would take advantage of that and take over whatever he could. It was really hard. Again, I should have filed charges and not had a single thing to do with him. It's a victim mentality and I think that's really hard to escape.

This guy I was with has gone on to do the very same thing, only worse, to his current wife and I'm sure he will continue to do so. It's an unfortunate cycle, as his father did the same crazy stuff to his mom. I believe a shelter is a good idea because there's a lot of support and resources available, and truly there does need to be some working on yourself, emotionally and psychologically, after enduring something like that. It's nearly impossible to just hop right back into life unscathed and unaffected. There's a lot to work on for yourself and your kids."

She ultimately moved to Austin to put hundreds of miles between them, and to show London that there is a better way than the path her parents laid out before her, and that the abusers parents laid out before him. She knew she was a strong, lovely, and intelligent woman. She wanted her daughter to have a happy and safe home. She wanted to be a secure, caring, and loving mom who would be a source of inspiration and a pillar of strength.

Even though those early years were extremely traumatic, there were still many good memories and celebrations. There were numerous friends and family potlucks and trips to the museums, with London being the center of attention. There were great band shows where Crystal bonded with her sisters and brothers in the scene. There was also an exposure to art, political and DIY thinking that would lay the framework for Crystal's future. During this period Crystal dedicated herself to parenting, music, and art, despite the hard realities she endured.

She taught herself how to play piano and then picked up the guitar. She fell in love with strings and took a class. She now has a range of music she enjoys playing including: dark experimental, hardcore punk, old blues, country and bluegrass.

She has also utilized her passion for art as a healing and reclaiming mechanism. She started off sculpting with traditional clay, making creatures, and then evolved to complex multi-media pieces. She likes to engage the senses in her art work, and will heavily rely on producing sound and layering textures. She likes the aesthetics of steampunk and incorporates a meshing of metal and Victorian ambiguity into some of her work with an emphasis on re-creating recycled art.

Her first few years in Austin, were focused on starting a new life with London and being part of a stalwart, supportive, and kid-friendly environment and social group. She reflects on the years that have passed since …

"I've come a long way. Whenever my brother died everything that I thought I knew about the world was destroyed. All preconceived notions were stripped from me. I no longer could look at anything superficially any longer. Everything became very serious, especially having a child so soon thereafter. It's kind of a blur really. I mean I was raised in this really static world—where it was just good to get by—and all this mundane shit meant something to everybody. No looking beyond day-to-day, or beyond the self.

I was actively searching out what the world was about, what else might be out there, when all of that happened. I became very aware of a lot of things that people just take for granted, or try to ignore. I was still so young, and trying to figure out how to deal with such trauma, as well as caring for a baby and working. Well, it took everything I had. So maybe personal development was happening, but still more than anything I was trying to survive and give my child the best I could.

Although at sixteen, when I ran away, I was involved with a counterculture community of punks, and of course in that inherently is a political statement, I learned the more intellectual side of politics at nineteen. That's when I began studying Goldman, Bakunin, Kropotkin, Lucy Parsons, and other anarchists and possibilities for self governance, which shed a whole new light on what could be.

Ironically, the very same guy who actually introduced me to Emma Goldman became abusive to me over the course of time; getting out of that was long, arduous and a somewhat confusing process. But I did it, and I learned from it. Although, I was learning so much throughout the years ... I never really just had a stable, calm space to expound on ideas and get to know myself and sort of synthesize everything. The past seven years have provided me with that and I have truly come to understand how much power I have, what I want and need, who I am—even parts of me I never paid attention to. It's been interesting and empowering.

Being a teenage mother with little education, or money, [suffering from] depression at times, I realize that at times in my life I have limited myself in what I thought was even possible, or probable for me to try and achieve. Getting beyond that was pretty revolutionary."

It was during this chapter of life that she met her life-partner and it was spontaneous attraction. He was a hard worker like her, sensitive and kind, anti-establishment, has great taste in music, and loves kids. He is also a meat/animal-eater which speaks to the opposites attract rule. [Same thing happened to me too.] London, after being raised vegetarian, decided to change teams and eat animals. Their differences and acceptance of each other makes their family whole. Not to mention it adds contrast to the household discussions.

When she learned of her second pregnancy, it too was also "quite a surprise," but she was much older and wiser. There was more questioning as to whether this would be a smart, healthy thing to do. She and her lover decided to be happy and to do this. He took London on as his daughter, who was then eleven, and they had Robby. The biggest fear they faced was: did they and could they have enough financial stability to be able to provide for two children? She was also concerned about starting school and having a new baby; she had literally just committed and enrolled. This changed everything. Her partner assured her they could do this, school and all, and with his encouragement, she found faith, "I had very sweet, loving support from Robby's father, who dreamt about his boy … even before we knew I was pregnant! He was enchanted in the whole process and excited about our impending arrival." She found support as well from her family in North Texas, but she has kept the distance between them to maintain her family balance and her peace of mind.

As a mom she expects herself to be nurturing, loving, and to provide the best she can for her children. She believes it is extremely important to be valiant for them and to lead by example; show them how to be good people. She is mindful of this daily in her interactions with others, knowing they are observing her behavior and discussions. She wants her children to be healthy, happy, fulfilled, and to be seekers of truth and justice in the world. She wants her children to have faith in themselves, and an inner reserve of strength and honesty, as an emotional and spiritual core, to get through life on. She is instilling faith in them by assuring them that they do not have to go along simply with whatever society tells them is the norm. They are empowered to question why and find a better way. She reminds us it's not as easy as it sounds, you must be mindful of your intent, and vigilant in your child-rearing, "Life can be hard and it's easy to get caught up in day-to-day life, just working to exist and survive, but it's imperative to keep that part of the self going for you and your children."

She describes her home structure as pretty laid back, and she tries to be flexible when necessary. She focuses her energy on what she can do to enrich her children's lives and hers. She refuses to buy her kids fast food, "no matter what little toy comes in the box." But the golden rule here is: she tells them why and gives them better alternatives. It's not a, *my way or the highway*, household. She explains the reasons behind their parenting decisions, and gets them involved in the discussion so that they can meet half-way. They discuss the big picture in comparison to the immediate need or desire. She makes a concerted effort to keep childhood innocence and the wonder of it intact, while still being real with them about what is happening in the world. It's a balancing act. She has learned too from trial and error not to lose herself in the process of mothering.

"I've gone through phases where I just have immersed myself in being a mommy. It's very easy to do—ignoring my own wildness, my own need to just let go, but it never lasts. It never could and doesn't work for any of us ultimately as a family. We have to respect our creative processes and personal needs in order to be the best person we can be not only for ourselves, but for our children. Kids need whole parents that are engaged in pursuing what they believe in and having fun with it."

She considers what is going on in the world, when shaping her outlook on the state of the children living in it:

"I tend to look at the world holistically, like an organism unto itself. Everyone and everything is at its foundation a part of the very same thing, all interconnected and woven together. What each of us does has a direct effect upon the rest of the world, someway, somehow. The little things we do in our everyday lives count enormously in the bigger picture, from simply reusing/recycling and making more environmentally/health conscious choices such as organic, or locally produced items like: food, art, and medicine; to empowering ourselves to create the kind of world we want to be part of. These things add up quick. As Gandhi said, 'Be the change you want to see in the world.'

I think that society has great potential and is slowly evolving, as hard as that is to see at times. Things have changed dramatically in how people see alternative ways of raising children (for the better) from the time I had my first child to my second. There's still such a long way to go. Children are awesome! They are the most creative and fun people you'll ever meet! I feel that they aren't necessarily considered [by society] at their full potential though. The work and foundation as a community that's needed to be able to raise these children as a whole is not there in the way it needs to be. Invest time, energy, thought, education and money in our kids, and our future as a society could only become better!"

Her optimism is balanced with realism as she shares the struggles that moms face,

"This particular society regards children almost as accessories, as something that isn't quite as significant as adults and they are only given moderate protection and nurturing from society as a whole. As something that happens, to be dealt with as quickly and efficiently as possible, to assimilate into a form of proper capitalist citizens, as soon as possible.

Society expects me to do this, as a mother, with little to no resources and no back-up, as sweetly and prettily as possible, and to conform to a set standard of living, or else face even more struggle and condemnation. Forget it!

We have the power to create a better world for our children and ourselves, and absolutely have to demand and expect it—for it to ever happen! We need to support each other as much as possible. Society must give parents and children the respect they deserve, and the resources to raise healthy, intelligent, and happy little beings."

It was this awareness in her youth that attracted her to the counterculture world; although it took experience to be able to articulate it specifically. For Crystal, there was no other way to exist that made sense to her. She also witnessed firsthand and up-close in her own home, the injustices forced upon women that stem from inequality. Rigid and outdated social values became more apparent, and repugnant to her, as she grew up. She gradually realized how the whole system really works towards women, children, the poor, the outcasts, minorities, and she knew that, "I could never have even tried to go along with the status quo, nor could those that I have surrounded myself with." She grew into a viable force as a change-agent in the world:

"I am an anarchist, an environmentalist, and I believe in equality and happiness for everyone, no matter what. I go through phases where I'm more active and less active, but really that just depends on how busy I am—doing everything I am doing. In general, I incorporate my political action into my day-to-day conscious choices: anything from what I choose to do with my free time, to what I buy and where I buy it. I feel that raising my kids in the way I do, and taking charge of my own health and bringing those options to others, is pretty huge. I try to support the people and businesses in my community that I think are trying to do good, and are good people. I also try to bring awareness of political issues to others attention whenever I can.

As a side note, I must mention that we have for a very long time been the outcasts, and that has often, but not always, been readily identifiable by our clothing, hair, music, etc. I feel like some of those things have in some ways been snatched up and marketed to the masses, minus the underlying causes: whether that's the rejection of traditional concepts of beauty or family values, or not buying into the capitalist way of life that we are force-fed from birth; the look of subversion without the teeth. It's insulting."

Community is an aspect of her life that she is now reclaiming and attempting to reintegrate into her family life. When they had Robby she was back in school, working, and raising a teen—so family life filled the periphery; there wasn't time for a meaningful social life. After doing this for six years, she knew she had to make some changes.

"I have just been trying to make that effort to create time and pay attention to my friends and their projects, be it their band, business, or whatever. It's not so easy when there's so much to do. I feel a little disconnected physically, and then I get so caught up in daily life (with the kids and my projects, business, and learning). I'm busy, but I'm taking more time for myself, because it's incredibly necessary! This is why I feel a really interesting and progressive community-oriented center would be so valuable, because there would actually be a space to work, teach, and offer free space and gardens for people to just do stuff together and connect more."

She reminds us as parents why it's so important:

"Make yourself go do something that involves friends and fun periodically! No matter how many millions of things you have to do. There will always be lots to do and going and doing something away from everyday life is going to make you feel better. It's going to give you inspiration, ideas, and help grow the communities that were trying to create. It's a fundamental part of what we have to do!"

Part of her village vision is to start a community center. She knows many amazing people locally, that although they are all busy and facing similar issues with "trying to get our shit together and take care of business," they are still able to support one another and enrich each other's lives when they can. A shared space would be an anchor for them.

"I hope to have a collaboration of involved herbalists and healers, activists, artists, teachers, builders, and others to form a community center for people to bring awareness, education, and viable options to people in regards to how they make decisions regarding the health of themselves and our world. I think a free/sliding scale herb clinic is sorely needed. We need a free space where there's access to information, people, and resources; to be able to create art, or play music, have classes, community gardens, etc.

It's in the works right now. I'm trying to figure out how to get this whole thing going. I have many like-minded herbalist and activist friends who are interested in collaboration. I'm currently searching out a space for this idea. It would be lovely if there were someone who had a centrally located space, or capital to donate for such a thing to really take off! I think that there must be some grants for this kind of thing also, but with the current state of politics here in Austin, I'm worried about that. (They're trying to shut down a large group of neighborhood schools right now, so I'm thinking families aren't on the list of top priorities right now. This is a really sad situation.) My hope is that we can pull together as a community and demand that our elected politicians support the needs of its citizens and not that of the mass of developers that have descended upon Austin."

She does have a close circle of moms that are part of her support network. Their withstanding connection is their "progressive and potentially subversive" ideas on religion, politics, and society in general. They refuse to let anyone make them feel like they aren't raising their kids 'right', if they don't abide by traditional and mainstream family roles, or values.

She relates to moms across varied spectrums through the shared experience of being not only a parent, but also a woman. She knows that we all have shared hopes and fears for our kids in this world, and that we have the capability to do something about it.

She assures moms of all walks of life, that we can have a more thoughtful, creative way of life. We can empower ourselves and our families. We can have a more engaging dialog on politics and life. We don't have to accept mainstream media, or traditional family values, and base our lives on those limitations. She tries to open other moms up to the possibilities if you look beyond those precepts. The world is far bigger than the box society says it is.

She does think that counterculture moms serve as a role-model for mainstream moms, because we provide different options for living, and creating our own tools in the absence of those options. She thinks it's crucial that we maintain a resistance to assimilating, and to keep our counterculture way of life going so that as a whole society doesn't stagnate—we can help push its ongoing evolution. She sees the need for more sub/counterculture moms and dads to be more organized and to truly redefine what it means to be normal. The purpose is to be better prepared for meaningful dialogue and debates. She thinks if society really analyzed what normalcy means in the mainstream context, they would be horrified at the abuses allowed in the name of exploitation and capital—under the guise of good manners.

> "In general, I think that mainstream culture in this country is concerned very little, if at all, with the shiesty behaviors of mega corporations, and politicians, and the major repercussions it has upon us as a culture. Not to mention other cultures which are impacted by our lovely foreign policies … As long as everyone has a Wal-Mart and a Starbucks to frequently drive to and purchase things, nobody gives a damn, not really. There's a complete disconnect with the reality of cause and effect.
>
> There's also this level of insincerity in general that's deemed perfectly normal, and lack of empathy, or concern for anyone, or anything, but themselves or their very own personal world, which drives us all into deeper isolation.
>
> I do not believe in the ways that a capitalist society conditions us and our children to behave and believe, particularly to be consumers of any and everything to extreme excess. To ignore the natural world around them and the repercussions of doing whatever you please, with disregard to others and the planet. I believe that we all have something unique to contribute to the world and that should be honored, and fed. Not shunned and denigrated."

She hopes all moms can be a driving political force for a better world and that her story can be one of enlightenment that will compel us to take action. She feels we must always strive to evolve, and learn from our experiences and mistakes, both good and bad. She knows it's equally important too, that we dedicate ourselves to what we believe in. And that we love and respect ourselves, and others, creating real and tangible values based on our chosen actions that can't be coerced—or sold. She feels that is what will make the difference in the quality of our lives and ours families at the end of the day. The context of her life has shaped who she is, and has given her an individualized discourse:

"All of my past experiences, good and bad, have created who I am today. I've had some very profound and some very interesting experiences, which have given me a unique point of view. I've had all sorts of jobs which have shaped the way I see human relations, from peep shows to clubs, restaurants, home health aide worker, care taker, landscaper, and community herbalist. I'm dedicated, compassionate, and ideological. I believe anything can be achieved with enough passion, dedication, and education.

I have politics. I have desires. I have a voice. I refuse to submit to any preconceived notions of what I should, or shouldn't be doing, as a woman and mother. I've worked hard to provide for my children a healthy and happy home, full of ideas and possibilities. I try to maintain that balance of having my own time to explore myself too and create room for growth.

I've raised my kids well and I'm very proud of them. I know that they have a deeper and more realistic perspective on society and the world, and what's really important in life. I also feel really good about going back to college, as well as herb school, and dedicating myself to furthering my profession in my own way and incorporating a grassroots and sustainable ideology into how I go about my business.

I appreciate the challenges I've made it through so far, the person I've become, and the sweet life I have with my family. I try to remember that when I feel like I'm not where I want to be yet in my life, or where I 'should' be."

Since becoming a mother, Crystal has had her fair share of challenging work, and such profound personal growth, in comparison to where she was at seventeen when she first became a parent. It stuns her when she looks back. She has hit "a few roadblocks here and there, but has picked back up and learned" from her mistakes. She was extremely proud of starting college in her late twenties and encourages any person who has the ambitions to do so, to do it! Don't let age be a deterrent and if you encounter any prejudice or meanness, just tell them, oh bollocks! She and I both have been the odd ones out in college classrooms, as workers, parents, and in our mid-to-late twenties. [And I am actually going back again to continue working on my bachelor's degree, now that life has resettled after this long project, many life-journeys, and some turmoil. I'm now in my mid-thirties. When you have obligations, and you're a working-class-kid to boot, you don't have privileges, you have necessities. Just hear Johnny Cash cooing "One course at a time and it did cost me more than a dime," and you will be fine. I never encountered any nastiness, and I was embraced by my much younger peers, and my opinions sought out. So maybe America's youth is isn't as screwed up and dismal as the media portrays, ha-ha.]

Crystal experienced a mixed bag of emotions, both excitement and fear, when she first stepped into a college classroom. It was hard on her, because it had been so long and it was physically demanding since her second child wasn't even one yet. In most of her classes she was the oldest one, but she assures us it was no big deal. She does emphasize though that as a parent you must have good childcare set up. She blended both online and in-classroom instruction so that she would have more flexibility for when the baby had a cold, or London was sick, etc. It helped her even out classwork by hoping online whenever she had a chance, balancing it with family and work demands. She cautions that in order for the online option to be beneficial, you must be committed in adhering to your own time schedules, and reserve it for subjects that you don't struggle with. If you're weak in an area, nothing will replace the advantages of classroom instruction and face-to-face help.

The newest element of motherhood that she has encountered is parenting a teenager! She shares her innermost thoughts …

"I guess it depends on the personality of the child; some teens are more-mellow than others. Mine happens to be very rebellious! I think just giving them as many opportunities as possible to do well and grow is important, like classes, groups, and exercises. Encourage their talents and give them as much praise as possible! Do things that will give them a strong sense of self and confidence. As they grow older it's important to understand that they're changing into their own person and there's this natural pulling away. They are trying to define who they are—it's easy at times to forget who we were as teenagers, but doing a serious reality check helps put things in perspective (for me). There definitely needs to be support for parents of teenagers, even if it's just moral support. It can get pretty crazy at times. You want to be open and let them experience the world, but still give them really strong rules and guidance to hold onto. Be willing to see them for who they are becoming as an individual and adjust your idea of how to work with them if necessary, to keep them on the right track."

One thing she has sacrificed for motherhood is her youthful desires to travel the world, but she hopes to make that a reality in the not-so-near future. She holds this dream dear to her heart and keeps it on the radar of possibilities to work towards. She wants to learn and teach different modalities of healing from different cultures. The places that hold the highest botanical interest for her are Peru, Mexico, and South America. She envisions specializing in ethnobotany and complimenting her herbalist practice with cultural anthropology.

What she is working on most immediately though is building a home for her family that is anchored in permaculture. She is student of permaculture design and landscaping, which is a system of sustainable living with the land, resources, people, and communities. She adds, "It's actually a comprehensive way of setting things up and quite in depth. There are whole programs and schools dedicated to this design technique." She notes wistfully though, that it's a struggle for her to integrate since she, "doesn't even own the land" she lives on. However, her family does what they can to create sustainable living such as: rain barrels, composting, organic gardening and companion planting. Currently, they are working on a greywater system (captured household water waste, excluding toilets, that is repurposed for landscaping). You can learn more about this cool concept and put it into action in your daily life, home, and parenting at: PermaCulture.org. There's an inspiring section on how to make it work for urban areas too, while keeping it simple.

How does she do it all you ask? As an avid activist, fantastic mother, diligent worker, lover, and a healer, Crystal finds she must make time to relax and just stand still.

She understands life is life, and she cuts herself some slack and compromises, or redefines, what is most important for that day, or that week. She holds her dreams close through hard work and a long-term vision. She also doesn't overburden herself with a bunch of really mundane and unimportant things that don't matter in the long run like: keeping a perfect house, washing the car religiously, or sweating over the dishes. The housework will get done eventually, with the help of everyone, but she isn't going to make those tasks more important than her essential work. To help her keep perspective, she bikes, journals, and practices Kundalini yoga. Overall, she concludes that being a mother is, "The single most important thing I've ever done in my life. It's been a challenge and has been worth every precious second. I'm a stronger, more creative, resourceful, and powerful person for having been a mom."

ജ്ജ

The Artists and Picture Takers

ജ്ജ

Have you felt empty, silenced, or restless? The women here will help you find yourself in myths, colors, and photographs.

Get ready to explore with these valorous artists the geography of the human heart, and both the magical—and not so magical—reality of being a mom, and a struggling artist. These moms have ventured into the darkness and the light ... with their spirits, imaginations, and efforts.

Check out the natural landscape with a cool earth mom who moonlights as a sleek fashionista taking urban nighttime pictures of downtime life. Get ready to home school while running a start-up art gallery. Step back into time and meet Minerva and the Spider Woman up close—courtesy of a brilliant NYC artist. This NYC artist tried really hard to be a real estate agent after having her daughter, but realized she didn't want that nutty life. She would have to find a better way to pay the bills. Share food and candles with the spirits of the dead through Day of the Dead art while celebrating a life worth living! This Day of the Dead artist will surprise you with her fighting spirit as she fights each day for happiness while being an awesome working stay-at-home mom! See an artistic renaissance that has swept the world off of its feet by one rocking Kansas artist! All she wanted was to be able to raise her son, and make a living from her art. She shares with you how she did it. No more factory work for her, finally! Meet an icon who is redefining what art is, and how it can look, and who women are and who they can be, while reshaping life as a single mom. She will open the door to passion and heady determination for you. Grab your paintbrushes and espressos ladies and ...

Be ready to be inspired. Welcome to the world of the Artists and Picture Takers.

"I express very personal stories and feelings through my artworks. I am a feminist. I am most interested in feminist myths, stories, and images in which the girl or woman is the hero."

Hayley
Feminist
Naturalist
Mythological Painter & Artist
Teacher
Cute-as-hell Curator
NYC, New York.

Hayley is a successful teacher and artist from New York City. She loves snowboarding, dancing, and being in the woods. She is a Scorpio who does everything with intensity including: loving life, teaching, painting, being a mother and part of a family.

Her art work currently is focused on colored pencil drawings on paper, but she mainly works with oil on canvas. She does a lot of self-portraits, and portraits of other women who are close friends and family. Her work has been described as folk art with a similarity to Mexican Retablos. (Retablos are a form of folk art unique to Mexico, Italy and Spain. They are votive offerings and commemorate meaningful events in life.)

She describes her work as a little morbid, a little quirky, and very intense. She tends to exaggerate the size of feet and hands in her work. Her work is stunningly intricate and detailed.

The supernatural and spiritual realms are a frequent theme in her work because she feels that the goddess and god are in us all, both on the outside, but most importantly on the inside. She feels if we all are aware of this presence and seek the wisdom it offer's, it can give us clarity and growth in regards to the personal struggles in our life. In mythology there is always a story you can relate to that is relevant to what is going on in your world, or that of others. This awareness is obvious in her self-portraits.

Hayley's *Self Portrait as Minerva*, captures her fascination with women and mythology. She wanted to do this painting because Minerva was intriguing, and she could relate to her character on many complex levels. Minerva is the Goddess of Wisdom, although she has qualities/impulses that also were contrary, which is the conflicting human element. In Greek myths, Minerva was often intensely jealous.

In the story of Arachne, Minerva finds out that a mortal woman has claimed to weave as well as her. Minerva disguises herself as an elderly woman and challenges the woman to a weaving contest. When the woman loses, Minerva reveals herself and turns the woman into the earth's first spider. Like Minerva, spiders are weavers. Hayley feels spiders are the most creative of the animal kingdom, "Spiders decide their fate and that of others by weaving."

Minerva is also said to have turned one of the Three Muses, who were Amazons, into Medusa. This happened because, allegedly, Medusa was flirting with her husband (in some tales she was actually raped by Poseidon). Hayley relates:

> "It is a quality about me that aggravates me [jealousy]. At times I think I am teaching the 'person' a valuable lesson, through acts of jealousy. Minerva was also the first Goddess to side with men. Minerva claimed to born out of her father's thigh, instead of from her mother. This aspect really disturbs me about her."

The disowning of the mother for the father is rampant in patriarchal society. It is related to the undervalued work of the mother, and the undervalued role of women, in both ancient society and modern society. Women tend to be strongly associated with negative *emotional* weaknesses and men with positive *un-emotional* intellectual strengths. It is no surprise that these aspects of society, including ancient and premature patriarchal society, found their way into the subconscious of the great mythological tales and dramas.

The disowning of the mother for the father is rampant in patriarchal society. It is related to the undervalued work of the mother, and the undervalued role of women, in both ancient society and modern society.

Women tend to be strongly associated with negative emotional weaknesses and men with positive un-emotional intellectual strengths.

It is no surprise that these aspects of society, including ancient and premature patriarchal society, found their way into the subconscious of the great mythological tales and dramas.

One aspect of Minerva that Hayley likes is Minerva's association with owls. Owls are associated with clairvoyance and the wisdom that comes from being able to perceive and speak the truth by, "seeing in the dark."

This intuitive wisdom associated with goddess culture, old and new, and that Minerva's story captures, is tribute to women's role as spiritual and social leaders from the distant past of matriarchal society. *[At the time that most of the ancient tales were born, or recorded rather, patriarchy itself was a newly developing way of society where women and children were subordinate to men. Aspects of the ancient matriarchal way of life found its way through. A common theme in mythologies is the conflict between women and men which is symbolic to the conflict of the old human society and the new male-centric society.]* This past does find its way into the western and eastern tales of goddesses and gods. And this past with its strong, ancient, and mysterious women are an attractant for Hayley's personality and that attraction finds its way into her art.

Hayley notes:

> "In the painting of Minerva, or I, we wear all of these stories on her dress like patches, kind of like 'medals'. I have a serious love-hate relationship with myself, and often feel the same way about Minerva. In art school all the teachers and students hated this painting, but when it is in a show everyone seems to like it best of all. It is also one of the best-sellers as a print."

Hayley further explores this relationship with herself, and women's past in her *Self Portrait as Spider Woman.* This painting is based on the Native American myth Spider Woman who is the Creator of the Universe. Her dress is woven with paint and threads that are as thin as spider webs. She wears the Tarot cards Strength and Stars on her sleeves. Hayley is a devout participant in the fields of astrology, tarot and palm reading, and talking to fairies (mystical creatures, commonly depicted in science fiction and fairy tales, which some spiritualists find real). Hayley recalls why she painted this,

> "I painted her, or me, in the city [New York City] when I first moved here, because I was creating a new life here. I was and am very hopeful about it. People stare at this painting for a long time usually, and tend to like it. People generally ask me a lot of questions about it. I needed to create this piece and others to own my own strength and to express my belief that the Goddess or God is just as much inside as it is outside. That no matter what a person has going on, there is a Goddess or God who's stories either mirror how to get though that struggle, or it is a metaphor on how to."

Hayley also has another complex art show favorite, *Self Portrait Myself over Myself,* based on her modern interpretation of the Hindu Goddess Kali. Kali is considered the Goddess of creation, destruction and preservation. She is said to be the force of Shiva. Kali represents the fear of life and the unknown.

People tend to be uncomfortable about this drawing, but gravitate towards it at shows, and the complexities of fear and curiosities it represents. Hayley never intended to show anyone this drawing which started out more as a journal entry. She had an art teacher who encouraged her to develop it more. She has this to say about *Myself over Myself,*

"It is a colored pencil drawing about my struggle with myself. It's about how I can keep myself down by being self-destructive. It's also about how women tend to keep each other down, because we are taught to be competitive with one another."

Hayley is a feminist thinker. This is paramount and evident in her art and the way she lives her life. It started eight years ago when she was an art student; she took a class called *Women in Art History.* When she started the class she was just coming out of an abusive relationship that spanned over five years. She began to read feminist literature and couldn't get enough. It opened her eyes to so much around her and within her.

She became friends with an amazing older woman who became a mentor to her and a patron of her developing work. The older woman was a writer and a story teller. Hayley showed her the paintings she had done thus far, and the woman revealed so much about their meaning to Hayley,

"I had no idea there was a female archetype, something I now know very much about. She on a whole has been my greatest teacher. Feminist thinking is now the foundation for everything I create."

Hayley shares a common reaction from people to her art work,

"I am annoyed when people act shocked, or act like they possibly can't understand what I was thinking. I do love it when people smile though. It is when people tell me they like the disturbing and strange ones that really keeps me painting and drawing. Because then I know that they are relating to aspects of myself that I didn't think, at one point, that anyone could relate to. It has made these 'aspects', or 'things' have much less power over me."

A true sign of an artist's impact is when a viewer can relate to these disturbing, conflicting human aspects and impacts of societal roles. It enables the viewer to participate, and free themselves mentally, spiritually, and emotionally from this bondage through relation, understanding, and recognition of the unspoken or subconscious world, that is now conscious and analyzed. You can view an array of Hayley's artwork at: HayleyHara.com.

Some of the artists she finds most inspiring are: Frida Kahlo, Alice Neel, Kiki Smith, and Kara Walker. She loves the poets Adrienne Rich, Kate Clanchy, and Maya Angelou. Authors she reads (and rereads) are: Louise Edrich, Toni Morrison, Zore Naele Hurston, Anne Cameron and Alice Walker. Hayley frequently reads a lot of non-fiction on feminist religion, myth and art. Musically, she loves Tori Amos, and punk rock, but she emphasizes it's the old stuff from the eighties and nineties that get her going. She likes a lot of hip-hop female vocalists as well, such as Ursula Rocker.

You can view Rebel Mom Hayley's mystical artwork at: HayleyHara.com.

The musician P.J. Harvey has had a huge impact on her. This is evident from an early self-portrait painting and a photograph collage book she made. The book deals with female body image and self-esteem issues. It is a critical self-examination of comparing ourselves to the body image that society wants from us, which is "large-breasted, skinny-perfection," with intelligence minimized. At the core of this image objectification paradox is submission and subdued self-destruction. Hayley looks at her reaction to this cultural expectation and the negative influences it has on women and girls. The book is a commentary on her personal struggle with, and against it, since it is internalized in women from an early age and onward. [There is a need to please others at our own expense, and to be physically perfect, and socially perfect, as semi-functioning second class citizens in a male driven society. Women are raised to please them, male and patriarchal institutions, even at our own destruction.] This book was a way to diminish its power over her.

P.J. Harvey addresses similar issues in her music. She has an ongoing dialogue with these aspects of the self. Harvey dances with it, teases it, banishes it, and destroys it. Her music gives women their own face they that can understand, and can scream at, and embrace as well.

Hayley had to exorcise these aspects out of her life and making this book was an identity and spiritual act of doing just that. Through it, she was able to regain hope and her own voice:

> "I have struggled with eating disorders, and how I get too crazy when I drink too much. I have also struggled with men in general, for as long as I can remember. I used to struggle with being different from most people. I now see it as one of my greatest attributes—it seems that other people do now too. Without my art, I'm not sure who or where I'd be, but I don't think it would be good. I think most people think of me as being a little crazy, or maybe bold is a better word."

Another person who has had a huge influence on her life is her grandmother. Her grandmother raised her. She was the first person to give Hayley paints and the encouragement to express herself through art, and creativity.

Hayley was twenty-nine-years-old when she met the perfect man for her. She describes her relationship with her husband, Ken as, "more like a dance than a struggle."

She was an art student in Brooklyn, New York when they met. They found out she was pregnant while she was still in school. They would have their baby two months after she graduated with her bachelor's in fine art. It took her ten years of going to school part-time to get her degree, and she continued to complete it while her pregnancy became obvious. (Hayley states, in retrospect, that she had planned to work on her career right away, after college, but the timing of the unplanned pregnancy was perfect.) She adds that,

> "I received a lot of support from everyone close to me. It was strange being in school with people a few years younger than me and being *so* pregnant. It seemed like they all felt sorry for me, even though I loved being pregnant. It was defiantly awkward. My main hopes were that I would have a girl who would be strong and

healthy. My main fear was money. I had no idea how I was going to afford anything, and also that everyone was going to think I wasn't ready. Our only plan was to move into a bigger apartment that cost less and we did."

Hayley attributes to pregnancy and motherhood the newfound ability to slow down and be more patient. She is more aware of what is going on around her now. She was much more self-consumed beforehand and anxious.

Parenthood shocked her expectations with all the highs and lows involved. She is filled with an enormous love for her daughter Sachie, whose name is Japanese and means Happy River. (One time on the phone with Hayley, I was able to hear Sachie's sweet high-pitched baby-toddler talk. As Sachie cooed in mom's arms, I heard Hayley's strongly soft voice turn serene while cooing back.) Sachie is over two-years-old now, and does manage to drive Hayley crazy. (I've been able to hear this too. Recently, Hayley and I were doing an update for the book, and Sachie started screaming demands with her new three-to-five word toddler sentences. Exasperated, Hayley had to let me go, but such is life when rocked with motherhood and parenthood.) Hayley did not expect to have to struggle to find time for herself for: painting, drawing, and focusing on her career.

Many moms have the idea that parenthood will blend in perfectly with everything else in our lives. This may be due to the popular magazine image of the Super Mom/Super Woman/ Happy Mom, but the marketing and cultural image is far from reality. When reality sets in, it's scary, especially if you do not have resources, or support. Making it work and finding balance is critical. Hayley makes it work with this mantra in mind:

"I expect myself to stay true to who I am, and to pass on what I value in life to my daughter. I expect to always respect myself and her father, especially in her presence. I think my parenting philosophy is to be happy and to do what I want, so long as I give her attention, love and respect. I hope she is creative, intelligent, respectful, loving, opinionated and strong. I hope to instill this by owning these qualities myself."

She adds:

"For all I have been through I have turned out very well. If there was a story about my life, I would want it to say that I was truly good, because in the end I think that is all that matters. I would want it to say that I lived a very full and interesting life. I would want it to be high drama, like the Greek myth of Persephone. Life is a rollercoaster, especially if you don't follow the rules.

I think this society doesn't know how to treat children like they are individuals. I think that mothers are expected to give up too much of their identity so that their child turns out 'right'."

One thing her and her husband hope for is that Sachie will know her Japanese roots. Her husband is half Japanese and he "just lights up, he gets so interested and excited," when reading about and hearing things about Japan. Her husband's father was very determined to be "American" and her husband is a little angry that he didn't get to visit more and learn more about his heritage and the Japanese culture when he was younger. This family dynamic has everything to do with the name they chose for Sachie.

Currently, Hayley is teaching American Art History to foreigners applying for United States citizenship. It is a job that exhilarates her. It combines three things she loves: people, culture, and art. After two years of being a working stay-at-home-mom she did a stint in real estate, but it was more of a frustrating rat race. She did the best she could, but knew she needed something more compatible with her soul-personality and life passion. Prior to parenthood, Hayley supported herself working in daycare & pre-school environments (She went to school part-time for ten years during this time).

"I think art and children are a beautiful and prefect mix. In all the pre-schools I have worked in, it seems that I was the only teacher to take the children's art seriously, and ask questions about it. I also encouraged them! They were never called smart if they drew well, except by me! Other subjects were considered more important. I think that artistic creations should be encouraged if only to give a child something to do other than watch TV, or play video games. I think the impact of the arts on humanity is much more complicated, but I can simply say that Frida Kahlo's art has helped me heal. I think that schools need to accept a wider definition of intelligence, so that our children are not afraid to be who they are."

Hayley knows a few other moms like herself. She thinks most moms are afraid of their children. There are a lot of moms who are worried about saying the wrong thing, or doing the wrong thing. (Hayley has a hard time being around moms who are anxious, both around their children, and other moms. The anxiety stems from that fear, which is also combined with the fear of other people's scrutiny of their parenting.) There are some moms she knows who are amazing, and she can relate to them, but they are few and far in-between. She feels the most uncommon ground she has with other moms is that she doesn't follow strict orders by her doctor or a book. She receives shocked disbelief and unwanted criticism from moms who parent by the book. She reads her daughter in different ways, but she is by no means stupid about it. She knows when to go to Sachie's doctor, and when to go by her own instincts,

"My idea of motherhood is treating your child like she is an extension of yourself, not something in a showcase. My role as a mother I think is to treat my daughter as if she is tough, strong, intelligent and very much aware of her surroundings all the time, as I have been since the moment she was born. I am an artist. I bring my baby to all of my arts openings, as well as other art shows and events. I don't look like a typical mom, clothing etc. I want my child to be exceptional, not like all other children.

I think that birthing a child into a classic family structure is extremely over-rated. I think that most counterculture moms are very accepting of a child as they are which will make a child more confident. I think that children who grow up with counterculture moms are more likely to be rock stars, protestors, and artists than to work for corporations. And we need more rock stars, freedom fighters, and artists, and way fewer corporations. The world also needs more talented women politicians who need to take charge soon."

I think that children who grow up with counterculture moms are more likely to be rock stars, protestors, and artists than to work for corporations. And we need more rock stars, freedom fighters, and artists, and way fewer corporations.

★★★★★★★★

Hayley was attracted to a subculture and counterculture way of life when she was eleven-years-old. Her best friend had an old sister who was a punk rocker that Hayley idolized. She started dressing like her and wanted to do everything like her. Hayley also loved the music. She, "felt like what was inside was finally on the outside." She started to pick up tarot at fourteen years-of-age and even at that young of an age liked to question authority. She thinks that,

> "Mainstream people are a little more content with the workings of the world, and more accepting of them [authority] in their personal life. I think that appearance-wise, the mainstream is afraid to put some creativity into their clothing and hair."

In addition to teaching, Hayley has been working hard doing numerous collaborative projects and arts shows. One such show included canvasses on subculture and counter culture mothers and their children. (Corbie and I were honored to be amongst the subjects!) There will be many more projects in years to come for her. Hayley takes Sachie to art shows and is appalled by the response she gets from some people:

> "Sachie is such a ham, so people love her for the most part. But I have been too many shows where I feel like people are wondering what the hell I'm doing there with a baby. I intend to keep bringing her until she tells me to stop."

Hayley is proud to be the confident woman she is. She has found a way to make artwork her living and has stuck with it, resulting in numerous shows and sells of her prints. Her goals haven't changed much since before Sachie was born. She has the same plans as before which are pursuing art shows and exhibits in Manhattan and Brooklyn, all over New York, and everywhere for that matter. She does want to do more free-lance illustration work, and commissioned portraits to have more money for Sachie's sake. Her plans are to keep doing shows and projects while being an awesome mother/mentor to her daughter. She ends our interview with this sentiment …

"My dream is to become a recognizable artist. I want gallery showings all over the world, and to be in the world through private collections and museums. I wish this because I feel that my art speaks universally to all women, and connects them by doing so. I wish and dream that my artwork inspires more people to truly express their stories because things have so much more power over us when they are hidden."

Her artwork and stories already have touched lives within subculture society, and will undoubtedly ripple out to touch the hearts of those who feel stifled or silenced in larger society.

**Since this interview: Hayley is now managing the NYC's Ashcan Studio of Art, as well as teaching. She was the 2007 recipient of a full scholarship to Omega Institute's Women and Power Conference (It was in collaboration with the Nobel Women's Initiative: Women, Power & Peace which features such celebrated faculty such as Eve Ensler, Jane Fonda, Sally Field, and Shirin Ebadi.) She and Ken have also had their second child.*

"My role is to provide survival and love to my babies. To make sure they are loving to others and that they know what prayer is."

Sarah Jane
Art Gallery Owner and Photographer
Home School Teacher
Gardener and Vegetarian
Night Time Fashionista
Holistic Earth Momma
Dallas, Texas.

Sarah Jane's photography captures the hopes and weaknesses people bring with them into the night life. Her photography has focused on the under-appreciated aspects of downtown life. She sees the reflection of struggling dreamers and forgotten innocence in both the faces and inanimate objects that fill the rooms of numerous Deep Ellum bars. Her work illuminates that young, angst-filled hope as it magically returns to her subjects.

Neon lights become spiritual Renaissances under her eye and camera.

She loves the color red and sees god in everyone. That sensitivity and awareness adds a soulful completeness to her work. Sarah Jane's photography is abstract, yet heavy—weighted down with the tension of life. Her work also highlights the simple pleasures of life in her family portraits and the essence of what makes us human in her self-portraits. She loves making pictures and she shares her work, which is very integrated, at: SarahJaneSemrad.com.

Sarah Jane is also the owner and curator of the Magnolia Art Gallery in Dallas, Texas. Her aim is to focus on and showcase regional art from all walks of life. She describes herself as:

> "I'm out-going, but in the most introverted way ever. I tend to be the leader in the group, but only out of default. I have a penchant for the bizarre in life. I enjoy seeing others reactions to my love of the bizarre."

She loves the color red and sees god in everyone. That sensitivity and awareness adds a soulful completeness to her work. Her work also highlights the simple pleasures of life in her family portraits and the essence of what makes us human in her self-portraits.

See for yourself at: SarahJaneSemrad.com

Running a gallery is an accomplishment that she has dreamed of since she was young. She hopes to be an inspiration to artists everywhere as well as being an artist's advocate by promoting them collectively. She feels that as artists they share the same spark, no matter how different the reason for that spark is, or what the final art form takes. She sums it up as:

> "I dream of making an impact in a large way on the art world. I don't have a specific view of it, just that it will be

HUGE. I'm open to whatever that may entail. I want to inspire great numbers of people to begin creating and to honor creativity."

Owning a gallery allows her to take her kids to work with her and gives her enough freedom to work at home with them full-time as well. They frequently help out at the gallery, and she and her husband home-school them. Every day is a learning experience of: making art, studying science, playing music and gardening. This magical home environment travels with them everywhere they go, the gallery, outings, and on trips.

Amongst her favorite artists are: Georgia O' Keefe, Diane Arbus, and poet E.E. Cummings, "I love E.E. Cummings, talk about bucking the system with poetry!"

Musically, she loves punk rock, old school country, indie, classical, and jazz genres. She fully appreciates the effort and soul that goes into all music by musicians. Her husband Paul is a musician and has been all of his life. One of his bands Course of Empire, Dallas based, put out numerous albums between 1990 and 1998.

Sarah Jane is strongly interested in gardening and research. She combines the two for treatments with natural medicine and herbal remedies. This love of knowledge and science is evident also in her seven-year-old daughter Eva. Eva is always exploring experimentation and theories. For example, one day driving in the car Eva was devising a vacuum to see what would happen to oxygenated and un-oxygenated blood. The question of the day was: would the oxygen leave the blood to form a gas? This is no surprise either because her mom Sarah Jane majored in chemistry in college.

When the family goes out publicly they don't mix well with the other parents or soccer moms, although they have tried, and are nice. Sarah feels that they look like freaks, and it outs them from the other parents each and every time, in addition to the difference in value systems, but she is okay with that. Sarah Jane and her husband have huge tattoos and the kids have punk rock haircuts. Their family is vegetarian and they refuse to put their children in school and learn mainstream values from other kids. Sarah Jane's perception of the values that she doesn't want her kids learning is:

> "Society at large scares the hell out of me. Americans in general are fat, greedy, and prone to be suckers and buy into anything they see on TV. I feel like TV and other dumb folks are out to coerce my kids to part with their money and the values we are instilling. I'm picky about who my children hang out with. There's some criticism about that from my family, liking I'm trying too hard to protect them and they won't be social in the appropriate way, it's not really about that. I want them to have respect for their planet and home, family and friends. At some point when I do let them go, they'll be in a position to pass these values on. Most other children I know are so incredibly affected by advertising, money, and greed, that they and their parents don't even see it. They're blind. I want my children to be the light.
>
> Here's the scoop with me, I'm no hippie granola eating militant. I'm a momma. And the thought of my babies growing up thinking they can have WHAT they want WHEN they want it, at the expense of not only our planet but those in lower socio-economic groups, keeps me up at night. The 'value' of self-entitlement is not going to happen in my house. Poverty and greed is the cycle that spreads the two problems farther apart. It seems to me there's enough for everyone and that's not our world's reality right now."

Sarah Jane frequently captures on film the effect that poverty, businesses and humans have on others, especially animals. She once found a newborn pup who was the only survivor of his litter after a demolition of a downtown building. Every action we take has an effect on others in the web of life, and that is the core of her parenting values and the overall message of her artwork and photography.

She does have several mom-friends like herself, and they are on the same page about some, but not all issues. But she tries not to make them wrong in their views, or vice versa, when they disagree on a subject.

She thinks the mainstream needs to take a break from McDonald's and mass produced culture. Their kids have never had McDonald's, nor drank soda. They don't know what designer label clothes are. The values they instill in their daughter Eva (age seven) and son Jiri (age five) are: a love for art, music and free-thinking. They want to instill in them the generosity of spirit and inspiration, and to be receptive to it from others too. Love is a big message in their house and they hope they love all their friends, family, and even the homeless guy begging for money. They want their kids to have the strength and ability to question the norm, question politics, question hair color, or whatever. She hopes to have, "Well read, well spoken little twits that are smart enough to know when to talk back. I instill it by example."

Their core parenting philosophy is: to simply be with their kids. She breastfed their children and the family co-slept together. The kids sleep together now that they are older. They decided to home-school their kids based on two things: the public schools that are available to them are awful (corporate advertising in the lunchroom, dark and musty hallways, and very mean children that attend who hit and yell) and they believe in child-led learning (which is the opposite of most public school curriculums—and certainly opposite of their assigned public school D.I.S.D—Dallas Independent School District) based on the unschooling philosophy of notorious education writer and teacher, John Holt. They are involved in all aspects of their life, including, work and play.

Now that the children are older, the couple's parents are finally beginning to see that their model of parenting really does work, including home-schooling and the elimination of sugary drinks and fast food. Sarah Jane's opinion is, "Though many may think that they can't change the world, the reality is that they can little-by-little." In our interview online over rushed internet exchanges, drying paint on her end, and cold coffee on mine, we are both are in agreement: change starts with how we parent the new/next generations, and how we conduct and live ourselves. Every time her family encounters a homeless person, Eva leads the family in prayer for them.

Sarah Jane and Paul eloped when she was twenty-one. Their dating was brief, but they were madly in love and knew they each were the one. They spent their honeymoon backpacking through Spain. Eva was a honeymoon conceived baby. Sarah Jane was sad, excited and mortified, all at once when she learned she was pregnant.

Sarah Jane was a child when her mother left, after her parents divorced. She was only two-years-old. She was raised by her stepmother. She was afraid she wouldn't know how to "mother" since she feels like she didn't really have one.

By the time Jiri was born, she was much more self-assured and confident. She gave birth to Jiri at home and by this time she trusted herself, her mothering instincts, and their parenting styles, and choices. She knew she could do natural birthing at home, by trusting her body and instincts. She beams when she thinks about that (having Jiri at home in the family bed), she feels like now she can do anything. (In retrospect, she has—including opening her own art gallery.) She is a self-proclaimed go-getter with an uncanny ability to get things done. "Being a mom is hard, but so worth it. I tend to move at lightning speed, and they [the kids] slow me down, this is a good thing."

Before marriage and kids entered the picture she always imagined herself running off to Africa and helping people. She was the first one in her circle of friends to get married and have babies, which no one expected, including her. She describes her relationship with her husband as:

> "My husband is very supportive. We tend to be pretty counterculture on all fronts and don't have support for the way we think except from each other. I'm glad he's in my life and eggs me on when our families frown upon yet one more thing we are doing that's not 'normal'."

As a married couple of almost eight years, they have grown together and understand marriage is hard work. Her husband is forty-two-years old and he still inspires her with his music and sideburns. She is thirty. They support each other fully and accept one another.

There was a previous marital affair and it has brought them closer together and they now know when ill-timed attractions occur they can work through it, but they have to address why it's happening—before it happens. Their acceptance of each other and love for one another makes their marital base strong, and enabled them to forgive and rebuild their relationship. He's nutty and she is witty. They are both brilliant and different, and they love that about one another.

She is currently working on creating an artist residency program in Oak Cliff, Texas. As far as the future goes she is going to keep doing what she's doing, and … "It's hard to go against the system and then not be able to back it up. If I can teach my children to be accountable, respectful, and well-spoken, then I've succeeded in this way of life."

"I never strived to be part of a counterculture. When I was little I used to read *National Geographic* and see pictures of women in Africa, with amazing body art, and beautifully wild hair. So I started getting tattooed and pierced when I was sixteen … My parents didn't object. So I wasn't rebelling against anything. I was just doing what felt right."

Kristen
Political Illustrator
Modern Renaissance Artist
Art-based Merchandise Company Owner
Record Lover
Foxy Full-time Momma
Feminist
Whitchata, Kansas.

Kristen is a laid-back artist who loves living life to the fullest and with a sense of humor. She makes enough money with her art and clothing/merch line business that she no longer has to have a day job. She wants to spend her days making funny pictures, hanging out with her son and husband. She doesn't care about being rich, or traveling, or fame, or even leaving the house for that matter. All she cares about is her boys and her artwork.

Her husband says she makes him laugh more than anyone he has ever known, her best friend says she is loyal like a pit bull, and her son says she is his favorite person. These are all the amazing compliments she needs from the most important people to her, to get through the world one-day-at-a-time.

> "I'm a mother first, an artist, and a feminist, trying to stay in the mindset of 'gender equality' and not 'female superiority,' but it is difficult. Loyalty, love and respect are the most important things to me, and I try to involve them in everything I do. I am horribly stubborn and opinionated, but always try to be cheerful about it."

Kristen loves good art, honest people, Indian food, and Kansas living. She is very fond of Hee-Haw reruns. She thinks the key to happiness for all people is finding stability through expression, living simplistically, being creative, and finding pleasure in everyday life experiences from making something, to eating your favorite food, completing a goal and hugging those close to you. What gets her excited about living is: politics, positive change in society, the growth of the underground art movement, good music, loyal friends, being in love, and free time.

She does have disdain for ill-behaved men, intolerant people, women who hate other women, anything pertaining to our past president George W. Bush, modern television (and our culture's addiction to it), and big dogs—they make her nervous.

She spends her days listening to music, "I listen to everything. If it's well done and stands out, I will enjoy it no matter what style it is." Music inspires and motivates her daily to paint, print-make, sew, draw, and play.

Kristen started her own merchandise business a few years ago. She didn't want to dedicate herself to anyone else's business anymore, so she made one of her own. Her art career has blossomed and she has been able to make her calling her vocation. After working many years for someone else's small business, and in factories, and having to delegate art to a part-time passion, she can finally devote herself entirely to it. She grew it gradually through word-of-mouth, years of effort with little sleep, and now she makes enough income to sustain her family while doing it.

Her artwork has a complex magical quality that transplants Renaissance art and religious symbolism with fairy tales while reducing sexist women's roles and images. Her art's commentary attempts to sever these roles from women, through evoking how they hinder and bind women in real life. This complex duality is fantastically mirrored back to the viewer to read. If there was a feminist rewrite of the Grimm's Fairytales, Kristen, undoubtedly, would be the only artist in the world who could succinctly capture the magic and the truths of the stories through illustration.

She cites her influences as Goya, Posada, Hieronymus Bosch, Albrecht Dürer, and her experiences both as a mother and a previous divorcee, and her having an intense emotional reaction to humanity (and the world at large).

Rebel Mom Kristen's artwork has a magical quality that transplants Renaissance art with pop culture fairy tales, while commenting on sexist women's roles and images. Check it out at: KristenFerrell.com

Her artwork is universally known and sought after, and has been shown in galleries internationally. In addition, to her work being subtextually feminist and punk, she has created explicitly cool and radical illustrations for magazines like *Punk Planet* and *Pistil*, for movements like the 2004 t-shirt design for the *Take Back the Night* campaign (A global direct action grassroots movement that started in 1976 against rape, and challenges violence against women. You can take a stand at TakeBacktheNight.org.) and logo design for bands like Citizen Fish and Leftover Crack.

She also has won numerous awards including the Charlotte and George L. Kreeck Award, Hollander Family Foundation Scholarship, Daniel Mac Morris Scholarship, and the Hollander Family Foundation Scholarship.

Her clothing line company, Kristen Ferrell Clothing, has become so popular that not only can you order her designs on t-shirts, but also dinnerware, bug boxes, stationary sets, kewpie dolls and quilts. Her line is sold at independent boutiques ranging from all major U.S. cities to international hot-spots like Dublin, Ireland and Berlin, Germany.

Take Back the Night is a global direct action grassroots movement that started in 1976 against rape, and challenges violence against women. Take a stand at TakeBacktheNight.org!

Her work has been featured in various magazines including *Juxtapoz*, a magazine on art and culture, and *Alternative Press Magazine*. Even bands are wearing her designs, like Homesick Abortions and Kamilla Vanilla (of the Horror Pops). Her customer gallery (on her website) has numerous pictures of individuals with her illustrations tattooed on. You can see more of her designs and check out her merchandise at: KristenFerrell.com.

Her work is demanding, but she juggles all the "full-time everything's," with a smile and occasional catnaps. She never imagined how busy her life would be with marriage, parenting, and work. When she had her son, Sully, she knew she had to figure out how to support him and accomplish her artistic career goals. She is astonished at how successful her efforts have become and couldn't be more satisfied, "There's too much to do, and not enough time to do it, so I'll rest when I'm dead."

She was a twenty-one-year-old art student when she learned she was pregnant. She was "just a kid embracing everything a young punker in college should be." She didn't have any real plans at the time, because she hadn't entered that stage of life called, "What I am going to do when I grow up?"

Kristen grew up in a very religious and quiet home, and when her family learned of her pregnancy it wasn't a question of, "Are you going to get married?" but "When are you going to get married?" She was a sophomore at this time. She didn't feel she had any choice in the matter and was pressured into marrying. However, her family was very supportive of her being a mother, and they have stood by her over the years, including her later divorce. For this, she can never thank them enough.

But in regards to the first marriage, she knows she was young and impressionable, and mistakenly thought she was in love. Their marriage only lasted a couple of years. She may regret the marriage, but not having her son. When they first met she was nineteen and he was twenty-six-years-old. Their relationship could be defined as drinking and causing trouble. When Kristen decided to have her son, she left that lifestyle behind for good. Sully's father tried to embrace the idea of it, but had a hard time letting go of the behavior (partying and mischief). After a few years, she had become a different person, but he hadn't … "I grew into who I was supposed to be and it didn't fit with the person he was anymore."

Kristen was in her final year in college when they divorced. The divorce was really hard on Sully, and he couldn't understand why daddy was upset all the time. She couldn't really explain the complexities of the demise of a marriage to a three-year-old. He was old enough though for it to affect him, but things have worked out well after the initial, and painful, transition period. It took a year of absence from Sully for his dad to finally become stable enough to reenter his life. Kristen is thankful for this period because, "He is now a good and active dad doing the best for himself and his son. A lot of guys never reach that level of maturity."

Both parents have happily remarried into healthy relationships. Sully has the best of both worlds in two productive home environments instead of one dysfunctional home. He understands now that mommy and daddy get along better as friends, and "All it means is that there is more people in his life that love him."

Kristen had to work out some emotional and mental issues first. Kristen's first marriage was a very destructive one and it left her with many issues regarding men—which she had to get over fast. She didn't see it as "healthy for her to be raising a son and hating men."

Her second husband, Brad, stepped into a "minefield" when he met her. She was a constant picture of exhaustion from trying to help Sully adjust and soothe him, while working full-time as a buyer for a retail boutique and promoting her art work in galleries, while resolving her own issues. She never second guessed her decisions though, "All you can do is make a choice and keep moving no matter where that takes you."

He was living in Los Angeles and she was in Kansas, so it forced them to take their relationship and dating very slowly. She wasn't going to allow another guy into her and Sully's life, until all issues were resolved. Brad had never been around kids and by taking everything laggardly, he was able to get to know Sully and figure out if parenting was something he was really into before he committed to it. But he knew the day he met her at the record store, that he was going to marry her. Sully and Brad ended up growing very close, and after figuring out the dynamics of their relationship, they now have a very wonderful one.

The family frequently does stuff outdoors together like swimming, skateboarding, and going to the park. A favorite weekend hobby is raiding the toy stores and loading up on comic books. There's a lot of involvement in music and art. Brad owns a record label, and is in several bands. There is no shortage of painting, or music-making, in their home. Kristen describes Sully as:

> "He is hilarious … but yet a handful. He's always been around adults—so he talks like one, which is a good thing, and a bad thing. I've never believed in dumbing anything down for him, and we don't have television (it's pure evil and produces mindless clones), so he entertains himself with books and educational computer programs. We've never really did the 'kiddy-music-and-playtime' stuff. So all the Barney sing-along crap really freaks him out. He hates it. I've always thought that stuff was insulting to a kid's intelligence, anyways. He would rather spend his time

watching documentaries about animals and medieval Europe than 'Thomas the Magic Railroad' any day. He's not actually able to relate to any kids his age, because he speaks over their heads. He's really 'advanced' for his age, but it makes things really hard for him at school. He gets bored easily and acts out. Since we have always treated him pretty much as an equal and with respect, he doesn't understand why there is such a dictatorship with his teachers. It's frustrating, because he's already fed up with school, and he's only six. But he amazes me every day."

She thinks that people underestimate children and what they are capable of doing and comprehending. She has observed that children are very perceptive, beautifully honest, and much wiser than most adults she knows. She thinks those traits are destroyed in the educational process because (like mothers) they are expected to look and behave in one particular fashion which destroys their individuality, "Being an outspoken individual is frowned upon when they get to school. It's really sad." Despite the school environment, she is providing her son with the tools to be anything he wants in life and to be secure and happy with himself. He knows no matter what he is always loved,

"All children want is to be loved, feel safe, and have fun. That's it. So I try to provide that as much as I possibly can. I am always showing him to be open to all situations, people and ways of life. I sometimes think there is a positive side to the aggression that we receive from strangers, because he sees my understanding and tolerance for others and their misconceptions. I fully believe in 'killing them with kindness,' because to react to someone who hates you because of how you look only reinforces everything they think of you. If you show these people that you are actually kind, educated, and confident in yourself, they may not be so quick to display that aggression towards the next person they see that looks like I do. My son witnessing that is an important lesson for him to learn. Tolerance for others is the only way we all will ever get along.

I want him to be happy and confident with the decisions he makes throughout life. I don't care what he decides to do with himself, as long as he is always respectful of himself and others, and true to what he believes. I think this is taught by example. If he sees me, and the people I choose to surround us behaving this way, he'll see it as how life is supposed to be: constant support, love, and understanding of his opinions, choices and ideas.

I have a tendency to be over-protective. I have to always watch my behavior so I don't keep him from experiencing life and learning from his mistakes, because of my own paranoia of the world and my emotional baggage. It's the difference of giving him advice and letting him choose whether or not he's going to take it, or making decisions for him. I think the future of my motherhood and parenting mainly consists of me learning how to do well in every situation. All we can do is give them the tools to function in society, help build their confidence to use these tools, and then trust them to use them properly … the rest is up to them, and all we can do after that is be there for them when things get difficult."

Having a little side kick is one element of motherhood she has enjoyed, a kind of, "Him and her against the world." She loves having him all to herself. Kristen and I bond in this moment for we both relate to the magical love we have for our children. It is all encompassing, and neither of us was prepared for such a profound deepness in it. It's almost suffocating sometimes. You expect to love your children, but not worship them. And there is no doubt in my mind that we worship our sons! We laugh over long-distance lines at this surreal revelation. (*Yes, when we interviewed basic cell phones were still an elusive and expensive accessory, ha-ha.)* She does acknowledge the feeling of isolation that comes along with such an intense love combined with single parenting. (Before she remarried it was really overwhelming at times, not being able to share all those little moments with anyone. Time has always been a major issue too—there's just not enough of it.) Before her career took off, freeing her up to work from home, she resented having to work full-time and long hours to make ends meet, when all she desired was to be with Sully every second …

"Motherhood is grossly underrated in our society as whole. It is our job to produce and mold these new and amazing creatures into something productive and thriving—while were fighting against every external element that exists, but with very little assistance in this job. It's the most important job out there, (to sustain a population of functioning, happy, and adjusted kids so the future won't turn foul) but it is taken for granted. And when women try to exist as an individual while embracing the occupation of 'motherhood,' it is frowned upon by men and women alike. All I want to do is provide all the necessary tools for my son to be everything he wants to be in life and at the same time maintain my own sense of self as an individual. It's not as easy as it sounds."

After having Sully, she had a newfound respect and sense of awe towards her own mother. Kristen says she was a "terrible kid that caused nothing but grief." She is adopted so she can also see the "insane act of selflessness" that her biological mother performed when she gave her up for adoption after going through the pregnancy and giving birth to a child.

She thought it was weird how she lost friends when she became a mom and that added to the initial shock of loneliness.

> "I was viewed in my circle as being a 'breeder,' doomed to domesticity. But I was also shunned from the parents groups because of my appearance. And since I was the first of my friends to have a kid, it was pretty isolating.
>
> Mothers can be like a coven of witches, if you don't fall into their specific guidelines on how to be, you are cast out of the group. Which is sad, because it's not about the mothers, it's about the kids. My son has always been excluded from playgroups, birthday parties, and after-school get-togethers, because I don't fit into their canon of what a mother should be like, even though my dedication to my son and his future is just as great as theirs. I think we all have the same hopes and fears as most parents … that they (the kids) make it through life happy and healthy. Most of the other mom's I have met are the stay-at-home soccer types … which it is totally great they have found happiness in that. But in order [for me] to function, I have to have my own personal dreams being fulfilled that don't necessary have anything to do with being a mom. A lot of mom's I have met don't understand that. They see it as me not dedicating everything I have to my son. I see it as bettering myself and my life for the sake of my son. It's just two very different ways of thinking that sometimes don't work well together."

Kristen is frequently grouped into the punk mom category, yet she doesn't feel that fits her since she isn't rebelling against anything. She just presents herself how she is comfortable, but the world has a hard time resisting the urge to categorize people, be it positive or negative, that doesn't fit the *acceptable* standard. [When it's a negative categorization, it's a cultural way of diminishing the individual's true normalcy and value in society; if people can be tightly labeled, belittled, and/or scrutinized as *abnormal, or poor, or rich, or black, or white, or this, or that* … it is to make them insignificant or unimportant. We have seen this behavior and attitude demonstrated at its worst, in regards to race and class, based on the indifference of the powerful: when the nation watched in outrage and horror as the people, the left-behind people, of New Orleans were left to die. We also saw, despite the lack of help from our leaders, our nation's people pull together to do what we could.]

She personally sees herself far more as a political mom than a punk one, which has everything to do with her political values, beliefs, and political activism, and nothing to do with how she looks. She is however always looking for a common bond with other women and mothers (regardless of appearance, or obvious lifestyle differences, etc.), but hasn't found many open-minded moms that live close to her. The few she has found, the family schedules are just too demanding and complex to allow frequent socializing. She adds that a definite plus kids get with subculture parents is:

> "I think that moms like me are a little more open to alternative ways of parenting, because they embrace different ways of thinking. Plus, with the adversities that we face in being shunned by people who are comfortable in the 'norm', we can offer more understanding and a tolerant way of thinking to our children. We can teach them to love people of all walks of life and appearance, even if it's not what we choose for ourselves."

Kristen is now thirty, and Sully is eight-years-old. Not much has changed in the world, but their acceptance of others is still the same and they feel this healthy way of living contributes to their happiness, and they are okay with who they are—even if the world at large isn't.

Kristen still struggles with not having enough time to do everything she sets out to, but she lives by a basic principle: "Life is short, so do it right! And the world is mean so keep your guard up … but smile there is no hell." She sums up her life as, "I lived hard, did it well, and will die peacefully in my sleep at the age of 145. That's all that anyone will care to know about me 100 years from now."

**Since this interview: Kristen and her family have happily relocated to L.A.*

"I felt maybe if I walked around a club nude, aside from having acrylics and undies on (for a body art canvas show), that I would be forcing myself to be comfortable with my body."

Jennifer
Mixed Media Artist
Icon Painter
Beautiful Earth Spiritualist
Canvas Body Art and Fashion Model
Cervix Industry Worker
Dallas, Texas.

Jennifer is a mixed media artist and college student. She employs a variety of material textures and mediums to create her art. She is a single mom raising two *almost* teenage girls. She struggles to find balance between all the demands of parenting, work and school. Her art keeps her mind focused when life is spinning out of control around her. She doesn't separate art from living,

"Life, I must create to function! It's like breathing. Regardless of how it is revealed (painting, photography, design, writing, music …) if I don't create, I die!!!"

Three of her favorite pieces as of late are a mixed media collage that depicts women walking towards blackness, a heavily textured acrylic face that ended up resembling Jimi Hendrix, and a line drawing that is a shadowy figure of a man's physical contours.

Music is a key component in helping her become centered and gets her in the artistic mood. The bands she frequently listens to are: Joy Division, Cocteau Twins, Bauhaus, Swans, Wolfgang Press, Le Tigre, Chicks on Speed, Arkane, Slits, Stranglers, and Siouxsie and the Banshees. (Which during the interview Jennifer proclaims spiritedly that Siouxsie has always been her Goddess! I second that!)

"As an artist, I am constantly attracted to that which is visually stunning. My series *Icons* is loosely based on the icons of the ancient Byzantium Church. Artists are usually socially aware individuals; I am one of these types of artists. Culture encompasses social activities: past, present, and future. In this series I am representing these themes as well as other social aspects involving spirituality, gender, and subculture."

As a mixed media artist, she combines a variety of mediums to make her masterpieces including: painted over photography, music backgrounds to accompany pieces, magazine pictures as paint backgrounds, and discarded objects for frames and points of attraction in her work. The objects can vary from tree bark to metal.

She balances the textures in her pieces which creates harmony. She relies on the colors black, white, and red to create a striking discord in some of her work. All of her creations stand uniquely on their own though, and if you look at her collection you wouldn't assume for a moment they were all done by the same artist. This makes her work even more distinct and diverse. Her collection varies from watercolors, acrylics, and paper, to wire-mesh collages.

Her photography encompasses the same variety and richness. Some of her photography is overtly political and serves as commentary on motherhood and women's subservient roles; others are highly sensual depictions of herself, which mirrors a self-love and a self-hate conflict.

She has recently completed her largest single theme series called *Icons*. Jennifer starts with a photo of a subject and immortalizes them with golden paint and bejewels them from behind with ancient Eastern Roman patterns. There are tattooed mothers with blue hair, individuals with mohawks, and living human goddesses and gods all blessed with halos. She also depicted me and my son in a Virgin Mary pose in the series. She describes the project and her role as the artist:

> "As an artist, I am constantly attracted to that which is visually stunning. My series *Icons* is loosely based on the icons of the ancient Byzantium Church. Artists are usually socially aware individuals; I am one of these types of artists. Culture encompasses social activities: past, present, and future. In this series I am representing these themes as well as other social aspects involving spirituality, gender, and subculture.
>
> Utilizing imagery and symbolism from the infancy of the religion that changed the world and made many cultures and faiths meld into one. I have evoked the spirits of the past, choosing my subjects from: ambiguous gender, to the dramatic imagery of contemporary subcultures, which set themselves apart from the 'norm' visually. Just as the 'saints' of the early church set themselves apart from the masses by images of themselves that created reverence among the masses. My images represent modern icons.
>
> My generation no longer clings to religion's robes. This generation seeks spirituality from within and from unconventional sources, fellow peers and friends. This is what the modern icons represent."

The three artists she credits for influencing her work are: Dave McKean, Vaughn Olive, and Picasso. She likes McKean's *Lovers* from the *Practical Tarot,* because he uses a unique approach to design colors and shadows. Vaughn Oliver also known as v23 or 23enevlope has a really fresh edge on design, and Jennifer views that as a unique challenge to apply to her own work, how to make it raw and new in a way that separates her work from others. She loves the obvious portrayal of passion in Picasso's pieces, even though, "He was a dick." Artists like Frida Kahlo, Floria Sigismondi, and Tina Modetti have also had a huge impact on her artistic style and psyche.

She considers her photography fine art, and stays away from 'boring' black and white and traditional photography. She will generally take her photography and canvas them, altering the space of the photo and changing the context of the subject. She does this digitally as well as through the old medium of paintbrush and paints. Jennifer's motto is:

> "You have to break all the rules to create! I love expressing myself through all facets of my life be it my clothing, my hair, my art, my writing, or my general being. I crave utter uniqueness. I crave open-minded thought. I probably take for granted the extreme nature of my interests since they are so everyday and common to me."

She hopes to achieve something revolutionary with her art. She "has to be somewhere in art history books, via infamy or originality!" It is her opinion that artists have a responsibility to evolve society's consciousness. The role of art and expression is a central structure in her household and she hopes it will encourage and enable her daughters to be broad-minded and independent thinkers.

Raising two daughters, Gabby and Arianne, on her own is a lot of work, but she tries to impart a bit of wisdom and culture to them, so that the next generation will evolve mentally and socially. She believes children are a tabula rasa, but are more complete as humans than any adult she has ever met, and she feels that is largely due to the fact they are born free and not yet poisoned by the world's hatred, biasness, greed and cruelty. [Tabula rasa is Latin for a clean slate. Humans are born like a blank canvas and their life experiences will become their window of the world and will gradually define and fill up their entire mental content.]

Her mantra is, "To raise my girls' right even if it's 'wrong'." Jennifer is a seeker of knowledge and wisdom and teaches her children by example. She knows this will make them strong and intelligent. Their ability to make decisions based on a variety of information manifested itself recently when another relative criticized the choice of books of Jennifer's oldest daughter. She was studying spiritualism and had a book on Earth religions and the older family member advised her that it was satanic and she shouldn't be reading that, but something Christian based. With the support of her mother, she advised the relative that she is a seeker of truth and knowledge, and it doesn't necessarily come in one form or from one belief system.

A favorite quote that Jennifer references frequently to her girls is from the book *Buddha Speaks* by Majjhima Nikaya:

> *"But what makes these 'experts' preach their opinion and call it truth?" asked the inquirer, "Is it an inheritance of humankind to do this, or is it merely something they gain satisfaction from?"*
>
> *"Apart from consciousness," answered the Buddha, "No absolute truths exist. False reasoning declares one view to be true and another view wrong. It is delight in their dearly held opinions that make them assert that anyone who disagrees is bound to come to a bad end. But no true seekers become embroiled in all this. Pass by peacefully, and go a stainless way, free from theories, lusts and dogmas."*

Jennifer's philosophy is that her daughter's points-of-view are as important as hers, and it is critical that she sees them both equally. She knows life is a hard balance, between responsibilities and dreams, but her daughters see her doing it every single day. "Making life what I want," which is an important ethic she wants them to learn. So that they grow up not only independent, but aware of life and conscious of their own choices in it.

She was only seventeen when she had her first daughter, and it was "ethics from the product of young love," that they decided to have her. She was afraid of having to grow up and that she couldn't do it any better than her mother. She had a lot of support from her family and still does to this day. The father Paul (and her teenage sweetheart) started distancing himself from his young family and eventually became unaware of what was going on in their lives. Sadly, he never had the chance to redeem himself; he was killed in a tragic car accident in Dallas. He was a pedestrian that mysteriously fell off the bridge, in the presence of his then-girlfriend, onto the expressway below.

Motherhood was a very scary concept to her, and it still frightens her ...

> "Will they [the government] take them away because of my beliefs? Am I good enough? Am I doing this right? And at the same time will there be enough of me to defend my girls if I am called to protect them from war mongers like [our previous president] Bush? How can I stop old traditions that kill a girl's self image?"

In her attempts to reconstruct her own self-esteem (that had been damaged by cultural beauty standards), Jennifer has modeled nude, expect for undies and paints, in a live body art show. She has modeled for photographers in art shoots, and lastly for fun fashion shoots. She also does self-portrait work. This is a frequent exercise she does to repair herself esteem when the world keeps shoving plastic tall Europeanized perfection down our throats. For anyone who is considering modeling she adds, "Remember who and what you are, and what you are doing it for ..."

By being a role model to her daughters, Jennifer shows them the value of self-love and self-beauty. Her household is an organized, uncluttered holistic sanctuary. Art decorates the walls symmetrically and her furniture is of the popular modern minimalist style. Her fridge is full of organic temptations and lively colorful Italian ceramics greet you in the kitchen. Lavender and Jojoba oils rest on the vanity in the bathroom. She relies on natural medicine and herbal remedies, for all of her family's needs, and she despises the United States excessive consumer culture which sickens the mind, spirit and body. Jennifer's biggest struggles with single parenting is time and money,

> "Well, if I had more time for just school and had living expenses paid for, I probably could be making a better living now. At the same time though, I am forced to be more creative to make my creations and myself, happen."

She does feel secure in the fact that when things fall apart, that she can always count on her friends and family to lend her a helping hand. She doesn't take this for granted because she knows single parents often don't have this built-in-help network.

For years she worked making minimum wage in the "Cervix Industry," (mostly women perform service jobs) and resents most of the people she has encountered and worked with.

> "I resent those who make a lot of money and take it for granted while you work for a lot less for them in the 'Cervix Industry'; and having to work/serve others who I don't feel deserve the things they have. I have to fight those thoughts a lot. Resentment is awful …"

About the overwhelming amount of women and mothers working in the Service/Cervix sector and the role of sexism involved in it, she notes, "Well let me just say this, I make less than any of the men that I work with regardless of how long I've been where I have been working." About the term she coined, *Cervix Industry*, [which is a term fitting for the reality that most minimum wage jobs are service jobs, and are disproportionably filled by working mothers and women] she explains with both agitation, and humored mockery (to deflect the serious reality all working class women and all working class mothers have to endure) …

> "I have worked with a few men and frequently have to pick up after their slack at work, 'Well, I'm a woman!' I should be familiar with cleaning, RIGHT? Fuck that. Most men I have met have been pampered by women their whole life and don't even begin to know how to take care of themselves, am I bitter?"

She is thrilled to now be working in a graphic design studio, even though it's a grunt entry-level position, but it's a step closer to where she wants to be. Finishing college is still a goal she gets closer to with every semester that she completes. She hopes to eventually have college funds for her daughters who are now nine and thirteen. Jennifer herself is thirty. She plans to travel the world with them for a while after they are done with high school, a chance for them (and her) to, "see and explore the world before they start college."

Before becoming a mother she describes herself as a, "Party girl, probably a bit of a slut and definitely a heartbreaker." She has become a responsible mother on her own though in spite of the distraction that life produces. Motherhood has been a period of constant growth and amazement for her.

She thinks all moms are frightened of raising children in this world which is full of violence and selfishness. She knows many moms similar to herself and they share very strong passions for: the arts, politics, being mothers, fashion, and music.

However, two things that tend to define them as a group (sub/counterculture moms), from mainstream moms she feels are:

> "The apparent and obvious drive we have and need for self-expression and having uncommon opinions; opinions that typically aren't even discussed amongst moms, or at least that's how their portrayed [as a group] in mainstream media."

Jennifer just shrugs off this apparent cultural difference in mothers and motherhood itself as,

> "It's just human nature, to have a rebel pack that is completely opposite to the majority pack that dominates the society and runs the system. What attracted me to the subculture way of life is my lust for expression and we have the wisdom of the real world because we seek truth. I refuse to live the 'suburban' clone nightmare. I strongly believe in breaking all tradition to create something new and possibly better."

★★★★★★★★

"It's just human nature, to have a rebel pack that is completely opposite to the 'majority pack' that dominates the society and runs the system. What attracted me to the subculture way of life is my lust for expression and we have the wisdom of the real world because we seek truth."

★★★★★★★★

Right now she just plans on taking care of herself and her children on her own, while fighting to finish school and producing her art, which has already begun to illuminate in the world.

**Since this interview: Jennifer has survived ovarian cancer, a job lay-off, and has had several successful and acclaimed art showings.*

"I love to create with my imagination, even though I do not have very much time and convenience for this. Adrenaline surges inside of me when I really get going in a creation of mine."

Cynthia
Day of the Dead Painter
Waitress
Fashion Maker
Saintly Seductress
Homemaker
Dallas, Texas.

Cynthia is a mesmerizing, homemaking siren who is building her fashion and art empire one piece at a time. She makes unique recycled art threads and sells clothes on eBay. She plans on expanding this to include shoes, jewelry and lingerie. The long term plan is to have a fully running internet store.

Most days she sews, paints, and cares for her two-year-old daughter Camilla full-time as a working stay-at-home mom. The struggle is finding time to create, while nurturing her daughter. She loves nature, reading, drawing, and animals. She battles with procrastination though, since she is compelled to do so much and to do so little, because she lacks enough personal time. She describes herself as an open-minded, witty, beautiful girl with a bite of sarcasm.

When she does find time to paint it's in the early morning, or late evening, or during Camilla's naptime. And it is a few moments of artistic genius that exhilarates her and renews her, enabling her to be a better mom throughout the day. Cynthia truly believes you are what you create. Her artwork has changed and evolved over the years reflecting all the twists and turns of her own life. Her portfolio consists of dark and bleak pieces, surreal, realistic, abstract, and mixed media from chalk, pastel, oil, etc.

Rebel Mom Cynthia is very proud of her Mexican heritage and that background provides her with cultural and spiritual paths to explore in her work. She's an admirer and studier of cultural art and history related to the ancient Aztec and modern Mexican Day of the Dead and Day of the Innocents celebrations.

Cynthia is very proud of her Mexican heritage and that background provides her with cultural and spiritual paths to explore in her work. She's an admirer and studier of cultural art and history related to the ancient Aztec and modern Mexican *Day of the Dead* and *Day of the Innocents* celebrations. She recently produced a wonderful piece on large plywood of a Day of the Dead scene. It is vibrant with colors and swells with mixed patterns and is full of flowers such as marigolds. She mellows it out with a huge bright sun and dancing pastel sugar skulls. It was commissioned for a popular restaurant, Guthries, but she is saddened by its commission because it's going to be hung outside on the patio and she knows eventually it will be weather damaged.

Another recently completed piece she is fond of is a grim green face that is painted onto framed window glass ... It is an acrylic piece and the face stares out the window at you in a tormented state. It's how she feels sometimes—trapped—trapped in either a marriage that is going through a stagnation phase, or trapped during cycles of heavy and exhaustive parenting with no break. It is in essence, the darkness within her.

Her favorite artists are Frida Kahlo, Miro, and Dali, "There is a strong sense of darkness and mystery to all of them. I love their unusual creations."

One of the bands she listens to in her artistic trance and on quiet evenings is the Cure. She loves how the lyrics are open, innocently tenebrous and playful. She feels the songs transport her to a completely other place, wherever the song is set at, and that allows her to find artistic nirvana. Shadow Frankenstein, and Bauhaus also cast an enchantingly serene spell on Cynthia while she is working. So does Alio di Ora,

> "I think they are from Italy. The album *'Door of Possibilities'*, is a collage of songs of pure noise and sound effects, like instruments, the ocean, etc. It sounds like music from a nightmare or something. I feel like I get taken to another world, a world of darkness and isolation when I listen to this. It's the ultimate. I extremely enjoy music that doesn't need words. I very much enjoy gothic-darkwave, industrial, and classical. I tend to like the gaudiness and mystery in this type of music. The instruments and words are so deep and piercing. There isn't music like that too much nowadays."

Joy Division is another band she loves, especially on hectic, frenzied days. She is fond of their song, *She's Lost Control.* She feels this way a lot when trying to juggle the demands between creating art, and taking care of her family.

Cynthia's life has become much more stable and quiet since having Camilla. A normal day consists of preparing meals, watching kid movies and shows like *The Wiggles*, *Barney*, and *Jay Jay*, as well as reading books. Throughout the day they take walks, visit family members, and go to the library. Consistently, she aims to create (and provides) an enjoyable environment full of activities for her daughter. She does all of her art work before and after Camilla is sleeping. She gets frustrated like any other mom, because parenting is a full-time job—but with no breaks. The naptimes tend to end abruptly while she is in the middle of work.

During the initial interview query Camilla had fallen asleep after lunch, and Cynthia showed me her art as we talked and enjoyed pastries and strong coffee in her pastel and brightly decorated kitchen (with awesome, contrasting, cabinets painted black). Just as abruptly as she fell asleep, Camilla woke up, and Cynthia put down her work, and didn't skip a beat in transitioning back to her role as mother and caretaker. [I have to admit, it's not as easy for me. I normally need a twenty minute decompression and I beg Corben for just one more minute …]

Before having Camilla, she was an angry and depressed person, and life just passed her by. Her depression started in childhood during longs periods when her father was absent, and her mother neglected her emotionally. Even though she had married the love of her life, she was still lonely and felt lost, and didn't have any plans for the future. She felt she had nothing going for her personally, and was, "just too childish and creating problems," with her husband. Her life seemed somewhat bleak to her before she found wholeness and direction with motherhood.

"I was depressed because I was not taking control of my life like I should have. Anything that was negative in my life, I dwelled on. I hated my sheltered childhood that my mother gave me. I hated the religion that was shoved down my throat. I hated my mother's husband and the lack of attention from her. I hated my family. I just wanted to be happy, and my happiness didn't seem very important. I wanted to pursue a fine art career and my mother was completely against it, and her lack of support in anything I did, was a negative.

My father's verbal abuse towards the world, his horrible attitude, and the violence on his side of the family, that I witnessed one too many times, affected me. I was rejected by his siblings because of the bad relationships he had with them. I was a 'nobody' in that family.

I have not been depressed ever since I had accepted my pregnancy. I feel purpose and love, now my child gives me reason and happiness each time I look into her eyes. I don't live in the black hole that I had created for myself prior."

She is now more relaxed, easy-going, and has a better, and happier, disposition about life now. She has a purpose and a tangible reason for finding rhyme and meaning, and staying positive. She smiles much, much more. Cynthia is very family oriented and it makes her work to be a better person, "even though [she giggles with a hint of naughtiness] it is not always that easy." She fights her tendency to procrastinate, or to be pessimistic, daily through being focused on art and her daughter.

Her childhood creates the frame of experience she references on *how not to parent*. Her own childhood left a lot to yearn for and she has created an atmosphere equal to her own childhood dreams for herself and her family:

"I understand the value and the blessing I have, and I refuse to take that for granted. I try to spend every moment I can with my child because in the end she will remember and realize how important she is to me. That is something too many children do feel (that they aren't important) or their parents don't realize they are taking them for granted. I believe 100% that parents are so very responsible for their children's happiness, health and future.

I hate it when moms have to leave their babies behind to go fulfill their personal needs, like to be with someone at that moment, go get wasted, or drugged, or whatever the interest is to satisfy, that comes before the child. I mean, fine go out once in a while without the baby, but don't make it a habit.

I despise parents who are abusive to their children (verbal abuse also is so much worse than what people think, I know this firsthand), who ignore their kids or their needs, or parents who put themselves first. I can't stand parents that smoke, especially around their children. The money for that habit could be used for something more productive."

Cynthia grew up with an alcoholic father and a Catholic mother. Her father wasn't the "physically abusive type of alcoholic," but a verbal one. He did make careless decisions due to his disease and had to go to prison twice for multiple DWI's. In spite of his absence during those periods, and his separation from Cynthia's mother, they maintained a close daughter-father relationship. As a teenager though, she resented him for not being there for her when she needed him most, but she still favored her dad over her, "paranoid, strict, religious, and overprotective mother." Cynthia says she was unfairly burdened with the exhausting task of raising her little sister and three brothers, by having to constantly care for them and watch them. She was given many jobs and duties by her mom, but didn't get much love or support from her in return. Her dad was a healthy outlet for her, despite his absences; because he gave her the attention and love she craved and needed, when he was around.

As an adult she has now articulated those childhood yearnings and has cultivated those buried hopes into the positive, warm, and loving home environment she provides for her family and the open, encouraging and trusting relationship she is building with her daughter.

> "My hopes are to give my child the comfort she needs from me throughout her entire life. My fears are that she might isolate herself for some reason from me, and I wouldn't know nor would she want me to. My plans are to give my child the best life I can and a very memorable one. I want to make my daughter to feel as comfortable as she can with me, to be able to come to me about any matter in her life. I want to develop a strong communication bond with her so that everything in her life is alright. I want to be able to care and nurture her without crossing the line, and be able to support her every choice in life.
>
> Motherhood can be the best or worst way of life, depending completely on the mother and her standpoints. I stand firmly on the fact of making the child's life safe in every way possible, and cleaning up their environment at home. I love motherhood and it has made a better person in a lot of ways. I believe children come first in one's life, excluding making their mothers life better for their children. My role is to educate mothers in the benefits of breastfeeding their children, or anything to make a child's life as superior as possible."

Cynthia had always wanted children, but never had planned on it being at the age of twenty-four. Camilla was unplanned and Cynthia was frightful of what pregnancy would do to her body. She and her husband had only been married a few years and they were hoping to have more time together before starting a family. Their life was one of intense love, but also full of conflict. When they married she was, "ecstatic to be marrying this man," but overall her life was, "hard, fast and very unstable." Even after marrying she still made, "life a complete struggle and everything I experienced had always been for the negative." She recalls how they met ...

> "We met at the Café Brazil in Deep Ellum. I was a waitress and he was a cook. He had just finished the midnight shift and I was entering for the early a.m. shift. We were alone. I was the only waitress there, and I saw him at a table waiting for his ride. I smiled a friendly smile and said hello.
>
> He wasn't talkative at all, which was a little annoying. He worked some of my shifts, but all I knew was that I couldn't stand the sight of him. I felt like he thought he was better. I eventually saw him at a train station and I passed him saying hello, and all he did was give me a nod. I knew for sure he was a jerk. A year or so later, I was transferred to the University Park location. Just like before, I came in, in the morning, and he was finishing from the night before. I sat to eat breakfast and he came straight to where I was with a huge smile. I didn't want to waste my time with him anymore, but eventually I gave in.
>
> I quickly started to realize how charming he was. I was in love. A co-worker was sending us both text messages trying to get us to couple up. Eventually, I asked him out and took him out for a wonderful time. The next day I went back to my boyfriend's place and broke up with him. Two months later I married that cook."

It took Cynthia a long time after being married to know what love actually is, in regards to trust, respect, and work. She admits she did bring her depression into the marriage, and at the worst times they became abusive to one another, and took each other for granted. The best times have been both more frequent and consistent since having a child together and more reminiscent of their embroiled romantic relationship at the beginning of their marriage. They spend as much time as they possibly can together, going on intimate walks at the lake, the arboretum, or for midnight strolls through nearby cemeteries.

Their closeness was sealed by fate when they both gazed into the richly caramel-colored eyes of their daughter (whom also served to slow Cynthia down a bit and making her more mentally and emotionally consistent and dependable). They were shocked to find everyone extremely supportive of them when they announced the news of their pregnancy. She never expected it to be such a healthy environment for her to have a child in. The reality of it wasn't too hard of a transition for her since she was very experienced with caring for children from when she was younger. Any aspects she didn't know she learned from doctors and books.

Her plans are to raise her daughter to be kind and without being a pushover. She wants her daughter to pursue anything in life that she desires that will bring her happiness. She will assure her daughter no matter what she will always be behind her. Camilla is three-years-old now, and Cynthia plans on showing her how to respect people and the environment, when the opportunities come though future encounters and interactions.

She doesn't know a lot of moms like herself, and the few she knows she feels are too extreme with their children in ways they shouldn't be, to strict or constraining. She feels a lot of moms she knows do not give their children the chances they deserve; the children are over-punished. She is not influenced overtly by counterculture parenting or mainstream parenting, and rejects what she doesn't like or doesn't agree with, from both.

> "I may not look like, or be, the yuppie mom, but like the rest of us, we are human too. I am a great mother and give my child the best I can. I try to make her happy and give her all the love I can. I do not let any *'culture'* interfere with me being a mother. She comes first before anything, any interest, any activity, and anyone."

However, Cynthia doesn't approach the world blindly, nor is she is naive enough to *not notice* the stares her fully tattooed and pierced family gets from strangers:

> "Society still doesn't understand that people will always be different, everyone still seems to have to be alike in every way to be considered acceptable even though that will never happen. Society is still very close-minded.
>
> I am an expressionist and I support a different way of thinking, individualism. I do not like to fall into the same category as everybody. Everybody else has interests that don't pertain to me anyhow. I just want to be me. I don't even like

the label, subculture, but I understand everyone comes with a label whether they like it or not.

Mainstream can be so blah. I hate the close-mindedness. One is not better than the other, (mainstream or subcultures) it's just different. What is important are people. People having: love, compassion, respect and understanding for one another, but many don't get it or have it."

She feels society hasn't progressed in its relationship with children. Society doesn't understand the fragility of every child. She feels society takes children for granted and they aren't respected and valued as they should be which contributes to the reality of children as prey for child murderers, kidnappers, and molesters.

The only thing she can do is try to protect her child vigilantly against the world, while still teaching her child how to safely embrace and explore it. She is still learning about herself as well, and as an, "artistically creative mother and wife," who is still searching for her personal happiness while maintaining the family balance and pursuing a developing career in art and fashion.

"I am what and who I am, because I have made my own decisions! You are in control of your own life! Do good, and do your best in anything that you want in life. Never be afraid to make your dreams come true. Where there is a will, there is a way, and anything is definitely possible."

I fully agree sister.

The Rockers and Music Makers

The women in this chapter will make you want to grab a guitar, learn chords, all the while standing up for kids and kicking ass!

The mothers in this chapter have been there and done that. All the while raising kids with a lot of heart and a lot of spitfire!

One helped start rock 'n' roll and was performing before Elvis Presley! She was forced to give up her career when she became a wife and mother. Another found her salvation and healing in New Orleans, and through fronting a band she exorcised her demons. An EMI signed bassist works with kids who have been hurt and abused by the system, and their parents. She needs her fun, spunky bands to take the edge off—even if Tripper Gore didn't get it. One mom stays clean and sober with the help of 'spitting' out fire balls on stage, and picking up the guitar and bass, which enables her to focus on what matters most: her family. Did you ever think Buddha would find himself smack dab center in a rockers life? You betcha! All it takes is being a rule-defying band-booking agent with a heart of gold! One rocker mom turns parking lots into playgrounds and gardens, and has very big green plans for her and her vegetarian son, while making the world a better place one plant, and one upright bass note, at a time. What does playing drums and toddler story time have in common? Everything when you're this awesome librarian! Speaking of drummers, you will meet the one whose band defied the Bush clan, and she stood up against her rapist and sought justice. Another mom's cello brings us to life while she shares with us that she gave her daughter up for adoption to be best mother possible. And last, but not least, this former Navy, Oakland P.T.A. anarchist mom, whose band has been compared to AC/DC, asks …

Are you ready to rock? Welcome to the world of the Rockers and Music Makers.

"It was really hard being a female to do this kind of music; they thought it was vulgar for women to move on stage. It's the fans that matter. It doesn't matter what men or record labels think. To be accepted by your fans, to hell with everything else."

The Female Elvis
The Original Queen of Rockabilly & Hard Rockin' Momma
***"Most Promising Female Artist of 1956,"* by Billboard Magazine**
Winner of over 200 Music Awards and Contests
Toured and played with Johnny Cash & Carl Perkins
Jumpin' Mother, Grandmother, & Gorgeous Great-Grandmother
Danville, Virginia.

Janis Martin is a musical icon who is a key figure in the birth of rock 'n' roll in the 1950s. She signed with RCA in 1956, and was hailed as *The Female Elvis.* The King approved RCA's promotional spin and linking of the pair, with a delivery of roses to one of Janis's first shows following her record deal. Janis's musical career however, had started years before the explosion of rock. She has recently rekindled her love affair with music.

Fans all over the world have been eagerly waiting for a release by her for decades. Janis just finished her first recording since 1977. She is currently looking for a distributor and label for it, but it has to be the right one for her. She will take her time searching. She is very excited about the new album, and is going to tour again to give her fans a chance to see her play.

Her new album, which is untitled at the moment, will be dedicated to her son Kevin, who passed away at the age of forty-nine, on the 27th of January in 2007. This tragic event combined with seven years of Rosie Flores (another well known later generation rockabilly/country performer) encouraging Janis, and "practically begging" Janis to come back into the studio, finally compelled her to do it.

Janis has been performing again annually since 1996, after a long hiatus due to motherhood, marriage, and sexism in the music industry. Most of her concerts have been limited to rockabilly festivals in Europe, where that brand of music is still greatly appreciated. She has played a couple of festivals and shows in the United States at the beckoning of fans.

Janis's music career started at home, at the age of four. Janis came from a family with a love for music and she was immersed in it very early. Her dad and uncle both played guitar and played frequently after dinner each night. It was a family affair and everyone gathered around to watch and hear. She was hauling her own very large guitar to the nightly dinners, learning to play. She had to play it like an upright bass, because in comparison to her four-year-old frame, the guitar was bigger than she was! She was also dared by her uncle to play the mandolin at one of these dinner gatherings,

> "I played the hell out of it … I think it's born in you, not something someone can teach you, it's your sound, not musical charts, which is what I liked about the early Nashville sound."

Janis was only six-years-old when she had mastered basic guitar chords and started singing. By the time she was eleven, she had already won two hundred music and contest awards. Before the age of fifteen, she had played with infamous artists such as: Glen Thompson, Bonnie Brown, Jim Eanes, Ernest and Sunshine Sue, and had been a regular guest on the Old Dominion Barndance in Richmond, Virginia. (The Barndance was the third largest stage show in the United States at that time, and the most popular second only to the Grand Ole Opry.)

Her mother Jewel (now ninety-years-old) was her biggest supporter and her career manager. In fact, during our phone interview, Janis and her husband Wayne were getting ready to go spend the day with her:

"My mom was the original woman's libber. Once she found out I had talent, she became the typical show-business mom. She was the driving force behind me. She still made me get an education while working together on my music."

Janis's mother also had a performing background herself as a high school actress. She would have liked to have gone on to New York to be on stage and pursue acting professionally, but like most women of her generation she started a family right after school—but when she saw this same talent in Janis, she nurtured it. For years Janis credited her mother as the driving force behind her, but eventually she realized it was herself. Jewel just saw Janis's talent and encouraged it when Janis was too young to fully discipline and push herself.

The priorities are completely different from when she was raised and how she raised her son. She sighs deeply and is troubled when we discuss today's children …

"I would not want to be a young person in today's society, with everything happening in the world. It all contributes to juvenile delinquency and there's no hope for the children. The family unit doesn't have any influence over kids anymore—and today's parents aren't setting good examples … putting their careers before children, not being with your kids … [She pauses and thinks of her own mom.]

No matter what you do in life—mothers are the same. No matter what their profession, that child must come first. Mothers are the most special person to a child and in their life. I think motherhood is a lot different than when I was growing up. Even though they have hockey games, SUV's, their careers, for lack of a better phrase not so much 'under their husband's thumb', like we were … But at the same time in our generation we couldn't just get up and walk away. We had to try to make it work for the children and be there for the children.

Even though I was a rebel as far as women's lib goes, I still think the old way is the best way (one working parent, one parent working-at-home). With the problem of latch-key kids and such, they're missing that critical need of the family to be there—they're missing that family time together, the family dinners."

> ***She knew becoming a married woman and a mother, would hurt her career, and would raise some eyebrows … but she wasn't prepared for the outright lashing the music world gave her for doing so. Being a woman, nonetheless a strong, opinionated, pioneering woman of rock was no easy feat in the fifties.***

Janis sees the dilemma that both families and mothers have been placed in together. She herself tried to combine her musical career, parenting and marriage, and she was rebutted for breaking taboos and roles. She was outright punished by the music industry for it. The world (social institutions, workplace policies, and cultural customs) makes it too hard to have both, causing undue strife for women and children alike.

Janis was on top of the world before her first marriage and pregnancy. She knew becoming a married woman and a mother, would hurt her career, and would raise some eyebrows … but she wasn't prepared for the outright lashing the music world gave her for doing so. Being a woman, nonetheless a strong, opinionated, pioneering woman of rock was no easy feat in the fifties. It may be easier for women to get into the music business now, than then, but opinionated women still aren't well received by the larger audience. This was demonstrated in our generation with the public outrage that the Dixie Chicks and Madonna (amongst others) received when they spoke out against the United States Invasion of Iraq.

When Janis explains to me what happened in those early years she clarifies that women performers in her day were pushed into the background—even if their records were outselling their male counterparts. This dilemma was the same regardless if it was tours, live or TV performances, or interviews. Women always had to be the show openers. They were never allowed to be the headliners. She illustrates this by the way women were treated in general in our society, "You have to realize that women were subordinate to men in every way."

When RCA Victor signed Janis in 1956 they cast her as a rockin' rebel teenage girl, that any girl would love to be, and any guy would love to date. The catch was she really wasn't supposed to rebel, or do anything that would break the image of teenage innocence and virginity despite the rebel yell RCA was selling as her image. Unlike her RCA protégé Elvis, she was a female, and females were expected to adhere to different standards. After her record deal, and at age of fifteen, Janis secretly married her childhood sweetheart, singer Tommy Ford. Shortly after that, she was pregnant. This was devastating to her employers. They had cast her so well as the rock 'n' roll teenage queen, she wasn't supposed to grow up and become a woman—at least not yet.

When RCA learned of her secret marriage they called Janis in for a meeting. Once they had confirmation that her marriage and pregnancy was indeed true, they proposed that she end the marriage through annulment and terminate the pregnancy to save her career. They made it clear to her that they still expected her to finish her contract and hoped she would consider their suggestions. When it became evident to RCA that she wasn't going to do this, they did try to recast her as a married woman, but the two images were to extreme from each other and the 1950s world wasn't ready for that. They certainly weren't ready for a mother-rocker-wife. The two worlds couldn't coincide. RCA was bitter by Janis's rejection of their proposal, and their failure to be able to successfully recast her. They did what the good ol' men's club always did: they 'blacklisted' her. This sting would be felt for many years, and every time she tried to re-launch her music career during different periods of her life.

Janis's first husband Tommy (in addition to being a singer and performer) was a USO Para Trooper stationed in Aus Bay, Germany. This is where they had eloped when Janis was fifteen, before the majority of Janis's RCA recordings were done. In 1957, Janis was in Germany again on a USO tour. She stayed as long as she could, and spent weeks over there with her childhood sweetheart-husband. It was during this time their son Kevin was conceived. As much as Janis loved music, and it had been her entire life, she was ready to take time off the road to be a mother and wife. Granted she wasn't planning on being completely expelled from the music world as she was for her choices in love, marriage, and parenthood. She innocently thought it would be a short and temporary leave. She imagined, as most of us do, that we would combine the worlds we love, but with our family taking priority and a larger share of our time over creative/work endeavors,

> "I was secretly married, secretly pregnant. I didn't think about it any other way. I wanted the child. Being that I had matured much faster than people my same age, I was ready to settle down after all the years of performing. I had hoped to combine the two. The label tried to recast me as a pop star/married woman, but the dye was already cast. I insisted on having my child and knew the consequences of the teenage image."

The sexism didn't begin nor end with RCA though. Prior to her first marriage, when Janis was on tour with several performers, the headlining artist punished her for being more popular and loved by the crowd than he was. (Just to demonstrate the virtue of Janis's character, when she told me this, she didn't say who the artist was. She kept it a secret.) After several nights of the crowd shouting her name after she left the stage as the opening act, the headliner told her she had to find a different ride on the tour, that she could no longer ride with him. Janis called her dad and he took a week of vacation to help her finish the tour, which she did despite the bad behavior and resentment from the jealous and spiteful performer. Janis did find support however, from one male peer Jim Reeves. He stepped in to take her under his wing, and protect her while she was on tour with him and performing on his show. Janis cut her last record of that time, at the age of seventeen, while eight months pregnant. She finished her contract with RCA with a final tour when her son Kevin was six-weeks-old.

Janis's music career after that quietly receded into the background, as she focused on raising Kevin. She loved being a wife, a mother, and needed a break from what had been a full-time lifelong music career. Janis and her first husband divorced after four years of marriage. He remained an important part of Kevin's life. During this time Janis made a home in Danville, Virginia and made a 4 song LP recording for Palette, a Belgian Record Company. It didn't do well since the popularity of rockabilly was declining and rock 'n' roll was evolving into something altogether different and foreign. The popularity of the Beatles and the Rolling Stones, in the sixties showcase this. Shortly afterwards, Janis married her second husband (Janis prefers I don't name him for his privacy) who didn't like the idea of his wife being a rock 'n' roll star. He did everything he could to hinder her progress and creativity.

Although they were married thirteen years, and Janis had two bands during this time, the tensions surrounding music grew between them. Her second husband felt threatened and insecure anytime Janis would make any attempt to revive her music career. He would frequently give her ultimatums to choose between their marriage and her music. Ironically, he was a musician himself, and clearly felt threatened by Janis's prior success and talent.

At one point she did lay down music to satisfy her second husband. This was an attempt to keep her home and marriage life together (and peaceful) for Kevin's sake. She comes from a time period and generation where women didn't divorce their husbands and leave them. Divorced women risked complete exile from loved ones and friends, loss of financial support, and would likely be disgraced and disowned by their families. (Janis however, didn't have to worry personally about the latter.) And she had already been through one divorce, albeit friendly, and didn't want to put Kevin, or herself, through another.)

Janis lived with a blended philosophy concerning marriage that was moderate and progressive for her generation: Instead of just staying married because of social taboos, Janis believed you should try your best to make it work, over and over if needed, for the sake of the family. But ultimately, when it's no good, know when to walk away. This was a radical choice and an unacceptable one in her generation. She sees this as different though from today's marital choices and outcomes. She feels couples now give up to easily and throw in the towel without ever really trying and working hard, to save their marriages.

Eventually, Janis decided she would no longer sacrifice music due to her second husband's fear of her being a success. He was very controlling, dominating, and instead of supporting her, he had in-effect caused her to give up music for far too long. Janis realized after thirteen years of not playing music that she missed it:

> "My second husband wouldn't even let me keep a guitar in the house. He gave me the ultimatum again in 1973 when I picked up the guitar and started my band Janis Martin and the EP Express. It was him, or music. I told him I gave it up one time, and I won't give it up again."

The animosity between them grew as Janis continued to play music with her band, and she started making TV appearances again in the early seventies. They finally divorced. During this time Janis had her feelings hurt again by the music industry, which kept releasing rockabilly collections, but leaving her out of them. She had her attorney look into the matter, and she was told by RCA they were not releasing any of her stuff, because they were holding onto her material for a future rockabilly revival. However, this is not the impression she got from the music labels and artists in Nashville (in 1977) when she tried to get back into the music scene,

> "I was blackballed by Nashville. I didn't have much use for the place anyway. Nashville is like a little clan in itself. I was told by Nashville that if I tried to come back I wouldn't be able to."

Janis is not one to take no for an answer and she started another band, Janis and The Variations, with her son Kevin (who played drums). Her close friend Chet Atkins also encouraged her to keep trying because rockabilly was making a comeback, especially in Europe. Janis started playing locally at small shows and receptions. True to Chet's word, in 1979 Bear Family Records of Germany reissued all of her RCA tracks introducing Janis to a new generation of fans. This was a great year for Janis as she was able to finally merge music, motherhood, and love with her son, new band, and new third husband Wayne. This is what she had wanted and strived for all along.

Janis's band with her son Kevin lasted until 1981. He continued to perform, and play music with his mom over the years nonetheless. Kevin loved his mother's music, and loved Elvis's music too. In fact, Janis adds that, "He was nuts over Elvis." As a teenager Kevin even dreamed that Elvis was his real dad, and his friends encouraged his parental conspiracy theory. [Oddly, I went through the same fascination as kid. But I knew Elvis wasn't my father, although I yearned for him to be. He seemed so caring and passionate, which was the opposite of my aloof, abusive, and mostly absent dad.] Janis reminiscences and laughs while telling me this story,

> "I took Kevin to see Elvis shortly before he (Elvis) passed away. Kevin used to wish Elvis was his dad. He would say, 'I look like him, I walk like him, my mom is 'The Female Elvis' … I had to tell him, no way, no way. I don't think so. You can look at your real dad and know exactly where you come from."

Ironically, Janis initially rejected RCA's proposal to link her music with Elvis's. Not that she didn't like him, (Janis had actually been performing rhythm and blues influenced music a couple of years before Sun Records signed Elvis's first song.) she loved Elvis Presley, but she wanted to stand out on her own talent alone. In the end though, RCA's marketing strategy won out and she succumbed to their wish. She did stop using the title for a long time after Elvis died, even though it is part of her musical history and legacy.

Janis's nostalgia however fades from laughter to sorrow after recalling this memory. She had many miscarried pregnancies. (She always wanted a large family.) She never contemplated her only child dying before she did. Her son Kevin just passed away earlier this year from a sudden brain aneurism. He had symptoms for almost a month before the tragedy occurred. Brain aneurisms can hit anyone at anytime, but most frequently occur to individuals between the ages of thirty, and sixty. Kevin's was induced by untreated high blood pressure. Sudden symptoms include: blurred vision, and vertigo. Brain aneurisms are disorders that occur when a weakness occurs in the cerebral artery or vein, which causes a ballooning of the blood vessel. In Kevin's case, it was a single aneurism that exploded his optic nerve. Kevin's aneurism was deep within the brain.

If there is one thing Janis could share with the world, it is this: If you have any of these symptoms, sudden vertigo and blurred vision, request an immediate cat scan to verify if a weakened blood vessel is the cause. In most cases a single aneurism caught within at least twenty-four hours before bursting, can be successfully operated on. Although, Kevin didn't get medical attention for his symptoms, Janis is certain that medical care and a brain scan can be life saving, especially if it is a shallow aneurism. (Kevin's wasn't. I verified this information with Kevin's daughter Lindsey who is a nurse.)

Janis was devastated when Kevin died, and felt like her life had ended. Kevin was her son, her drummer for eleven years, a father, a husband, and his life was cut short. He was a, "Happy go-lucky type. He lived wide open, lived life to the fullest." Janis's friends tried to comfort her, but no one had lost a child before, and couldn't relate. Janis had to stay strong for her family including her granddaughter Lindsey, and great-granddaughter Kaylee. There was hardly a dull moment in Kevin's childhood with the Female Elvis as his mom. Janis has a lucid parenting style that has flowed over to her role as grandmother as well:

> "If you're a rock 'n' roll mom … you're maybe more interesting than a church-going-bible-spewing mom. My son used to tell me, that his friends would say, 'No one has a mother like him,' and he was real proud of it."

Janis was frequently dragged out in her pajamas in the middle of the night to hang out with Kevin, and his friends, as well as Lindsey's as she got older. Kevin felt, that a party was not a party at all, if mom wasn't there. Janis's parenting philosophy is pretty straight forward just like her life philosophy, "If you say you're going to do something, do it." Janis showered Kevin with love, but also if she said she was going to punish him, she did it. A central and critical component to their mother-child relationship was honesty. Janis never lied to Kevin. This factor of honesty and respect is also what enabled them to have such a close and loving friendship as adults. She was always positive with him, but always honest. Janis confesses she was never the SUV-driving type-of-mom we see today, nor was she ever the June Cleaver mom of her generation, "My own granddaughter would tell you I don't sit at home and bake cookies." Janis never felt awkward merging motherhood and work with rock 'n' roll, but sometimes it did produce some gauche moments at work:

> "The only time I felt weird was, I had a career managing a Golf and Country Club for twenty-seven years, and they never knew anything about me! I would just take my vacations to go play shows [Janis frequently played in Canada, Spain, Denmark, France, U.K., and Holland.]. Sometimes I felt kind of funny, when someone would find out I was going to do rock shows, and they saw me as a business woman."

Janis is a very private person, as we see with her separation of professional and artistic careers. However, she quickly opens up and warmly shares her heart and mind with anyone she is talking to on a personal level. For the last three decades, Janis has successfully managed balancing motherhood, grand, and great-grand-motherhood, with a full-time management career, marriage, all while performing concerts locally and abroad.

In her third husband, Wayne, she finally found her life-partner, "the right one." They have been married for twenty-nine years now and he is very supportive of her. He frequently travels with her on road shows and concerts. She loves him and his support, and he is very respectful of her as an artist too. He comes to all of her shows, but doesn't interfere, nor does he try to control what she does, as an artist, or as a woman. Most importantly, he accepts her and loves her for who she is: guitar-player-singer and all. Wayne loves her even though she is opinionated, goal-oriented, and stands her own ground. She is Janis. He can relate—he's witty, strong-minded and a former café owner and chef himself! During the interview, Janis told me that although she is an Aries, "I am very easy going," which Wayne humorously retorted in the background, "shit." They both started laughing together, and their understanding and love for each other was obvious. Janis added that,

> "I'm wide open. I'm not very domesticated. I don't like housework. I'm not your typical housewife. If I feel like writing a song I will stop whatever I am doing, and go to the basement to play, and emerge four hours later."

Janis feels that no one, spouses included, have the right to tell someone what they can, or can't do, or how they should live their life. She also feels that,

> "I think all of us have a god-given talent. It's a sin to suppress your natural talent. You end up miserable and make everyone else around you miserable. Do what is your god given talent, as long as it doesn't hurt anyone else."

Janis explained to me how she felt when she picked up the guitar again in 1973, "Like I was at home, and the old bug got in me, and I haven't laid it down since." Janis talks about her first large concert since the 1950s on her forty-second birthday. There's pure excitement in her voice as she recalls this event:

> "Chet told me it (rockabilly revival and craze) was happening over there in Europe and I agreed in 1982 to go over there and play. I was in a band and had been playing gigs like wedding receptions, not concerts; I was scared out of my mind! When I stepped on stage it was like I was where I was supposed to be. I haven't

stopped since. I played more shows each summer overseas, including an Americana mix of rockabilly and a show with June Carter's daughter Colleen Carter.

I'm sixty-seven-years-old and still going strong. Old male rockers have already passed. They lived hard, and passed. I came along, and I was the first (female) to do this, and the fans realize we suffered the abuse (sexism and rock 'n' roll criticism) to get the music out there."

For Janis, it has always been about the fans, and she doesn't regret her life or her choices at all. She received affirmation that she did the right thing by picking up music again (despite the music industry backlash, and the earlier marital discord it caused) when a fan came up, a twenty-year old girl after a show who hugged and squeezed Janis. The fan cried, telling Janis how happy she was, because she had finally found the music she had been looking for all of her life. Fans like her compels Janis to keep going, and also served as the inspiration for a historical documentary made by Beth Harrington (released in 2002), that featured Janis in it, titled: *The Women of Rockabilly: Welcome to the Club*. Janis was shocked when she learned during the filming, that all of her early performance archives had been destroyed by the music industry.

"When they were making the film *Welcome to the Club*, they couldn't find any of the archives from all the films and shows I had done—but when you buck the system—there's a price to pay. But I came back at the right time and I'm having a great ride."

The PBS documentary does showcase a recent performance of Janis's at Viva Las Vegas (an annual rockabilly festival) and an extensive interview with her. The movie also includes peers from the same genre and time period like: Wanda Jackson, Charlene Arthur, Rose Maddox, and Barbara Pittman. You can learn more about the documentary at: Pbs.org/itvs/WelcometotheClub/.

One of Janis's career highlights was sharing a stage with her musical idol Ruth Brown a.k.a., Miss. Rhythm, who was an early rockin' rhythm and jump-blues singer from the 1940s and 50s. Janis started listening to her in 1953 around the age of twelve and fell in love. Janis played and performed Ruth Brown covers all the time, and she cites Ruth Brown for having the largest influence on her musically:

"I did a show with her three years ago. I finally got to meet my idol. Tom Ingram from Viva Las Vegas filmed it. We did her song, *'Momma, He Treats Your Daughter Mean.'* I cried at the end of it. When she passed away I got phone calls from all over—including from friends in France. Everyone knew how much I loved her and idolized her."

Even though Janis just completed a new album recording with talented modern rockabilly musicians in Austin, Texas—she was literally just finishing the recording in Austin when I spoke to her—she's not very fond of modern music at all. She doesn't listen to the radio, and loathes what is called "new country" music. Janis doesn't like anything expect rockabilly and old school rhythm and blues. She feels in general most current artists that are popular just simply lack real talent. And that they are selling attractive vices in lieu of talent, to the kids:

"When we were first there in rock 'n' roll, we were cursed by the church and media and we were told we were Satan's music. We were just kids having fun, but today is different. Kids are the same, but the music world is selling sex instead of talent. I almost got canned several times back then for saying some of the things I said, but frequently now everything is out in the open, back then it wasn't. Kids see their idols doing drugs, and having kids out of wedlock. Today's music is more 'satan' influenced than ours by far."

Check out Janis Martin's awesome music at: Myspace. com/FemaleElvis. And don't forget Beth Harrington's historical documentary: *The Women of Rockabilly: Welcome to the Club.*

Janis feels when people have real raw talent they don't have to rely on selling explicit sexuality, or over the top lifestyle's (doing drugs blatantly and sleeping around) to get attention or to make money. Their talent should be good enough to sell itself.

Janis is perplexed by the virtual reversal of virtues that occurred in the last few generations, and doesn't understand how this degeneration has happened. She doesn't feel women gaining more of an equal status or rock 'n' roll, at least in its early form, are to blame, but she does feel parents shifting priorities where children are on the bottom of the priority list, and not the top of, does account for most of it. She also feels that the self-destruction and the general nihilism that is reflected in the behaviors of young music stars today accounts for some. She cites their extravagant behaviors that reflect a lack of concern (or responsibility) for their fame and who they influence. Our children (and teenagers/young adults) are of course most susceptible to the worst of these popular behaviors and imagery that is cast by stardom.

She is relieved that there are modern performers who are noteworthy and deserving of their acclaim and she cites Rosie Flores, Marti Brom and Candye Kane. All of which, she has had the pleasure of working with and personally mentoring two of the three.

She acknowledges that today's rockabilly is different from her brand of original rockabilly (for it too has been sexed up, although still more constrained compared to other styles of modern rock or rap), but also that other music genres have been confused with it. She clarifies this point with the use of the steel guitar, which traditionally was used in western swing, not rockabilly. Yet the two are interchangeably labeled rockabilly now. Formally speaking, it's incorrect … "Don't get me wrong, I like western swing, but it's not rockabilly. Rockabilly is lead guitar, rhythm guitar, drums, and an upright bass."

Her upcoming album is pure rockabilly and it's recorded live at a ranch in Blanco, Texas. There are no individual sittings, and few retakes. She also credits Rosie Flores, whom she did a duet with in 1996, for not only dragging her back into the studio, but for also coproducing it.

Rosie shared with Janis that all the musicians she was playing with were not only fans of hers, but also hoped to have her energy, love of fun, and good disposition at sixty-seven too. When Janis cut her new record she got, "nine rockers, and one ballad, and I didn't even really want to do the ballad, but Wayne and Rosie talked me into it." The band and Janis focused on songs from her generation, that hadn't yet been covered by a woman. Janis is very excited about the records upcoming release, and plans on hitting the road, and touring once it is distributed. To check out music samples, album release information, and tour dates go to: Myspace.com/FemaleElvis. I don't know where Janis will turn up next to rock, but I will be watching, waiting to see her … since she is one of my hero's. Janis closes our intimate and fun interview with sentiments about the amazing life she has lived thus far,

"I have been so blessed, that the interest is still out there after all these years. If I get to the place where I can't go out there and give it everything I got, then I will stop. I'm not planning on doing it, once that happens, until then I will keep going."

"I'm just me, good or bad. I'm an Aries. Ray Hall said, 'Willie Nelson was not the first outlaw, you were'."

In memory of Janis Martin

March 27th 1940

—

September 3rd 2007.

Janis Martin passed away from sudden terminal cancer a few months after this interview. The world is saddened over the loss of our beloved musical icon.

"Life is all these amazing chapters, know when to walk away."

Corey Parks
Clothing Designer for Vision Skate Wear line: Deconstruct
Fire-Eating Bassist for
Nashville Pussy
Die Hunns
Charley Horse
Tattooed Rocker Momma
Los Angeles, California.

Corey Parks is probably best known to everyone as the rocking bassist and one of the founding members of the band Nashville Pussy. Although she is no longer a member of the band, it was her introduction to the world as the fire-dancing and fire-breathing bassist (who also made out with the guitarist on stage) who really got the pit moving and got everyone in it, including guys *and girls* (myself included, when I saw them perform at Trees over a decade ago). Corey called me from the road where she is on tour with the Die Hunns, and is having a blast being pregnant and playing shows. She is definitely getting the star treatment as a mom-in-the-making.

Corey has been playing bass and has been in bands for over thirteen years now. She is a self-taught musician. She can't read notes, but can play anything by ear and develop it. The bands that have had the strongest influence on her playing style are: ACDC, the Ramones, and ZZ Top. Picking up a bass was an easy choice for Corey. She could play any note by ear, had long arms and fingers, and was inspired by the big boom of female bass players—which were showing up everywhere, on every coast, and in every scene. There were women rocking out all around her. It was a great thing to be around and she wanted to be part of it, and as a participant—not just a spectator.

There is a lot on her mind nowadays besides just basses, bands and music—motherhood. Corey is thirty-four and expecting her first child with lover and fellow band member Dwayne Peters.

She is going to be a mom—a Rebel Mom—who says no to the government and bullshit standards. She has always been defiantly anti-government, although intrinsically patriotic (for example, understanding and supporting Vietnam veterans, but critical of the government who sent/drafted/forced them to go there). She has been questioning the control of motherhood by the government and its negative impact on motherhood (and children) from welfare 'reform' that cuts essential needs, and the lack of social policy that supports women and children, including financial and adequate job protection, for women becoming parents. *[The U.S. social policy is primitive compared to other first world countries that provide subsidized maternal leave for as long as six years recognizing both the demanding need primary-aged children have for their parents, as well as the community's need for well-cared for and loved children that grow into caring, productive, and social adults. For example, according to Washington D.C.'s Center for Economic and Policy Research (C.E.P.R) report The Parental Leave Policies in 21 Countries: Assessing Generosity and Gender Equality, the U.S. ranks 20th for leave for new parents in comparison to other first world wealthy nations—which means we've worked pretty hard at ostracizing and punishing our moms and kids at best, neglecting them altogether and taking away their access to essential needs at worst, during these critical early childhood years. If you're lucky enough to be Spanish or French the subsidized leave is as long as six years, or three years for paid leave for both parents, Germany and Greece average three years, Japan, the U.K., and Australia average one year, and almost everywhere else averages a year or more paid leave, except the U.S. and Sweden (Sweden has 14 weeks paid leave compared to our legal maximum of 12 weeks of FMLA unpaid.) Most of these countries excluding the U.S. and Sweden, also count parents (primarily women) working as stay-at-home parents as part of their gross domestic product/GDP. Elder care is also counted in the GDP.]*

She also worries about the intrusion of the government on family life, in addition to its control of essential resources. [The government is very intrusive and if you happen to be lower class, and in need of social services, such as food assistance or need help getting child support from a delinquent parent (normally men); it's at the risk of being scrutinized, and your children possibly being taken. This happens mostly to poor women in the U.S. who are judged for both being lower class and dealing with the lack of resources (and additional obstacles) that that entails. Or if they piss off their social worker(s) for defending themselves (and their children) against above prejudices, or if they have an unapologetic anti-authoritarianism value system and a different way of raising their kids, like Corey will, they can be subject to ridicule and risk government abuse, and that is one of her primary concerns.] She wants "The government to stay the fuck away from her and her family to be." She sees that there is nothing but harm that they can do, from policies to stereotypes, to intrusion.

She is self-described as a true patriot, and she defines that as the opposite of nationalism—which is where people follow blindly, or fearfully, the leaders of government under the guise of 'for country'. She is "anti-establishment, pro-bill of rights, and pro-constitution." She views the (now former) Bush Jr. Administration attempts to change the constitution by outlawing gay marriage as just a step to make all other laws that protect liberty and freedom null and void. As an extreme, but plausible scenario, if she didn't have fame and fortune to protect her (somewhat) publicly, could Bush, or any other president, pass a federal law that would allow states to seize children of women that play aggressive rock 'n' roll (or rap, etc.), or are vocal activists, and/or that have tattoo's because they (the law/government) views them as a threat, a threat to consumer 'lifestyle', and to government/corporate policy? Could her anti-government beliefs alone be enough to sanction such action? It sounds wild—but when you consider the Patriot Act, secret surveillance of citizens, and everything else that the recently previous Bush Jr. Administration had done, and other administrations in the past, and what current governments and corporations are doing now, it's not far-fetched.

She's no fan of the Patriot Act, which side steps the Bill of Rights and our constitutional protections for the sake of 'national safety'. She is shocked that homeschooling is defined as a terrorist act under the bill—it's fitting though since institutionalized schooling typically includes indoctrination. The fact you have to annually sign a rejection wavier that forbids your child's school from allowing military personnel to meet with them (for promoting their later enlistment), demonstrates this. I have had to sign one each year Corben is in public school thus far. Her concern is grave as she expresses this, and her voice becomes hardly audible as she whispers into the phone; this is among many other things labeled as 'terrorism', including the right to protest and dissent, or participating in acts that question the actions and policies of our government and business leaders. The bill actually lists many well known and well received U.S. lobbying organizations as terrorist groups under the act including: the Green Party, Planned Parenthood, and the National Organization for Women.

The scary thing about the Patriot Act is that you (U.S citizens with constitutional protections, as well as people without) could be 'taken' (and held in detention with no legal recourse) under the bill and no one will ever know, because under the act you have no constitutional rights at all. She wirily concludes, "We are being policed." [In 2009, Obama had been elected president and ordered the closing of Guantanamo Prison in Cuba, and well, it's still open for business.]

Corey believes we are being pushed into a One World Order whether we want to be or not. This is to abolish local and state governments that are more aligned with the local citizens. *[Clinton started the dramatic financial segway with the NAFTA bill and the forming of the World Trade Organization. If there is no limitation to power, and without proper checks and balances, we will be abused. History, modern and historical, captures this reality of exploitations and atrocities that occur to the majority, who aren't the upper or ruling class, by the minority, the few that 'own' and control everything (From Kings to CEOs). The Seattle Riots in 1999 against the WTO is a demonstration of this. The mislabeled 'water wars' between civilians of a community and bastard corporations substantiates these concerns. The only ones who will benefit from this are the private interests of the few, at the expense of the many. If you control food and water, essentially you will have slaves.]* Corey feels the so-called Iraq War and the oil companies are a grotesque example of this abuse of power, and removal of authority from local citizens. It is commercial and corporate warfare and welfare at its worst, which is why these civil liberties groups are blacklisted on the bill; they challenge corporate dominance at the expense of personal and local community liberty.

There is one source she cites as very credible to expose media lies and government/corporate spins which is Info Wars (.com). It's made by a journalist named Alex Jones, who is trying to, "wake people up." He is a well known documentary filmmaker and a talk show host on a nationally syndicated show simply called, *The Alex Jones Show*, which airs via the Genesis Communication Network on over 60 radio stations across the country.

Corey is currently five months pregnant and the government control factor of our lives has made her determined to, "find a way to beat the system," when it comes to the birth of her child and how she raises her child. Her voice is strong and determined when she states this, and matches her powerful female warrior build and strong personality. Corey Parks is a Rock 'N' Roll Wonder Woman in every sense of the term. The show she played tonight has left her exhausted, but ready for more, before the baby gets here. Her determination to protect her forming family from the government, and it's spying and denying tendencies, is both urgent and evident in her tone and speech as we talk over the phone in a loud club. She frequently pauses during the interview to grab some cold water, and push back her walnut and chocolate hued hair that sticks sweaty to her face. Corey believes that eventually the government will track everyone through microchips, and vaccinations are the key to getting microchips into everyone through syringes. There is varied debate on the subject, and the intention of human micro-chipping is very real. Tommy Thompson, former Secretary of Health and Human Services with the Bush Administration, publicly endorses the government micro-chipping the population. He sits on the Board of Directors of the U.S. Company called VeriChip—whose purpose is to do just that. He has used his Bush Administration connections to publicly endorse the company.

VeriChip was publicly rebuffed for attempting to *give* free microchips to patients at the Orange Grove Center in Tennessee, with only the administrations consent and knowledge—not the patients. The IBM Corporation is a big investor in VeriChip, and they have a human chipping test facility located in Austin, Texas. According to AntiChips.com (which has some amazing news and provocative essays) even (then) Senator (and now U.S. Vice President) Joseph Biden commented to John Roberts during his 2005 Supreme Court confirmation hearings that, *"Can a microscopic tag be implanted in a person's body to track his every movement? There's actual discussion about that. You will rule on that, mark my words, before your tenure is over."*

Corey feels that, just like the Patriot Act, vaccinations and thus micro-chipping would do more harm than good. For example, finding kidnap victims through chipping would be salvation for parents and children who are victims of a predatory crime, however, Corey is concerned that the intent of chipping humans will not be for our safety, but for spying and controlling us through tracking (Similar to how corporations track our 'psychological' spending and buying patterns through our debit card use, etc.) and it would be a gateway to other physical manipulations. Her conclusion is that the potential civil liberty abuse would exceed any potential good, as it did under the Patriot Act, and would give our government the ultimate ability to terrorize its citizens through physical tracking.

She is not going to have her child vaccinated, and this is her right as a parent, even if she has to fight the state for their rights to be respected, as more and more middle and lower class parents are finding that they have to. [Medical evidence trumps the argument that the group (community) has rights which supersede the individuals.] She also has studied the medical side of the debate, and that also has influenced her decision. It's no secret that autism and vaccinations are closely linked—hence all the recent heated discussion. She also noted that in Japan they changed their medical practices, and as a result SIDS (Sudden Infant Death Syndrome) has decreased over eight percent. Instead of starting vaccinations at birth forward, Japan now starts giving vaccinations at the age of three, and not all at once. A big theory on healing-arts.org/children/vaccines/vaccines-auto-immunity.htm is that in the U.S. we give a large amount of vaccines which introduce multi-viruses into babies and toddlers, and autism (and other related conditions) results from an auto-immunity backfire triggered by the multi-viral attack on premature immune systems. Her mid-wife has two kids who eat healthy and are treated by their mom with herbs and vitamins. She states that her midwife's children have never gotten sick, no chicken pox, no flu, and they don't have vaccinations, which supports Corey's thesis.

Corey isn't just sickened by the vaccination indoctrination, but is also outraged by the way women and mothers are treated in the United States by the Medical Profession:

"Cesareans are so high here, robbing women of their right to give birth. My mid-wife has had over seventeen years of experience and she has delivered all kinds of positioned babies including breached ones. She has never had a mother who had to get a caesarian. In fact, delivering in the hospital is just a factory delivery. Only in America and Canada are mid-wives not involved in delivery of the babies. But in Germany it is law; the mid-wife must be present and 80%-90% of births are at home. In fact, only high risk pregnancies are at the hospital.

What's really scary is in California, social services is connected to the hospital to such a degree that if you have had a baby (and the baby is fine), you can't check yourself out of the hospital without them seeing you first. If you refuse to take anything they [the hospital] gives you—including medication or formula—they will call Social Services up immediately. They don't let you trust your own bodies and instincts."

She recalls a story of a heavily tattooed couple she knows who had a hospital birth. They were great people and just because they looked out of the norm, "They were treated like the enemy. They were being judged while trying to deliver the baby." She doesn't like the medical establishment anyway. She adds, "The American Medical Association is hand-in-hand with the fucking government, no money in cure but money in meds." The medical, pharmaceutical, and insurance scams are literally killing and bankrupting us she feels. (Michael Moore's exposé film, *Sicko*, came out after this interview, but adds statistical large-scale findings to her conclusions.)

Corey is going to avoid stereotypes and abuse/exploitation by skipping the medical industry and hospital altogether. She is going to have a home water-birth with her highly experienced mid-wife. Safety, calmness, and comfort are the focus of the upcoming birth of her child. She is going to have a surreal and spiritual encounter with her child for their first face-to-face meeting. It will not be perverted by the judgments of hospital staff, the chaos of a hospital delivery, the financial exploitations of a capitalist medical business, or the electronics of a hospital room. She notes that women have been doing this for millennia and mid-wifery and dulas are:

> "A matriarchal approach and it's about giving life to the whole experience, not just a fucking medical procedure. When the medical industry came around they started telling us how to do things and they started fucking things up."

She is also aware that,

> "It takes a pretty selfless human to be a mom, and it's a thankless job. No one is every ready financially or otherwise. I have been having crazy dreams that I am not prepared for this, and I go to breastfeed my baby and no milk comes out. I am preparing for the birth, but I'm not prepared for her after. I am very attached, and I think it's going to be a girl."

She has no idea what to expect and won't know until she gets there. What she is sure of though, is that she can give this baby unconditional love and affection, and just learn the rest as she goes. She cites her mom Deborah Parks as her role model and mentor:

> "My mom raised me single-handedly. One thing that was very important is that she never tainted my ideal of my father, and she loved us unconditionally. She laid a lot of tools at our feet and let us decide. She exposed us to Eastern Philosophy and meditation in Sunday school. We had a beautiful concept of God and spirituality. My mom was very open-minded.
>
> My dad didn't pay any child support and my mom worked two jobs both as a construction worker and as a cocktail waitress. But we never felt like we went without. Mom never judged us. She never judged me even during my nine years of addiction. She just did what she could do to help and make you feel better. She believed in you. My mom supported me when I was a twenty-two-year-old drop-out drug addict. She was a working woman living paycheck-to-paycheck. She is my role model."

It was at this point that Corey picked up the bass and kicked drugs for the first time [addictions typically go through variations of relapse and 'start-over-relapse' is part of recovery—even if there are years in-between]. She learned bass with the help of an ex-boyfriend and got into a touring band, before she helped form the band Nashville Pussy.

She was in Nashville Pussy for the majority of her musical career and did not have a "girl persona." She did not encounter some of the sexism that other female musicians get from men in the same scene, from the music industry, or from people at shows. She attests this to the fact that, "I definitely don't give the impression of a chick in a dress on stage … I played like a guy and mostly guys, musically, have been my influence."

She does acknowledge that she has a very dirty rock 'n' roll persona that is sexually charged on stage. A lot of 'smoking mirrors' is her key to success and confidence. She played six nights a week all over the country for years. She describes it as, "Times have really changed for rock 'n' rollers. I could spend ten months on the road and make a lot of money. And it was a very exciting time to be part of the band."

She eventually had to leave Nashville Pussy for her own health and sanity. She was really strung out again and before she walked away, she was a "therapeutic junkie." There was bad blood about her leaving but she knew she had to. She joined Alcoholics Anonymous and sobered up. She had actually started the process before quitting Nashville Pussy. She had a low self-esteem when she started the process, but is happy now (not only with herself, but also with the direction her life has taken since).

She found herself sober and healing. She needed a job and that's when the band the Die Hunns came into play. They needed a bassist. She met Duane Peters from U.S. Bombs (and the Die Hunns) and it was love at first sight. She adds:

> "I had wanted to be a mom for a while and I found a man I want to build a life with. Not a logical step, but a wonderful gift (the pregnancy and love) that landed in our lap."

"Mom never judged us. She never judged me even during my nine years of addiction. She just did what she could do to help and make you feel better. She believed in you. My mom supported me when I was a twenty-two-year-old drop-out drug addict. She was a working woman living paycheck-to-paycheck. She is my role model."

Her first record with the Die Hunns was *Long Legs*, and she thinks it's the best that she has done musically. She has also shared the stage with Lemmy from Motorhead, the Horror Pops, and Dave Navarro (of Jane's Addiction). Following this she developed a fashion and skate line for Vision Skateboards and Skatewear called Deconstruct, and has since started her own independent line of punk and metal fashion wear.

She runs her clothing studio from a garage at her house. Famous stars have even gotten in on the southern punk rock gear she makes including: U2's Bono, Lenny Kravitz, Lisa Marie Presley, and Britney Spears.

The band and the couple have bought a house in Austin, Texas, which was the best the place for them to be. The first three months of her pregnancy they had been on the road. She found out she was pregnant in Berlin, Germany. They just had a record come out and still had three months of shows booked.

As she tells me stories of their European tour, Dwayne urges her to wrap the interview up because everyone is on the tour bus and ready to go. He teases her because she is still on the bar phone talking to me. She excitedly reminds him about the interview and we say our good-byes, but not before I ask her one more final question: What are her plans for after the baby is born? "More tours across Europe, and with my mom on board as nanny."

Rock On.

**Since this interview: Corey actually had a boy and they named him Clash. I couldn't resist making a photo of them the interview photo, although it was afterwards that she gave birth. Recently, she's been playing upright bass in the band Charley Horse and playing in a very cool cover band called Chelsea Girls. Duane and Corey wed, and the family moved from Austin to LA.*

**"Stay-at-Home Bomb takes the whole mom thing and housewife stuff and puts it into music. Our songs are about clotheslines, baking cookies, and we play solos with blenders on.
The band is an ideal aggression towards the stereotype."**

Sharon Needles
Educator of Asperger Teens
Caregiver for infants with A.I.D.S.
Mentor/Counselor for Runaway Teens
Awesome Actress
Guitarist/Bassist for:
Butt Trumpet/Betty Blowtorch
Stay-at-Home Bomb
Legal Weapon
Two Drink Minimum
God Riot 73 and many more ...
Hollywood, California.

Sharon Needles is a rocker, mother, and wife all rolled up into one. She spends her days raising a two-year-old, working with children and teens, playing in a band and hanging out with her friends and her husband.

She has been in over twenty-five bands, of which some have been quite notorious. As a child she mastered air guitar and was always pretending to play. She later picked up various instruments in school, and joined choir. She finally found her destiny when she started playing bass at the age of seventeen as a senior in high school.

Her first band Flesh Weapon was formed a year later and was influenced by the Ramones and the New York Dolls. Her guitar player taught her how to cheat on the bass by using half scales and going forwards and backwards on the strings. Her first band lasted about three years, and she went through some more until she found a home with Butt Trumpet in 1993.

Butt Trumpet was the first punk band to be signed by EMI Records since the infamous Sex Pistols. The band lasted until 1997, and is known by their silly, and offensive, lyrics and antics. The titles of their songs include: *Clusterfuck, Dicktatorship, Funeral Crashing Tonight, Pink Gun, I'm Ugly and Don't Know Why,* and *Primitive Enema.* Lyrically speaking, some could group them in the same category as G.G. Allen, but with a significant difference: they were taking stabs in a fun way at sexism and society without even meaning to, and without throwing feces at their audiences.

The demise of the original Butt Trumpet line-up occurred after the EMI record deal. Thom the singer quit the band, and fellow band member Bianca stepped up and took over vocals. EMI was trying to change the band after just one record on their label, and none of them could take their "stranglehold." They finished one last tour with the Meatmen, came home and called it quits. This was around 1995. During this time they came under the scrutiny of Tripper Gore's censorship efforts, because of one of the songs Sharon wrote called, *Ugly*, which is a song where a young female tries to initiate her first sexual encounter, and she's rebuffed for being ugly. The song cries that it all started in third grade, and she makes up for being 'ugly' by getting back at those that put her down, essentially.

After Butt Trumpet disintegrated, Sharon moved on to play with Legal Weapon. The band was a generation ahead of her former one, but she had gotten to know them previously on different tours and playing gigs together. Occasionally, she would fill in for them which led to her joining the band later. Legal Weapon was a southern California band originally formed in the 1980s. Sharon was excited to be playing with a band that she loved when she was a teenager. The band did a European tour.

"Playing in East Germany with them was interesting. There was no wall (the Berlin Wall) left anymore, but the whole vibe of the wall was still there in the cold cities. Broken down cars and abandoned police cars lined the streets. The clubs had to put up barricades to keep the Nazi skinheads out. I was really worried because I was dark skinned, and our bass player was black. Everybody in the club was Anti-Nazi but the threat of them busting through the barricades were real. The shows were some of the best I had ever been a part of though, because everybody was really into politics over there. It was nice to have conversations there with everyone.

Spain was also a very political place; I had a lot of good conversations about politics while drinking beer with everyone. Pat (Legal Weapon member, now part of the band Gun Club) was there for this too."

Their debut album Get Off was produced by Gun-N-Roses bassist Duff McKagan. The singer Bianca was molested as a child by her stepfather and this was her fuck-you ode to him. Betty Blowtorch gained a huge following all across the country even though they received little airplay by any mainstream radio stations. They were known for opening their shows with, "We're Betty Blowtorch and we're from Hollywood and we don't give a fuck!"

In 1998, when she got back home from the Legal Weapon tour, she and three former members of Butt Trumpet decided to forge a new band called Betty Blowtorch, which was more metal. The wild stage antics and sexually aggressive personas were turned up some too.

> "We were a spirited and sarcastic band pushing 1980s 'Sex, Drugs, and Rock 'n' Roll'. The funny thing was none of us did drugs, some used to a long time ago, but here we were pushing the stereotype and doing the whole 80s thing and faking it. The whole sex thing was an act too, we were four prudes, but it was a fun persona."

Check out Rebel Mom Sharon's awesome bands like Butt Trumpet, Betty Blowtorch & Stay-at-Home-Bomb!

Order the Betty Blowtorch movie at: CinemaLibreStudio. com.

Check out Stay-at-Home-Bomb at: WarningLabel Records.com. And hear an mp3 at: AliceBag.com/ media.html.

Their debut album *Get Off* was produced by Gun-N-Roses bassist Duff McKagan. The singer Bianca was molested as a child by her stepfather and this was her fuck-you ode to him. Betty Blowtorch gained a huge following all across the country even though they received little airplay by any mainstream radio stations. They were known for opening their shows with, *"We're Betty Blowtorch and we're from Hollywood and we don't give a fuck!"*

Even though too hardcore and controversial for the mainstream, Disney/Touchstone featured the band in their film *Bubble Boy*. Sharon herself has also acted as an extra in notorious films like, *Sid & Nancy* (The movie about the relationship and demise of Sid Vicious of the Sex Pistols and Nancy Spungen. It also has Courtney Love in it as an extra too.), *What's Love Got to do With It* (About Tina and Ike Turner) and *Neon Maniacs.*

After the release of their second album, *Are You Man Enough?* and only four years of being together, Betty Blowtorch was ended by a tragic accident that took the life of their singer Bianca in 2001. She was killed in an auto accident in New

Orleans, Louisiana. Sharon grieved the loss of her friend and band mate, and it was a horrible time in her life.

Their legacy however has continued with a large fan following, and an award winning documentary that was released on CD in 2006. The acclaimed documentary about Sharon's band, and their singer Bianca, was filmed by Anthony Scarpa, and distributed by Cinema Libre Studios. You can order the Betty Blowtorch film at: CinemaLibreStudio.com or check it out at: Myspace.com/TheBetty BlowtorchMovie.

Sharon met her husband Scott before the tragic accident occurred. The door guy/bartender at the club where the band played frequently always gave Sharon a hard time (playfully). One night one of the girls from Betty Blowtorch said there was a guy who wanted to meet her and learn more about her. It was him, and they dated for a few months before becoming exclusive.

They waited a few years before getting married. They had always wanted kids, but Sharon wanted to play music until the last minute. Between their work schedules and the music, it just didn't seem like the right time to have a baby yet. Her husband works several jobs, including the club, and video editing at a post production company. Sharon's work is very demanding and time consuming. She has worked as an educator and advocate for children with disabilities since she was seventeen years-old. Her band was her other full-time job. Sharon at times would like to be more politically involved, but she does feel the work she does caring for children with learning difficulties or social problems is a 9to5 advocacy.

Sharon was born in Amsterdam, Holland and came over to the states as an adolescent; she still carries her green card and is not a U.S. citizen. She doesn't want to relinquish her right as a citizen of Holland, so she is okay with her current U.S. status.

She currently works with ninth graders that have Asperger Syndrome, which is similar to Autism, but generally the causes are believed to be genetic. Sharon got into her line of work right after graduating from high school. Her first job was through an agency as a sitter for autistic children, of which some were blind and/or deaf. She was going to paralegal school, working with children, and working in a law firm. She knew ultimately she wanted to continue to work with children with special needs and play music, so she made those her main focuses.

> "I was on shift 24-7 and the agency didn't ask for much experience except for working with kids and be willing to watch kids with special needs. I went on to care for babies with A.I.D.S. I later applied at the school district and started working with runaway teens. Most of the work with the teens was positive, taking them to universities, on walks, and playing basketball with them. I was able to listen, and give advice and relate to a lot of them because of my interest in music. A lot of them were abused by one of their parents; parents that used drugs or alcohol, or didn't take care of them or kicked them out of the house."

She loved working with kids, and got used to some of the problems uniquely had by runaways, and also when working in a different setting, the challenges of caring for those with disabilities or terminal illnesses; but she never got used to losing one of them. She became attached to the children she cared for, and that was her job, but she was never prepared for them to die—even though she was supposed to be.

One of her favorite kids Ezekiel, whom she met ten years ago, was a child with AIDS that she had been caring for since infancy. When he passed at the age of two, it devastated her. She didn't know anything about his parents; they could have been dead, on drugs, or in jail. He had been in this group home virtually since he was born. She and her husband later named their child Zeke in honor of him.

Their son Zeke is now four-years-old and she was a working stay-at-home mother for the first year, but now works part-time with the school district in the Special Education Department.

When Zeke was only three-months-old Sharon had to have open heart surgery to replace one of her valves. For four months post surgery she couldn't lift or hold him. It was incredibly hard for her and it broke her heart. She found out about her heart problem originally while on tour with Betty Blowtorch, and it was then diagnosed as a mild heart valve problem from rheumatic fever she had as a child. A few months later she had to have surgery. Her friend and band-mate Bianca's death occurred shortly after her surgery

As a mother her hopes for Zeke are simple: for him to be happy and respectful of everyone. She wants him to find what makes his heart happy and to go for it. She thinks if she gives him her love, encouragement and support as well as living by example, she will be able to instill this. Mothering has been the best experience for her and she wishes sometimes she would have started earlier, but it also has been full of challenges. She loves being a mom more than anything else.

Her husband works nights and she works days. Zeke is at Montessori school while she works and her husband and her meet at a halfway point and swap while she goes to band practice with Zeke, and he goes to work.

Her current band Stay-at-Home Bomb plays only once or twice a month, but they have tons of fun doing it. They are a whimsical, sarcastic group of rockers, with blacked-out teeth, rollers in their hair, who threaten you with burnt cookies. Their stage antics are reminiscent of GWAR, but in line with the stay-at-home mom grimace. Imagine the Lunachicks suddenly armed with strollers, diapers and bottle-grenades.

The other band members are Alice Armendariz of the infamous late seventies L.A. punk band, The Bags, Lysa Flores and Judy Molish from Betty Blowtorch. Their stage names are: Betty Blender, Judy Polish, Mortha Stewart and Sharon Sewing Needles. Their first album was released in the fall of 2004. You can hear an mp3 at: AliceBag.com/media.html, or contact the label for ordering information at: WarningLabelRecords.com.

Some of Sharon's favorite bands/musicians are: AC/DC, Dead Boys, Plasmatics, Adolescents, KISS, Aerobitch, Al Green, and 999. When Sharon isn't playing with her band, or rocking out to tunes by the bands she loves, she enjoys hanging out with her family and reading. Currently, she is reading a book called, *Cinderella's Big Score: Women of the Punk and Indie Underground.* It's a book written by Maria Raha, and it's about women like Sharon and the women who came before her. It is a documentary of women who shaped rock and punk that were neglected or sidelined (like women in every field) from their male counterparts. [I later checked it out, after we interviewed, and it's an awesome book! It became one of my needed 'break-time' books when I was burnt-out on writing and working.]

Her family usually spends the weekends going to BBQs and surfing. They love traveling, but will gladly spend weekends at the beach or going to Disneyland since both are nearby. In addition to rocking and challenging the Betty Crocker mom stereotype, Sharon is going to keep doing what she loves best, "I'm expecting that being a mother will continue to be the hardest thing I'll ever love to do."

**Since this interview: Sharon is now playing with the band Psychostar, and Stay-at-Home Bomb has recently disbanded after rocking hard and throwing cookies for almost a decade.*

**"No matter how bad the taste in my mouth is,
I have to take something from it, to learn from it."**

**Beth
Vixen Vocalist for Rubber Bullet
Musician
Social Advocate
Education Reformist
Law School Student
Hypnobirthing Momma
Fort Worth, Texas.**

Beth has traveled down many roads which have led her to holistic living and wholeness, living in balance with herself, and the earth. This path has included artist, New Orleans gutter punk, rocker, lover, psychology major, mother, wife, and law student.

There were several factors that compelled her to start law school. When she majored in psychology it was for her, a natural springboard to law. She had been working as a field researcher in social work and child psychology. She saw the social worker as an advocate for the child. There were two to three family lawyers involved in the process and most of the time that was just on the states side. In her opinion, both the social worker and lawyer make a difference at the end of the day, but one makes monetarily so much more money. She wants to feel like she is helping kids, not just making money, but as a mom, and a humanitarian, she needs to do both. She has to be making a positive contribution in the world, "I have lived a colorful life and don't want to check that in at the door for a diploma. Choices you make give you a lot of life experience and you want to honor those."

"I have lived a colorful life and don't want to check that in at the door for a diploma. Choices you make give you a lot of life experience and you want to honor those."

She is an education advocate for the child and is adamantly opposed to the *No Pass No Play* system used in most Texas schools, which also has gained popularity throughout school districts nationally. *No Pass No Play* penalizes students by removing an extracurricular activity (gymnastics, sports, band, chess club, etc) if they have a failing grade in any class, in any six-week term. The intent of the legislation is to compel students to achieve passing grades and therefore pursue the things they enjoy academically. However, it is flawed because it fails to recognize a student's struggling areas where they may need developmental coaching instead. Perhaps the schools/teachers need to approach the individual students with a custom plan or strategy, or recognize if there are socio-economic factors that could be contributing to their failing grades. Why strip the students of their strengths, when you can help strengthen their weaknesses instead?

Beth also approaches children in a psychological fashion, and would like to see that done at school as well. She believes in Maslow's *Hierarchy of Needs,* which is a theory in psychology. The theory proposes that at everyone's emotional/mental and physical core there are five primal needs that have to be met in order to grow as a person, or as a child. Part of this growth aspect is learning. She feels most kids whose grades don't meet the requirements to participate in other school activities like sports or drama have one or more primal needs not being met. These five needs are: clothing, food, shelter, love and emotional resource. There can be a healthy-minded parent who lacks support systems or resources and even this can impact the child's five needs. For example, the divorced mom who is taking care of a family of three with no outside help from her ex-husband, family, or friends. The parent can be loving, which is clearly important, but obviously resources will be strained and emotional resource and time may have to be depleted from the household in order for the single parent to work two or more jobs just to meet the first three primary needs.

Often in these situations one of the children, if not all, may be falling behind in school because they are taking care of the other siblings (and additional adult-like responsibilities). The above example is of course the best-case scenario for why a child falls behind. The scenario can be much bleaker with abusive or neglectful family members and parents.

The *No pass No Play* system is too frigid and overlooks these situations. Beth believes that by participating in play-based school activities, beyond classroom academics, it could actually benefit a child whose grades are suffering. It helps give them that time to play and be creative that their home life may not allow.

When Beth grew up those five needs weren't adequately being met, and she was not learning, and was falling behind in school. It is through the five primal needs she was later able to articulate, grasp, and grow from her teenage and young adult experiences.

Her childhood was a very traditional and upper middle class one with a two-parent household. She was raised by politically and religiously conservative parents, despite primarily her father's "hypocrisies and lustful sins." She and her siblings all attended Catholic school. Her mother was unhappily married for twenty-five years to a "philandering and womanizing father." Her mother had a master's degree and had three children. Her father was a college professor. Beth (as was well as her mom it seems) had been emotionally neglected for most of her life by her father. Her dad moved out when she was seventeen.

At this time Beth decided to move to Dallas with her best friend who was then nineteen. They did everything together from eating, sleeping, drugs, living together, and dating. When her best friend died from a heroin overdose she didn't have the emotional tools to deal with it. She took off to New Orleans in search of salvation.

She spent a year and a half as a gutter punk there. She doesn't regret her time in the Big Easy at all. She lived day-to-day stealing from tourists, drinking shots, and eating food left out for the homeless by the local restaurants. If there was ever cash it was spent on booze and cigarettes, not for nourishment.

The defining moment in her life came when she was about to steal a van and head off to Canada with her friends. She called her mom, and for the first time in her life, her mom asked her to come home. Her brother had already gone to prison at this point. Beth had developed ulcers from going hungry frequently (and drinking heavily) in New Orleans. But the city taught her so much about the human spirit that by the time she got home she was on a spiritual, emotional and intellectual quest: "I was really hungry. And I had to learn ways to deal with it [life], and deal with the loss of my best friend and that's when Rubberbullet came into play."

It saddens her to see homelessness criminalized now in Dallas. The reasons for homelessness are so varied that criminalizing it does nothing but perpetrate it. She feels we all go through sagas, quests, and life circumstances (including job loss, war, abuse, and hardship) which all can contribute to homelessness, and no one should be put in jail for lacking a place to call home.

When the band Rubberbullet started she did not know how to write lyrics, "but a lot of beauty came from that," since she had no instruction. Being in the band helped to cleanse her soul, and rid her of her turmoil and youthful confusion. She got it all out by detoxifying through creating jazzy-noise-rock songs. [Don't let my inadequate description deceive you—these songs were fast and compelling, but with a poetic and clamoring surface, creating a musical juxtaposition. I had their album at age twenty after I moved back to Dallas from Cincinnati.] Beth enjoyed pursuing an artistic vocation and the built-in comradeship she developed with her band-mates and peers such as: MC 900 Foot Jesus and Seal. Of course, there were still some negative stuff going on in her life like excesses in the party/band scene, family trouble, and boy trouble. But she was learning, growing and getting it all out, "No matter how bad the taste in my mouth is, I have to take something from it, to learn from it."

With that in her emotional toolbox she was able to start respecting herself and respecting her body. The right foods were in the refrigerator, she was getting her body-in-shape and she was meeting her own needs physically, spiritually, mentally, and emotionally.

It was at this time in her life that she met her husband Todd. He was very self-sufficient and very independent, and so was she. They were both working toward getting their college degrees, and they were both in rock bands, he was in the Toadies, and she was still in Rubberbullet. (She also later played with another Dallas band, Pinkston, in which her vocals got rave reviews.)

They were married in 1998. Their first five years before starting a family were dreamy and wonderful. They still are very much in love, and with their daughter Ruby it has truly made them one person.

Ruby is like an amazing work of art that runs, jumps, and is full of colorful personality. Ruby is playful and robust with energy, but Ruby is also well-grounded and not prone to temper tantrums; they feel a lot of this is due to how she was born.

Ruby was born using a naturalistic womb-oriented birthing plan called Hypnobirthing. This is where you have your baby in a very relaxed room. The ambience is quiet and tranquil. You bring yourself into a state of meditation with no pushing. Your body simply becomes a medium in which the child delivers themselves. There is no noise, no activity … nothing that disturbs the transition from womb-to-world. The child goes straight to breast feeding. In all the research Beth did, as well as in their personal experience later, hypnobabies rarely cry. This is because of how calm and soothing the birth process is for both mother and child. The important principle is to replace negative with positive.

Their parenting beliefs are very wholesome. They minimize television in their house and minimize exposure to commercialism. Beth said, "Ruby has to have love, laughter and optimism in her home and in her life." This is their focus behind everything they do as parents. Commercialism and television tend to contradict that focus. They work to maintain their focus on love, laughter, and optimism. That is regardless of money, income, or other life stresses like work, school, art, and music.

Charity work and volunteer work is a common event in their house both because of Beth's personal experience being homeless, and her belief that all things run in circles (karma) and that it's critical to give back. They want to raise Ruby with: awareness of others, and with kindness and sharing as a core life value.

Right now they get by on her income as a waitress and her husband's royalties from his band the Toadies. When life pushes hard with its demands, they pull together instead of being pulled apart. They make necessary compromises and plan together as well. (They have really dug deep into themselves and have pulled out those qualities and strengths and have used them. They have found out what they are really made of together in times of difficulty.) At the end of each day they can say they have done a good job and all was well handled.

At the time of this interview, Ruby was two and Beth was thirty-five. A frequent night in their house is sipping milk and watching fun, educational, and non-commercial/non-violent movies together on the couch.

She approaches her life as a parent, and as a wife, differently from that of her parents. She respects her own body and mind, and her husband respects himself in the same fashion—and their relationship is built on trust and mutual respect and consideration of each other. They don't abuse their bodies with alcohol, or drugs (including pharmaceutical prescriptions) nor do they abuse each other, emotionally, or verbally. Faith and communication are the cornerstones of their marriage and that approach also helps them see and understand one another. No philandering in their household.

They have gotten frequent questions, and slack, about why they won't have a second child. They don't want one. People are always giving them their opinion on the matter insisting Ruby needs a brother or a sister. Sometimes it makes her second guess her choice. But she has real reasons behind it: finances and time.

As Beth goes into her new line of work in the legal system, she isn't worried about all the tattoos she has, or peoples responses to them:

> "I am not defined by my tattoos. They are a marking of where I have been … if it's all about appearance and tattoos, you are leaving out and leaving behind a lot of good quality people."

She may get back into music someday, but for now she is content to pull out her Rubberbullet and Pinkston records, and listen to them from time-to-time, knowing she did that and was part of it.

Right on!

**Since this interview: Beth changed course and went back to her first love psychology. She now is a marriage and family therapist who focuses on "unconventional approaches to life's conventions" with her own private practice called Mistletoe Family Therapy Group. You can view their site at: MistletoeGroup.com.*

"I like the Punk Rock. I like it because it's political and socially aware. I live for music and can't imagine life without it."

Picture by Angie Taksony at PunkRockNight.com

Selena
Drummer for the band Menstrual Tramps
Recreation Leader & Mentor at a children's shelter
College Student
Outdoor Enthusiast
Strong Single Momma
Feminist
Minneapolis, Minnesota.

Selena is a thirty-year-old quiet and shy drummer that lives in the Twin Cities. The most important things in her life are: Lavender (her daughter), her friends, family and music. Second to those are learning about new things, helping children (which she does working at a children's shelter) reading, checking out punk and mariachi bands, cooking, touring, and nature. She tries to be outdoors as much as possible and loves waterskiing, basketball, tai chi, biking, swimming and skateboarding.

She doesn't know how she ended up in Minnesota, considering she loves the ocean and the mountains. She feels connected to them through her Mexican and Native American heritage and history. She learns more about herself, her family, her people, and her land daily, through the informal study of anthropology and specifically her indigenous culture. When she is exploring nature she feels a powerful connection to her past, and to her ancestors. I envision Selena standing erect calling the spirits of the past to her in the middle of the forest, leaving her empowered. Much like when I summon the goddesses under the night sky.

Music, feminism, and literature are the driving forces behind the social-political punk rock she plays. The artists that inspire and motivate her are: Maya Angelou, Mahatma Gandhi, Margaret Mead, Judy Chicago, Alice Walker and Emma Goldman. Selena counts on them during hard times. When she starts to feel cynical about the state of the world, or her own life, she remembers Meads words, "*Never believe that a few caring people can't change the world. For indeed that's all who ever have.*" She also leans on Gandhi's wisdom to sustain her, "*You must be the change you wish to see in the world,*" and she just changes her own disposition. When she needs to forgive herself, she understands both human potential and human experience through Angelou's wisdom, *"I did what I thought was best, now I know better."* She cites these artists as true philosophers and human angels whose work both awes, inspires, and shocks the world, while provoking anger in some, and giving hope to others:

> "Emma Goldman is my hero. I love her little anarcho-feminist thoughts. I love the artist Judy Chicago. Anyone who spends that much time and energy making a Dinner Party for all these different women and makes the plates into different vaginas is awesome in my book."

Selena's favorite read is Aldous Huxley's *Brave New World.* It's a fictional account of a future utopian state that is erringly benign. It's a caste controlled world where all human expression is censored, and where subversive artists and thinkers are banned to an island, non-violently. It's a politically infused philosophical fictional exploration analyzing the hope of national peace through governmental control, but it's ripe with contradictions and strife. It compels its readers to ask at what expense can we hope for peace and is it a deception?

Brave New World helps Selena think about humanity on broad universal lines, although written in 1932 it's far from out-dated; but when it comes to daily living all she needs to get up and get going is one universal truth written by poet Maya Angelou, "*I love to see a young girl go out and grab the world by its lapels. Life's a bitch. You've got to go out and kick some ass.*" It's this element of pro-female action and aggression that she brings to the band, Menstrual Tramps. They describe themselves as, "*The chicks you love to hate.*" Selena has been with the band since the late 1990s. Everyone in the band is now a mother. Musically, they are an in-your-face-three-chord, hardcore punk trio with a distinctive metal edge and a confrontational feminist demeanor reminiscent of Riot Grrrls and early punk.

Menstrual Tramps.
"The chicks you love to hate."

They are a punk trio with a distinctive metal edge and a confrontational feminist demeanor reminiscent of Riot Grrrls and early punk. You can check them out on Facebook or at: Myspace.com/MenstrualTramps.

Their stage presence is incredible and strong. I saw the band play at Bar of Soap in Dallas and felt power and hope for females in rock as I danced with the crowd, and felt the crowd's excitement surge the place. I felt the presence of the female activists and musicians who came before them and helped pave the way to where they stand, loud and outspoken, on stage. You could see the struggles and dreams of many ancestral women merged into the expressions of their faces as the band played.

Chyna's intense deep growl fighting to get out as she sings and shouts the lyrics while playing guitar, her bleach blonde hair exploding around the thrusts and shaking of her head and body. Val's sweat rolling down from her red-auburn hair, and powder pale face, clinging to her biceps and forearms, making her tattoos glisten, as she plays bass; her lips curl in a smirk, and her long skinny fingers curling around the neck of her bass. Like a symbolic feminine triangle positioned on stage Chyna and Val are supported by Selena, who like a triumphal arch, supports the sound and progression of band's musical structure, and visual perception. Her amber face masked by fury and fervor as she pounds away on the drums. Her long twisted dreadlocks slapping against her back and chest, as her face and upper torso is tensed in a frenzy of excursion.

This empowering moment of seeing the band play comes to a grinding halt suddenly. A male friend of mine quirps, "I wonder which one I'm going to take home tonight?" I am dumbfounded and expressionless. Why can't women rock without being seen as sex objects for the pleasure of men? His sense of entitlement leaves me feeling degraded and it takes me days to figure it out, address it and get over it. It's a common perception that men share, that we (females) are here to sexually please them, and this expectation is paramount in general in societies and cultures (universally), not just in music, even when it's a sense of entitlement from otherwise allegedly enlightened counter-culture modern men. I feel conflicted shame though too, because I realize now that when I was younger, I acted the same way about dudes on stage. Sexism and exploitation (it can be subtle, outright, intentional or unintentional) are what the band stands against and challenges.

Selena and the band have had several releases including the most recent album, *No Hesitation, No Defeat*, and two prior 7-inch records, *Toxic Shock* and *Late Night Riot.* They consider their recent release a big *fuck you* to the Bush legacy. The band views the entire clan as exploitative and abusing power starting with senior all the way down to junior. I smile warmly as I envision the band striking a pose with hips thrust out, fishnets and boots on, giving the bird to the Bush presidents as the chorus, *fuck you, fuck you, and fuck you*, rings loudly behind them.

The band has done over five tours on both coasts, and they manage their own material and merchandise, maintaining complete artistic control. The band takes several mini-tours a year and a long tour during the summer. They incorporate friends and family for childcare during the shorter tours and sometimes will bring the older children on tour during the summer for longer tours on the coasts and through the South. (Lavender who is eleven, frequently sells the merchandise for the band during shows.) Since the band is a complete DIY band and they manage themselves, they work harder, but they make all the rules. You can check out the band at: Myspace.com/MenstrualTramps. You can also check them at on their Facebook page.

Music is what led Selena to the path of motherhood. She was on tour, seeing the world and playing music at the age of eighteen. She had no desire to go to college because she felt it was, "a load of shit" and she didn't want to, "Go out and do what everyone said I should do. I wasn't going to conform to what society said I should or shouldn't do." She was on a visionary quest to live and explore life which is something she felt you can't find in a college classroom. She was barely eighteen when she first had the impression of how different the world is just outside the U.S. border.

> "I remember Vancouver, B.C., Canada and the special café they had there. I liked that place a whole lot. I was amazed that cafes like that existed where you could order up a vaporizer or hookah. I guess I was a product of the War on Drugs generation. I remember getting harassed more by the U.S. Border Patrol than I was ever was by the Canadians. That bothered me. I'm an American citizen, why were they fucking with me? Was it the green hair? I had a quick lesson in profiling and it left me sick."

She wanted to live life free and open. Selena and her boyfriend had more plans for traveling and exploring the world when the pregnancy occurred:

"I was traveling across the U.S. in a van when I found out I was pregnant. I was in California at the time and I decided to continue on the trip and then go to Alaska where my mom was to have the baby. We didn't talk about any other options. We were young and in love. I do remember crying though. It was like your whole life was about to change."

Initially, she was afraid to tell her family, but once she did they gave her their complete support and love. The young couple had a lot of normal fears like, could they do it? Will they be good at it? But they were determined to provide their child with a healthy and happy home. They stayed together for four years, which originally Selena believed the fairy tales children (girls in particular) are raised on: ideas that romantic love is eternal; it never occurred to her that they wouldn't be a family forever and live happily ever after.

The couple split up after they moved from Alaska to Minnesota. Selena was sexually assaulted months after their move, and it left her empty and in pain. As Selena tells me this story online I can see her smile crumbling, and shadows clinging to her face, every keyboard key touched in dread and hesitation. Even after the rapist was convicted it didn't stop the rage from boiling over, and the hurt from drowning her soul. It was as if she had been stolen from herself. To calm and contain the pain Selena started drinking heavily and her boyfriend started using heroin as a means to cope. Realizing their life was out of control, and their family in danger, they both started treatment. It didn't save their relationship, but it did save the family. A few years after their split, he moved back to Alaska and she stayed in Minneapolis. Parenting however took its toll on her, especially after the separation …

"Once I became a single parent it was all about no sleep and lots of work. Work as in at home and at the J.O.B. It seemed like I was always working. Then I realized I wasn't doing anything for myself. I was unhappy. I put myself into ultra-mom mode. I needed to do things for myself too. I needed to find a balance. I started playing music again after quitting for a few years and it was like I was reborn. I needed the outlet and creative force in my life. I realized I couldn't be the best mom I could be, by suppressing myself, and the things I wanted to do. It's a balancing act. Spending time with my daughter, spending time with myself, and then there is everything else."

At that time she put up a flyer advertising herself as a drummer looking for a band and that is how she met Chyna and Sigrid, and they would later become the Menstrual Tramps. She feels very fortunate to have not only grown up per se with the band, but she has also been able to count on them as friends and confidants, and now as moms too. She has several good friends that are parents and they help each other out and lean on one another during good times and hard times. A majority of them are single moms so sharing resources and time with each other is a huge help. They are always searching for free activities for the kids, health care on a sliding fee, and scholarships for their kids. They frequently trade childcare amongst themselves as a viable solution. Selena has taken her friends kids to music class with her when they needed a sitter and her friends do the same for her. They turn to each other for advice and problem solving. This back up is essential for single moms,

"Society has little to no help or support for single mothers like myself. I get thrown a little crumb at tax time for working and having a child and that is supposed to keep me quiet and happy until next year. The support I have has been through my friends and family. I don't feel supported by society as a whole. Maybe if I lived in another country this would change. Single moms should get double the sick days and lots of childcare help. There are so many ways society can support single moms and their children, but it just doesn't seem to be there."

Selena's frustration has also been with her ex-spouse who doesn't help out as an equal parent. He maintains a presence in Lavender's life (and Lavender adores her father) and he spends time with Lavender when he can, but the distance between them makes it difficult. Regardless of his love for their child—his financial child support has been rare. A common dilemma many moms endure. The only reason why Selena is now finally getting some child support from him is because child support enforcement caught up to him and the alternative to financially caring for his child was to go to jail. Although she is finally getting child support, legally enforced, the fact is that Lavender is eleven-years-old, why did it take this long? Is it because children are seen exclusively as a woman's responsibility? Is it because children are seen more as objects than people who need to eat, have shelter, and have care? Selena thinks the apathy, or indifference, society has towards children is due to the enduring ideal that children should be seen and not heard. *[A part of sexism that society reinforces on to children, as it is expected of women, whom incidentally are largely the care-givers of children: motherism.]* She feels society doesn't put its money where its mouth is. *[Case-in-point: children are priceless, yet our public schools have minimal funding, and according to a recent CNN Health report by Elizabeth Landau, "About 21 percent of children in the United States will be living below the poverty line in 2010, the highest rate in 20 years." That means a lot of hungry and needful kid's right here in our own backyards. And let's not even get started on childcare/latchkey kid issues and lack of medical coverage! Not to mention record breaking profits for oil companies like Exxon and Chevron), GE, and others, while enjoying a tax free corporate income for 2010, 2009, and so on. And according to the Daily Comet and the New York Times we actually paid them! And contrary to public opinion most Americans who receive help through government housing or food assistance work—and work for these greedy giants!]*

Selena encounters children every day in her line of work that are homeless, neglected, and that are waiting to be adopted. She also meets a lot of loved children who suffer from not having any medical insurance while having physical or mental impairments. Society's indifference, or even hypocrisy, is a large part of the problem (in addition to our evidently corrupt tax system!).

"Society talks about loving and caring for children, but they don't want to talk about what's wrong. There are so many children waiting to be adopted yet there are billboards proclaiming an embryo is a baby all along I-35! Don't get me wrong here, I'm all about choice! It's just that I work in a children's shelter and see the pain of neglected and abused children every day. Children, who need and want homes, but have behavior problems or the wrong skin color. But we just want to talk about how cute they are and how they are our future. In my opinion society is not putting enough time and energy into 'our future'. Children are at home alone because parents have to work two jobs. Parents have to work two jobs just to feed their children. The television babysits and we breed drone consumers. I'm not saying there aren't good programs out there; they are just under funded. It just sickens me we can spend millions on a war against terror, yet children still go to bed hungry … hey but they're still lookin' cute, right?"

Selena also feels our indifference and refusal to thoroughly acknowledge, or adequately address the abuse of children, is muting entire generations and maiming them:

"Based on my experience, we as a society need to start looking at child sexual abuse for one. It is a silent killer of our children. They are losing their spirits. We don't talk about it and we don't have stiff enough consequences for offenders. I also think we need to go back to the old saying 'It takes a whole village to raise a child,' if there is to be any lasting hope for our children [and for parents]."

This general indifference towards children has compelled Selena not only to work with kids in need, but to make it her second career. She currently works as a recreational leader at a middle school and at a children's shelter. She is working towards developing a multi-layered career combining the essential elements of being a guidance counselor, social worker, and a psychologist. She is currently attending college to obtain the required degree(s) for this quasi-profession, even though what she already does encompasses this work. Her opinion on college hasn't changed necessarily, but due to bureaucracy she can't get higher pay or recognition for her work without the degrees and formal titles. Selena knows this is needed work and she loves and respects kids,

"I was the oldest of four kids, and with my mom being a single mom as well, I was always helping out with the other kids. I love kids. I'll probably always work with children. It's very challenging, but very rewarding. Hanging out with homeless kids and giving them my time and making them feel as safe as possible, and then getting their respect or a smile in return. Knowing that I'm hanging out with a middle school girl who could be doing other things she shouldn't be doing, is pretty damn rewarding and worth every second."

As a single mother, Selena is acutely aware of society's contradictions and lack of community help and involvement. She wants her daughter Lavender to learn to be herself, and go after her dreams, even if people/society tries to get in her way. She hopes her daughter will do her best at everything she tries. She is instilling an authentic respect for diversity by teaching Lavender about different ways of living, and cultures. Selena is also laying the foundation of Lavender's self-esteem by teaching self-respect and respecting others as an essential and defining principle. She is teaching Lavender about her ancestral heritage and hopes she takes an interest in it. Lavender is also free to express her own opinions, even if they do not mirror, or conflict, with Selena's; as long as they are expressed and shared in a respectful fashion. Lavender recently displayed not only confidence in her own opinion, but the ability to scientifically reason about evolution and religion with her Baptist grandmother …

> "Lavender loves plays, so I took her to see 'Inherit the Wind', and she was telling her grandmother about it. I smiled to myself as I heard her tell her grandmother how silly it is for us to believe that we all come from Adam and Eve."

Selena raises Lavender with a feminist consciousness,

> "I took her to see the Guerilla Girls [Political anti-sexist art 'commentary' via ads and graphics] when they came through town. She loved it! She also hears it [feminism] everyday in my conversations with friends, band-mates, and my boyfriend. I guess now that I think about it, her and I talk about feminism quite a bit. I never let her have Barbie's growing up. Did it make a difference? Well, I slept better at night, and she isn't losing sleep over it."

Her main parenting philosophy, which also extends to her professional work with children, is that children learn by doing. She feels it's a healthy part of their development to push and test boundaries. Selena is laid-back in her parenting so that her daughter feels secure trying new things, but Lavender knows that mom is there to catch her. Selena emphasizes that every action has a reaction or a result. (She doesn't interrupt this process unless Lavender is doing something innately dangerous, or totally off-the-wall.) The most important piece of parenting advice she has is, "I've learned to pick my battles, respect is important, and communication is huge. Without them there is no parenting." The main expectation she has of herself as a parent is:

"As a mother I always have to stay informed and teach my child the age-appropriate things I know. To always be there for my daughter until the day I die. To set an example of a strong independent woman who is capable of doing things (for herself) or finding ways to get things done; to be myself so that my daughter knows me and respects me. I want the stories of how I overcame obstacles in my life, and the adventures I took, to help my daughter. These are the stories I want my daughter and her children to remember so that they can look back on them and gain strength from them when they need it. That's what I do. I gain strength and motivation from my mother and grandmother. I am proud to be a single mom raising a creative, intelligent young girl. It's been a struggle financially and emotionally, but I do it every day and I do a damn good job too!"

As a single mom Selena juggles all of the responsibilities of being a full-time parent, mother, worker, teacher, student, artist/musician, and activist. Selena however, in the midst of all of her responsibilities, takes time-out to nurture her soul and spirit. She shares a one-bedroom apartment with her daughter, and Lavender has the bedroom, while Selena sleeps on the futon in the living room. Critical to Selena's spirituality and essence is sexuality/sensuality which is hard to explore in such a small environment. Contrary to society's confusing messages about sex, Selena feels it is one aspect of life that is essential just like all the rest, despite the Victorian contradictions our culture has, or the sexism normally attached to it. Trying to have a sex life as a single mother in a one-bedroom apartment does sometimes create some humorous moments though,

"Sex is very important to me and I'm not afraid to admit that I really enjoy it. Sometimes it really sucks cause it's late at night, and I have to try to be quiet so I don't wake Lavender up. No kid wants to hear her parents having sex, but it happens. Just the other morning she asked me if I could keep it down at night. She had a hard time sleeping. So you have to be respectful, and you have to talk about it with your kids. You can't just stop having sex! Shit, that's how we get our beautiful little angels!"

Besides breaking taboos about women in general, from female rockers, female educators/mentors, and the virginal dichotomy of motherhood and the sex(less) taboo for mothers, Selena has also faced some personal struggles concerning substance abuse. She has used drugs and alcohol in the past to medicate herself when faced with enormous life-challenges. At one point she had to have her mom take care of Lavender while she went to treatment. It was something that started when she was a teenager, turning to stimulants, or depressants, as temporary band-aids to help her manage stress and emotional rollercoaster's; then it would subside with a bout of willpower and life working itself out. In the world of music, performers are glorified for habitual abuse, but Selena's situation was far from regular, or constant, and definitely not glamorous. The United States has a complex and torrid love affair with, and a dependency on, alcohol and drugs (both illegal, and legally controlled substances), but it is more acceptable for male addicts (our society has more sympathy for male addicts than females) to reach out for help than women. Compounding this situation even more is the reality that once a woman becomes a mother these problems are suppose to just disappear, and stay gone. They aren't discussed because they conflict with the sacred immaculate expectations and images of what mothers, and motherhood, are suppose to be. When Selena realized her occasional use had become a serious problem, she did what most wouldn't have had the courage to do (due to fear of ridicule—or the very real fear that the state would attempt to take her child) which is seek help.

It takes a lot of strength to acknowledge you have a problem and then to do something about it. Selena still occasionally struggles with it, as most people who have had abuse problems do, but she remembers that,

"It just tells me I need to step back and figure out what is going on in my life, what is bugging me. I can't just shove it way down or I'll be in trouble, and I know that."

> ★★★★★★★★
>
> ***She still gets plenty of disapproving looks …***
>
> **"Why? Because we don't celebrate Easter, we celebrate May Day … because we don't bake cookies; we bake cupcakes with skulls and crossbones on them … because I look different than your everyday suburban soccer mom. I have tattoos, piercings, dreadlocks, and sometimes purple or red hair … because I don't go to aerobics; I play in a band and go on tours with my girls."**
>
> ★★★★★★★★

She gets her share of shocked looks and reactions from others when they learn she is a parent. Selena's life is a constant taboo breaker, from a woman playing drums, to a woman who acknowledges the importance of her having a life beyond just mothering. Selena is a renegade mother who doesn't feel her personal life has to come to an abrupt end just because she has a child, even though society expects her to. She still gets plenty of disapproving looks, even from successful 'post' feminist mainstream moms,

> "Why? Because we don't celebrate Easter, we celebrate May Day … because we don't bake cookies; we bake cupcakes with skulls and crossbones on them … because I look different than your everyday suburban soccer mom. I have tattoos, piercings, dreadlocks, and sometimes purple or red hair … because I don't go to aerobics; I play in a band and go on tours with my girls."

Even though she knows at first glance she is stereotyped, she tries to refrain from doing the same and stays receptive to people from all different cultures, including mainstream, because you never know who they may be under the surface. She encounters a lot of moms at her job. Some are responsive to her feedback; others are in a big hurry. As a mother herself, she always tries to give them the most information she can because that is the same respect she would like. She definitely knows that being a subculture mom, she feels freer to be herself and that's what attracted her to it in the first place:

> "I can express myself the way I choose to with few reservations and pressures. There is more openness. Mainstream feels fake … do this because everyone else is, or says so. There is less individuality and more numbing of the mind in the mainstream world. There is also a lot of money and power involved and whose best interests are at stake? The people with money and power."

Selena thinks that subculture parenting offers children acceptance and teaches them the ability to think for themselves, which is an underrated social value in our society. She sees children and teens everyday that worry about not fitting in. These kids lack the confidence to think for themselves and to act decisively with courage and conviction. She feels that, "People who are different from each other can always learn from each other. If nothing else they can learn tolerance and respect for their differences."

She is content openly embracing life while raising Lavender. She is going to live life her way: breaking rules and rocking out while helping the kids who need a hand. Now, that's what I call a Rebel Mom!

"I am a single mom, so in this society I am pond scum. There's a certain freedom in being pond scum. No Joneses to keep up with, no man to displease, no fear of having said man leave you."

Picture by Jeff Gracianette at ThePathtoAll.com

Mother Nature
Sexy Sailor
Anarchist
Singer/Guitarist for the band Placenta
Published Writer in:
***Slingshot* & *Hip Mama* Magazines**
Classical Music Major
Performer for the Berkley Women's Community Orchestra
Owner of a Home Cleaning Business
Oakland, California.

She goes by the stage name, Mother Nature, as in "Don't Mess With!" She plays with and fronts the band Placenta. It's an all moms band whose ambitions are to write and perform really good, meaningful, and complex rock songs about the entirety of the female experience, including mothering. They are recording again and they briefly had a Canadian reality TV show, but it was canceled after the station realized that they weren't going to be able to gentrify them into suburban upper class moms (that occasionally picked up an instrument in-between the nanny arriving with the kids from private school, and the moms putting down the guitars, to run household errands). They had something to say and it challenged people's brains unlike most reality shows which get people to buy-in and be clueless or petty. Mother Nature writes most of the songs and she draws her inspiration largely from her political activism:

> "Given the fact that all the band kids are mixed race, and given that I am so involved in the lesbian/gay/trans community, I am a leftist activist, and a performance artist, and I try to be present and unafraid in my songwriting as much as possible, my subject matter runs the gamut [of everything counter to mainstream American society]."

They have two albums out *Placenta*, and *Chocolate and Heroin.* The songs vary in subject matter, but the song titles will give you some insight on what to expect: *Single Mom, WTF Went Wrong? Super Gender Bender, Ugly, Oakland Unified School District, Laundry Song* and *Too Much Woman.*

She hopes her band will be influential, and Placenta can have a huge impact on people and the way they live and think. She tries to live courageously, and write and perform, to the best of her ability. She hopes to inspire other artists and musicians. She would like for someone really famous and powerful to say they admire her songwriting, singing, performing, and general aesthetic:

> "I want to change people's lives because of one tiny thing I've said. I want them to look at the world as a place that can be changed or improved, or ripped apart as the case may be."

Placenta has been featured in countless newspapers and magazines, including the *Wall Street Journal*, *Chicago Tribune*, the *London Telegraph*, and the *New York Daily News*. Most of the articles have had a condescending air to them, and Placenta has been lumped into a movement with other mom rock bands, or bands that happen to have moms in them. Mother Nature feels the general media's attitude is, "Moms with guitars, how cute." Placenta states it clearly on their webpage that if you're looking for a mom band that sings about spilled spaghetti sauce, or picking up socks, this isn't the band for you. They are a political activist rock band, and coincidentally they are all mothers, so women's and mother's issues finds its way into the music since: being both a woman and a mother can be a transforming political experience, especially once you step out of the mold of what is acceptable for either role. Placenta has received some great meaningful reviews that are a stark contrast to the former. *AfterEllen.com* said, *"Definitions of sexual-orientation (if not civilization itself) break down and crumble before phenomenon like the California based band Placenta." Contra Costa Times* said they are a … *"Blend of rock and power punk that takes on such issues as war, domestic abuse and even the Oakland School District."* (Mother Nature has had to battle with the school district over dress-code, getting classes and help her kids have needed academically, while fighting overwhelming homework loads that infringe on her kid's family time and time for them to pursue personal interests.) Mother Nature's favorite quote was from the cover of *USA Today*, *"The rules of motherhood are being radically rewritten—with a snarl, cymbal crash, and power E-chord that would makes the lads in AC/DC stand and salute. Placenta is blowing like a Hurricane."*

You can check out the band at: PlacentaMusic.com, or at: Myspace.com/PlacentaMusic. The band is trying to build a coalition with other girl bands so that they all can get booked together for playing shows. This is one way to strengthen their line-up and deal with the obstacles of getting passed over for male bands in a music scene, even punk, that is still largely dick oriented. She hopes to create her own showcase next summer. For the most part though, they have enough clubs and promoters that dig them that they do get regular bookings:

"I guess we might get passed over for some gigs, because were girls, but it's kinda hard to know that for sure. There are jerky guys/bands to be sure, but I don't know if they are more jerky to us. We're pretty tough. There's a lot of penis politics, but we just don't deal with that. If we get shat upon by a club, we don't go back."

Originally, Placenta was called the Lactators. Mother Nature has been in a few other bands too, including a hardcore punk rock band called the Iraqi Liberation Front. She has been in a country band called the Whoreshoes, and a band called the B-Cups.

She likes emotional music and relates more to music with meaningful lyrics. She likes everything from Tool to Tuvan throat singing. She has a weakness for good show tunes; anything that seems like it could work as the soundtrack of her life. She loves the Beatles and as a kid, she would lose herself in their music, and her own make-believe world, "Where people wore groovy clothes and traveled to India and made art, that said 'yes', and people wrote songs about things that were happening around them."

She has a background in classical music and has played with the Berkley Women's Community Orchestra as an adult, and as a teenager in the Colorado Youth Symphony. She majored in viola and jazz in college. She has a long history and exposure to world music. Among some of her favorites are: Indian Ragas, Polynesian Music, and African Polyrhythmic. This musical exposure came from her childhood. Her violin and viola teacher, Mr. Smith, has had a great influence on her tastes. He was a "virtuoso on the viola." She doesn't know how he got stuck in Greeley, Colorado (where she grew up) because he seemed meant for so much more, somewhere bigger, but there he was in this small rural college town teaching. He taught her a lot about technique, how to break a piece of music down, to learn it, and how to *fake* it.

Mr. Davis, her band instructor, taught her about jazz and blues, and how to play chord progressions. This was critical to her development of her own style of rhythm playing.

A recent mentor and friend, Lana Shively, has helped influence the shape of her newest musical projects. She taught her about theater and how to be truly expressive without censoring oneself due to fear of others or their reactions.

Mother Nature has a high energy level that comes from fear, angst and survival instinct. She frequently encounters men who have a hard time with it, or with interacting with her, because a majority of men are used to and expect women to keep their energy focused on The "make-up counter, or for making perfect pies, or something." Some men really dig her though because she defies the stereotype of what a woman should be in our culture. More women seem to respond and appreciate her very present energy and sense of self.

"The rules of motherhood are being radically rewritten—with a snarl, cymbal crash, and power E-chord that would makes the lads in AC/DC stand and salute. Placenta is rocking like a hurricane." —USA Today

Rock out to Placenta at: PlacentaMusic.com, or at: Myspace.com/PlacentaMusic.

Her parents have a lot to do with her survival instinct and her determination to live by her own accord. They were "cruel and neglectful" which forced her to survive and get by without them at a premature age. She blossomed despite them. Her father has a long history of disappointing her and abusing her. After his last act of harassment, she wrote him off for good.

"I just broke things off with my dad, formally, this past year. I hadn't talked to him for a while, but Placenta got on the cover of USA Today [with an article on rock-mom bands written by Marco R. della Cava], so he found our band email. His 'congratulatory' email suggested that we change our name to the Cock Stoppers. He sent pictures of naked women with rifles and other violent porn. Then I asked him what, exactly, it was he wanted. He made up some bullshit about wanting to put me in his will, so he needed all my personal info. I told him goodbye, and what a fucking relief! He kept sending violent and sexually inappropriate emails for a while, cuz I'm not the one who owns the band email. I felt bad for my lead guitar player, having to see that, but at least someone got a taste of his shit, so I didn't feel so alone."

Her relationship with her mother is just as awkward and awful. She has never confronted her mother about the stuff she let her father get away with, or about her (mom's) own behavior, because her mom won't ever acknowledge that she has ever done anything wrong, or made bad choices, or decisions. She adds, "I just don't allow her in my house and I don't visit hers. My life is beyond her realm of comprehension anyway."

She realized when she was much older that she had never been a wanted child, or a wanted pregnancy. She learned later that her dad had abandoned her mother when she was in her last month of pregnancy, "He hated me before I was even born, and she was always afraid to love me." He came back shortly after her birth, and both her parents made her life hell all the way up to adulthood.

Finding out the truth as a teenager put her into a state of shock, but it gave her a much clearer picture of her life. She realized her father would have never liked her no matter what she did, and that's why her mom always treated her (and everything she has done), as if she was scared to death of Mother Nature. Her mere existence represents danger to her, and the threat of her husband leaving again. (Her parents did later finally divorce when Mother Nature was a teenager.)

This realization affected her subconsciously for years, and she figured out recently it was childhood bondage and parental rejection that drew her to men who wouldn't like nor respect her, and caused her to excessively worry about frightening or hurting women. As a child, "I could never measure up; it's the whole lack of a penis thing."

She has always felt alone and it's a feeling she still can't shake. She asserts that her parents are racists, so when Mother Nature had two Filipina children, it sealed her fate as an outsider to her family. Her mother has gone so far to alienate Mother Nature and her two children by 'adopting' two white kids as grandchildren. Some of her most shocking and vicious memories of her parents are:

"I remember when my mother called the cops on me for the first time. I was nine and went to the school yard (two blocks away) without telling her. They (the cops) followed me slowly as I walked home, weird. I remember I had to promise my dad that I would 'do something' with the music lessons he paid for, heh, heh. I remember when my dad beat me up (I was fifteen.) and dragged me out of bed to go to his house in the middle of the night because my mom had rolled her car on an icy patch, and she wanted me and my brother to be 'safe', or maybe she thought I was going to throw a party. I remember the last time my mom called the cops on me. I was in college. She told them I had a shotgun in the car and that I had said I was going to run down the cops. They handcuffed me and took me to the psyche ward. All I had in my car was statistics homework and an unopened bottle of Tylenol. My mother then told the family doctor I was on drugs, so he recommended that I stay for a week. I lost all my financial aid."

Mother Nature is still baffled at how her parents could have hated her so much that they would deliberately sabotage her college career. They way they have treated her over the years has been with acts of vengeance and hatred, even though she asserts she has done nothing for them to despise her so cruelly. She had to get away from them, and since college was now ruined, she joined the Navy as a final escape from them, and to create a means of getting a college education.

She was in the Navy when the U.S. invaded Kuwait, under Bush Sr., and she didn't see the logic of us invading them, "I couldn't see how this country getting involved in the affairs of other countries could be wise for our military." It made sense when one day one of her co-workers was applying chap-stick to his lips, and he looked at the lip balm and said, *"This is why we're going to war."* As she recalled these events, I could imagine her shaking her head, with her blonde hair hugging her cheeks with an absolute dismal look in her eyes, because our poor have to trade their lives for college and war. [My own father was a Vietnam Vet. As a teenager he had nowhere else to go, abandoned (and abused) by his family at the age of twelve, and like Mother Nature he had no other resources. He enlisted as soon as he legally could to get off the streets.]

"I remember how my dad's neighbor (an ex-Marine, Vietnam War Vet and the only Rastafarian in my hometown) told me that the U.S. Military is not really a volunteer outfit. If you require people to be degreed in order to have decent jobs, and the only way for poor people to get a college education is to serve in the military, then it isn't really AN option: it is THE option. So you have a military of poor people who have no other options—disposable people to fight wars for lip balm. And I was one of them."

Mother Nature has the same opinion of both the invasion she was involved in and the current, Iraq 'War'. The invasion she was involved in wasn't about noble deeds or protecting Kuwait from Saddam Hussein, it was about protecting our capital interest in their resources, and the oil companies investments. Instead of the oil companies using their own CEO soldiers, they use the poor of the United States with the blessing of our government to fight for their companies. It is eerie how history repeats itself when now we are doing the same thing again, compliments of Bush Jr., for oil companies, in Iraq.

Overall, she was surprised by the childishness of the Navy personnel. People were always gossiping about each other, and there was a complete lack of privacy. The misogyny was incredible. (Mother Nature understands that the military is a codified strictly-enforced version of our societal structure and layers, from class, to race and gender, all confined by uniform, but your status is dictated by the former. You don't find rich people dying on the battlefield; you find them running the show from the top.) There was one thing she liked about the Navy though which was the ocean …

"The ship itself smelled like diesel and the water tasted like diesel, but, oh my, being at sea was so wonderful. The ocean is so dark, it's not really blue, it is black. It looks like black obsidian. You really can see the curve of the Earth, and you get a very, very clear idea of how small and insignificant we humans are, floating around in a little tin can. I saw orcas, sharks, flying fish, and humpbacked whales. I have often thought about going on a regular cruise, just to get back out on the ocean."

It was during time that she learned she was pregnant, and she was able to leave the Kuwait Invasion and the Navy behind her. If you are planning on continuing a pregnancy, you are discharged from your duty. (However, the military will let you continue to serve if you have an abortion—they just won't pay for it or provide any related medical care. It's kind of like the policy for gays in the military, "Don't Ask, Don't Tell," anyone about your abortion.) They were both young and Mother Nature was only twenty-three-years-old when they married and had their first child. The first few years of their nine year marriage she obsessively strived to be the *perfect* mother and wife (as society expects us to be), but for some reason never measured up to the expected images. She was very unhappy, *which seemed contrary to how she should feel,* according to the magazine and car ads of smiling, youthful and affluent moms with prefect hair, perfect kids, perfect cars, perfect careers and perfect make-up. She also got the same reaction from others when she expressed her unhappiness—she should be happy.

She wanted her child (at that time they only had one child) to know that she was loved and wanted. Mother Nature thought that if she achieved the expected perfect mom/wife role that she would be conveying that. On the outside, her marriage seemed perfect, but she was unhappy with an unsupportive spouse who took her for granted (and he was content to play the traditional roles to the extreme—at her expense), while completely neglecting her, and using her as a wifely sex-toy that did all the work, including child-rearing. After a few years of never giving herself breaks, being hard on herself, and never taking time for herself she was burnt out on parenting and marital martyrdom. She found herself exhausted and therefore desperate to create a real life full of meaning and hope, one that would acknowledge: her unhappiness, the subservient role she found herself married to, the

She found herself exhausted and therefore desperate to create a real life full of meaning and hope. One that would acknowledge: her unhappiness, the subservient role she found herself married to, the second and third shifts she was working, and empower her to do something about it.

second and third shifts she was working, and empower her to do something about it.

Her second child was unexpected, because shortly after having her first child she had to have an ovary removed. It was an, "Oops! You're pregnant! Hey, you aren't supposed to be able to do that! Now you are the darling of the Berkeley Infertility Community!" She was very confused with the second pregnancy and hoped her child would not be some freak of nature. She had also hoped she could mend ties with her family and they would be more involved than they had been with her first child. She yearned to have a boy (she had another girl), and wanted her life to, "Stop sucking, and not to be poor, and not to be ill and tired, and for the father to give a shit about me." She feared going through postpartum depression again which lasted for several years the first time around. [The longest medically documented case lasted for five years, and I as a mother suffered from it too, for almost four years … although more intermittent now, it seems to be persistently present form time-to-time. My doctor will disagree however, and label it just regular depression now, since my son is now older.]

With both of her daughters she practiced attachment parenting with home-birthing, breastfeeding, and wore them close to her all the time with baby-slings that were fashioned after the baby wraps of both ancient and tribal worlds. For her daughters she wishes:

> "I hope my daughters can better navigate the choppy waters of being girls in a non-girl friendly world than I have been able to. They are so smart, so I feel very good about that. But, I want them to be able to do better than I have; I want them to not be poor and alone, and pissed off at the world when they are in their thirties. I try to expose them to all sorts of experiences, music, art, dance, political protests, and gardening. I discuss the way the world works all the time. I want them to have their eyes open, to have analytical skills."

Mother Nature started realizing what she wanted out of life by communicating her newly articulated philosophies and values to her daughters, but she knew how her own life was falling short of her own developing expectations. She wanted out of the loveless marriage, and was going to stop giving so much of herself away, and letting things go (like being walked on by her spouse, and suffering her parents ridicule). She felt for so long that she didn't have any value (further complicated by postpartum depression) and let the people closest to her treat her badly. Bit-by-bit, she started listening to her inner voice/self more and gradually started doing more things for herself. She felt she kept trying and the world kept taking from her, so she decided she had to do something frank, "The one thing that this society hates most, especially from a woman and a mother, is unapologetic honesty. I had to talk and be honest." The one thing she felt the world couldn't take from her was her musical talent and she eventually used this as medium to connect to others.

Before getting to her currently successful, self-content and self-reliant point in her life she first had to complete the transitional phase. She had to find out who she was, and who she was meant to become, and if anything salvageable remained under the façade of her marriage that had been maintained for over nine years.

She was beginning to start the closure process for her marriage when she learned that she was pregnant for a third time. She had already undergone multiple surgeries for dermoid tumors in her uterus and on her ovaries, which is what originally resulted in the loss of one of her ovaries, and the prior diagnosis of infertility.

Her doctor advised her, the best case scenario was that she would grow a baby along with a tumor, have the baby, then have surgery to remove the tumor, and what was left of the half of an ovary she had. So she would have a new baby and be going through surgical menopause at the same time. The worst case scenario would be that the tumor would burst during pregnancy which could potentially kill her and the baby.

She realized she didn't want another child with her husband, especially a high risk one that threatened her very life and her being there for her daughters. Her husband refused to talk to her about any of the issues related to the pregnancy and the decisions that needed to be made, so she decided to have an abortion and scheduled the surgeries immediately to remove the fetus, and the tumor, and to save the last of her remaining ovary.

When it came time for the abortion, her husband had made no plans for childcare, or for her transportation. Even though she wasn't supposed to, she drove herself home since he failed to pick her up, or to even get her a cab. While she was recovering the first night, he was online in a Catholic singles chat room discussing the evils of abortion, *and what he had just gone through.*

Shortly, after her first surgery, she had to have the second surgery to remove the tumor. While she was in surgery, he went home to hang out in the chat room again. This time at least he showed up to pick her up. She had to have several days of bed rest and with a respirator placed down her throat. He rigged her up with some ties and bells so she could ring for him if she needed him since she couldn't speak, but he was so engaged in the chat room that after a few rings the first day he stopped coming to her aid completely.

As she got her health back she started practicing yoga, meditating, and eating macrobiotic food. Macrobiotic followers view the world in terms of yin and yang and they eliminate all foods and substances that are not whole, or in its natural state, or that is processed, toxic, or animal-cruelty based, like meat, from their diet. Mother Nature's goal now was to build a healthy life for herself and her children that focused on holistic naturalness. It was around this time her husband started having an affair with a woman he met in the Catholic Single's chat room. They divorced five months later.

Prior to the surgeries, and all the changes she made in her (and her children's) lives, she suffered a great deal from Post Traumatic Stress Syndrome, depression and borderline A.D.D. (Attention Deficit Disorder). She still battles with those issues, but they are becoming less frequent and severe as she learns to let go of stresses and things beyond her control, and to just love herself a little more day-by-day,

"I can't get over the whole not-being-wanted thing. Sometimes I have a hard time feeling that I have a right to breathe. I feel that I have to earn everything that I don't deserve anything. I don't feel that way about my kids—they deserve the best the world has to offer, but myself? Other times I get really pissed off that I, amongst all these other human beings, do not deserve to breathe, to live. And then I write pissy songs and shave my hair into a mohawk, and TAKE. When I perform I scream that I am alive, that I deserve not only to be alive, but to be feared, and listened to, and worshiped!"

Another reason she embraced a more natural way of life is because she is allergic to most western medicines. The philosophies behind living naturally are more peaceful and earth-friendly than the current Western-consumer-medicated, over-stressed lifestyles that dominates the average U.S. American. Mother Nature feels that, "The Earth is alive and she is pissed. She'll shake us off, soon enough." This way of life, also led her and a friend to starting a natural non-chemical cleaning company.

"I clean other people's toilets for a living. I started this biz about three years ago, with a friend. We were both fat and getting depressed cuz we were poor and had to eat poor people food. So I thought about what we could do to lose weight, and make money and not be depressed. She and I had cleaned before, for her ex-girlfriend, so I suggested starting a cleaning company together. She only cleaned one house with me, and I just kept doing it myself. It's not rocket surgery, but you do have to run it like a business, even if you're running it under the table.

I advertise every week (even though I am over-booked right now). I follow up with every prospect, I show up for all my appointments, I do a good job and I charge a fair price. It's a great business for single moms, for subversive types, or for people who don't want to deal with the man anymore. Start-up costs are low, and you hardly have to maintain any inventory, I have one small closet where I maintain all my supplies.

I am like a cheap visiting therapist for my clients. They don't care what color my hair is, just as long as their house looks good when I'm done. I do get to go into some of the most beautiful homes around the area, and make them more beautiful. There are many, many resources for starting a cleaning business and for getting good quality earth-friendly and people-friendly supplies. There are books and websites devoted to how to do it right."

If you're interested in going eco-friendly for your cleaning needs in your home, or starting your own business, you can check out these awesome sites: DeliciousOrganics.com, *GreenCleanBook.com*, or make them yourself at: *TheGreenGuide.org/article/diy/household.* You can learn more about natural living at: *MotherEarthNews.com*, and natural mothering at: *Mothering.com.*

She hopes to expand the business to include three full-time employees so that she can have more time for her band, instead of being a musician with a full-time day job. Right now, she does everything from being a full-time worker, musician and a mother. She receives no help or support from her family, or her kids "dead-beat dad." Being a single mom is hard, especially financially, and her kids get to see, "The good, the bad, and the ugly of life." She doesn't sugar-coat life, because she wants to prepare her daughters for the world, and hopes they will be more enabled to make better choices, with more wisdom and knowledge, than she did when growing up and into her own.

Want to go green for your cleaning needs? Or start your own cleaning business?

Check out these awesome sites! DeliciousOrganics.com, ***GreenCleanBook.com*, or make them yourself at: *TheGreenGuide.org /article /diy/ household.***

Learn more about natural living at: *MotherEarthNews.com*, and natural mothering at: *Mothering.com.*

When she started over, she was shocked to find her prior world (of submissive marriage, and conformity-authoritarian parenting) was the actual real world. She had expected her prior life to be the exception, not the rule:

> "This society hates children. This society hates mothers. I can't figure out which is more hated. My neighbor across the street thinks it's all about misogyny, and especially fear and hatred of the sexually mature woman—the opposite of the cult of virginity. Children are proof of a woman's sexual maturity.
>
> I, however, tend to think we are a society that hates ourselves. The people on the top see the rest of us as objects (think Babs Bush at the Astrodome) either to be

used, or moved about. Children are more objects to be controlled, a nuisance. If they are lucky, the people at the top, they can get us to spend all of our money buying shit for our kids, so we stay poor and indebted, and easy to control. But children, take parents away from the work force, makes us more in touch with being human, makes us less easy to control, so that's bad.

Mothers are the source of children. Women who become mothers become decision makers, and that's bad for people who want to control us. So, we, mothers, must be controlled. They tell everyone that mothers are icky in some way, not too bright, overbearing, irrational, etc. So, we can tell things to our kids, but not to the world at large. Of course, this means that if we, mothers, break through that wall, we can come into our full potential as human beings.

I had no idea it [motherhood and society] would suck so bad. I thought I'd find, or create, a loving, caring community. I didn't realize just how much of a child-hating society we live in. I've tried living in shared housing, with other single moms, joining L.L.L. (La Leche League), the P.T.A, the Girl Scouts, everything. The only place where I get any sense of that I'm somehow okay and accepted is in the freaky arts community. I mean real artists, not family funded pot-head poseurs.

It's okay though. It's the return to being a freaky artist myself that's very nice. People dig that I do my thing and have kids at the same time, and there's no artificial separation between the two. I think the marginalizing of artists in our society goes right along with the marginalizing of mothers and children. I think that separating artists from children and expecting artists to just hang out with other adults and to be unhealthy and chemically dependent, creates this ACHE for contact with healthy aspects of human existence—and children tend to be rather healthy."

She found a home in the Bay Area arts community for her and her children that contradicted the rest of the world. People, even some outsiders, started listening to their gut feelings, became brave, and they started standing up for themselves and for others. The world changed a little for the better. The cooperative she is part of is called the Otherworld and is based in Oakland, California. It's a small world and Mother Nature gets to go to great art-friendly pro-Oakland places like the coffee shop Momma Buzz.

She has turned to other artists and has developed close friendships with them, and they have helped influence her life, as well as helped fill the dad-less void for the children by becoming surrogate aunts and uncles.

A friend of hers, Lolo Shantung, a performance artist now living in Mexico, was such a mentor. Lolo doesn't have kids by choice, but loved Mother Nature's daughters and did parental-type activities with them, such as getting Chinese food on weekends, taking them to Fairy Land (and even advising and offering help to runaway teen friends of her daughter's). There are many other friend-family members that are a big part of their lives and vice versa, and the most important thing is that her kids know that, "There are people around who care about them. I encourage my kids to build their own relationships with adults I'm cool with."

Mother Nature is concerned with some of the problems this art community has, like most others, which is its reliance on drugs, and the "Provincial, emotional attachment to Burning Man as the 'neat thing' to do or be a part of, and the poseur element."

There is a societal expectation for artists to be self-destructive, as if that gets them in touch with their emotions and creativity, similar to the notion that to be a female poet or artist, you have to be suicidal and weak, a.k.a. Sylvia Plath, or Anne Sexton. Both of these notions are sick cultural myths that have disempowered potential artists making them mere commodities with lesser impact, to be awed at as weekend amusement, or simply in a college textbook in a classroom.

Mother Nature does point out that there are a larger number of artists that are healthy though, and it's a definite plus for her to be hanging out with them. She and her kids get to see their work, and more importantly their works-in-progress. Many artists have rejected the self-destructive role that is expected of them to focus on the act of creation—which in itself is "addictive and satisfying."

Another thing that perturbs her about art and society is:

> "The society that we live in is very sick, I mean ill. The so-called patriarchy is just a symptom of a bigger problem. The fact that we don't support the arts at all, I mean, there's no viable artist class, means that we don't value our own humanity. We are so detached from our spiritual purpose. We are killing ourselves.
>
> Don't watch TV, or read the newspaper, or even peep at the ads on the computer or play video games, or go the movies for a month. Read books, draw, cook good

food and hang out with your friends. Then, turn on the evening news. Not a sitcom, not Kung Fu Theater, but the evening news. And you will get a shock about how bad things are. Humans are sensitive things. When we see death and violence and hatred all the time, we absorb it and it kills us."

Through our numerous computer interactions, brief phone talk, and the very cool Placenta package Mother Nature sent me, I gleefully conclude that the thought process behind her art is … the unique lens in which she views the world and interacts with it. Mother Nature's approach to living and looking at the world is in an artistic manner. Stop and think about it for a minute—it's a truly divine and radical concept. It also makes for good songwriting. It further explains why her projected image frequents between Marilyn-esqe rocker and a Mohawk Momma. She is always changing, and her mindset fluctuates between aggressive/outspoken and introspective/contemplative; it's also suggestive of her sexual nature: combatively sexy.

She keeps a book on 20th Century Art in her bathroom for quick moments of solitude and inspiration. She looks to others to help enrich her life (and she returns the favor) and finds the most love from friends who are artists, authors, spoken word artists, dancers, poets, musicians, hair stylists, and fashionistas. For her, their lives capture the element of human sensitivity, contrasting so many who live with it diminished by greed, corruption, strife or struggle. Inadvertently, they have the potential to impact others profoundly, because they live colorfully and boldly (despite who and what society tells them they should/shouldn't be, and what they should/shouldn't value).

In her world, she doesn't spend a lot of time worrying about the newest technologies, or whether her social class will reject her. She spends her time just trying to survive and beyond that making art to give her life dimension and meaning. Mother Nature also uses this perspective to shape her parenting and the relationships she builds with her children:

"We talk a lot about how the world is. My folks never analyzed anything; they never broke anything down for me. I try to talk to my kids about advertising and corporations and the government vs. art and breathing. I try to tell them how much the system tries (and succeeds!) to control us. I try to tell them how hard, yet important, it is to try to be yourself in a world that hates individuality. I guess I won't know the final impact until they are older."

Mother Nature participates in subversive political activism in which she involves her kids. They will illegally sticker up public places with political slogans and band stickers late at night. For her and her kids, it's just something they do (and that she does), like gardening, the kids coming with her to band practice, and seeing her band play. It's family-time, Mother Nature style.

Her family specializes in running social experiments that range from running around a really posh shopping center dressed as Mrs. Claus, two weeks after Xmas, or she and the kids will videotape themselves cutting in line at the grocery store. One of their favorite routines is telling people that their 85lb. Pit-Bull is a Chihuahua. They have run fake ads on Craigslist, or they will make flyers for an event that doesn't exist and put them around town. The family likes juxtapositions of the expected and the unexpected, but all with a social purpose: to question what you presume you know to be truth or reality.

They like to bring to light the oddity of social expectations, and to have fun while doing it. Why is it weird to dress like Mrs. Claus after Xmas, but not during? You're still dressing like someone else, so what's the problem? People don't react negatively to Mrs. Claus during the holiday season, but they don't like seeing her run around any other time of the year. Why are we limited to dressing in costume on only certain dates like Halloween, or for special occasions? Who wrote these rules, and why? And who said we have to obey them?

Mother Nature more poignantly expands the juxtaposition to illustrate that you are expected to behave with manners and consideration in public, but it is okay for your employers to treat you badly and disrespect you, or for our government to bomb and kill people. Some people that her family has pulled the 85lb. dog switch gag on have actually started to believe her. It shows the power of propaganda, or marketing, or myth, or stereotype, that if you tell someone a lie over and over, even when showing them the truth, they will believe the deception. Her anarchist beliefs and life are at the core of her writing. She has written pieces for zines like *Hip Mama*, and *Slingshot*, which is an anarchist newsletter.

Hip Mama is an awesome online and print magazine whose audience is the marginalized momma, and whose aim is to provide support, debate, discussion, inspiration, and sharing. It was started by Ariel Gore (another righteous Rebel Mom in this book) in 1993 as a school project that evolved and blossomed. You can check out the online version at: *HipMama.com.*

Slingshot contains very profound reading, ideas for inspiration, and engages you in active critical thinking and living. Most of the articles reflect a need for community building instead of community breaking down, which is why Mother Nature, as well as myself and many other readers, like Slingshot so much. For example, one article by a writer named Breezy asks the question: If eating disorders are largely the result of how woman are depicted in the media as having an ideal dress size of five or less, but yet most women aren't, what causes the media to portray women this way knowing it hurts them? And why do women strive to be that, even if they have to hurt themselves to achieve it? The answer simply is capitalistic: profit and control. If people buy things to make themselves feel better, because marketing makes them feel bad, it's a cycle that continuously repeats itself. This is just one example of many subjects that the zine scrutinizes. The newsletter not only asks the question, and logically analyzes the answers, but collectively brainstorms for viable solutions to the problems that everyday people can participate in, which is why Mother Nature likes the writing for them, in addition to its hands on

Slingshot contains profound reading, ideas for inspiration, and engages you in active critical thinking and living. Most of the articles reflect a need for community-building, instead of community breaking-down. Check out the magazine at: Slingshot.Tao.CA.

And for the momma-in-you check out HipMama.com!

anarchist approach. You can check out the magazine at: *Slingshot. Tao.CA.*

Her kids get a certain amount of street credit for having the mom with a pink/green/yellow mohawk. Now that the kids are older, twelve and fifteen, they are becoming aware that not everyone's parents, "have friends who are transgender, not everyone goes to anti-war protests, not everyone has amplifiers and guitars all over the house."

Mother Nature feels her oldest daughter is pushing herself really hard to not be like mom, and doesn't want to be defined by a punk rock way of life (which is mom's personality/ lifestyle). Her oldest daughter shuns shaved heads, and bright colors, but she thinks about what is going on around her. She is blossoming into a naturalistic, non-aggressive, nature-oriented intellectual who has an anarchist way of living. The youngest daughter used to occasionally ask, *"Why can't we be just like everyone else?"* She understands now the fact that most people lose their true sense of identity when they start seeking approval by fitting in, or become numbed to the mainstream, or commercial, way of life including its indulgences and ingredients (excesses, exploitations and cruelty), but she still yearns to fit in and minimize adversity. This is a basic yearning we all have, teenagers or not, to fit in, be loved and be accepted; but at what price? That is the adage Mother Nature is instilling in her girls.

Mother Nature is, "An old Punk Rocker, the girl that never fit in, the sensitive artist, the genius with weird hair and a leather jacket." She didn't intend on not being part of the crowd, she just never was part of it. She fell into the counterculture life because public policy and commercialism disturbs her, so naturally that's where she belongs,

> "I don't live the way I do because I think it's cool or because I have wealthy parents to support me and against whom I rebel. I'm sort of here by default. I am married to a gay man from Taiwan so he gets a tax break, and I get medical and dental for my kids. I have Amerasian (Fil-Am) kids. I front a rock band. My kids take hip-hop dance and watch Anime. I have stretched earlobes and green-yellow-pink hair.

I am poor and I am not trying to get rich. I don't watch TV or read the paper. I don't pay much attention to celebrity gossip. I swear like a sailor. I was a sailor. I write articles for anarchist papers and counterculture parenting zines. I'm starting a counterculture zine. I dumpster dive, I mean, I drive around the back of any building where I'm about to go shopping before I go in—and I sidewalk dive. I make stuff instead of buying it. I am crafty, but I never use kits to make crafts.

I am a performance artist. I am the woman who had a home birth—who had two, and who filed a complaint against the second midwife for emotional abuse, who breastfed, who tandem breastfed, who breastfed toddlers. I am the woman who got her earlobes stretched as a celebration of turning thirty. I am the woman who left a physically, verbally, financially, and sexually abusive partner after nine years of putting up with his shit.

I was an unwanted pregnancy. I started a movement of mom rockers. I've had national and international press attention. I still have a hard time getting my band booked locally. I made the lead singer of Green Day pay full retail for one of my band tee-shirts. I wrote a song about his brother the school janitor.

I collect blue willow china and mismatched sterling silver. I make quilts. I read to my kids. I wish I were famous. Then I read about fame and I'm glad I'm not. But I still wish I were. I look like Marilyn Monroe, but I scream and groan and yell and belt it onstage. I hate crowds unless I am performing in front of them. I just live sort of sideways from the rest of society. I can't seem to fit into the usual little boxes, so I gave up. That's the thing; I gave up trying to fit in!"

In addition to playing in a band, writing and mothering, she also loves gardening and blogging. She paints furniture, and on the side teaches violin lessons. One thing she is really proud of, that she feels is very significant is creating human life inside her body, twice. Mother Nature has always been frustrated by the roles that are set forth for women, especially the one that says you're supposed to be a coveted virgin, who teases, or a slut who pleases/who asks for it, then later a mother/wife who is a saintly nun who lives only for that purpose. Her very nature, persona, and values reject and defy those notions:

"Motherhood rocks; you fuck someone, then you create a human being inside your body, then you help that human become the best person that he or she can be. What sucks about motherhood is the bullshit expectation that we, moms, are supposed to become bland, sexless doormats the minute we give birth—through our sex organs, hello! And our decision-making should be limited to just what kind of fucking peanut butter we buy for our children!"

She doesn't know a lot of moms like herself with the exception of her band-mates (to whom she turns to for support as well as her non-parent friends within the music and art scene that she lives in). She definitely feels that we (sub/counterculture mothers) negotiate things on our own terms, and "Teach our children to differentiate between messages that come from within ourselves and the relentless messages from Big Brother." She feels counterculture mothers/parents teach our children to see what others consider to be trash as raw material for art, decoration, and for living. Most importantly, she thinks we teach our children by example, and that it is possible to live a meaningful life without buying a bunch of junk.

Mother Nature thinks kindness and openness is warranted for all moms towards one another and valuable insights can be shared amongst ourselves regardless if they are mainstream or not:

"Mothering, loving our children, that crosses all kinds of boundaries. We can learn how we all have similar fears, but they buy things to assuage their fears while we, do what we do. Maybe we can teach them to walk away from messages telling them they suck, or that we suck. I have a cleaning client who is very well-to-do and looks to have married the 'perfect' man and has a new baby, and I'll be damned if she isn't moving away from the mainstream idea of distancing herself from her baby (to teach him 'independence') and moving toward attachment parenting. And she consults me about it, because she sees that because I do it, it can work. That's my tiny bit of influence."

Being a mother is a common ground amongst women that can bring them closer instead of further apart; however, Mother Nature herself knows sometimes you aren't able to connect with someone who is, "Trying hard to fit some sort of an idea; they're doing what they consider best to do." She knows they (mainstream moms) love their kids, and that they are doing what they feel they must to survive. Sometimes they may "freak out" about how she lives her life, but she doesn't trip on how they live theirs, even when they are intent on spending an excessive amount of money on their kids.

She normally conceals herself around mainstream people because there generally isn't a point in talking about things beyond casual conversation. She has come to this conclusion based on previous reactions. She can have meaningful conversations about age appropriate behavior, or parenting concerns, without delving into the counterculture too much, but if she becomes semi-personal, or close with a mainstream mother her true identity will emerge, and the conversations become real and meaningful.

Mother Nature hopes through her band Placenta more moms will become radical activists for change not only for the future of their children, but for themselves. It is in this ideal that she feels the bridge between moms can strengthen since humanity is something we all hold sacred, and feel it is worth fighting for, and the Earth worth saving.

She is now thirty-nine-years-old, and in so many ways feels like her life has just begun again, and she is hell-bent on ruling the world and taking over,

"I want World Domination through Rock 'n' Roll!!! On the mom tip, I'm preparing my kids for college and life beyond. I'm teaching them to become entrepreneurs so they don't have to work shit jobs in college. I'm teaching them not to expect that a man will come along and make everything wonderful. I am doing this by dating every asshole on the face of the planet, apparently. Just kidding, but I'm trying to move forward with my band, writing more pieces, more magazine articles about being a mom and a rocker, and how that is in direct conflict with the imposed societal views about motherhood, as well as rock music."

Hell Yeah!

"I'm on a constant search for the truth and happiness in the endless piles of bullshit."

Nana
Vixen Vegetarian
Recycled Art Gardner
Upright Bass Player for Sik-Luv
Rad and Rocking Mom
Palo Alto, California.

Nana is the songstress (with a pleasantly pinched vocal timbre that hangs above her bands guitar and slap-bass rhythms) and rowdy upright bass player for the incredible band Sik Luv (deeper-pitched modern rockabilly with a hint of Mars madness) from the West Coast. She is the gregarious mother of Manny, an amazing budding musician himself, who is eight-years-old.

Nana is also a leader in community activism in Oakland with her socially-infused recycled art gardening efforts.

Nana's day starts off very busy at 5:00 A.M. She gets Manny up for school, and then prepares herself for her work day as the Garden Coordinator for the Palo Alto School District. Her weeks quickly hurdle into the weekends, which are filled with Manny-time, playing shows with her band, gardening, and hanging out with her fabulous new boyfriend, a vegetarian chef for Facebook. (Nana didn't give his name to keep it private—she is very private about her personal life—it took me over a year to convince her to let me interview her for the book!) He also has a daughter the same age as Manny. Besides her boyfriend and her son, her heroes are Barack Obama and Howard Stern.

She gets down to 70s Elvis, feels deeply with Tom Waits, and laughs with George Carlin. Her favorite movie is the *Fight Club*, and she scrutinizes the intentions of the world at large through the lens of the infamous line from the movie, "*Advertising has us chasing cars and clothes, working jobs we hate so we can buy shit we don't need.*"

Nana and her son Manny are vegetarians. Manny has been raised as an earth-conscious vegetarian since infancy, and Nana herself became one at the tender age of seventeen. She was searching for answers to the big questions in life. She related to the information that she got in the mail from PETA (People for the Ethical Treatment of Animals). "Everything seemed so screwed up in the world. Animal rights and the end of animal brutality made sense to me. I found some answers I needed *in not eating* animals." Like most kids Manny is a finicky eater, and frequently claims to be allergic to vegetables, but can't get enough of the soy hot dogs. He is also very sensitive to the mistreatment of animals, especially poor and homeless animals trapped in the confines of the city.

Being vegetarians is one way of giving Manny (and the world) a shot at a better life. The other part Nana planned out was moving from Oakland to Palo Alto when she accepted a recent job offer as the school district garden coordinator. She wanted her son in a better school district and this was her ticket. The position, which sounds like a dream job, is of course fraught with difficulties including: limited budgets, no school input, and lack of district communication, feedback and involvement. So she flies solo at the schools with a small budget and tries to get teacher and student/parent involvement at the schools, so that the gardens are a lasting success.

Nana loves gardening and being a mother—but without one, she wouldn't have found the other. It was as a new mom that she found gardening and that gave her a real defined sense of purpose,

> "Moms were staring at me after I had my son. I didn't know what the fuck I was doing—taking him home alone, and I didn't know any moms. I started gardening in the backyard, and it changed my life. I ended up starting a community garden across the street in the vacant lot, and it grew so huge, so fast. People were getting involved, tons of parents and kids. There's a playground now too."

Manny has been raised as an earth-conscious vegetarian, and Nana herself became one at the age of seventeen. She was searching for answers to the big questions in life. She related to the information that she got in the mail from PETA.

"Everything seemed so screwed up in the world. Animal rights and the end of animal brutality made sense to me. I found some answers I needed in not eating animals."

Although Nana has moved out of Oakland, she is still involved with the community garden and playground she started there. The Oakland community keeps pulling together to take care of it. Oakland holds her best memories. She misses home so much that she wrote a kick-ass song about it, and it's my personal favorite Sik Luv song.

Nana moved to Oakland in the early 1990s when she was

eighteen, and made a life for herself as a Gilman St. Punk. She felt alive and awakened by Gilman St.'s activist community and anti-establishment decree. She was involved with many of the bands that played there including Blitz, Rancid, and Green Day. She worked at the venue as well. When she feels alone and needs inspiration, she pulls out her Gilman St. memories to revitalize her commitment to doing things right and with meaning. The spark that attracted her to the subculture scene, and that shaped who she is, became a driving force for her life: seeking truth. For the first time she felt like was being told the truth about things.

> "I always thought everybody was full of shit. From the dead dog lying on the beach, to grandma dying and no one wanted to talk about this stuff and then I heard Jello Biafra (from the Dead Kennedys) and everybody was unsettled and wanted to know more—why weren't we being told the truth?"

Although she lives in Palo Alto now, she goes to Oakland every few months to check on friends, the garden, and to hang out at the Gilman St. Venue (the longest opened independent music venue in U.S. history—1984 to current; it's a volunteer run venue and non-profit). She still sees a majority of the same people hanging out and helping run things that were there in the beginning. After having Manny, she also started having community vegetarian BBQs and was teaching the kids about respecting the Earth through fun garden workshops. It was very natural, the kids responded excitedly to it, and Nana worked her magic with them. This is why she misses Oakland so much; the heart of Oakland is raw, energetic, and organic. Palo Alto is the opposite with its historic Craftsmen homes, and very smooth, planned urban existence. Palo Alto is perfection, and Oakland is fused with spontaneous and diverse activity. Parents tend to have a more holistic connection to children in artfully spontaneous environments and Nana has observed that the parents in her new neighborhood miss this connection by replacing it with artificial means of avoidance (toys, electronic gadgets, etc, instead of time nourishment and hands-on involvement).

Nana learned she was going to be a mom while working as a bike messenger in Oakland. She was so surprised; that she had the dispatcher at work call her then-husband and tell him he had to come pick her up—she was pregnant! She suddenly felt both euphoric and frozen in time. She felt that she couldn't ride her bike anymore, the traffic frightened her, and she didn't want anything to happen to the life inside of her. She was literally a walking 'bike' messenger for seven months thereafter.

Manny's father and she were ecstatic. Their relationship was both passionate and relaxed. Their lives literally lived and thrived on the moment and enjoying simple pleasures and parties. This was something they wanted to do together, and it seemed like the perfect time …

> "We were both really excited. We both wanted to home school him, and he was going to work, and I was going to be at home with our son all the time. But the relationship turned out being so bad. I have had to be very adaptable to the situation since it turned out differently than planned."

During her pregnancy Nana kept a journal of her daily thoughts, hopes and plans, and was looking forward to becoming a mother. But she couldn't shake her fear of not knowing what she was doing. She felt she should be the last person on the earth to take care of a baby, although she really wanted to. She just resigned herself to be open to the unknown, and learn as much as she could.

At the time it felt like the right thing to do, and hence Manny was born. Her family and friends were very supportive, although they didn't think the dad-to-be was the best choice in a mate or a father, but she ignored their obligatory warnings and dived right in to love and parenting. She didn't realize until afterwards that maybe she didn't choose the right person to do it with after all. Nana and Manny's father tried everything to make it work from following the old-school marriage tradition of sticking-it-out to the new-school co-parenting ex-spouses sharing a divided living space. Nothing worked.

"When we finally divorced, there were lots of drugs involved and he (Manny's dad) wouldn't clean up. I was sick of it. We had done several rounds of him cleaning up and us trying to make it as a couple/family again and it just didn't work out. Even after calling it quits, we still tried to co-parent in a house he owned when Manny was almost two, and we were always clashing and screaming. He was still intrusive even though we were divorced. Now we co-parent from different and separate living spaces, and it's great."

During the interview when Nana said "it's great" about living separately from her ex-and co-parenting, her voice was shrill with exasperation and imbued with laughter. She has a great sense of humor and a witty sarcasm that burns a little while doing down, think a whiskey on the rocks. However, in order for her to stay positive with an unchangeable situation, she must find humor in the irony of it. Nana cannot stand her ex's parenting style (something from a 1950s sitcom, but without the balanced TV temperament) and she doesn't like Manny being around his older half-sister. Manny spends most of his weekends with his dad, since Nana has him during the week. Manny's dad believes in parental corporal punishment and spanking, Nana on the other hand does not. Nana also disapproves of her ex's lack of exertion in controlling his older daughter's abusive and physical attacks on the smaller and younger Manny. She says her ex simply dismisses it as sibling behavior and thus acceptable.

Nana tries to install logic and reason into her parenting with Manny, which is the opposite of his father's,

"I want him to know the reactions of what he chooses to do, but for some reason it is hard—to raise him around good people, and raise him to be a good person while being comfortable with himself and vocal. I want him to appreciate the smaller things in life, and the special moments that occur each day that we don't notice out of habit anymore. It's the small moments that make life."

One word of advice she offers all new parents is to remember what it is like to be small. She learned this the hard way when Manny was a baby and he rolled off the bed. She wants to spare you this lesson. Some additional insight is: the P.T.A. will never take you seriously.

She has seven years under her belt now as a mom, but still faces difficulties and challenges, largely from others ostracizing her. Where she most expected support, from punk moms, she found none. Her conclusion is that the rawness, openness, and challenge to society that was the basis of the early punk scene, seems to be pretty much forgotten amongst the newest generation of. The focus now seems to be all tattoos and trends—major label red carpet, ala carte commercialism. There is a 'punk' mom whose son attends one of the schools she gardens for and acting out of camaraderie Nana reached out to her and greeted her. The 'punk' mom looked her up and down *(As if she, the 'punk mom' was in Beverly Hills 90210.)* and dismissed her. She added insult to injury by turning her back on Nana and just walking off. Nana was initially shocked and enraged, but after stewing on it, shrugged it off as what happens when the real thing becomes a buyable commodity—rock glamour, packaged goods, a fashion trend, etc. Nana's school mom is the outcome of a water-downed version of punk becoming just fashion for the masses.

Speaking of assholes though, one thing though that never gets easier though for Nana is people looking down on her for not having enough money:

> "The less money you have, the more people look down at you, and especially if you are a single mom. I snapped at a cashier (who obviously felt very high-up on the social-standing scale) who snickered at me for using food stamps to pay for our food. I screamed at her—I do pretty damn good here, can you give me a break?"

Like most work that is essential and beneficial to kids (and society), it's grossly underpaid. Although her title is very impressive and implies that it would be high-paying, it's not. She doesn't make enough take home after-taxes to make ends meet and put food on the table. It's not a matter of lack of wealth in this country; it's a matter of distribution, period. When, and if, the tax (and social) infrastructure changes to be more socially equitable, those of us who do essential work may actually get paid for what it is really worth. But Nana is prepared for the last laugh on capitalism (and in line with her green parenting philosophy),

> "Even with capitalism collapsing, people are still refusing to learn how to just do things for themselves, and if people just took care of their own shit instead of living in a throw-away society, then maybe. With global warming, and rising water levels, it is expected for California to be swallowed. And no one is doing anything about it. When everybody else panics and the Stanford Scholars are swallowed, I will be in Arizona at my greenhouse. I took some courses on ecology at the San Jose State University, and the professor there said it's too late to save the state (and maybe the world), save yourself. A while back I bought some empty land in Arizona, on eBay, with the intent to build a green house with solar panels and composting toilets, etc. I plan on gradually migrating Manny and myself there and building it. You know, it's great to see all these people buying green products, but they are still driving everywhere. I feel privileged to see the world come to an end, so I will build our green house away from California, and just have fun in life …"

And to top it all off, from class polarization, to so-called punk moms rejecting her because of lack of wealth/social-standing, and the end of the world looming—the P.T.A. still won't take her seriously and mocks her. She had blue highlights in her hair, and the P.T.A. ignored her input and what she wanted to see achieved at the school—and this is with her being the *School District Garden Coordinator*! Nana even dyed her hair black, 'normalizing' herself so that they would take her seriously, and they didn't; they treated her same. Her motto is the P.T.A. is a pain-in-the-ass. I second that—they are self-defeating when they act like privileged cliquey-CEO-Queens (It took four schools before I met a man on the P.T.A. board) and run the association as if it was an invite only private social club. It's dehumanizing, and I conclude that, that is the point so moms *like me and Nana* feel excluded and therefore won't participate; if they are lucky, ha-ha. We aren't wanted because we are not like them, nor are we in the same upper tax bracket as the majority of P.T.A. CEO-Queens we have encountered and tried to work with. Classism + Egoism=Most P.T.A's.

As a parent Nana has had to face a lot of battles, some expected and some not. When Manny was diagnosed with A.D.H.D. (Attention Deficit Hyperactivity Disorder) it took her by surprise, but it helped explain his constant behaviors. She hasn't placed him on medicine, because she questions its effectiveness and from her research concludes it isn't warranted. The benefits (if any) would be outweighed by its harmfulness. She watches his diet and limits his sugar and she ensures that his refined/processed food intake is minimal, because of the physical reactions he has to it. (Plus, it's not healthy for any of us!) She also has to remind him to keep on top of things. She will send him to go brush his teeth for school, and instead she will find him playing finger puppets. He has a tutor that comes to help him with lessons once a week, but to make his education successful, with A.D.H.D, and with no medicine, his education has to incorporate movement breaks and exploring outside. Nana wishes she could afford to, or had the resources, to home-school him. It took her three years to get his school to meet her halfway concerning Manny and adhere to the I.E.P. meeting (Intervention Education Program) guidelines, and for him to get some support and intervention/adjustment in learning, and for her to get some understanding.

> "Most teachers think that children are meant to sit in a desk for four hours and not move. A child without A.D.H.D. can't do this—or one with! Most districts have school health counseling for kids with special needs that can help get the classroom adapted to be beneficial to the child with different needs. You just have to keep pushing them. The school psychologist kept blowing me off and I finally had to raise my voice to get a response back."

Her final words of advice (on dealing with schools and children's needs) are: be brave and remember your doing this for your kid, and the children of others. This is just another reason for them to ignore you—don't let them.

Besides Manny and animal rights, the other thing that Nana is very passionate about is her seductive [my word—I love upright basses and the female curvature] mauveine pink upright bass.

Nana grew up in a musical household, so it's no surprise that she picked up musical playing later in life. She also has passed down the generational love of music to Manny. Growing up, her house was always full on the weekends with relatives getting together playing music, cooking and singing. Her dad, who plays guitar and harp, bought her an acoustic guitar for her seventh birthday, and as an avid KISS fan, she was disappointed. Her young motto was, "Electric guitars rock, acoustics do not." She didn't embrace the lure of acoustic strings until she was twenty-five.

> "It never really occurred to me until then that I could do it. My friend had an upright bass and I was encouraged to play. I bought one and would occasionally play. When I was contacted by a guy on Myspace who needed an upright bass player for his band, I just stopped thinking about it and did it."

The story behind her joining Sik Luv is one filled with both humor and pain. She had only a few weeks to learn the songs, and her ex was helping to teach her how to play. (Manny's dad is a drummer and multi-instrument musician.) During this process she broke her ankle in a roller derby match (She did a brief stint as derby girl to break the isolation surrounding her as a new parent.) and had to figure out how to learn her bass lines on the upright, while being bedridden. She literally just brought her bass into bed and got comfy. She taught herself all the needed jump bass lines by ear, and ironically the broken ankle gave her the time to learn all the songs in a compact period.

Her band has been on-and-off-again now for a couple of years, but she loves playing and it definitely gives her the breaks that she needs as a mom. The Cramps are the largest influence on the band, and although

"A whiplash collision of whiskey, heartache and hellfire, fueled by the passions of love and hate."

Check out Rebel Mom Nana's band Sik Luv at: Myspace.com/SikLuv!

it's branded as rockabilly, she doesn't feel this niche defines her, she just wants to do her own thing. The band now has back-up singers, the Cold Hearted Dames, which add to the allure, and adds a demure outer vocal layer, but for Nana it's about having fun, and having fun with her upright.

Sik Luv has played with notorious bands and acts such as: the Meteors, Devil Doll and Chop Tops. They have gotten some excellent reviews by the press, ranging from, "*Roots based rockabilly at the speed of punk*" (writer unknown), to *"Greased up horror-rock, with Nana hitting the upright bass like it owes her money,"* by reviewer Ryan Osterbeck. Even the infamous director of *Pink Flamingo* and *Crybaby*, John Waters, has stopped by to check them out, and James Hetfield of Metallica is a huge fan. But I think their self-description of the band being, *"A whiplash collision of whiskey, heartache and hellfire, fueled by the passions of love and hate,"* sums them up the best.

Nana's favorite show with the band, thus far, was the Creepshow Peepshow. It was a Halloween show in July! There was a big fake meat grinder with meat hooks in back, and she was picking up members of the audience and putting them in the faux grinder and fake blood and guts were flying out everywhere. There was one girl she did this too, and the guy holding her up didn't realize it was all fake and literally freaked out. She felt like GG Allen at a Blood and Zombies dressed up affair, and loved every minute of it.

They have an (incredible!) album out and you can hear songs at their website on Myspace.com/SikLuv.

Manny loves going to band practice with mom, and also playing his drum set at his dad's house. (Manny is now on his second drum set after thrashing the first one his dad gave him at age two.) Manny is also a gifted singer who is now taking a vocal class and learning and signing opera. Manny's life is well-balanced with lots of love, music, Star-Wars, dinosaurs, family, and veggie dogs. And Nana wouldn't have it any other way.

Her future goals include creating a fun vegetarian cookbook for kids and a kid-friendly philosophical gardening book, "I think about what happens when action and reaction happens, and I totally get it. That's why I want to teach kids the web of life with through good food and gardens." But for the summer, all she wants to do is spend time with her son and boyfriend, and take a much needed break from planting seeds and playing music.

Hear, Hear!

"There aren't enough of us out there, women in music. We must realize that we can do it. This business is a 'man's' world. But that can change."

Jenise
Renegade Rocker
Righteous Mother
Record Label Promoter
Band and Venue Booking Agent
Buddhist
Detroit, Michigan.

Jenise is a divorced mom to three amazing children, one is an adult, and two are teenagers. She is a free spirit that works in the music industry. She has always been into the punk and rockabilly scenes, and she loves everything from Gene Vincent to 7-Seconds.

She is a Buddhist that loves reading the writings of monk's from various cultures and ways of life, from European to Oriental. Her favorite book is the *Siddhartha* by Herman Hesse. She collects Tibetan art, which she finds soulful, powerful, and soothing.

Music, mothering, and Buddhism have helped her survive an abusive marriage, stay strong through a lover-related kidnapping of her child, a rape attack and health problems. Her friends always comment on how, "She just takes life as it is and stays positive, just grabbing the beast, or bull by the horns," and how she lives life with a sense of humor. She keeps her friends and family close to her, while they all share and provide each other with a strong, loving support network for one another. Jenise describes one of her foremost priorities as, "The happiness of those who are closest to me, that doesn't just include my kids."

Jenise has never been someone to take no for an answer, and that attitude is what has kept her going, and also has allowed her to make a career as a venue and band booking agent in the music industry; despite the fact that the industry prefers women who are docile, eye candy, or pleasure objects. The music industry is known for not wanting strong, viable women *(i.e., women who aren't here to turn men on)* as part of the show, nonetheless running it.

She fell into the music industry on accident. She was selling merchandise for a band at a local event and she met a guy who became one of her closest friends, but also introduced her into working in the music field. He taught her the ropes and she gradually went from selling merchandise for bands to booking their shows. This was a comfortable transition from participant/fan to insider for her, since she has always been involved, at least on some level, behind the music scenes of punk and rockabilly. These musical cultures/genres have always felt like a home for her, filled with loving and hard-working people, despite the sexism and youthism that is common place.'

Jenise acknowledges the lack of women in the music world, and that disparity is even more pronounced behind the scenes than it is on stage. She says that women on stage don't get the same respect as men on stage, but the lack of acknowledgement for women in music intensifies for non-performing women who work behind the scenes. Her general sentiment is that women are needed, but our presence is always taken for granted, no matter what we do. She wishes that more women would cross that line from audience participant to behind the scenes worker/promoter. If strong minded women were more visible in the music world, it may help weaken the sexist rock 'n' roll stronghold choking music today. Most women are treated like sex toys in the music industry; it becomes more visibly perverse the more well known the band is, or if it's affiliated with major labels.

Jenise has observed that even in the anti-corporate world of punk, you still find a majority of punk guys betting on which girl they will get to take home tonight, and that's all they care about, trying to screw this female rocker. Some men treat women in music as if they were sexual servants, or if they were at a strip club not a venue, and not as their equals, or peers. It may not be as blatant as groping women in the pit or surfing on the crowd, or raping them, but the lack of respect and sexual manipulation games is repulsing. This difference between politics and behavior is hypocritical of the lyrical stances of most punk bands.

The womanizing known in the rockabilly realms fare no better, even though historically some of the major players have been women, such as: the Queens of Rockabilly Wanda Jackson and the Female Elvis Janis Martin. Today we also have incredibly strong, empowering, an vocal women in all aspects of music, including punk and rockabilly (and its many spinoff's) such as: Suzy Q and her Be Bop Boys and of the Hot Rod Trio, Patricia Day of the Horror Pop's, Brody of the Distillers, etc., but the sexism in music is still heavily relevant both in mainstream music and subculture music scenes.

Jenise credits Exene Cervenka from the band X as a breakthrough performer and one of her favorites, "She did what many (women and men) wish they could have done. She made an impact on music itself." She wishes we could see more women like her fully engaged in all aspects of music, but a majority of women are intimated by the sexism and exploitation of it all, or get sick of it, and are worn out by it (and leave) the music scene.

She acknowledges it is her strong personality that has allowed her to work in this industry, as well as come out ahead in life even though it has been extremely difficult. The challenges, emotionally and physically, that Jenise has endured is heart shattering, and brought me to tears when we interviewed. There have been times she didn't think she would make it in life, or music, but she always pushed her way through.

Jenise has never liked what the mainstream has offered musically, or religiously, which she finds both to be very sexist, and that they ignore the real general experience of women while berating us. She feels the mainstream is religiously controlling and awkwardly connected to the marketplace. She is a Buddhist and has been since 1997. She was in desperate need of something and her life felt empty …

> "I never could understand, or really accept the Christian explanation of anything. When I began to read about Buddhism, I had an overwhelming sense of being at peace with myself that I hadn't felt in a long time. It is very basic: you get in life what you put into it. That is what I live by and that is how I feel."

Her kids are free to do whatever they want with religion, be it if they choose to follow Buddhism, Judaism, or become Agnostic. She knows it is up to them to find what is right, "I can only guide them on a path; they need to decide which fork in the road to take."

Her favorite tattoo that she has is of the Buddha. It reminds her that life is special and precious. Never take anything for granted, and whatever good thing you have done in life you will reap the benefits someday.

Jenise's faith has gone through several horrific trials, the type of fears every woman dreads: being raped and the kidnapping of a child. She has also survived an ordeal every person with diabetes dreads, the loss of a limb in order to continue to live.

The rape occurred in 2004, she never saw the attacker. She was taking a walk and was grabbed from behind and dragged into an alley. The rapist pulled her shirt up over her head so fast that she knows nothing specific about the man. He said awful things to her like, "*I know this is how you like it.*" Jenise frequently thinks about relocating, because every day and night she relives how he terrorized her, but she is trying to recover and heal,

> "In some ways I am doing a lot better now that I've had a few years pass. I am starting to be able to sleep at night, and I don't jump as much from loud noises. But there are times when I am out that I get creeped out by a guy looking at me in a certain way. I am not bitter against men in general; I cannot blame the entire species for one man's stupidity and the need to feel power over someone who couldn't hurt anyone."

For anyone who has endured a rape attack these are the only words of hope she can offer:

> "I just know that you have to be strong and don't accept that it was your fault or that it could have been prevented. The person who does that to you is a sick fuck who needs to be caught and punished to the full extent of the law."

The police and court system did nothing for her, and they were very ugly in their behavior and innuendos they implied. They didn't pursue any type of significant criminal investigation, and they interrogated her, as if she provoked the attack from simply being female. The indifference towards, and the blaming of the rape/abuse victims by our government/institutions and society is very common in a *she-deserved-it-society* (or he/she also deserved it if they happen to be gay/bi/effeminate/transgender). *[This enables predators to not only justify their actions, but to feel entitled to violently hurt someone else. Woman are presented and accepted by the majority in society as somehow sub-human/ inferior/ here to please, making them exploitable by those who feel egotistically in power, or above them. We are objects to be consumed, or hurt, for someone else's gratification or insecurity.]*

Jenise acknowledges that without her support system, it would have been hard for her to make it as humanly intact as possible. She credits her faith and close friends like Joe Scharf, Paul Einhaus, and Jeff Bitzinger. They have continuously been there for her, especially during the ordeal she endured following the rape attack. They also helped her through some challenging health problems as well.

Jenise has been diabetic since she was nine-years-old. She lost her lower left leg to diabetes recently. There have been moments where she was temporarily blind because of the disease. Before her surgery, she almost died due to her heart and kidney shutting down.

Shortly after her amputation, she broke her right leg, foot, and ankle in a bad car accident. It was during this time her youngest son, Trent, was kidnapped. She was hospitalized for four days and she needed bed rest upon return. Her ex's were to pick up the kids, who are part of a blended family. Her oldest children Justin (then fifteen-years-old, and now eighteen) and Mackenzie (then eleven-years-old, now fourteen) from her first marriage were picked up by her ex-husband, and their nine-year-old half-brother [I personally as a writer and humanist loath that term for siblings, but have included it just for the sake of understanding the family relationships/lineage.] Trent was picked up her ex-domestic partner, who kidnapped him.

> "I had no warning, no nothing. I had to stay in bed and couldn't take care of the kids. If I would have known that was the last time I would see him I would have done so many things differently. I can't explain the grief or loss that I feel knowing that my child probably thinks that I don't love him anymore. I cannot even imagine what his dad has told him."

Her older children were shocked and it was comparable to a death in the family. To her dismay eventually her immediate family and her children stopped talking about Trent. Jenise eventually stopped talking about him because it made everyone uncomfortable,

> "Well let me tell you, I am not, or ever will be ok, or comfortable about this, and I think everyone needs to stop feeling that it is better for them to not talk about it, because it makes THEM feel strange. I need to talk about my son. I need to remember what it felt like to hold him and hear him tell me how much he loved me. I need him to know that not a day goes by that I don't think about him and that my

love for him is as strong as the day I gave birth to him. My biggest fear for him is that he will grow up and be a bitter man about me and women in general."

Jenise, like most women, never expected her ex-domestic partner to kidnap their son out of animosity towards her, and the break-up of their relationship. Nor did she expect her first marriage to be one that became abusive. She married young as most women of her generation did, right after high school. Jenise (at the time of this interview) was thirty-seven and she married at the age of eighteen, and never planned on becoming a mother.

> "I honestly never wanted to be a mother. I was amazed with what my mom had gone through, even having a husband around. I never thought that I could be someone's role model. My role in being a mom is to try to raise my kids with the smarts they have been given, and hopefully guide them on their way to becoming a good person."

She learned she was nine-weeks-pregnant a week after she married. They had no idea she was expecting prior, and hadn't given children much thought. Suddenly, she found herself fantasizing about being a wife and mother. That was how she was supposed to feel according to the world. They were surprised, but quite happy about the pregnancy. Their family was disappointed because it was so early, and they hadn't had the time to discover themselves yet, and explore life together.

All parents wish for a happy and healthy pregnancy and delivery, but Jenise had several complications and Justin her oldest son was born six-weeks early. It was really hard for her to see other moms taking their babies home and she couldn't. Justin was premature and had to be kept in the neonatal unit. Her daughter McKenzie was born through an emergency c-section due to the umbilical cord being wrapped around her neck. Trent was also born three-weeks early. Her fear for all of the births of her children was that they weren't going to make it.

She had support from her family for her first two children, but they (and her doctors) disapproved of her having Trent because of the severe health problems she had due to her diabetes. During her pregnancy with him her family became really cold and distant towards her. Although they love Trent, she gets the impression that they wish he hadn't been born.

Jenise found herself, as a mother, unprepared to provide everything for these tiny people, and it didn't matter if it was one or ten children, "The reality is you are never prepared for what happens in your life or prepared for what you need to do." Initially, she felt the only way she could be the parent she wanted to be was to lose all self-centeredness since her children depended on her for all the answers. Her expectations of herself as a mother have evolved since then.

> "I thought in the beginning that I would give birth to this perfect being and that I would do them no wrong. I expected that they would never think ill of me and that we would be best friends, as well as have a parent/child relationship."

She discovered, and was quite surprised that children develop their own personalities and tastes—early! On a less amusing note though, she also learned the world at large isn't very amicable to kids and a one-size-fits-all approach doesn't work. She also realized the working world ignores and

Jenise has never liked what the mainstream has offered musically, or religiously, which she finds both very sexist, and that they ignore the real general experience of women while berating us. She feels the mainstream is religiously controlling and awkwardly connected to the marketplace. She is a Buddhist and has been since 1997.

Her kids are free to do whatever they want with religion, be it if they choose to follow Buddhism, Judaism, or become Agnostic. She knows it is up to them to find what is right,

"I can only guide them on a path; they need to decide which fork in the road to take."

is counter-productive to the parent/child relationship. She has missed an excessive amount of time with hers kids, because of full-time work demands born of economic necessity, and because of her illness.

Despite these missed moments, she is very close to her sons. Her daughter McKenzie and her, however, have opposite opinions about things and aren't normally agreeable on a wide range of subjects. Although, there is personality clashes that cause distance between them, their mutual love and affection is no less. They have learned to respect their differences and each other, which is sometimes a challenge, but a frequent practice of self-discipline and open communication between the two.

When she ended her marriage, she was worried about how her divorce was going to affect her children, but after years of abuse she had to leave. Justin and McKenzie were disappointed, but children sometimes don't understand the dynamics of abuse especially when the abuse is subtle (mental), or the physical abuse is hidden.

> "My divorce was due to abuse. Yes, it affected me in several ways. It made me feel worthless and like nothing at the same time. I don't care if you're married fifty years, or one year! It will make you feel like something is not right."

As a divorced mom, she has learned the importance of supporting herself and her kids, not just financially, but spiritually, and emotionally. She understands the importance of unconditional love, not only for them, but for herself. Her three priorities for her kids are to make sure they are happy, safe and healthy. She hopes her kids evolve beyond humanities perceived limitations (negativity and selfishness). According to her Buddhist beliefs, one's journey never ends and the path to enlightenment is varied, constant and ever-changing, as is the person. How open and aware of the process you are, the more peaceful and gratifying your response to life's experiences and lessons will be. She will support them in whatever path they choose. What is important to her is that she has tried to instill in them the desire to choose good careers that are healthy for the world and for humanity, which will bless them and the world around them.

It's important to her that they live meaningful lives, act with real morals, and integrity. She also insists that they always stay true to themselves, and that no one can make them happy, but themselves. To help keep their perceptive balanced she does emphasize that they need to remember that everyone they meet on their life journey is a stepping stone closer to who they are. She also warns never assume people know you, always appreciate them, and never take them for granted.

Her parenting philosophy is:

> "If you treat a child like they are stupid you will make them that way. I have never hit my kids, or talked to them like they had no clue. I don't talk down to them and I have one steadfast rule: as long as you tell the truth, you won't get in trouble. That may sound easy on them, but I can honestly say that they have never been in major trouble and they don't lie to me either."

In addition to instilling trust and honesty in her parent/child relationships, the kids also see her growing and taking responsibility for them as a family and herself personally:

> "It took me a long time to arrive at this conclusion; you get out of life what you put into it. I can't say it anymore simply than that. Never let anyone tell you that you cannot overcome adversity. Always take your life into your own hands and always follow your instincts. Keep on going; you can always overcome anything that stands in your way."

She follows this belief, and she credits it for allowing her to find happiness while she pursues her life's destinies. For what she has she both endured and accomplished, she undoubtedly believes the power of its meaning: which is empowering, encouraging and optimistic, not only to her, but also for those around her. Simply, despite what you have to go through and what you want out of life—just keep going and reach for it. She thinks that one problem with the world is that not enough people take the time to stop and truly listen not only to others, but to themselves. Everyday when she wakes up she is happy because she chooses to be, and she sees her life and her kids are true gifts and she never under appreciates that. It excites her to live another day. This excitement has impacted her kids, because in general they have positive views and a love for life and its blessings, as well as its challenges.

★★★★★★★★
"I took my kids to their first day of kindergarten and stuck out like a sore thumb. I was the mom in a t-shirt and jeans when the rest were in dresses and high heels. My kids were amazed when they went to school. My son Justin asked me, *'What was wrong with the other moms?'* I asked him what he meant. And he said, *'The other moms have no tattoos.'* I then explained to him that I was the exception to the rule and they weren't. He said, *'Well, I am glad you are my mom.'* That is when I knew I did something right."
★★★★★★★★

Jenise always had these yearnings for spiritual philosophies and knowledge; it just took years to articulate them. It's the sense of longing for something with more meaning and natural purveyance that attracted her to a subculture way of life. She never fit in with the popular group of kids, who seemed cruel and shallow, at least on the surface. When she met kindred spirits, those who possessed a beauty of open-mindedness and acted with sincerity, she felt accepted for who she was. There was no pretense needed. She knows tons of kids succumb to the peer pressure to fit in, but she felt stronger than most. At a young age she chose a higher path: to hear her own voice and follow it.

It makes sense to Jenise to accept people who are different and to realize that it is a blessing; which is also something her kids know about firsthand. She has over one hundred and forty tattoos, works in the rock 'n' roll business, and is a Buddhist. All three defy society's stereotypes for women and mothers. Jenise remembers the first time her son Justin sensed something was different.

> "I took my kids to their first day of kindergarten and stuck out like a sore thumb. I was the mom in a t-shirt and jeans when the rest were in dresses and high heels. My kids were amazed when they went to school. My son Justin asked me, '*What was wrong with the other moms?*' I asked him what he meant. And he said, '*The other moms have no tattoos.*' I then explained to him that I was the exception to the rule and they weren't. He said, '*Well, I am glad you are my mom.*' That is when I knew I did something right."

This knowledge and experience with her children is critical because people just assume that people (like those with tattoos and work in the music industry) shouldn't be around kids. But she disagrees with the world at large in general:

> "I think society is in a place where we still haven't learned that's it's not okay to give children everything that their hearts desire. It seems we have raised our kids to be all about themselves, rather than what they should be contributing to the world itself. We live in a place that doesn't reprimand our kids for unacceptable behavior and I feel that is why our future generations will eventually have no morals whatsoever.
>
> My feelings of kids in general are: I love my kids, and they do know what is right and what is wrong. But I'm tired of hearing about someone's child, who is very young, being in jail for whatever reason. I am finding that I do not like most kids simply because they appreciate nothing and are not well mannered."

Jenise has made an effort to relate to mainstream mothers, but the majority that she has gotten to know seem to be overly concerned with appearances and keeping up with the Joneses, which has no value for her. Despite that she continues to be receptive to new encounters and possible relationships with people from all sides of the track of life. She reasons that surely there must be great spiritualist/activist moms living in that world (that are from different walks of life, and different from her), just as surely as Buddhism itself varies greatly. She likens it to her experience with teenagers, many of her contemporaries may hide behind wealth and image, and may be afraid of breaking the standard and coming out.

With her oldest son entering college soon, McKenzie becoming a teenager, and continuing her search for Trent, Jenise plans on just taking life one-day-at-a-time. She will continue to live by example, and wishing for the best for her family's future,

"I want to see my children grow up and have the life they want and deserve. I want to grow old and have a life like my grandparents. They have been married over fifty-four years and have never stopped for a minute to let life pass them by. I hope that I can be successful in work, but if not I will take what I can get. I am happy for what I have right now."

**Since this interview: Thankfully Trent has been safely returned home.*

"I didn't realize that it would be so hard to juggle a job, and parenting, and homemaking. After I had become a librarian, that's when I got the biggest shock about how hard it is to be a parent and have a full-time job. There was little flexibility. It was hell."

Suzie
Librarian
Story-teller
Crafter
Foxy Filmmaker
Visionary
Founder of and Drummer for Frump
Dallas, Texas.

Suzie is a fun-loving punk goddess approaching her early fifties. Suzie digs her drums, her French lover and their vegetarian life, and pondering solutions to the one of the biggest obstacles that faces parents and kids: how to find work that allows us to be parents (and how to shape work that allows businesses to flourish while we do). Her secret calling is to be an economist who dabbles in politics, so she can fully explore her rhetorical solutions and make them a reality. Her three daughters, Cecil, Daisy, and Polly, are her life's work, and her girls compliment all of her artistic achievements as a filmmaker and a musician.

She looks to Andy Warhol, KD Lang, and Koko the Gorilla for inspiration. When she needs to just chill out, she checks out: Johnny Mathis, the Ramones, the Monkees, and Eric Satie. She also enjoys reading the punk-infused Buddhist writings of Noah Levine, which helps her stay positive in a not-so-positive world.

What gets her excited, besides her incredible family, is her books! She is the world's coolest librarian, and she would easily give the ancient caretaker of Cleopatra's infamous library at Alexandria a run for their money. She has always loved libraries, and they have been a source of comfort, solace, and inspiration for her in times of need. She spent the days of her youth day-dreaming and researching at libraries without ever knowing the day had slipped by, until the sun was setting. She loves that someone can find what they need, right there in a library collection, and that it is a beautiful and organized landscape of art and ideals. She has been a librarian now for over twenty years. Had someone told her that she would become a keeper of books when she was twenty, she would have thought they were nuts. Life always has a different path in mind, than the one we do.

When she initially became a mom, she was a young, ambitious filmmaker who was finishing up school. She was in a content relationship with another artist, and their job was making short independent films and video installations at the now infamous 1980s Dallas Starck Club. [Yep, the one that had Grace Jones, Madonna, and Stevie Nicks perform at it. This club could have easily been cast in *Desperately Seeking Susan*, and it put Dallas back on the map for the film industry and celebrity drop-in's. It even had old-school beatniks swinging by, a.k.a. Allen Ginsberg. I was fourteen-years-old, when it closed in the mid-nineties and by the time I was old enough to be snuck into it, the greatness of it was long gone.] Suzie recalls "The eighties had so much money going around; artists could find work and get paid." Suzie had just changed colleges, moved from Austin to Dallas, when she and her boyfriend happened to be in the right place at the right time. Short and independent film was a new art form, and they had the right vision that the club was seeking. In college, she had always envisioned, "A place that I would always be upstairs and could come down anytime I wanted to, to the party, and contribute my art." The Starck Club was her place and her party. She "just wanted to be a starving artist" while she was figuring out what she wanted to say. Then her life spoke for her.

She and her boyfriend learned she was pregnant when working at the club. She jokes that, "Nothing could hold Cecil back—not even birth control!" She was excited about having a baby. She had always loved kids, and babysat all through high school and occasionally in college. They were employed, had their art, and were happy. They married, and tried something new and experimental: family life.

> "For the first year, my [1st] husband and I worked at the same job and we had very flexible hours. We made our own schedule and brought her to work with us. When she started walking, we needed a babysitter. More and more, I found myself at home, taking a backseat and opting out of opportunities, because it was just easier. Then the place we worked at said that they needed to eliminate one our positions. To their credit, management left it up to us. They said you can either both go part-time or one of you can be laid off. It would have been better for our careers if we had gone part-time, but we could keep our health insurance, and collect unemployment if one of us took the lay-off. I had been thinking about returning to school and he had become more necessary at the job anyway, so I took it, and went back to school to be a librarian."

The introduction to motherhood was daunting for Suzie. She suddenly found herself needing to sacrifice work, career opportunities, and economical worth in order to be a present parent, but it was the relentless physical demands of caring for a young baby, and trying to juggle it all, that left her dumbfounded …

> "Okay, I did not expect to NEVER be able to turn away from the baby to take a shower, talk on the phone, and even think. It was stressful. I didn't realize that it

would be so hard to juggle a job, parenting and homemaking. After I had become a librarian, that's when I got the biggest shock about how hard it is to be a parent and have a full-time job. There was little flexibility. It was hell."

Suzie feels that although women's lib made numerous advancements for women, and she is thankful for that, it has neglected our roles and needs as mothers. Society does not value the most difficult and important job in the world that we do as mothers. She has experienced firsthand that, "Mothering and home-making are not valued. We have taken them for granted." She had always wanted to be a working stay-at-home mother, and it makes her very sad that once children did enter her life she couldn't do that, economically. Suzie and her 1st husband went on to have two more daughters, and she became an assistant manager librarian at her home branch in Lakewood, but that doesn't mean it got any easier doing it all:

"At first I worked part-time as a librarian while I was getting my masters degree, and that was tricky. When I went full-time, it was a shock to not be able to juggle my parenting and my work. I had hoped once I could afford ballet lessons I could take my girls [to class]. Well, now I could afford it, but I couldn't take them because the work schedule was inflexible. People are tightening their assholes all the way around and becoming more rigid, especially in the workplace. We need room to be parents. The FMLA act serves as a box to force us in, and it's better than not having any leave on the law books, but parenting is more than [kids] being sick."

Suzie still appreciates her more favorable circumstances, although it was excruciatingly hard for her and her family. She knows there are more families with fewer resources and options, meaning the kids have to be neglected/latch-keyed for work, in order to pay bills and buy necessities. She and her family luckily didn't have to go down that road, but it did not make it any less of a struggle.

"Most of the time we staggered schedules to be able to do it. It isn't ideal, because the families aren't spending a lot of time together as a family, as a whole, and the couple doesn't ever get to be together as a couple, but that was the only option we had. My [1st] husband ran his own business, and he had a store, so he was able to drive the kids to ballet lessons. Overall, there was just a lot of patching together as we went, surviving transitions, lay-offs, and multiple children."

Her experience at the library, both as a member of management and a librarian, was a complete contrast to the flexibility she had as new mom when she was a filmmaker. She had incorrectly anticipated more flexibility working at the library, since modern libraries have generally been left to women to work in (similar to the teaching field for students from elementary through high school), but she found it choking and stifling instead. She has given the matter much thought over the last twenty years and is adamant that it is time for politicians and big business to stop with the lip service, and to really create family friendly work environments:

"Frankly, what I think they are going to need to do, and it's not considered politically correct, I think businesses need to recognize that people are at different life stages, and tailor jobs to different life stages. There are mega-jobs like CEOs, where you can expect to work eighty-hour work weeks, and get midnight calls. Then you have the 8-5 job where you never get called in, but you are full-time. Then there's the job where you do have a life outside of work: parent, care-giver for a parent, or you're a student, or an artist. When you are in that life stage, working forty-hours a week doesn't make sense, but you should be able to make livable wages and get benefits, because it's more full-time than part-time. Then there is *true* part-time work like ten hours a week and it can serve as a pool for people to get a call in to work.

It's silly to ask a person who has all these things going on in their lives to give 100%. They can lie and tell you that they will, but they won't be able to. We need to be honest about who we are, and where we really are, and employers need to expand on these options because it is real life, and there are stages accordingly. The other thing is we need to have some national health care and a lot of people who work at full-time jobs need access to that."

This conversation on workplace policy, and the impacts it has on the quality of family, personal, and community life, started over a spicy vegetable curry. Since she lives locally, we met up for dinner at one of our mutually favorite vegetarian restaurants, Kalachandji's in Old East Dallas. Our book interview turned into a brain-storming for national solutions to national problems that impact women, children, and business. There's this old boys club line of thinking that constantly gets in the way—that you can't be profitable and good to your employees and community, at the same time. This need to exploit (and quite often break existing labor laws, both out rightly and subtly) and wear down your employees for *slight* variance in *today's* productivity numbers, and profit margins is archaic; i.e., it's ultimately meaningless (but demoralizing) and the quarters you profit today from bad practices will cost you dollars tomorrow. Small business is just as guilty of this as big business.

"At first I worked part-time as a librarian while I was getting my masters degree, and that was tricky. When I went full-time, it was a shock to not be able to juggle my parenting and my work. I had hoped once I could afford ballet lessons I could take my girls [to class]. Well, now I could afford it, but I couldn't take them because the work schedule was inflexible. People are tightening their assholes all the way around and becoming more rigid, especially in the workplace. We need room to be parents."

The oxymoron that Suzie and I are just as perplexed by is: why wouldn't business want to just do the right thing and build long term investments and relationships that benefit both employees and clients/customers for sustainable revenue, tenure, and commitment? From both parties! It's a win-win! But you can't have that if: a) your nickel and dimming them and b) if you give no authentic consideration and care to the needs of the people and the parents that work for you. It seems a no-brainer, but it goes against almost everything I have ultimately seen done by executive and upper management and have heard flow from business management meetings despite the occasional pro-employee jargon. You just have to sift through actions vs. lip-service and you will see how businesses really conduct themselves and how this impacts your community. For Suzie, she is a librarian who has faced the typical business paradigm: as an employee your parental obligations are irrelevant to your paid work ones. Bad business practices and bad family practices in the long run undermine sustainability for business and family alike. And that impacts everyone.

Another thing Suzie and I shred into over dinner is, since when did part-time with no benefits morph from under twenty-hours a week to almost forty? I was fifteen when I had to start working full-time, and back then part-time was anything under twenty-hours a week, which makes more sense. 'Part-time' work is now full-time work with no benefits, and our laws and businesses are behaving scandalously and bankrupting the American public.

Suzie and I, and our guests at the table, realize that what we need is a real national platform with a truly diverse spectrum of thinkers to really plug away at this. I envision a roundtable consisting of Hilary Clinton (My hero of course.), President Obama and his family (Children and spouses need to be part of the discussion.), Warren Buffett, Bill Gates, Dr. Taj Anwar, Kimberly of Warrior Mammas, Crystal, and other Rebel Moms,

"I follow this philosophy of nonviolence. I learned parenting from that. It comes down to treating others as you would like to be treated.

Yelling at kids, or spanking kids, is ridiculous when you think about it. It doesn't work. You may get compliance, but you will distance yourself from your child, and that disconnect will be lasting.

You get much more of a connection with compassion and respect. That is true with people in general."

awesome Dallas based socialist-activist-dad Stephen Benavides, Arkansas Senator Blanche Lincoln, notorious and self-proclaimed Chicana Feminist Martha Cortera, Newt Gingrich (for kicks and giggles—as well as opposing theory) and so many more. This roundtable needs to be a huge and varied discussion to come up with viable solutions that work for everyone, both business and family alike. For it be truly inclusive, all attendee's would need to include their children, their hired help (if there is any) and the children of. It would be necessary to pull in random workers from all stages of life and occupations, and strata's of society. We could kick it off with a survey similar to the in-depth employee surveys administered by large companies, to help give our dialogue the most elementally necessary areas of crucial focus. Then get to brainstorming and work. Suzie pulls me out of my Sabji-induced trance of political inspiration and hope, by reminding me that it is almost 10:00 PM and the restaurant will be closing soon.

Suzie is stumped at how we could make this a reality, staggering work to accommodate life-cycles and different stages, while being receptive to the needs of parents, and the needs of business. She dreams that maybe an economist could latch on to the idea, figure out the long-term numbers and balance, and who could be high enough in the administration to make it a reality with changes in the labor and tax laws. I suggest France, where her second husband Frankie is from, as an example for a starting point in comparison, to draw upon ideas that could work if at least partially incorporated here, modified based on our realities, and needs. Ultimately, her idea is that we need more part-time professional/skilled jobs with higher pay and benefits so that both parents could work less and have more time for a home life. For that to be an American reality we have to move away from the 10% rule. Meaning, that 90% of the wealth cannot be kept by only 10% of the population. Those who run and own companies, have to share more equitably … what we workers earn for them. Say a 50/50 rule as a starting point. We close our conversation on national labor and business reform, to focus on the nuts-and-bolts of daily parenting.

Suzie has successfully raised three children, Cecil who is now twenty-five and has graduated from college, Daisy, who is seventeen and on the cusp of transitioning into adulthood, and Polly who is twelve-years-old and is about to step into the world of teenagers. Her overall child-rearing philosophy has evolved since she first started out in the world of parenting.

"I follow this philosophy of nonviolence. I learned parenting from that. It comes down to treating others as you would like to be treated. Yelling at kids, or spanking kids, is ridiculous when you think about it. It doesn't work. You may get compliance, but you will distance yourself from your child, and that disconnect will be lasting. You get much more of a connection with compassion and respect. That is true with people in general. There are a lot of people who think that this is just crazy talk. But as far as field work, I did the traditional way of parenting (authoritarian/ control) with Cecil and she had some temper issues. My two younger children, where I took the better way and parented with respect and care, don't have core anger issues. You are still a responsible parent, and kids want that, it's parenting with structure, guidance and safety, but with compassion and care. It's giving boundaries in a loving way, not in an angry way."

Some tools that have helped her navigate parenting, while making better choices, is the website CNVC.org (The Center for Non Violent Communication), the book "*How to Talk so Kids will Listen and Listen so Kids will Talk*" by Adele Faber and Elaine Mazlish (Which she swears by as an absolute life-saver!), and Maria Montessori's principles of teaching adapted for parenting. Suzie's overall parenting mantra is, "Respect kids. Don't bully them."

> **Some tools that have helped her navigate parenting are: CNVC. org (The Center for Non Violent Communication), the book "*How to Talk so Kids will Listen and Listen so Kids will Talk*" by Adele Faber and Elaine Mazlish (Which she swears by as an absolute life-saver!), and Maria Montessori's principles of teaching adapted for parenting. Suzie's overall parenting mantra is, "Respect kids. Don't bully them."**

She wants her kids to be peaceful, and she aims to empower them, while helping guide them on their path. Her purpose is for them to be true to themselves, without "enabling slacking." To achieve this takes focus and dedication to your parenting and your kids—good old fashioned effort. She tries to parent as peacefully as she can, while staying as "loyal as possible to non-violence." This includes parenting without coercion, demands, punishment, etc. She emphasizes that, "I am not perfect! But I try." To help illustrate how this parenting can be not only achieved, but beneficial to the family and kids, she shared some tangible real-life situations and parenting-in-action for us:

> "I heard a great example on the radio the other day, but it was true and just happened in my own life. My daughter Daisy was applying for colleges. To a point you back off and let them take care of things. The mother realized that were deadlines involved, and you are present and on top of it with your children, versus being absent and letting a life-lesson happen, which could be very counter-productive to their life. For my daughter, she is great at math, but hates essay. When the day came that the application was due, she hadn't written her essay yet. I had plans to go somewhere, and several weeks prior we went over a checklist together. I periodically kept going over it with her to keep an eye on her progress. And she had to work on getting her act together, and I kept being around to help her out if she needed me. Then the day it finally had to be finished and turned in, she had it half-written and couldn't get it done. I stayed with her, and she needed me there. It was really hard and foreign to her; had I not canceled plans that submit button may not have gotten pushed. One of the tricks to get into college is being able to get your shit together and getting it all in on time."

Suzie observes where many parents go wrong: either doing the task at hand for them, or forcing them to do it but in a way that is demoralizing, not supportive, or just leaving it completely up to them and letting what may happen, happen. She sees this frequently with parents of very young children and teenagers [The two most challenging stages, for adults and kid's, ha-ha—the growth spurt periods.] It's the approach that is all wrong, and that greatly influences the outcome:

> "Realize first: don't try to overpower them (physically, emotionally, or intellectually). You can't really make anybody do anything. I see a lot of parents get

into conflicts with their kids over this, and it's a losing battle, with butting heads. Respect them, as well. If you issue ultimatums and strict rules, try to communicate with them before becoming the enforcer. I heard once on TV some advice on teens; with teenagers you just really have to be available when they are ready to connect with you. You can't really drop short notice talks on them, especially when they are about to leave, etc. Secondly, make your life as such, that you are around, so that when they feel like talking you are there. If you are always on the go and busy, and not noticing that they are ready to open up, you won't be there. Parents tend to disappear when kids become teens and become independent, but then the parents aren't there to talk out situations with before they make a decision as a teen. Some of these can be pretty serious, like doing a drug, or having sex; how can they make a better choice, if you don't know what's going on?"

Speaking of sex, Suzie thought she had the perfect dialogue plan worked out to have with Cecil, her oldest girl, who in turn taught her a life-lesson:

"The third piece of advice for teens—is to have the sex talk way early. I thought with my oldest daughter I would just have the talk when she started to ask questions. And suddenly she was twelve, and didn't want to talk about this. And I was like, but wait, you weren't old enough before! I think eventually she figured it out. We put her through a great sex-education class at the Unitarian church. One moment they don't care if you're alive, there would be more space in the house if you weren't there, and the next they are crying because they need you."

Suzie had a more comprehensive plan with her other two daughters, to engage with them on the subject earlier. She put some tidbits out there, creating a safety-net and a warm environment where they could ask questions, and come to her intermittently. Suzie also revisits the topic as situations are observed and interweaves information and knowledge. Sometimes it leads to an in-depth discussion, sometimes it doesn't, but it's creating an on-going and evolving dialogue, which is what's crucial as opposed to a one-time 'big' discussion that may or may not be well-received by a child/pre-teen. As parents we want to be a pillar of strength for our children, and a safety zone. We need to be a sounding board for them to bounce things off of, to counter the peer pressure, and the negative examples of 'role-models' that our society fleshes out for us.

Suzie grew up in a loving and supportive household and knows firsthand how crucial that is to kid's development and self-esteem. It also plays a role in the choices they make, which can have pretty stiff consequences if the parents aren't parenting with heart, direction, and an open mind. She feels lucky to have had the parents she did, and she was raised a Unitarian, so questioning things is what she has always done, and that has enabled her to be a supportive parent to her girls, because she gets it. She's still question things, because well, so many things are just ass-backwards in the human societies and structures that we have built. But that doesn't mean it's easy for her, nor was it easy on her parents.

> "My oldest daughter has been more challenging and there have been times that she and I have had conflict, and that has been challenging. But one of the most surprising moments in parenting is that, I'm amazed at how good my daughters seem to be doing. I just think back to when I was growing up, and my parents were pretty challenged by me as a teenager. You hear these stories about teenagers who are difficult. I am really surprised at how well they are doing. My youngest daughter, Polly, is about to turn thirteen and she tells me all the time how happy she is, and that's not where teens normally are. I'm surprised too by my oldest daughter who is now grown, that she's been able to transition into an adult and take on additional responsibility. The transition has been very well. This is a very big surprise from what I had expected. It's just surprising when you see them become mature adults. I think the extended maturity years have added to this, because kids are more prepared intellectually and with more maturity to bear the financial and ongoing responsibilities of [adulthood]."

Suzie thinks the good, strong foundation set by her and her first husband minimized the toll their divorce had on them on later. These are three great, strong, and happy kids who even in the midst of a not-so-nice divorce didn't lose control and become wild; making detrimental choices that would have reverberated throughout their lives—which seems to be the fate of many kids who go through parent separations.

"We were married eighteen years, and I finally just got brave enough. We created a life, and had two more kids. I was really into the relationship for such a long time. The band, Frump, once I saw that I could do that, it gave me the courage to ask to change the relationship to make it better. I addressed those concerns, the relationship was pretty much over, but he didn't want the relationship to end. The divorce wasn't as friendly as I hoped, like us all getting together for Friday night pizza …

It's very important not to demonize the person you are divorcing. Some of my friends were real negative, and it was unnecessary, but I also understand they were attempting to comfort me. My lawyer was also being real negative, but I think he was used to being the adversary for his clients. I wanted more of a collaborated divorce, and there is such a thing out there, but the few attorneys who offer it are extremely expensive. I also should have spoken up more to my friends and family who felt they needed to defend me, to say this isn't how I want to frame this."

This strong foundation helped set them up for later success when they became a blended family. Suzie is still knee-deep in parenting, and one thing that shocked her about parenting is how normal it makes your life, "way more normal" than she ever planned. She adds with a touch of sarcastic humor, it also has left her "way more broke than she ever planned to be." It's a mixture of love, high-stress, demands, compromises, hope, and normalcy.

As a kid herself growing up in Texas and Oklahoma, she was a dreamer with her head in the clouds, and laughs that her high school class would have voted her "more likely to be a poet or a heroin addict than a librarian." She initially resisted the idea of becoming a librarian because it seemed so far from her original vision of life as an artist. But she knew as a new mom with new life demands, including financially, she had to change course and figure out a different way. She read a book (It always starts with a great book!) written by Dick Bolles called *What Color is Your Parachute?* The career assessment kept telling her what she didn't want to hear.

"The book kept coming up with librarian, but at first I kept thinking/saying, 'No. I'm a filmmaker and artist. And soon I realized that I loved the library and this was my calling. I had a part-time job there and loved the beauty of the place, and helping people. Not to say that film-making for me is over, and art, it's not. It's just something I can return to later."

The book has had an annual edition published since its first publication in 1974—so it has much to offer, and it is a trusted resource for career and work change direction. The writer has created a fully comprehensive website with many tools you can utilize, including job hunting in today's world at JobHuntersBible.com.

One thing she loves doing is the toddler story time that she developed and implemented at her branch. She gets to dress up as different, crazy, and cool characters for the readings, including a princess, a cow, and other creatures/animals. But as a budding filmmaker turned librarian (that has dedicated her life to children and books) she suddenly found herself in her forties with less child-rearing and work demands and she had something she hadn't had enough of in the last twenty years, time! She wanted to do something more adult-centric and dexterously artistic. The opportunity to play drums again was a needed venture back to her pre-motherhood adventuress-self.

"I first had learned how to play drums when my neighbor in Austin played drums and taught me. I spent my youth in Austin, going to all the punks clubs, and checking out bands, and playing drums looked like so much fun. There was a gal named Kathy McCarty who played in the Buffalo Gals, and they were three women who barely knew how to play their instruments, and they just got up there and played. It was real inspiring.

When Cecil was a teenager, I would go to drop her off at a friend's house, and they would be playing drums and guitars. My daughter dated Anthony who would later be the drummer for [Dallas's very awesome but now defunct] Spector 45, and he would let me play his drums. And one day my neighbor was driving off with a drum set, and they were returning the drum set, so I called the person who owned it, to see if I could buy it. She sold it to me. So now I had this drum set, so I had to start a band."

And that is exactly what she did. She reached out to some moms with an interest and background in music that she knew from church and from her daughter's school. For most of the moms, it was a great opportunity to rekindle their love affair with instruments that were laid to rest when motherhood and the necessity of regular paid work came knocking at their doors. Suzie cleared out her dining room and converted it to a jam room. They had gotten together every Sunday and went at it, as the kids played and ran around the house and outdoors. The mantra they all agreed upon was motherhood is tough as hell and that yields some fun, and loud, rock 'n' roll. They decided to make motherhood, which is such a huge part of womanhood, their primary musical focus. However, motherhood, being a serious role, had been mostly all work and no play for them, so they decided to take the songs they love and remake them with whimsical child-rearing moments in mind. Frump's band motto was: *The All-Mom Garage Band was a group of women who needed to make some noise.*

They blessed their band with the name Frump, since that is what society tends to deem us middle-aged moms as, and as a modern adjective it is taken to mean a woman who doesn't take interest in being sexy or 'womanly', and according to the Merriam-Webster Dictionary frump means, "A dowdy unattractive girl or woman, or a staid old-fashioned person." They adapted a cooler-than-cool Rosie the Riveter logo for their band, going back to their mutual *Bondage, Up Yours!* roots.

Their first-full length album featured such parodies as *Pick Up Your Socks*, *Vasectomy* (A take on the Ramones's *Teenage Lobotomy.*), *Shove It*, *Mommies Are People* (By Carol Hall for *Free To be You and Me*, adapted by Frump.) and *We're Really Beat* (A take on the Go-Go's *We Got the Beat.*). You can order their album, hot pink and black band t-shirts, and very special *Frump You* bumper stickers at Frump.com.

During the five years they played together as a band, they played birthday parties, and festivals, including Mamapalooza [You must check it out, Mamapalooza.com.], and various local shows. Suzie was broken-hearted when the band broke up due to conflicts over their future direction. She is thrilled, however, that she did it and she still beats away at her drums. Now she is just taking the time to get ready for her next project, as the kids leave the nest one at a time.

Suzie suggests for any projects on a tight budget that CafePress.com is a wonderful starter point for designing and ordering merchandise for your band, collective, solo project, etc. Especially, like the moms in the band, if you're already stretched thin with time and money. Cafe Press charges on a per-order basis, and it is virtually free to use and set-up shop on. They make their profit off of the printing and shipping of your items. So yes, you will not build a lot of revenue from your merchandise to put back into your band, but you will earn some, while providing options for merchandise to your fans, that otherwise you may not be able to. [For the same reasons as Suzie, I set up a merch line for Rebel Moms at CafePress.com too. I had big visions and plans for celebrating Rebel Moms and creating cool gear, but with far less money to launch it, I had to come up with a Plan B.] She also suggests you find a local printer for local events so that you can have items for sell to promote your band/project without having to pay full retail on them, like you do at Cafe Press.

> **Frump's full length album features such parodies as *Pick Up Your Socks, Vasectomy* (A take on the Ramones's *Teenage Lobotomy*.), *Shove It*, Mommies Are People (By Carol Hall for *Free To be You and Me*, adapted by Frump.) and *We're Really Beat* (A take on the Go-Go's *We Got the Beat*.). You can order their album, hot pink and black band t-shirts, and very special *Frump You* bumper stickers at Frump.com. Also, don't forget Rebel Mom Suzie's insider tip when starting a merch project on the cheap—Café Press.com!**

Frump is what gave her strength to seek change in her 1st marriage, and when it became evident it was not going to work, to leave it. Had she not done the band, and sought change in love, it would have never opened the door to her meeting the love of her life, several years later. Of course, she is not psychic, so she had no idea that this is what the future would hold, as it unfolded. Nor does she regret her first marriage, because it had its place and time, and yielded three awesome kids. She wasn't seeking romance when it found its way to her.

Frankie, her second husband, saw her profile online and he knew it was fated. He had to meet the girl who loved Dr. Seuss, *Tig Nag Ham* (a Buddhist book) and the Ramones, as much as he did. He was already living in the U.S., in fact, right down the street practically! He left France when his job moved over here to DFW. His dad was already living here. He had reached out to her, and it was love at first type. She thought, "He was a really special guy, and he thought I was a really special girl. And we just feel in love."

Frankie had joined us at Kalachandji's for the first interview, and they are really cute together, reminiscent of one's first teenage love; wholesome, trusting, adorable and sweet. They are animal-right activists and rescuers, vegetarians, pacifists with an angry punk streak (because of all the unnecessary nonsense in the world), and lovers of kooky, unique, vintage, and fun things. She loves going home to France with him occasionally, and they plan on retiring there. When I was trying to get the love story behind 'Suzie and Frankie' during the second interview over the phone, Frankie joked at my reference to all the love stories with the name Frankie in it, that "Nothing with name Frankie in it is a happy story, but theirs is." They have been together for two-and-a-half years now and recently wed. Because her kids were just getting used to their parents being divorced for a few years, after a long marriage, they took their time and were careful with introducing their relationship to them. Suzie shares:

> "During the transition, the kids knew we were seeing each other, but he would only stay over on the nights they were at their dads. One night, for some reason my middle-aged daughter Daisy was not going over to her dads, and I needed to have the big talk with her on the fact that Frankie and I were together, and he would be over tonight. When I went to tell her, she said, 'Mom, I already know. We figured it out when the toilet lid was left up."

Suzie and I erupted in laughter as she shared this. Kids are so smart, and who knew a toilet seat would be the one oversight that spilled the beans. She adds:

> "Luckily they liked him right away. We were together all the time. It was such a struggle getting him back to Euless from Dallas in time for work, etc. Shortly afterwards, just for efficiency, he moved in. Then we got married."

Suzie has made several milestone transitions in work, parenting, love, music, and life. Lately, she's been just enjoying love, writing and sewing. For the future she will probably work on a music project with Frankie and just see what happens.

Roger that!

"It was painful. That's the only word I have for it in every aspect: pregnancy, motherhood, adoption. Painful."

Marea
College Student
Ambitious Dreamer
Birth Mother
Traveler
Cute-ass Cellist in Breadlines at Gunpoint
Dallas, Texas.

Marea is a wonderful and gifted musician with a passion for animal print who comes from the Mid-West. Her sense of curiosity and adventure has led her all over the United States, but she has made Dallas a make-shift home while she finishes her associate degree in music. She is an avid music-lover whose repertoire includes the greatest of the eighties: Madonna, Bauhaus, and Siouxsie and the Banshees. Her introduction into punk music is defined by her love of Crass and Conflict, as well as some lesser known bands that started in the late nineties from her hometown of Minneapolis, such as the Menstrual Tramps (whose drummer is a Rebel Mom in this book!), Husker Du and Onward to Mayhem; but right now she is all about strings, strings, and more strings!

Marea was one of my first few interviews for this book and we meet through mutual friends one evening out. I knew her story was one of valor shaped by her tumultuous spirit. The story of her life, her daughter Tovah's life, and her music, begged to spill forth from these pages! She has an unshakable drive and a huge heart. She felt that to be the best mom possible she should give her daughter up for adoption into a mature, resourceful, and loving family. She is a Rebel Mom with courage and soul. Our interview was make-shift since we were both incorporating meaningful projects into our very busy lives. I drove from East Dallas to Carrollton to take her to school so that we could get together. We taped the interview while driving in the car and my son Corben was asleep in his car-seat. Where there is a will, there is a way! We opened the interview on the subject of the love of her life … her cello.

She remembers being fond of stringed instruments in elementary school and had played the violin briefly in second grade. Due to a lack of money her family couldn't afford to buy her a stringed instrument, so she learned to play the piano since her family already had one. She was following in the generational footsteps of her mother and grandmother, whom both are pianists.

She finally had an opportunity to pursue stringed instruments as a junior in high school. She feels very behind now as a college student cellist, because she got a much later start than most. She also tutors children on the cello who have been playing since the first grade. It blows her mind to think about what these kids will be like when they get to be her age. She tries desperately to be happy for them though, and to not let envy or bitterness get her down—but she fights that feeling of jealousy, since their families could give them more opportunities than what hers could. If she could change just one thing about elementary schools today, it would be to budget in more money for a string session so that all kids, not just a lucky few, could be empowered to pursue classical music. She has been playing cello for six years now.

"Playing the cello is a very profound thing. It's the same passion anybody has with their own instrument. If you're really into it and really dedicated to it—and it's real serious—it's a huge part of your life. It's kind of an issue also of what you're willing to share and what you're willing to give up. Like right now I probably shouldn't be seeing someone and dedicating myself to the cello. I feel guilty if I go out to the bar one night with friends and I think I should be at home playing solos. I don't know if other people feel the same, but I would assume so. There's a difference between dedication and discipline. If I could learn how to battle discipline ... That's where it gets really tricky, and that's where the guilt comes in. It also depends on what your version of reality is—and mine changes from day-to-day.

It's also an issue when I see another cellist perform, like when I saw Lynn Harrell perform. He's one of the top twenty cellists of today, and you know that going in. And when I saw him, and heard that first chord, it was just astonishing! I was taken away, tears in my eyes. But as soon as it was over and he left the hall I got really depressed and I collapsed and felt guilty all over again, about how I'm not there. Will I ever be there? What do I need to do to get there? And again that's where I didn't start early enough, and there are just some things that aren't attainable."

She knew at an early age that she had "big aspirations" and wanted to be a performer. She wasn't exactly sure what medium, or how to make it happen, so she kept her dreams a secret and didn't share them anyone. She wanted to create music with a message, but hated everything she saw and heard on MTV; which seemed shallow. She wanted her music to be fun, but the meaning important.

Initially, she had been accepted at Berkley Music College in Boston when she graduated high school, but she made the decision to take a year off from school to live life a little. That choice would later have huge repercussions. She was hanging out in the city trying to figure out who she wanted to be. She was enjoying going to shows and parties, but was still trying to define her values. Then she met the young man who would be her first boyfriend. Their short relationship was calamitous, and they were "falling apart as soon as they got together, and were not meant to be." However, like most first relationships they dragged it out way longer than they should have and finally broke up. They were relieved and happy to be moving on when Marea got some shocking news:

"Once I became pregnant everything sort of stopped; I totally shutdown. I didn't want to be around anyone anymore, and even then a lot of people I was hanging around with were basically just people to go drink with and do whatever with. They weren't really friends, just people to hang out with at that moment. I knew no one was going to talk to me anymore once they heard. I knew everyone was going to look at me and judge me. The worst part of it was that I was so ashamed of myself. I had never even had a serious boyfriend up until Kevin and I hadn't slept with nobody up until him. The first boyfriend I get, I lose my virginity too, and that was kind of pathetic. And I didn't want to do that. And the first boyfriend I have I end up getting pregnant. I guess I hadn't thought too hard about my future and what I wanted my life to be. But I never imagined being down that road! I wasn't the girl that got pregnant. That happened to other people in high school—but that was not me. And all of a sudden it was me. I didn't leave my house for a month."

"I knew everyone was going to look at me and judge me. The first boyfriend I get, I lose my virginity too, and that was kind of pathetic. And I didn't want to do that. And the first boyfriend I have I end up getting pregnant. I guess I hadn't thought too hard about my future and what I wanted my life to be. But I never imagined being down that road! I wasn't the girl that got pregnant. That happened to other people in high school—but that was not me. And all of a sudden it was me."

She moved out of her shared apartment, opting for her own private space when the lease was up. She didn't tell anybody why she was leaving, where she was going, or what she doing. She exiled herself. The only person she had any communication with was Kevin, and she leaned on him for as much support as he could muster. When she reached out to her family, sadly, they disowned her. She was in an abyss of despair, but tried to rationalize the situation and believed that somehow she could still do everything she had planned to do prior. Reality was somber and the direction of the wind changed despite her forceful efforts.

"Well that was the summer right before I was supposed to go to Boston. I was trying really hard to get out there, and everything I was trying to do failed, the loan and everything. It was a sign that I needed to stay. I didn't want to and I just knew I was going to be stuck here forever. Kevin is a very nice person, but he was not ever what I would want for a father to be."

Kevin wanted either for them to stay together and have the baby, or for her to get an abortion. He wanted the child to be either here with him, or not here at all. Marea was conflicted. All the circumstances were wrong, the person she was with was wrong, and although at this point she never had given much thought to marriage, or children, she knew that this wasn't what she wanted. She had planned to see the world with her cello by her side. It's much more difficult to make that your reality if you are a parent, and she didn't even begin to have an idea of how she could reconcile the two. She found herself knee-deep in life's biggest questions,

"Before I was pregnant, I never wanted to have children. I never wanted to be pregnant. I never wanted to be married. I wanted to make sure I was as independent as I possibly ever could be. So I wanted to make sure I didn't have any attachments.

But also, I didn't want children because I didn't like the way that the world was turning out. I didn't want to put anyone in that situation. I was really young anyway, so at that point I had no idea how I was going to instill any morals, or theories on life, for someone else when I couldn't figure it out for myself. I started to reevaluate everything in life and what I thought about bringing a child into this world and what I thought about marriage. It was never an issue to have an abortion. It was never even a thought. I had never formed an opinion on whether I was pro-choice or pro-life, but then all of a sudden I was pregnant.

Part of me died, but that was a part of me that needed to die—the immature kid who just ran around. I got her over with and ran on auto-pilot. I had to start thinking about someone else and everything I did concerned someone else. You can't be selfish. I mean, you can, and there are people that are selfish, but I just didn't work that way."

She survived the daily motions by throwing herself into work while tabling the decision that needed to be made—to be a family or not? She knew an abortion was out of the question and told Kevin as much, but she couldn't yet emotionally or intellectually think beyond that. Instead she put it off by working sixty hours a week, and was concerned with just taking care of herself.

Eventually, time caught up to her as she entered her second trimester. Kevin and her two best friends, Mark and Sarah, urged her to think about what she was going to do. She finally came to the decision that the best thing to do would be to give her child up for adoption. Over time it made sense to Kevin too, as he and Marea looked at the dismal reality of what kind of a life they could offer a child. They were young, unstable, had no resources, and they didn't even love each other. Many young parents find themselves sticking together and starting a family with no resources, but have love as the necessary glue. Marea was plainly honest with him and herself, this just cannot be (them raising a child together). In her view it meant having to raise a child under challenging circumstances with someone she had fought antagonistically with constantly during their brief and immature courtship. She also felt she would never be able to achieve her goals and desires if she became a young mom with no college education, and didn't want her life determined by this unfortunate circumstance. Kevin in time reluctantly agreed with Marea, and the adoption process was started.

They worked with an agency and looked at pictures and bios of many families seeking to adopt. She saw pictures of their houses, and really, she says, "It was like shopping. You picked what you liked." She met with several different families, and was looking for the type that could provide the life that she wanted for her child—preferably in uptown Minneapolis. She didn't want their child to be denied any life opportunities due to class or lack of wealth. In essence, she wanted her child to have the comforts and privileges that she couldn't give and never got herself. However, it was more than material wealth that mattered to her. You could give a child the world, but without love, support, and positive disciplining you have done that child no justice with embellishment. She sought a structured and loving home environment, plus amenities. There were some families she met that were great and it seemed a perfect match, but something just didn't feel right for either party. She was beginning to worry that she might not find anyone to adopt her child, when just one month before Tovah's birth it finally happened.

> "We ended up finding her parents, the right ones, and they are really nice people. They are a diverse family and really open. So I'm not too concerned with anything really. I trust their judgment. They may have different feelings on things that are different than my own, but it just comes with the territory. There's no way it will be exactly as I would want it to be, but they will be good, thoughtful, caring parents, and that's a good thing."

When she went into labor it was horrifically painful, and the hospital staff made her feel like she wasn't doing it right, "I was using my veins and every orifice of my body was pushing. Then I would have to start all over." She also didn't know why there were so many people in the delivery room that she didn't want to be in there: more doctors than she could count, at least four nurses, the adoption agency, Kevin's family, and all sorts of friends that she never saw when she was pregnant. She felt there was an excessive amount of medical personnel whose only purpose there was to watch. She had spent the whole nine months alone, basically, and the only people she wanted to be in there was the essential medical staff, Mark, Sarah, and Kevin. That's it. It was treated more like a horrible sci-fi film event than a private birthing. She was near the end, when finally Tovah's head emerged and Kevin became very excited about their child being born. Marea, on the other hand, was in no mood for celebration.

"This is so painful. It hurts! I just want it to come out! I know it's supposed to be miraculous, but that's only on one end, and on the other end is where you are sitting and it's not beautiful or miraculous. It's only miraculous that it ends! Afterwards I just sort of laid on the table. It's a feeling you can't describe, literally empty. Your body has just been through the most traumatic experience it will ever be through. And you're just laying there like oh my god. You're scared to move. You're worried that something will fall out. It's just awful."

She was hesitant to decide if she should see Tovah or not, and debated. She knew that "she existed for a long time, but now she has a face." Marea had no idea what she was going to look like, and suddenly there was a physical child to imprint into memory "from this mystery." It jolted her with a different perspective,

"First they put her on my stomach, and I didn't really look. It obviously felt like a baby, but I didn't really grasp it. I didn't even realize what gender she was until someone told me—and I think it was the start of being really in tune with myself. I knew it was going to be a girl, and furthermore it was going to be Tovah. When I see her now it doesn't surprise me, I assume of course that's what she's going to be like. And I couldn't say now what she will look like at twenty, but when I see her at twenty it will be like of course that's what she looks like. And that's because that was always how it was going to happen. So her being a girl, I kind of knew that in the back of my mind. But I still had mixed emotions on it because I had to be sure that I got as much of her as I could, because I only had two days. And then maybe I shouldn't get any of her because I only have two days."

Marea was crumbling on the inside as she was pushed around in the wheelchair. She was holding Tovah and was anguished with despair. She was the only mom in the birth ward who was troubled deeply, while the other moms were surrounded by balloons, flowers, and gifts. The spirit of joy filled their rooms skipping Marea's entirely. She felt "depleted just holding her" because she knew it wasn't going to last. She knew nothing about being a mother, but had resolved to be the best mother she could for the two days that she had Tovah.

> "Whatever luxuries you have in the hospital, like a bath, or whatever moms do, like be totally pampered, I didn't have that at that point, because I couldn't take a moment of being away from Tovah. I desperately tried everything I could to make her aware of me; even though I knew it was kind of a moot point. The Kangaroo thing, where you put your baby on your bare chest, I did that. I made sure Kevin did that. I wanted her to have this connection with her parents. I was exhausted, but so scared to sleep. I was afraid I would wake-up and she would be gone. I was a mess."

Kevin's parents made the transition additionally difficult, because they insisted on taking family photos. Marea just couldn't bear it, insisting that: "We weren't a family. She is not ours." It was a decision they had made before Tovah was born, that she would be adopted. Marea struggled with the commitment, but she was certain that it was the best possible situation for them and their daughter. She was preparing herself for Tovah's arrival to her adoptive family:

> "I didn't breast feed her because she gets more connected to you as a mother, and I didn't want to imbalance things, and thought it wouldn't be a good idea. Suddenly my two days were up and it was time to move on. I used baked cabbage to let them [her breasts] down. It was really tough lactating and no baby."

The first few months after her daughter was adopted were like an eerie dream for Marea. She thought it would never be possible for there to be life after Tovah. She had pictures everywhere, and tortured herself with her memory. She eventually put them away and started reclaiming her life one day at a time. After a year of occasionally visiting the adoptive family and her daughter, Marea decided it was time to let them be a family. She did not want to be a constant reminder to Tovah's new parents that she was her birth mom. She squeezed her girl tight as they all promised to stay in touch, at least on birthdays, and she packed up her stuff to head south.

She ended up in Texas at the age of twenty. She found work at a pizzeria and re-enrolled in college. Here she found her way back to her first love, "I always thought the cello was the best symbol for a woman. It just expresses the greatest emotions and has such fantastic symbolism. It's just so fitting! And it goes right between your legs!"

She started playing cello in a punk rock band. She clarifies in the interview that she was not the first cello player to do so—her friend Lisa from Guns on Bosnia was. The concept blew me away! I would've thought she was the first since it seemed such an unlikely marriage (classical music and anti-establishment rock-n-roll), but then again, so does motherhood and rebellion. One often does not exclude the other, but rather enhances it. Things aren't always as they seem on the surface, and often times one must look deeper in order to get to the real grits and butter of something or someone—including parenting and music. She has had struggles with the band, however; they more or less want her front and center singing and jumping, pushing her cello to the side—but that wasn't the deal. She is fighting to keep her cello center stage, and she has even added pick-ups to it. The band has helped her develop musically though,

★★★★★★★★

"I always thought the cello was the best symbol for a woman. It just expresses the greatest emotions, and has such fantastic symbolism. It's just so fitting! And it goes right between your legs!"

★★★★★★★★

"I'm learning how to project myself and be active performance-wise. I like being hyper, and having it there with me, and not having it break. As far as technique, there is no technique. I'm a music major, so I've been learning things like major seven, dominant chords. So the guys are like, 'play this: chun, chun, chun.' And so I'm trying to figure out what chun, chun, chun means in chords. So I'm kind of digressing in that sense, but one of my goals is to become a studio cellist and I'm going to run up against a lot of people who don't know a lot about music, even though they're in the music business. So I have to be able to know what chun, chun, chun means. So that's what playing in Breadlines at Gunpoint is like, ha-ha. I'm hoping to get an electric cello, but of course it costs money.

I'm also playing chamber music now. When I was younger I never wanted to play in an orchestra, it just seemed so very boring, not any excitement. Now that I've gotten older, I would actually like to play in one. Nobody expects me to say I like classical music, or that I play the cello for that matter, because of my appearance. I don't fit the description of a classical player at all. So it's sort of interesting what my choices are and how I'm going to be perceived. I keep having a feeling I'm going to have to dye my hair black [from blue] just because I want to play. But where else can I go? I'm just going to have to do it."

Marea is facing the reality of having to censor herself to meet a need. Marea explains:

"I've had blue hair since high school, but the truth of it is—I love blue! I love having blue hair! It doesn't go further than that. And it's unfortunate that people want it to be something other than that—which brings a lot more determination towards being able to play. There's nothing like showing up and them thinking, 'She's nothing! She's not serious.' Then I sit down and do my thing and blow them out of the water. And to be soooooooo good, they can't turn me away, and I look however I want to. And that's where the discipline comes in."

She says people in the classical world always seem to think she is trying to stand out, or that she's doing it because of her friends, but that just makes no sense to her. She only wants to be able to do what she loves expressively, including playing music professionally, and being herself. It sounds simple enough, but social structures tend to be hell-bent on control and authority. That's the real heart of the matter when it comes to professions, jobs, roles, schools etc: without dominance how will anyone be controlled?

Marea is still in touch with her daughter and the adoptive family, but it is annually now versus every couple of months. Whenever she does travel home to Minnesota, they all get together, every single time. She's horrible at writing and battles guilt when she doesn't send a birthday card home for Tovah, but she is torn. How involved should she be? So she keeps herself at a distance. When she does talk to them she lets them know how much she loves Tovah and how this is, has been, and will continue to be the best thing for them all. Tovah is very blessed to have two wonderful women in her life that love her very much—her mom and her birth-mother, Marea. The relationship Marea has with Tovah's family is honest, respectful, and considerate, which is a defining characteristic of an involved, committed, and successful open adoption. For Marea, it's not an issue of forgetting … just needing to move on. And she is making sure from here on out that what she does counts. For her future she says, "If I give myself to the cello, she will give herself to me, and take me wherever I want to go."

**Since this interview: Marea has graduated from school, fallen in love with motorcycles, and moved to Norway.*

ཐ ཆ

The Designers and Stylists

ཐ ཆ

Are you all work and no play? These moms will remind you to have fun, and glam-it-up a bit. They work hard and so do you. Let them show you the world of style!

The moms in this chapter will give you an inside peak into the world of high and low-brow fashion and design, and in their world it has to do with self-love not self-loathing, and on the cheap and on the fly.

Did you ever want to start your own business, but don't know where to start? A rad stylist mom does just that while giving you her blueprint! She also introduces us into the world of 50s cool and her story produces proof that single moms can make it, and do find true love again. You just have to keep your eye on the ball and keep truckin'. If you never have been on the wild side, it's okay. One L.A. designer to the stars will take you there.

Speaking of wild, they will all help you find ways to create unconventional work and child care that works for you! One mom will assure you that it's okay to be fabulous you while still being the greatest mom on earth! Her story is also a testament that we can somehow pick up the pieces of our heart from the floor of hell, when the worst tragedy a parent can ever imagine, happens. A kids clothing designer will show you how to make a few dollars crafting cool clothes from home while being a working stay-at-home parent. Ever want to transform your living space into something truly freakin' awesome? Or better yet want to get into the industry? The world's coolest interior designer shows you how while battling chronic health problems. Are you fed up with a crappy school system? One mom temporarily retires from the world of make-up and hair to go the unschooling route and shares her insights into all of it—life that is. Get ready for the ride on the wild-side as you step into …

The world of style and fashion with the Designers and Stylists!

"A mother is never done working; a mother is never, not needed. She instills in her children values, ideals, and goals that are kept and remembered for their entire lives. That is why our role as mother is important."

Stephanie
Gorgeous Cosmetologist
Moxie Salon Owner
Vincent Price Enthusiast
Beauty Book Author
Avid Snow White Collector
Children's Advocate
Hyperemesis Survivor
Grand Rapids, Michigan.

Stephanie is a newly remarried, daring, giddy, and fantastic retro-mom who has also recently added successful business owner to her list of accomplishments. Besides her family, the things that she loves most are collecting "everything Disney" (snow globes, figurines, lunch boxes, stamps, ornaments, and books), Vincent Price (she has a large tattoo of him with plans for more) and vintage juice glasses which are overfilling her cabinets like an overstuffed tofu-turkey. But this is just the tip of the iceberg—Stephanie has such a huge passion for life that I cannot even attempt to begin to describe her vivacious spirit within the confines of an introductory paragraph.

Stephanie spends her weekends dreaming about cowboys and pirates while sipping Diet Vanilla Pepsi and running vintage-style salon booths at festivals and events doing everybody's hair from B52's Kate Pierson, the crew on Ben Stiller's film *30 Minutes or Less,* and getting everybody dolled up for Viva Las Vegas. She has been on, or done the styling for models, for numerous magazines covers including *Tattoo Savage*, *REVUE*, and *On the Town*. She loves listening to music while working since it helps keep her and her clients pumped up. She frequently rocks out to her favorite musicians/bands like Morrissey, the Damned, Elton John (She loves hearing the piano!), Patti Smith, Wanda Jackson, Reverend Horton Heat, the Yo-Yo's, the Stray Cats, Billie Holiday, the Ramones, Rufus Wainwright, and Harry Connick Jr. Her life's work is dedicated to the glamour of the pin-up lifestyle and to raising her son with panache. When she isn't working she loves spending time with her two main boys: Vanian and her new second husband Steve.

Stephanie was amongst one of first ten women I interviewed for this book, and when we initially interviewed she was just defining her dreams, and had started cosmetology school. In the short six years since then all of her dreams have come true … with a lot of hard work, effort, and a dash of luck. I reached out to her as I was editing and revising her story, to let her know how damned proud of her I was, and to get the info you would all need! How did she get from A-to-Z? She got there because she has a good heart, she had a solid plan, and she wasn't afraid to keep trying. She also stayed positive while having the support of friends and family. We will start with A however, and what the beginning was like …

When we met she was working as a retail manager, and was twenty-five, and a newly divorced mom to Vanian, then three-years-old. She was already a diehard "fashion geek who loves handbags, shoes, and hair styles!" Life had thrown her a curveball, so she threw it back.

"I worked my retail job part-time, read fashion magazines, and read about fashion shows, etc. I wasn't sure that I would extend my boundaries much further that that career-wise, at least not for a long time. I assumed that I would have more children and being a mother would be #1 and my 'career'. Life has taken unexpected turns and has brought me to where I am now. I am recently divorced. I have the responsibility now of caring for me and my son financially. Since I have no schooling and no real career options available to me, I had to take a hard look at the future of my son, and I. I have no skills, no college degree; I don't even know how to type! Working retail is not what I want to do for the rest of my life. So I have decided that now is the time to pursue my love of the world of beauty! I am very excited about this new stage in life and the opportunities it may bring. It will be a process of learning something completely new and broadening my horizons. I never thought I would go to cosmetology school and have jumped at the chance!"

She had married young the first-time around, and didn't really have any set plans before becoming a mom. She laughs with acknowledgement, "My focus was mainly on myself. I don't know that I considered other people's feelings or needs as much. I think I was pretty selfish." She has become more aware of the needs of others, since having a child is like having a mirror that reflects your actions back towards you. She was like most young adults, working wherever and just planning on moving up the ladder there. She envisioned herself eventually being a clothing buyer or a music buyer for a company. She and her first husband had romanticized the ideal of moving to California, but never made any real efforts towards it. Then they learned they were pregnant.

"My pregnancy was not planned, but very wanted. My first husband and I were thrilled. Our families were thrilled and supportive. I had no idea what to expect! I had never been pregnant before so I wasn't quite sure what the nine months would be like. I never would have thought that I would be so sick! I read a lot of books on pregnancy and babies. Later in my pregnancy we took Lamaze classes. Although, the breathing techniques didn't help me, the class did prepare me for what to expect. I recommend taking the class. We took several other classes as well, Infant C.P.R.

[Cardiopulmonary Resuscitation], and another class on caring for infants. I think I was so concentrated on getting through the nine months that I didn't have time to be afraid of the delivery! After I became a parent, it set in that this thing isn't easy! You won't know until you experience parenthood for yourself how difficult it can be. Especially in the first few months when you are recovering and tired, but your baby needs you twenty-four hours a day. I remember thinking is he warm enough? Is he hungry? Is he sick? Is he comfortable? So many things go through your mind! Even now there is this fear that I'll fail in some way. I'm hoping this is normal! I want so much for my son to grow into a happy, healthy, confident person. All I can do is my best."

Stephanie was very ill during her pregnancy. She had hyperemesis which is a severe form of morning sickness with extreme nausea and vomiting. She felt like she was dying, and it was a terrifying physical ordeal for her.

"It was a scary time. I also think this gave me a huge wake-up call and I saw what was important and what wasn't. I realized that analyzing every little thing about my figure what stupid. Don't look in the mirror and tell yourself, how fat you are! Be thankful that you have food and can eat it! I could not keep food down for several months! I was fed by an I.V. Health is important. I thank god that I made it through and my son was born healthy."

She is frustrated that many women suffer from this and their doctors either don't know about it, or fail to take their concerns seriously until they end up in the hospital with an I.V., like she did. She wants every mom-to-be to know that there is morning sickness, and then there is *morning sickness*, and if you feel like you're dying and it's unrelenting, seek help since this condition can lead to fetal damage as well as miscarriage. She is an active member of the Her Foundation [Hyperemesis Education and Research Foundation]. You can learn more about this daunting pregnancy related condition at Hypermesis.org.

Stephanie embraced her new life as a mom and it opened her up to the wonders of the world that she had forgotten about like: going to the zoo, being outside in the spring and summer enjoying nature, and observing our role as mothers in life:

"Motherhood is the greatest experience and the greatest role a woman could have. A mother is a teacher, protector, provider, comforter, advice-giver, disciplinarian, friend, all wrapped up in one. It's a tough job to measure up to, but it's great at the same time. I watch as my child learns new things everyday. The simple things I never notice he learns for the first time, like a ladybug, or building a snowman. He always notices ants and follows them as they crawl along the pavement. All these things around me I start to see through his eyes.

Everyone has a mother and we all need them. Even though I am older, I still need my mom! I call her for advice or to tell her the latest news. A mother is never done working. A mother is never, not needed. She instills in her children values, ideals, and goals that are kept and remembered for their entire lives. That is why our role as mother is important. Since we remember what our mothers told us and taught us, we have to be aware of what we are telling and teaching our children. What we teach them about life, and about other people, and about themselves will be carried with them their whole lives. It's a big responsibility, but it's a responsibility that can lead to change, to more compassion in this world, to better self-esteem for our children, and respect for others. Mothers can change the world."

"I was in a verbally abusive marriage and didn't realize it. I felt completely overwhelmed by sadness and confusion. I had started to lose hope of having a happy marriage. Marriage counseling didn't help me and it left me without any answers as to what was happening in my marriage. Then I found out about Patricia Evans and her books on verbal abuse and her site VerbalAbuse. com."

Motherhood opened her eyes to so many things that she didn't see beforehand, including a failing marriage and escalating verbal abuse. She isn't sure if it had started before they had Vanian, or after when the pressures of supporting a family became apparent. What she does know though is that it hurt, and then it hurt worse, and eventually her self-esteem had gotten so low she didn't feel she could ever have happiness and was starting to lose her ability to function and cope. That's when she became aware that this was a problem and it wasn't just hers alone:

"I was in a verbally abusive marriage and didn't realize it. I felt completely overwhelmed by sadness and confusion. I had started to lose hope of having a happy marriage. Marriage counseling didn't help me and it left me without any answers as to what was happening in my marriage. Then I found out about Patricia Evans and her books on verbal abuse and her site, VerbalAbuse.com. To make a long story short, her books addressed every issue I was dealing with and clearly described what verbal abuse is. I recommend her books to anyone who thinks they may be in a verbally/emotionally abusive relationship."

The marriage wasn't salvageable, so Stephanie left a bad situation. She found herself divorced, suddenly homeless, and with no financial support. She felt as if she had "tripped over a huge rock and fell flat" on her face. Her life had fallen completely apart, with a toddler-in-tow. She didn't realize how amazing her parents and three brothers were until this happened, and they took her in. She feels very fortunate to have them and loves them deeply. She was starting over and she had the best support system ever, her family, and feels blessed, since she knows not everyone is that fortunate. Her words of advice for anyone in this situation is,

"I do know that sadness can have a nasty grip on you. Hope and looking ahead, not back, is the best cure. I looked to what the possibilities were in my future. I worked hard on keeping my self-esteem good, keeping my stress-level down and fighting loneliness. I hadn't had the greatest time battling those the past few years, but I did a lot better. I realized I have to find and accept what is truth, not what I think may be true, or what someone else tells me. A verbally and emotionally abusive relationship can really make you think things about yourself that aren't true, but at the time it's hard to see it. As far as loneliness is concerned, a person is sometimes lonelier in a relationship than out of one. I had the guts to face life as a single mom. I also had the guts to say I won't take abuse anymore. You can too."

Stephanie relied on music as her therapy tool. I think most of us can relate.

"Music is my place to go when life is good, bad, sad, happy, confusing, and stressful, or I'm in love. Songs like Social Distortion's *Reach for the Sky* and *Angel's Wings* and Horror Pop's *Emotional Abuse* have been played repeatedly in my CD player in the past. When a person relates to a song, it has healing power. I cannot watch the Johnny Cash video for *Hurt* or listen to him sing it without feeling touched, or tearing up. It's so emotional. He sings that song from the core. There's something about Dean Martin's voice that makes me smile every time I hear it. He sings so effortlessly. If I put the Misfits on, suddenly I'm like a rock star—pumping my fists in the air! Music is a constant in my life, because it resonates so deeply with me."

Music was her therapy, and art and prose articulated her longings for the future as she moved forward in her life, and put the past abuse behind her. She thinks there are two books that should be mandatory reading in high school which are *Tuesdays with Morrie* by Mitch Albom, and *Ragamuffin Gospel* by Brennan Manning, both works she cites as life changing. She is compelled to read biographies, which help her to place her experiences in perspective and context. Some of her favorite stories are the lives of: Ronald and Nancy Reagan, Traci Lords, Lauren Bacall, and Audrey Hepburn, "She was an incredible lady! She had such a big heart and did so much for UNICEF (United Nations Children's Fund). Every woman should read about her life." Her favorite poets are: Emily Dickinson, Edgar Allen Poe and Percy Bysshe Shelley. Shelley also wrote her favorite poem: *Love's Philosophy*.

Art helps her envision her passions and what she is attracted to in life which is romance and fun. She enjoys the art of Jack Vettriano, a handsome Scottish self-made artist who rose from the mining labor world. Her two favorite pieces by him are *The Last Great Romantic* and *The Road to Nowhere*. She also adores the work of Roy Lichtenstein; an iconic comic book influenced American pop artist, and the illustrations of Shag, a famed tiki-loving artist from Southern California.

She was empowered by the work and lives of her adopted mentors, and she found the courage to keep going after her dreams, while rebuilding her life and her son's. It was scary at first, but she knew she wanted it too much to let it overwhelm her, or to let fear stop her:

"My life's dreams kept me going day-to-day. My career dream was to complete school and open a retro-inspired salon and boutique with lots of pink and leopard print, with fun retro-barber chairs, selling vintage inspired cosmetics and beauty products!"

She kept telling herself, "Someday Steph!" and she did it! She took it one step at a time while keeping her ultimate goal in mind, and breaking it down to mini-milestone goals in between to ensure she got there:

a) Completed school.
b) Got a job in the field.
c) Got a place of her own for her and Vanian.
d) Specialized in retro-design and built up her skill-set.
e) Paid off her school debt.
f) Started to save money for the long-term goal of opening a salon.
g) Created an additional income stream while establishing herself as an expert in her field by creating two cool retro-style books for men and women. *(She had taught herself how to build websites and create graphic design lay-outs with a now defunct, but early motherhood, social site for vintage lifestyle moms called Strollerville.com; which was crucial to her being able to design and create style manuals. The books took minimal investment since she printed them on a pre-ordered basis with a local printer and she and her second husband Steve collaborated on them together doing all the work themselves.)*
h) Laid out her business plan for her salon.

Basically, Stephanie worked studiously, built-up experience, networked, and gradually saved money from doing hair and the sales from her books *Set & Style* and *Grease it Up* (which feature great illustrations by Steve). She raised capital so that she could come up with a down payment on her salon location while buying what was essential for the interior of the salon and starter gear, and doing the interior design herself. Steve had suddenly walked into her life a couple of years after she finished school …

"Then there's this thing called love. Of course I didn't want to be alone for the rest of my life. But I wasn't looking for just anyone. I think that's in a Morrissey song! Anyway, it's true. I didn't seem to do very well in this department, ha-ha. But then again there seemed to be a lack of quality fish in the sea. I wanted to be in love. I dreamt of that shortness of breath, heart stopping, and melting into the floor kind of love. Something I had never known. I dreamt that there was someone out there who thought that his life just wouldn't be the same if I weren't part of it."

When she met Steve, he was the man of her dreams, and he wasn't afraid to be a real man—he put all of the other fish in her sea to shame. He is a stand-up, righteous, intelligent, hot-rod loving man with a strong work ethic, and he is caring, considerate, heroic, sweet, romantic and loving. Like Stephanie, he has splendid fashion flair, and he's an amazing step-father. Vanian knows him simply as dad, proving love and family is much bigger than the limited concepts of blood or water. Steve has been very supportive of Stephanie's dreams, and talents, and has been her right-hand man ever since they fell in love—and her co-parenting partner. They married in 2007. It was her second shot at marriage, but she knew without a doubt that he was the one, and that everything in her life had led up to her meeting him, her opening her dream business, and her being a wonderful mom to Vanian:

> "Becoming a mother changed my view of life. Suddenly the focus was taken off myself. I had received my answer as to what I was supposed to be in life, a mother. I have always had a love of fashion and beauty, but I initially set that aside when I first became a mother and wife. It was important to me to be home with my son. Of course things changed when I left my first husband, but when I became a mother it's almost like I became a new person in a sense. I was now protecting and caring for a little person. Life becomes a little brighter and a lot more meaningful. With the good times and the bad times I've had, his love and my love for him has been constant. His hugs and kisses are the best! Anytime he says, 'I love you mommy' it doesn't matter what happened that day, I melt and my day is brighter."

Stephanie does feels that mothers are devalued in society and that, "Stay-at-home [working] moms are great women, and working moms are great women. They are both important." She doesn't like the misleading stereotype that implies that stay-at-home moms have it easy, and feels that, "It's a tough job that doesn't get much notice." She has been both and can speak from experience. She also thinks kids aren't faring much better either.

"Children in society have a bumpy road. There are so many things that our society throws at children. There seems to be a pill for every problem. Medicating kids seems too common and accepted. There is a big problem with child obesity and diabetes. Kid's health is going downhill. I took a nutrition course and it helped me understand food and how it affects our bodies. I would recommend it to other moms. It can help you know how to be balanced with your food choices and teach your children good food choices. There is a lot in our grocery stores that are harmful.

Kids also need real role models. All the Brittney Spears's, Christina Aguilera's, and other half-dressed with no talent singers there are now, just don't cut it. How do these people become role models for our kids?! Maybe things really haven't changed from when I was a kid. But I didn't know what Playboy was when I was thirteen, and there's no way I would wear a Playboy t-shirt at that age!

I think society's constant need to stay young and thin is influencing younger and younger girls. Plastic surgery seems bigger than ever. I do think girls learn how to view themselves from their moms. Perfection in beauty becomes an obsession and it gets passed down to our children."

As a mom, she expects to be able to provide a home environment that is: loving, safe, and secure. She teaches Vanian that, "Life is hard but it doesn't have to beat you." She hopes to be the person he comes to for advice and help. She wants him to value himself and others. When her first marriage fell apart, she was placed on a "huge guilt-trip" that her son's life would be ruined and he would be stricken with behavior problems and learning disabilities. She ignored the curses of doom and dismay and did what was best for her, and him, and he is a very happy and physically healthy child. In fact, he's a great kid with good manners, probing curiosity, and a sincere, sweet disposition. Stephanie knew this would be the outcome all along if she raised him in a sound and healthy environment, which made divorcing his biological father even more necessary:

"I knew my son was not a reject of society. I knew he had, and has, potential beyond anyone's limits. He can be whoever he wants; the doors are completely open to him. I hope as he grows up he will continue to find what makes him happy, and what he is talented at and pursue it to the fullest. My hope is that he becomes a man who is courageous, confident, and compassionate. I want him to be successful and happy in life, not to prove certain people wrong, because I already knew they were wrong, but because happiness is his to have and he isn't beneath those things."

The core of her parenting philosophy comes from her ideals and her experiences.

"I am a person who hates to give up without a fight, without trying. The one thing I tell myself, and instill in my son, is to always try. Reach for the skies, give 'em all you've got, and then go back for more! When things have fallen apart, or didn't turn out like I had hoped, I had to keep on going. It can be hard to keep keepin' on when life throws a curve, and I have found myself at what seemed the bottom of the barrel.

When I first divorced, I had moved to a new place, and realized how hard it was being on the outside. When you don't have friends, don't know the right people, start a new job, and don't quite fit in. I know also how it feels to be treated cruelly, to feel invalid, to have someone make you feel unimportant. I think it is so important to stop and think about how we treat other people in our day to day lives. It's easy to hurt someone with words. I also think it's important to stand up for yourself when someone tries to intimidate, devalue, or disrespect you with words. People tend to be so rude to others over small things. That reflects on our children. They watch how we treat others and they in turn treat their classmates or playmates in that manner. I'm a big believer in the importance of a simple please and thank you.

I'm also a very giving person. I would much rather give something to someone in need than buy something for myself. There are several charities I try to send donations too regularly like Children of the Night [.org]. They help rescue kids from prostitution. They supply kids with a place to stay, food to eat, schooling, and essentials like: soap, toothbrushes, clothing, etc. It goes right along with thinking of other people and valuing their lives, like you do your own. I hope my son will grow up to see how important it is to consider others who are in need."

As a subculture mom she gotten some interesting reactions from others and has had some downright mean encounters with other moms:

"Most moms I meet think I'm strange simply because they have never heard of rockabilly or psychobilly! The music alone sets me apart from most people, especially other moms. My son is named after David Vanian, lead singer for the Damned. I did not name my son Vanian because of a crazy obsession, or to be 'scary' or 'gothic'!

I simply love the name and they are a favorite band of mine. My son's name is very personal and special to me.

I am a mom with tattoos. I am asked daily if they are real! My son and I go to the library often, and one particular time we were there, a mother made her son go clear across to the other side of the room to stay away from the 'scary' lady! Vanian and I were playing with a puzzle. I was so disgusted at what she just taught her child. Never teach your child that someone who is different than you is 'weird' or 'scary'. Differences are a good thing. It keeps things from getting boring. Uniqueness is good.

★★★★★★★★★

"My life simply reflects who I am. I have become a mother, but I hold onto my interests, music, beliefs, loves. My car still has Nekromantix, Social Distortion, and Tiger Army stickers on it! My son and I play air-guitar and sing along to Brian Setzer and the Bouncing Souls. I enjoy my hobbies, interests, and clothes. I embrace life! I think sometimes mainstream thinking, or what I like to call small-town minds can kill a spirit, lead to hate, and squander the arts. People tend to really fear difference."

★★★★★★★★★

I am a mom who loves all things classic, vintage, antique and art deco. I enjoy the 1930s through the 1950s. There are many treasures to be found in the antique shops and thrift shops of America! I love old Hollywood with its glamour, and its classy dames and handsome leading men.

I don't meet many moms whose dream is car is a 1959 Cadillac! I have no skills of my own when it comes to cars! However, my father and grandfather are auto body repair men. I grew up around cars and watching them restore classics. I remember helping my father paint one of his cars and I accidentally put a big smear across the hood! Man that was not good! I think I was sixteen or seventeen-years-old. I definitely have an admiration for classic cars and the talented people who restore and customize them. I am amazed at what my father and grandfather can do with cars.

I have meet moms with similar interests through the site I had, but didn't know any moms where I lived until much more recently. It was nice to finally meet some other retro-moms I have things in common with so that Vanian could play with friends and relate to them as well.

Sometimes I get asked, 'When are you going to grow out of all this?' Or someone will say 'Just wait until you have kids, then you'll be boring like me!' It's assumed I have not grown up or matured, if I don't seem like the typical soccer-mom. It's often a surprise to people when I tell them I am a mother [and now a successful business owner]."

Stephanie isn't sure what drew her to a subculture lifestyle, but somewhere in the early days of high school she started listening to punk and the rest is history! She values uniqueness, creativity, and expression, and that may have sparked the initial attraction. She also thinks sometimes parents, out of fear, will squash a child's natural deviation towards what suits them best *[For example, if you a have son who is more inclined to be a dancer {or a pastry chef, florist, drag queen, social worker, actor, etc.}, but you worry he will be labeled and ridiculed … and as a parent, with good intentions, you may try to force more 'masculine' sports/electives on him, like playing football or becoming a Marine. Normally, in the long run much more harm is caused than good. You also have to scrutinize your intention as well—are you doing this to shelter him, or to protect yourself from the ridicule of your neighbors/peers and what they may think? It takes bravery and fortitude to do the right thing as a parent and a person.]* Stephanie feels fortunate that she had a family that loved her just the way she was, and she was allowed to mature into herself.

"My life simply reflects who I am. I have become a mother, but I hold onto my interests, music, beliefs, loves. My car still has Nekromantix, Social Distortion, and Tiger Army stickers on it! My son and I play air-guitar and sing along to Brian Setzer and the Bouncing Souls. I enjoy my hobbies, interests and clothes. I embrace life! I think sometimes mainstream thinking, or what I like to call small-town minds … can kill a spirit, lead to hate, and squander the arts. People tend to really fear difference."

She is bemused at the influence of celebrities on society. She cites for example when rapper-extraordinaire P. Diddy wore a Von Dutch hat, "The next day it suddenly becomes a 'designer label' in the media and everyone and their mother has to have one!" What stymies Stephanie is that no one even takes the time to find out who Von Dutch was (artist Kenny Howard) and people *just have to have* the jeans and hat, because suddenly a star wore them and now everyone else is wearing them! "Everyone's brains get morphed as soon as a celebrity is mentioned! It seems like everyone tries hard to be a celebrity." She passed on the ugg boots craze with miniskirts spawned by mass culture consumption of celebrity fashion. Suddenly, everyone was walking around in eighty-degree weather with heavy, warm, furry boots on that are meant to be worn in near or below freezing weather. She also knows though that not all of mainstream society endorses or just jumps on the band wagon of popular culture, or accepts everything at face value, and it's important that we as moms scrutinize what is being promoted to us and why, but even us cool, kick-ass moms, have to remember to keep our minds open as well:

> "I think subculture/counterculture moms understand the importance of accepting people for who they are. We know the importance of letting our kids be who they are. I think we may see things bigger, more opened up, instead of in a tiny box. We encourage our kids to be into the arts and music, which I think are key outlets for them to expand their minds and express themselves. I think there is always something to learn in life and we can learn from anyone.
>
> I must not be close-minded because another person or mom seems 'square'. I've been treated rude by other mothers and my son has been treated poorly by their kids—but it doesn't mean that every mainstream mother is that way. If I want other moms to be accepting of me, I have to accept them for who they are as well. That is how we will teach our children to care and think of others, even those who seem different."

Stephanie is a vivacious mom and woman and has successfully worked hard to rebuild her life and her son's from the rubble of a young marriage turned bad. She shows us that no matter what is thrown our way, we can overcome it, and still achieve our dreams, while being an incredible parent. Her son has been the highlight of her whole life and she never wants to go a day without his kisses and hugs. Or her husband Steve's for that matter. She remembers where she has been, and hopes that her story can help you hold on to the faith if you find yourself in need,

> "We simply do the best we can as parents. My philosophy on life is basically that life can be tough and uncertain, but you have to keep going. Family and friends are the most important, so hold them close, especially in tough times. Never give up. Health, happiness, and family … are our treasures."

And if you are ever in Grand Rapids, Michigan and in need of some quality mom-makeover time, be sure to swing by and see Stephanie at her vintage beauty parlor, Moxie! Just tell her Rebel Moms sent you. It will make her day, and her vixen style team will make yours, pampering you like the queen you are!

"If you were to drop by on most days, more than likely, the BBQ and stove would be going, the glue gun would be plugged in, and fabric, feathers and rhinestones would be flyin' around."

Winter
Fashion Designer
Fetish Model
Damn-hot Dominatrix
World Explorer
BBQ Chef
Los Angeles, California.

Winter is a forceful storm rocking through town on a smog-filled, hot, summer day. She lives in Los Angeles and designs crotch-less panties for the superstars and has for over ten years.

She loves bright colors, good people who are a little bad; being at BBQs filled with meat and ribs, and music, music, music! Winter loves old punk, old honky tonk and country. Her husband has also played with the Avengers and played guitar for Chris Isaac for twelve years. They have only one household rule: no techno allowed.

She describes their lifestyle as eccentrically entertaining. They try to maintain a healthy balance of partying, working and parenting.

She loves creepy-crafting, cooking, and playing with her glue gun. She loves motorcycles, cars, racing, and demolition derby. She always knew, deep down, that she wanted to be a stock car racer, and someday plans on getting behind the wheel. She also wants her own punk rock cooking show, which was in the works before becoming a parent. Winter describes herself as:

> "My legs are six-inches too short, arms three-inches too long, freckles on my knees, beer in one hand, and a cigarette in the other. I am 100 lbs. of loud American Punk Rock trucker-mouthed momma."

Her favorite artist is a friend of hers named Elizabeth McGrath whose style is, 'both cute and disgusting.' Her favorite book is called *Geek Love* written by Katherine Dunn. Her favorite poet is Shel Silverstein who also writes children's poetry.

Winter has been designing for over ten years now for Trashy Lingerie. She started off in L.A. as a seventeen-year-old runaway who had drug problems. She landed her first job in the fashion industry at that time. Initially, she was paid $5.00 an hour to get lunch for the designers, runs their errands, and rip out the company's ads from magazines for the company's portfolio.

In just three years, she worked her way up to a textile designer and got her first loft in downtown L.A. By the time she was twenty-one she had a job as a head designer and was making tons of money, traveling the world, and living the life of a Hollywood superstar. The parties were outlandish and would last for days on end. Winter was hooked on the great party themes. She kept this up for five years until she developed bleeding ulcers and then decided she needed a break from designing and the lifestyle that came with it. This is when she became a professional dominatrix.

It came pretty natural for her since she had also worked as an art and fetish model for famed erotica photographers Gary and Pierre Silva. She had been doing nude shoots for them since she was eighteen-years-old. When she quit her career as a fashion designer she convinced one of her slaves to invest $20,000 in a dungeon for her. She loved it. She made $250.00 dollars an hour to 'punish' men and got fabulous corsets and boots as gifts.

She eventually became bored with this and wanted to get back into fashion and took a job at Trashy Lingerie, where she still works now. She designs custom clothing for movies, television, celebrities, and the wives of rich men in Beverly Hills. One of her favorite designs came from a dream …

> "It's nothing special, but I own tons of them now and wear it a lot. I had this dream that I was freezing cold and looking in this store window at this track suit. It was big, fluffy and in the softest fabric. I wanted it so bad, I woke up bought some polar fleece and sewed one myself … We sell them like hotcakes in the store now!"

She made an amazing dress for Linda Blair, the horror movie queen and U.K. actress. It had birds all over it and Linda wore it the British Comedy Awards. She also had tons of fun turning Michael Jordon's old jerseys into a dress for Mariah Carey. Winter even once had to make a sports jacket for an orangutan. You can check out her designs at Trashy.com.

Her words of advice for anyone wanting to get into fashion design, is to work your ass off. You will need to stay focused and free in your creativity, and 'dress up' your resume some. She exaggerated a little here, and a little there, but it helped her career instead of hurting it, "I'm really proud of my career, considering, I'm a high school dropout. I don't really resent anything I've done, even the tons of nude modeling photos."

Speaking of awesome nude photos, Gary and Pierre Silva released a book called *Delicious* that has over nine pages of

Winter. Her husband was not too thrilled about it, but Winter was stoked! She can't change what's in her past, and the photos are great, and she is really happy she did them. You can check out the book at: SilvaPhoto.com.

Her job as a designer has taken her to faraway places like Hong Kong, Korea, and Brazil. She says the perception of Americans overseas isn't real positive, but who can blame them? When you consider the negative impacts our capitalist ways have had on their economies and quality of life:

> "The Orient looks to America as a major asset obviously, that's their industry, manufacturing plastic garbage for the masses. They are very polite to Americans, but it's really sad to see the common workers there. I went to sweat shops and factories. It's sad. I saw the way they live. Dilapidated sky rise apartments, buildings with tiny rooms. Each room has one window with a big long pole sticking out of it with all their laundry on it. It's quite a sight to see, a twenty-five story building with hundreds of poles full of laundry coming off the sides! I was there right before the communists took it back in 1997. I remember being really drunk in a taxi cab and asking the driver about his country turning back communist. He started screaming in Chinese and English. I couldn't understand him but I got the jist.
>
> Brazil though is very European. They don't care much for snooty, uppity Americans. They have all their own resources, they don't need us. It's a great place ... there is very little English spoken there and it is virtually uncorrupted by America. I highly recommend Brazil! It's heaven on Earth. I have been back there twice and am looking right now for properties to buy, so eventually I can move there. I need to travel more to elaborate even more here, but I will say this, I've left the U.S. enough times to understand why the rest of the world hates us so much."

Since Winter has become a mother she works part-time at the studio, and works the rest of the week from home. She makes the patterns and designs, and has over forty amazing seamstresses!

She is really frightened of daycare and didn't want her kid in a "disease pit." He is over two-years-old and hasn't been sick yet. A great thing happened for them though, making managing work and parenting easier. Her husband Jimmy works for a big ad agency in Hollywood and a lesbian couple there were expecting their own baby at the same time they were. The two couples hired a full-time nanny and set up a mutual nursery in their office. The nanny works with the kids there while they work. Jimmy takes little Waylon to work with him three days a week. It gives Winter a chance to work at the studio. The two couples split the cost of the nanny. The rest of the week Waylon is home with Winter.

Their son Waylon is named after the late and great outlaw and performer Waylon Jennings. He is the guy that sung the Dukes of Hazard theme song. Her husband Jimmy has played guitar with little Waylon since day one and now their toddler is obsessed with it! Winter describes Waylon:

> "He's a really good baby. He's very tolerant, loves to be passed around, and loves people. He's the kind of kid that makes people who don't want kids want one … like all my friends. He has red hair, blue eyes, and is silly-as-hell!"

Winter met her husband, Jimmy, in the now famous punk rock bar, Al's Bar, in downtown L.A. Shortly thereafter, he moved into the loft with her and they threw many parties and tore up the town. They recruited several strippers from local clubs for their parties and even had a dancing pole installed in their kitchen. This period lasted for five years and came to an end when the city shut down the building where they lived forcing everyone to move. They had had big plans for the dancing pole though,

> "I had a stripper pole installed in my kitchen, because of my plans to do a rock 'n' roll cooking show, me cooking, and I would have strippers named, Beef, Chicken, Pork and Fish, and a different live band every week. I had crap loads of folks ready to shoot the pilot … then we got kicked out of our loft! I still plan on doing it. It would be a big sacrifice now though. Even if MTV picked it up, it wouldn't pay for shit and would be tons of work! Right after we got kicked out we moved into a house in the hills and wham in two months, we were pregnant! We are happier than ever now though!"

It was an unplanned pregnancy but, "life is so short … how can we plan?" (Winter likes waking up in the morning and just deciding life one-day-at-a-time.) She was thirty-four then and the clock was ticking so it was, "now or never." She pretty much decided now was the time to become a mom, "A void has been filled that I never knew existed. I've never felt so happy and complete."

She hopes she sheds a new light on parenting, as we know it, and at the same time raises a child who is a free thinker for a new generation … and a rock star! She can't expect anything from herself as a parent except that she will live for her boy, and hopes he loves her. She hopes he finds a way to be happy in, "a fucked up world." She hopes he never has to see a war draft, and she hopes the current 'war' we're in will end. Winter makes it a point to be as happy as possible, and tries to show strength, exercise freedom, and introduces knowledge, to her son. She believes if you just be yourself and be happy, your kid will love you for it; "Life is too short, so stop SUCKING!"

> **"I was scared shitless, scared of maternity clothes, scared of soccer moms, scared of ME not being accepted into the 'mommy-world', because of who I am. I was scared of losing who I was. I was scared of play dates and Gymboree. I was scared of nannies abusing my baby, scared of molesters and drugs. I was scared of raising a child in the time of war. I was scared of my karma. Then I realized who I was and I could do this on roller skates."**

The fact that she never wanted a kid before having one blows her mind because she is so happy. Life can be pleasantly surprising. Her husband was her life force and support during the pregnancy. Her friends went into an emergency state of shock, but that weeded out who her friends really were. Pregnancy and motherhood was daunting nonetheless.

"I was scared shitless, scared of maternity clothes, scared of soccer moms, scared of ME not being accepted into the 'mommy-world', because of who I am.

I was scared of losing who I was. I was scared of play dates and Gymboree. I was scared of nannies abusing my baby, scared of molesters and drugs. I was scared of raising a child in the time of war. I was scared of my karma. Then I realized who I was and I could do this on roller skates. I just hoped I could make other parents realize that changing who you are because you've had a child, only makes the child miserable because you are. I had a plan to raise my child in my wonderful world and not listen to everyone's bullshit. I read so many books on so much complete bullshit and that state of panic was so unnecessary. The only reality I deal with now, and did not expect, was this insane feeling of natural love for my kid; total animal instinct that is completely overbearing!"

About her observation of motherhood in general she has this to say,

"I think motherhood is a very serious choice. I think a lot of women don't realize how tough it really is, and I have a lot of respect for a woman who chooses not to have a child, because she realizes she's not cut out for it . . . one less child with a shitty upbringing in this world! Fucked up people need to stop breeding. I realize this statement sounds harsh, but if you can't commit, then don't do it. Like how many times do we have to be told to NOT leave the fucking baby in the car in the middle of summer while you're getting a fuckin' pedicure? ARRRGHHHH!"

Up until recently, she didn't know other moms like herself. She thanks the internet for changing that situation. She became acquainted with PunkyMoms.com and became involved in the online community and made strong friendships that were sealed with interstate flights and play dates, plus nights out on the town with no kids. The community became such a part of her life, that when the founder Jessica Seymour wanted to move on to a different project, Winter and two of the other moms bought the site and community-indie-business, and revamped it with the slogan "Punky Moms—Kicking Motherhood in the Ass!" Punky Moms is also how I met both Winter and Jessica, as well as Rebel Mom Carol.

She is really blown away that there aren't more moms like herself in Los Angeles, "parents with a force" she means. She knows a few limited ones locally like Slash's wife who took over running Heidi Fleiss business while she was in jail, and her initial dominatrix teacher who is an amazing stepmom. Her close friend Tracy is a teen psychologist, punk rock as hell, and an awesome mom too. That's the gamut. Most moms she meets recoil in horror from her, yet are intrigued by her, and treat her as a scientific subject to be quizzed:

> "They take one look at me and see satan. They never give me a chance, if they only knew ... idiots. It's funny cause other moms always ask me what I am doing to have such a good, happy, baby? Cause obviously, they think I'm a fuckin' junkie or something, cause I smoke cigarettes, WHOA ... I just tell them, I never changed who I was because I had a child. Why should we all be miserable?"

Winter's concedes that her kid will have the freedom to be whoever he wants, just like her. She's all for what's in the heart. She feels moms who have lost themselves to trying to confirm to this suffocating perfect/normal/self-sacrificing/self-censoring-mommy image will teach their children only shame, because many of those kids are forced into doing things they really hate in an atmosphere of negativity. Winter's fear is that children of this sort of parenting will in turn force that shame onto other children through teasing and bullying, leading to a vicious and violent cycle. She doesn't want Waylon to fall victim to kids like that. Her solution is to prepare him to be brave and aware while allowing him room for growth in a supportive and creative atmosphere, the type of environment Winter herself had, but with improvements in the awareness/attention/love department.

In elementary school, Winter was the "total geek-nerd-freak" that collected bugs and loved science and geology. Her parents never forced her into doing stuff she didn't like, but they didn't pay her much attention either. "I'm sad because I've never been close to my parents. I was an accident after they had three kids and I was very neglected, and still am."

"Punky Moms—Kicking Motherhood in the Ass!"
PunkyMoms.com

She gives credit to her siblings for raising her and that's why she turned out so kick-ass. Her favorite older brother was into rockabilly, and her sister was a 1970s glitter punk. As a kid she always wanted to be the Dolphin Girl at Sea World, "The one who does hand stands on the dolphins and says … Taaa-Daaa!" However, she skipped majoring in marine biology though for a fun life of a designer in Hollywood.

She thinks it's funny just how commercial and mainstream "generic punk rock" is these days. *[It would be great if it was having a serious impact, but it's becoming profit-driven, and retooled/sexed back up, reflecting antiquated sexist mainstream 'values'. Same thing can be said for the spin-off of radical movements, once marketing gets its hands on it, it becomes feel-good stuff for the mainstream that re-supports capitalism and exploitation making the original movement far less effective and reinforces the status quo it originally challenged. It still has the potential for good and impact, but only if you dig deep past the 'new' hype. Think of the novel, "Citizen Girl" by Emma McLaughlin and Nicole Kraus, which humorously illustrates this point in general for the feminist and non-profit social crowds and movements. But I guess for trends, at least it's swinging in the right direction when you take into account vegetarianism, Buddhism, goddess-worship, the green movement, indie presses, punk rock feminism, feminist parenting, etc.]* It wasn't like that when she was starting out, and everyone that was 'different' got their asses kicked. She strives to stay as non-mainstream as possible. For her every day is a challenge with her look as a subculture parent, period. As a designer, and a punk rock mom, fashion and attitude is everything.

Winter loves themes and here lately her thing has been "Hollywood-white-trash-cholita." Her husband is a country musician who likes to wear, "nudie suits with rhinestones." Sometimes she works in a 1940s style cholita-cowgirl outfit for fun inspiration. She also loves adding fake blood dripping from her ears "cause that's just damned cute!"

She eventually wants to get her cooking show off the ground, and also sing in a band, because she's so good on stage. She admits though that she needs to learn how to sing first. Her big frustration is that there is so much she wants to do, but not enough time. Her closing thoughts are,

"Society SUCKS! I'm a Punk Rock Mom! I enjoy walking down the street in high-heeled boots and big fucked-up hair and tons of make up with my happy, giggling baby on my hip! Women resist me at first, then wind up asking me what I do to have such a good baby who never screams. It's simple. Don't change who you are. Be a person."

Amen sister.

**Since this interview: After thirteen years at Trashy, Winter has now left and is designing for Leg Avenue. She has also started a specialized custom design line under the alias Creepsuela Switchletto.*

"I am proud of my life. I know a lot of my family doubted my marriage, me having children, and me being a hair stylist. I have shown them that I can make it and have a wonderful family despite my alternative life style."

Dawna
Inked Intellectual
Pop Mod Momma
Art Lover
Healer
Hot Hair Colorist and Stylist
Erie, Pennsylvania.

Dawna grew up inspired by the art and lifestyles of some of the most notorious artists and writers of the twentieth century. She loves Picasso, Van Gogh, Warhol, Monet and Anais Nin. She admires Nin and views her as an amazing and strong woman for her time, and ours.

You take this formula, shake it up with Oi music, sixties British pop, northern soul, and bands like The Smiths and The Cure, and you get a colorful Dawna martini. Dawna is full of life and always embraces living with a lovely bite and a playful twist.

Her love of art is colorfully displayed on her body via tattoos. Her love of living is symbolically marked by piercings on her temple/body. Her love of color and texture is why she chose to be a hair stylist. It allows her hands to create living works of art for people and the image they want to project. It makes her feel great to have clients that trust her, and include her in their vision of themselves. She knows when she is commissioned to do someone's hair it so much more than just a color or style, it is creating magic for the client in her chair. She has been doing hair now for ten years, of which many have been spent at Studio Hue, an upscale couture salon in the heart of Erie.

Dawna loves working at Studio Hue since the owner, Judy Meyn, was trained in London under the great Vidal Sassoon. Dawna practices and adheres to his art-hair philosophy of smooth and geometric lines. She also loves bringing people to life through surreal and intense coloring adaptations. They carry exclusive organic Italian color lines that make their clients feel both eco-friendly and pampered. They love their clients and although the studio is refined glamour, with a penchant for edge-y fun, they make sure everyone feels at home, and treat their clients to gourmet coffees and pastries in addition to relaxed and individual consultations.

Dawna also enjoys making clocks, painting, refurbishing vintage furniture, and exploring the world with her kids and husband. Dawna describes herself as:

> "I am me! I am a strong, smart, open-minded, loyal and loving woman! I am me, I have always done things the way I wanted, like with my clothes and hair, and to this day I still do!"

Dawna had a wonderful childhood and recognizes how lucky she is to be able to say so. She did have some personal battles as a teenager, (like most of us) that she had to deal with. She overcame eating disorders in high school, which came from the need to be thin at all costs and beautiful. *[Beautiful in the context of the image that sells magazines. Images of women who are: overtly tall, unshapely thin, and exotically gorgeous and wealthy, or so they are portrayed. These images have a negative impact on self esteem in adolescents, who aren't able to achieve this body image, that lifestyle, or that perceived value.]* She and all of her girlfriends in high-school started a variety of anorexic and bulimic behaviors when normal eating and exercising wasn't achieving the look they wanted.

Dawna finally did deal with her eating disorder and her perception of body image. In fact, it started her love affair with art, because suddenly women were portrayed shapely and realistically. She became comfortable with herself and developed a deep sense of self-respect and healing that enabled her to make the transition from teenager to woman. Out went Cosmo, and in came Impressionism and modern feminism. This cross-over gave birth to self-love that started in her later teen years and also helped her end a teenage relationship with an abusive boyfriend.

She never had to rebel against her parents to get their attention. Because they were so open-minded and loving, she never had to pretend to be someone else in an attempt to make them happy, or meet exact expectations as far as what kind of person she should be, or what she should like or not like. This is a lesson she thinks mainstream parents can learn from, to be truly supportive of your child and embrace them for who they are, not who you want them to be. Dawna had an awesome childhood and

Dawna finally did deal with her eating disorder and her perception of body image. In fact, it started her love affair with art, because suddenly women were portrayed shapely and realistically. She became comfortable with herself and developed a deep sense of self-respect and healing that enabled her to make the transition from teenager to woman. Out went Cosmo, and in came Impressionism and modern feminism.

wants to give that to her children. The strong framework her own parents gave her opened the door for her as a parent,

> "I would say we offer support of allowing our children to be who they really are, not forcing them to be like everyone else or better than. We are not afraid of culture, art and music."

★★★★★★★★

"I think society never focuses on the good points of motherhood and parenting. They always focus on how uncomfortable and 'ugly' pregnancy is, and how expensive raising children are, never the beauty of it all."

★★★★★★★★

It is important that her children know every part of society around them, the good and the bad, and to be open-minded and non-judgmental. She knows that,

> "When I have a mother as a client we talk the normal baby talk, but a mother in public would never approach me and talk about parenting. They probably think I am baby-sitter or a bad mother."

As a tattooed parent, she takes her children to shows and festivals. She allows them to have mohawks and dress the way they want. No traditional gender coded coloring, like boys in blue, for Dawna and her family. However, she does have some traditional parent practices. There are rules. She rewards for good things, and punishes for bad things. She balances this with giving them lots of love and respect. She stays patient and strong even in the most stressful moments of parenting, such as tantrums, and trying to make school, work, and money balance. [She and I fully bond at this juncture of the interview. For me, parenting and taking care of a family of three on 14.00 dollars per hour, before taxes and insurance premiums, is pretty damn hard. She can fully relate. We agree that juggling it all too can be quite daunting. As her and I trade parenting advice (mainly me getting and Dawna giving) Corben goes into tantrum mode and dad whisks him away. I let Dawna know that my time for artistic commitment today is going to have to be cut-short; luckily, as a mom of young children she fully understands.] Her hopes for her children are for them to live happy, healthy lives and that they will live life to the fullest, like she does.

When her husband and she started their family they were fortunate to have support from all their friends, family, and even co-workers! This helped take the fear out of the unknown. She knew she wanted to be a mother and was going to make it work no matter what. The reality of motherhood has been pure happiness and amazement. It astonishes them that they created these wonderful beings …

> "I think society never focuses on the good points of motherhood and parenting. They always focus on how uncomfortable and 'ugly' pregnancy is, and how expensive raising children are, never the beauty of it all."

Her worst fears during pregnancy was that something devastating may happen, or losing their children afterwards. Their daughter Aislin died at the age of nineteen months due to a neurological disorder. But they have had to keep going for their other children Baylon now eight, and Alton now three. The loss of Aislin drives them to live life with more intensity, and with happiness, for both themselves and their children. Dawna truly appreciates how precious a gift motherhood is, and what a gift children are and can be. What's the most important thing she can feed her kids? Knowledge and love! Her role as a mother is to be the best she can be and to nurture her children the best she can. She is a feisty woman full of warmth, energy, and hope. She is a sweet and cool-as-hell Rebel Mom!

Dawna has bright plans for her future. She plans on traveling the world and exploring this amazing, crazy thing called life with her family and eventually opening up her own salon, "Since becoming a mother my life is full of true happiness. Watching my children grow is amazing. Yes, life can be very hectic, but when I look upon my children sleeping at night, I smile knowing it's all worth it."

"I believe that most people in society would rather not deal with children at all. They are too concerned with material possessions, careers, and vanity. Women are supposed to be career-oriented and if they are 'mothers' they should have a good daycare, or a nanny, an SUV and a great job."

Juli
Interior Designer
Pouty Painter & Artist
Kute Kitsch Enthusiast
Oi Skin
Chicago, Illinois.

Juli is a goofball, who can be a (self-described) pessimistic, jaded, tough ass. She can also be a sweetheart who will be your best friend until you cross her. She is "loud and obnoxious," but hides her sensitive side who is a "tattooed, chubby loudmouth with a good heart, and a love of animals, but I'm not a big fan of the general public." Before having her son, art and music was her life.

Juli loves pop culture, architecture, interior design and true crime. Kitsch is one of her favorite arts [which is tiki, low-brow art, and 1950s and 1960s interiors]. She paints and draws frequently and has been told her work is very good, but she chooses not to pursue it professionally. She does it for herself only, and she wants to keep it that way.

Her favorite artists are Salvador Dali, Picasso, Shag, Frida Kahlo, Lexander Calder, Andy Warhol, and Keith Haring. She likes them all specifically because of their impact on the art world, and they all changed it radically, and feels that art has never been perceived the same since.

Her favorite bands and musicians are DRI, GBH, Black Flag, Misfits, Desmond, Dekker, Laurel Aitken, The Specials, Madness, Les Baxter, Motorhead, Probot, Celtic Frost, Billie Holiday, Josephine Baker, Dizzie Gillespie, Cab Calloway, Frantic Flattops, the Trashmen, and Black Sabbath.

Juli has over seven tattoos including matching ones with her husband Manny. She looks at her tattoos fondly because each one marks a time in her life. She also loves sharing autumn with her family, getting new tattoos, changing her hair color, meeting different people, driving fast cars, and seeing great movies over and over again.

Before becoming pregnant and deciding to work at home as a full-time mother Juli was in school to get her Bachelors of Arts degree in interior design, and worked full-time as an interior designer for hotels. Her career seemed to have been on the fast track and it was exciting.

Initially, she was working for a national and large hotel as the administrative assistant to the vice-president of merchandising. She met Carol, the interior designer for the company, who befriended her. Once the company started a department strictly for design her friend took Juli under her wing and become her mentor. Her new title officially was, interior designer assistant, and they had a mentor/protégé relationship. She learned all she knows from her. They would go to hotels and assess their needs, then start selecting: carpets, wall covering, furnishings, lighting and so forth. They would make design boards and submit it to the clients and begin the pricing and approval process.

The challenge for Juli was learning the entire process, but it was very pleasurable as well. She worked for a very open-minded, diverse company and her desire for a career in design allowed her to be progressive and different. Her words of wisdom for anyone wanting to get involved in that field are:

"Learn all you can and don't be closed to constructive criticism, like in the art world. Interior Design is subjective and every person has their likes and dislikes. Take every opinion with a grain of salt, and don't take anything personally."

Juli was eventually promoted to interior designer, and did that for several years until she learned she was going to be a mother. She had a lot of support from family, but not from her friends or co-workers. She eventually left the field to stay-at-home with her son, Vincent, who is three-years-old now. Raising her son was her first priority, and he will always be. She plans on eventually working part-time again, but for now her career can wait.

"My life has completely changed now. I can no longer have any inkling of selfishness, but I don't mind, because my son has become the world to me. I used to be a working girl with much independence. Since becoming a mother I'm still having a tough time being housebound and attached.

I believe that motherhood is the best thing that can happen to any woman. I didn't realize I'd love it so much. It is so important to me that my son knows I will always be his friend and the one person in life he can come to for support and love.

Now that my husband is clean and sober he is an amazing father! He works his ass off for us so that I can stay-at-home and raise Vinnie the right way. Manny is an extremely intelligent and a 'blow-you-away-with-talent' guitar player who always sells himself short. He's my best friend in the whole world and we have the same brain. His family thanks me daily for 'saving his life' which I'm not sure I did that, we help each other through everything in life."

At the time of her pregnancy it seemed they were growing apart. They never tried to conceive they just let 'fate' decide. Her initial fears were that her husband was going to run, or that she wouldn't be able to handle the challenge of motherhood. However, they had been though many challenging moments together. They grew up as adults with one another after meeting in the skin/oi scene as teenagers, and battled addictions and self-esteem issues together. As Juli is sharing this with me, her Chicago accent becomes real evident, and her voice strong and confident, "We were still trying to find our niche in life, but I didn't really realize what I wanted until my son Vinnie was born." They didn't have a plan, they were just happy to be alive, and relatively happy in life.

At this point in their lives, her husband had been a recovering heroin addict who had recently quit methadone. She also feared she wouldn't live to see her son Vinnie grow up, since she has Crohn's disease and ulcerative colitis, both of which are inflammatory bowel diseases and can result in cancers, but she decided to not let it control her life.

The parenting principles Juli and her husband Manny share are: to be as honest with Vinnie as possible, and let him explore life and his desires with their continued support and guidance. Love, communication, and respect define their world as a family.

They hope he has a more realistic view on life, better street smarts than they did, and open-mindedness. They also plan on teaching him to analyze the value and meaning of life, personal relationships, and his interactions with others, in the hopes he doesn't fall victim to consumerism, ego, greed, or neighborhood drug pushers. They plan on exposing him to a broad spectrum of art and music. They hope he will enjoy life with all its wonder, and not fall into a self-loathing depression which Juli feels is common for people raised by absent, neglectful, controlling, or depressed parents. (This is supported by the findings of noted North Carolina therapist Kristen McClure in her essay "*What is the Cause of Depression?*" She states specifically that, *'Family or origin is very often a cause of depression. Any history of neglect, physical, emotional, or sexual abuse is a risk factor for depression. The building blocks for how you feel about yourself are initially laid in your family.*" See more at her insightful site Kristen-McClure-Therapist.com.)

Juli herself has battled depression all of her life and it runs in her family. Her mother frequently walked a fine line between sadness and despair, while grasping for seemingly elusive joy. Her mother struggled with it, and despite of, created a great home environment for Juli. She grew up in a very progressive town on the outskirts of Chicago, Illinois. The town had racial and social harmony, and she was raised by two Northwestern graduates who were intellectuals.

Her parents owned their own business so she was always with them. They were intellectually and socially progressive, with a taste for politics, and a busy social life, but she could always go to them—which was the key in their successful parenting. She rebelled not against her parents, or community, but against the jocks and preps in her school that she got a lot of flak from for not being one of them or like them.

She was introduced to the punk scene by her best friend's mom who was living with Pierre Kezdy, the bass player for a very popular Chicago punk band named Naked Raygun. She was a wide-eyed kid ready to learn everything and he exposed her to all kinds of different music and scenes. She was about thirteen at this time. Juli steps outside her red brick home with creamy white siding to take a smoke, and I decide to go with her. We're in different states on the phone, but we are both animated and excited about our first encounters with punk and share stories.

She started going to shows with her best friend and then later found her mom reading the book about Nancy Spungen, *And I Don't Want to Live This Life*. It seemed to her that it was her destiny to have a life in punk and music. Juli read the book afterwards, and she was on a mission to learn everything she could about punks, who then could be best defined as loudly and crassly anti-culture (and upper class totalitarianism), and musically, they were raw and had confrontational politics—the refusal to be suppressed, exploited, or to 'stay in their place'. The mainstream despised punks and their politics (or threat to the class system) and certainly didn't idolize them, as is done with fashionable knock-offs today. The boldness, energy, and rejection of elitism fascinated her and it became part of her life. She was hooked and grabbed every record by the Sex Pistols, the Cramps, CSNY, and B-52's. It was the early 1980s.

She was gradually starting to hang out in the punk scene and had a red, white and black catwoman hair style; the infamous punk hairstyle named after London's Soo Catwoman of the 1970s. She fell into the anti-racist working class skinhead movement and found that was more for her liking. She felt they were scarier and tougher than punks, and she was attracted to that alley machismo after being picked on for so long by others. She yearned to feel safe and confident, and before long shaved her head and started hanging out with the bomber boys and other 'independent' (non-defined SHARP [Skinheads against Racial Prejudice] or ARA [Anti-Racist Action] members, etc) skins. She drank, smoked, and skanked her way through the remainder of high school and the eighties.

She still has a love for all things outside the norm and its attraction has lasted even into her mid-thirties because she has found that while not everyone likes what she does, the people in the scene share similar views on life and like the same music:

> "Most people think that all the old punks and skins didn't survive, much less procreate, that is if they knew about us at all. I look relatively normal now too, so I'm not sure why the stares. I usually get a nervous hello from normal/mainstream moms after I give them a big smile."

"Most people think that all the old punks and skins didn't survive, much less procreate, that is if they knew about us at all. I look relatively normal now too, so I'm not sure why the stares. I usually get a nervous hello from normal/mainstream moms after I give them a big smile."

Juli feels if you view the world in a historical context, it is better off now than ever. She feels lucky to live in America since we have the luxury of "whining about the condition of the world." She thinks the world is a beautiful, strange place (that she is thankful to be in). She does have concerns about parents and kids:

"I was pleasantly surprised that motherhood has come more naturally to me than I initially thought it would. I also don't have the stomach for some of the things I used to. I'm so in love with children and become enraged now at how children are treated in this world; whereas before I thought things were bad, but I was passive.

I believe that we as a society are sacrificing children's innocence and sense of wonder for greed and celebrity. Children need our guidance and unconditional love. I believe society would rather point a finger at video games, television, music, drugs, for the way children are now behaving, like guns in schools, sexual behavior at a young age, etc … rather than the fact that eighty percent of children come home to self-involved parents that ignores them, or no parents at all."

This problem is compounded by the fact that our society doesn't have family-friendly policies from work practices (kid and parent friendly) or kid-need based school practices and legislation, to enforceable child support, or even shared child rearing standards for both genders.

Juli doesn't know many moms like herself, or from comparable backgrounds, in fact the only ones she has met have been on Myspace and Facebook. She does hangout with some local moms and they let their kids play together, but the conversations are pretty much limited to diaper and tantrum stories. When she walks around their neighborhood with Vinnie in a stroller she gets a lot of looks from other mothers that make her feel like she has a shaved head again. Juli however, is determined to overcome stereotypes and hopefully engage other parents in dialogue that will make the world a better and freer place for kids and moms alike.

As for her future, once Vinnie gets older, she plans on resuming her career in interior design and incorporating graphic design into it as well. Manny and her also plan on having another child in a few more years too. Her final words on life are, "Life is what you make it and things will not come to you. You have to go out and get what you want." Sounds like a rock solid philosophy to me.

**Since this interview: Juli and her husband have moved to Buffalo, New York, and indeed did have their second child, a beautiful little boy named (after dad) Manny.*

"I would want people to know that I am a normal ev just like the next one. I do believe I have a lot to offe they should look more at *who* people are, not *what*

Sarah
Good Listener
Record Collector
Vintage Shopper
Furniture Restorer
Head Cashier
Accounting Major
Curvy Children's Clothing Designer
Fort Worth, Texas.

Sarah is a Nevada girl who traveled to Texas at twenty-one to find love, adventure, and a college degree. When she was twenty-five she became engaged and had a baby. Sarah runs an internet group helping subculture moms connect with each other; she also makes cool clothes for cool kids. She is a recovering accountant and business major who gave up the life of crunching numbers for mothering.

Sarah is now doing something more creative with her life; however, she still works with money as the head cashier at a local arts and crafts store. She lives for thrifting, collecting, and one can always find her rummaging through forgotten treasures at estate and garage sales. Sarah also has a doo-wop and Elvis vinyl collection that is just to die for. She is defined by her uniqueness and determination in life; she is a strong-willed woman with a gigantic heart, and a swooning smile.

When Sarah is not changing diapers, she gets a few minutes to herself. She enjoys playing the piano and listening to some of her favorite classical artists like Chopin, Beethoven, and Rachmaninoff (their works conjure up romantic, thundering interludes for her). She escapes into the mischievous grim world summoned up Stephen King's novels. She also is a fan of the morbid and sociopathic world created by famed Hannibal Lecter writer and creator, Thomas Harris. Like Harris, Sarah is jovial, caring and kind. Although her reading interests run deep and serious, she balances it out with the fun and energetic sound of traditional rockabilly, which is her favorite musical genre. The music she proclaims has "such a raw sound, and is so happy and upbeat! It can definitely brighten my mood!" Her favorite performers are Wanda Jackson, Janis Martin, Ronnie Dawson, and Hank III.

Sarah and her fiancé Marc are the proud parents of six-month-old Grace. They met online while she was still living in Vegas and plotting her way out of it. She was headed for Los Angeles with her best friend before the two connected. Her best friend decided Texas sounded better; neither of them had ever been here, and they figured, why not? Within two months they packed up their stuff into a Ryder truck. Sarah and her best friend came to the only state in the union that negotiated the right to secede with no military backlash. The first couple of years were hard on her, because she terribly missed her family back home, but she knew she wanted to stay.

> "Ahh ... it was hard. I got homesick, had to find work, and get settled. We had an apartment [her best friend and her] that we lined up before we moved, but bills were coming fast enough, and we were running out of money. We ended up getting

jobs at rinky-dink places though and made it. I loved it here. I love the people, they are so friendly. Fort Worth is such a large city, with a country feel; very different from Vegas."

Sarah grew up with very loving and very Mormon parents from Salt Lake City, Utah. Sarah normally doesn't confide this to people because she doesn't want to be judged on that, because there are so many different misconceptions about the religion, "There are plenty of Mormon bashers out there, heh." She returns the favor by not judging other's religious beliefs, and/or the environments they were raised in, as well. Her mom did expect her children to respect their beliefs, but they weren't forced to embrace the religious temperament, if they didn't want to. Sarah's father did not attend church, but her mom did, and it kept things in perspective:

> "I believe my parents raised me well and taught me to be a strong person. I was raised in a highly religious household, and even though I do not follow everything along the religious lines, they did teach me to be a good person. I am a well-rounded, open-minded person myself. I'm shy—but not afraid to hold my ground. I can speak up for what I believe in and fight for causes that I believe need to be taken care of. I want the best for myself, as well as my child, and will do what it takes to get it done. I am a good friend and listener. I will do anything for anyone I possibly can. I have morals and high expectations."

Her upbringing also helped define her views on motherhood and what she can contribute to Grace's environment. Sarah believes that motherhood plays an extremely important part in everyone's lives and that it is the most amazing experience someone can ever have. [I am inclined to agree; although a tour of Europe, the Mediterranean, and the Persian world would come a very close second, for me, ha-ha.] Sarah plans to shape her daughter's personality, hoping she will be open-minded, nonjudgmental and an overall well-rounded person. However, when she did learn she was pregnant she was scared to tell her folks, since they were very conservative. She feared they would disown her, which did not happen. When she did finally confide in them, Sarah was four-and-a-half months along.

Sarah was young, having fun with new friends, and Marc, before becoming a mom. Her loneliness for home and missing her family eventually made it extremely hard for her to stay still. She lived for seeing bands, getting out and about, and soon enough became a barfly.

"I went out almost every night and got drunk. I went to a lot of shows, basically any one I could get to. I went to bars and drank the night away rather than be at home. I did have responsibilities, I kept a job and paid the bills, but I would rather go out to drink away the loneliness and problems than be at home."

She views her unplanned pregnancy with Grace as fated.

"When I found out I was pregnant I decided maybe there was a reason behind it all. I saw myself getting worse and worse with my drinking and I just couldn't think of not having the baby. I strongly believe that people should have the right to do as they chose (as far as abortion) however I knew I didn't want to do that myself. I was very scared of rejection from my family, with them being strongly religious, and not believing in things such as premarital sex, but I went ahead with the pregnancy. I have learned to put someone else before me and I know everything I do is going to affect her in some way. I have to think before doing things and make sure I am doing the right things. No more crazy bar nights if I know I have to drive home; no more binge drinking knowing I have to wake up and take care her of her. Basically, I would say I've definitely grown up."

Sarah wants to show Grace a great life and to teach her about everything. She also wants to instill an innate acceptance of different people and variant circumstances, so that Grace is compassionate, considerate, and loving. She wants her to be very analytic and observant, and to see beyond and deeper than the everyday normal things that go on. She simply wants her girl to love and enjoy life to the fullest. Sarah's introduction into parenting though has been rocky, and she was, "so scared and still am at times," of all of the elements beyond our control as parents:

"Honestly, it hasn't been easy. Both me and my fiancé Marc lost our jobs when our daughter was three-and-a-half-months-old. That was horrible to come home and not know what we were going to do for food for her and diapers. It made me feel like a failure very early in her life. It was very, very hard. We were worried about paying our rent, and getting groceries. We barely had money for gas to go look for jobs. Luckily, my parents and our friends loaned us some money to help us and to make sure we didn't lose our place. Ramen definitely isn't a nice thing to go back to. It definitely has been harder than expected. It wasn't really real to me until I had to get up in the middle of the night, or balance our income around her needs. I do believe though, despite our rough start, with losing our jobs and going through that, and having to find work again, that it is actually better than I could ever have imagined."

Her advice for any parent who finds themselves in such peril is just to take life day-by-day, and try to do your best each day that you possibly can. That is all you can do. It is important to stay positive, do not let things beyond your control spoil, or ruin, the things within your control … like your children, home environment, and your relationship with your spouse. She's been there, and I've been there, and due to corporate greed, and the greed of our country's richest upper class, over ten percent of working Americans (i.e., roughly ten million families) are there right now. We just have to learn to work through this, while maintaining our dignity, and the health, safety, and morale of our families, while doing what we can as a community to support

"Honestly, it hasn't been easy. Both me and my fiancé Marc lost our jobs when our daughter was three-and-a-half-months-old. That was horrible to come home and not know what we were going to do for food for her and diapers. It made me feel like a failure very early in her life. It was very, very hard. We were worried about paying our rent, and getting groceries. We barely had money for gas to go look for jobs."

each other, and nonviolently fight for social and class justice and monetary/tax/personhood equality.

The rocky start with them losing their jobs put everything into immediate and sharp focus for Sarah. She knew two things: she wanted to stay-at-home with their girl and she needed an income to do so. One advantage of where she works now is that she is immersing herself into craft and textile design, and she gets an employee discount on supplies. Sarah is also drafting the blueprint for launching a clothing line, *Mommies with Monsters*, for kids next year. The theme is anchored in fun, and the style is tongue-in-cheek.

> "My daughter has motivated me to get things done, and I want to be able to do things so I can provide a better life for her. I hope to get this children's clothing line off the ground. I hope for it do well and stay-at-home and raise my daughter. I would like to finish college as well."

She had been going to school to become an accountant, with a minor in business, but has since realized that she needs to have a creative outlet in her day job. She's not sure how this will pan-out, so she plans on resuming school soon to continue her core credits, while she launches the clothing line, and she will take it from there. Sarah will readjust her vision as needed. If it works out as she hopes, she will go to school, and will just build her home business. Her fiancé's plans are to start building custom cars, which he adores, and selling them. He is a wonderful father to Grace, and she means more to him than anything. Like Sarah and her fiancé, Grace will know that life is broad and big:

> "I want to teach her about life, and living, and seeing things. I want her to know it is okay to like things out of the ordinary, and you don't have to fit in with the crowd. If she chooses to like what the public is choosing at the time, so be it, but I want her to learn about art, history, music, and subcultures. I want her to know it is okay to stand up for herself and her beliefs. I want to teach her to be proud that she is female and not let society tell her she can't do something because of that. I want her to have the best possible life I can give her. I don't ever want her to have to need something that is a necessity. I want to be able to give her everything I possibly can. I think I got a lot ahead of me."

She also feels how we live our lives will influence our children,

"I hope I can teach her to be an admirable woman. I want her to have high morals and expectations. I want her to be intelligent and have goals in life. Whether she decides to go to college or not, I want her to achieve her goals in life. I believe her seeing and watching things I do myself is going to be the best way to instill this in her. I want to be a role model for her, which I need to do a lot myself to be a good one. I want her to learn from me, as well as her father, and our friends."

Sarah believes that, with children, one cannot be afraid to say no, and that they need to be taught to have respect and manners. She feels too many parents are lenient, or indifferent, with their children and give them everything without instilling a sense of appreciation and responsibility. She thinks the best way children can learn respect, including self-respect, is by the adults in their lives modeling that towards their children, to one another, and others. She is certain if parents would just turn the TV off and interact with their kids consistently, that most of the world's problems could be solved; especially if we are doing things to interact with them such as: painting a picture with them, taking the time to read a book to them, etc. She wishes more parents were prudent in how they behave around their kids; be careful and take the time to think about their actions, what they do around their children, since children mimic adults and parents are their primary teachers. She also thinks society has some work to do too:

"People now look past the way I look and whatever I am wearing, when they see her. It's funny how rude people were to me when I was pregnant. They just looked at me like some tattooed white trash pregnant girl. Now they hardly even notice these things because of the baby. I actually feel society accepts me for other than my looks when I have her with me, and I find that sad. People are far too judgmental and think because one looks a certain way they are going to fail as a parent. I read to her daily, and get her things that will help her become an intelligent child. I refuse to let the TV raise my child, and I think some people are surprised that I am like that.

I believe a lot of children are overlooked. It's sad to me how many children these days are abused and raised by daycare and babysitters. I'm not speaking of the parents who have to have daycare and babysitters because they have to work to provide for their families. I am speaking of the ones who don't want their children around, and would rather drop them off somewhere rather than raise them themselves. I love children, and I believe they all deserve a fair chance in this world and should be given that."

Sarah believes that we as a society need to do better and do right by our kids—and that we're not … as parents, as legislators, as business leaders, and as individuals, doing our fair share for kids. She wants us to stop wasting so much time stereotyping and to focus on doing the right thing, "The world right now is a mess. I believe people need to open their eyes and be more accepting of others. They need to learn to let people believe what they choose and accept them for who they are."

That sense of acceptance is what subconsciously drew her as a fifteen-year-old to a different way of life, "To not be afraid to be who I am and worry about what everyone else is doing." There was an aura of strength that captivated her by those going against the grain, "People don't have to follow what everyone else's beliefs are. They were not afraid to say what they think and do what they want." She found herself at home, with the fun, the music, the politics, the dancing, and all the amazing bands she saw like Murphy's Law, Bad Religion, and Agnostic Front. As she got older, she did become more intrigued by the retro-music scene, and fell in love with multiple subcultures that overlap and form an awesome international and diverse community.

She has met very accomplished individuals over the years, which has inspired her, and gave her the DIY footing once she became a mom to figure out a better way to combine parenting, work, and creativity, by starting her own kids fashion line—selling one piece at a time. She believes a unique advantage Grace will have, is that she will be raised around many different people, along with their different lifestyles. Grace will learn about art, history, music, and other hobbies, and not just those interests that are deemed commercially okay, which will help her navigate and experience life more holistically.

Sarah feels fortunate to know many moms that she has common interests with, and they help provide each other with emotional support, babysitting, and play-dates:

"A lot of my friends are parents, but not necessarily into the exact same things as me. It's nice because they can appreciate the things I do and buy for my daughter while others might think it's odd. They can appreciate the way I have her room decorated and the clothes I put her in. However, a lot of us do have different views on different subjects. They might not feel as strongly as I do about different parenting methods, or they have different ideas on how to raise a child, and that's okay."

Sarah knows that we as moms have a lot more to share with each other when we open up to one another.

"On the surface, I'm not a carbon-copy GAP-style mom. To look at me, I suppose most people wouldn't even think I'm a mom when they see me. I love all sorts of music and styles, and a lot of things in my life are based around those. But I'm a mom just like the next one. I can sit around and talk about how my daughter threw up on her dad's face, or dealing with babysitters, and changing diapers, and getting up in the middle of the night. I can talk about my child teething, throwing fits, even at her young age. I know what it is like to know that every choice I make in some way is going to affect my daughter. I'm sure most parents whether subculture or not have those same thoughts."

It's true that the bridge to engagement is being open-minded and looking past socially taught stigmas. Sarah has faith in humanity, and I have found since I started writing this book I do too. This is the mainstay of her parenting philosophy, and her take on the world. Grace is not even a year old yet, but Sarah is determined to make her goals happen and be a working stay-at-home mom with a successful indie clothing line. There is absolutely no doubt in my mind that she will make it happen.

**Since this interview: Sarah's now defunct Mommies with Monsters group and fashion line did enable her to work from home and finish school. She merged her business degree with photography, and opened up her own traveling studio called Dynamite Dames. Her business is wildly successful and specializes in pin-up portraits. She does carefully coordinated and frequently sold-out sessions all over the U.S! You can check it out on Facebook! She and Marc married and recently had a little boy named Chap. She is still a stay-at-home mom who works from home, while traveling for her business seasonally.*

"I didn't have a lot of direction, but then you have a baby, and good-god! You suddenly want to give that person, the moon, the stars, the planets, and the whole damn solar system!

Lola
Retired Hairdresser
Stay-at-Home Working Mom
Un-schooler
Lovely Laid Back Catholic
Home Remodeler
Rockabilly Momma
Richardson, Texas.

Lola is a relaxed, down-to-earth, witty, and rocking lady who grew up in San Diego. She's decked out in colorful tattoos and awesome cat-eyed 1950s glasses. She is a fun loving mom who feels it's important that parents are actively involved in raising their kids and being there in everyday life. Lola fulfilled her career goals, and then stepped out of the world of glamour and good tunes to raise her toddler-aged daughter Hannah. She also wanted to be fully present for her teenage son, Ian. She is happily married to a wonderful man and father, Liam, and family life is her thing.

Since Liam was making more at work as a traveling salesperson, and they wanted another child, they decided that now was a good time to move and buy a house. So they resettled in Texas. Lola confides that, in California, no one can afford a home, even in the ghetto, unless they are making at least two-hundred and fifty-thousand dollars, or more, a year. Since they didn't, and they wanted to broaden their horizons, they moved here and fell in love with Dallas. Lola likes the cosmopolitan feel that the city has, and the fact that everybody seems so friendly and says hello to you. This blew her away, since "nobody does that in San Diego."

"I'm going the un-schooling route with Ian. I think kids tend to gravitate towards what they are really interested in when not being slammed with homework and subjects at school. He's actually taking a pre-engineering class with the City of Richardson and learning to build robots. It only costs sixty dollars. There is no stringent curriculum we are following."

Lola spends her days raising her kids, fixing up the house, and going to shows when her husband is in town. She and her son have discussions on politics, music, and life, of which dad pipes in on when he's not out working. Hannah is gradually being immersed into the dialogue. Ian likes a little bit of everything, but she drew the line with Tupac, insisting that, "He didn't need to be listening to that, see parental advisory number one warning label." Although, Tupac descended from amazing activist revolutionaries, and was an extremely talented, educated and trained performer, she didn't want Ian immersed into what his rap career focused on (as opposed to his early performances in jazz, acting, dance, and drama) which was largely coastal gang and music rivalries, violence, and self-proclaimed 'thug life'. She's grateful that teenagers have short attention spans, and he has moved on to Run DMC instead. She feels that she is a pretty open-minded mom, but that there is a place and time for everything, and at thirteen, there is only so much he needs to be exposed to. Lola is home schooling her kids, but in a John Holt way.

"I'm going the un-schooling route with Ian. I think kids tend to gravitate towards what they are really interested in when not being slammed with homework and subjects at school. He's actually taking a pre-engineering class with the City of Richardson and learning to build robots. It only costs sixty dollars. There is no stringent curriculum we are following."

Lola is very proud of her son, and feels that they have done a great job. Ian has made really good choices and is a very good kid, who is also out-going and can adapt to any situation. Because of this, when he came to her and wanted to dye his hair a bold color, she had no problems with it.

"He has green hair, and he gets questions like, 'Were you the Incredible Hulk for Halloween?', and he's like, 'Umm … no. I wanted green hair and my mom let me.' And of course, then I get funny looks. To me, it's more important to let them do their creative things than to have to worry if their out strung-out on crack or something. The color of your hair has no bearing on what kind of person you are, same with tattoos."

Ian has been in and out of tattoo shops his whole life. He's been propped up against a soda machine in a car-seat watching Liam or Lola get tattooed, and once he started walking and talking, he simply came along to hang out while they got work done. As he got older, he also got to know many of the artists in the shops they went to. He had an opportunity to ask many questions about the culture of, and the profession of the inked arts. She adds:

"The thing is we talk a lot to Ian, and he really listens. Well maybe not to me, since I'm his mom, ha-ha, but I know he does even if he doesn't act like it sometimes. He picks up pieces of information, and later he will say, 'You know, remember this …' We've never kept him from other kinds of people, or what society calls 'other kinds of people', tattooed freaks, or whatever, as long as they are good at heart, that is all that matters to us."

Unfortunately, most people aren't that loving and accepting of people, as Lola and her family have experienced personally. They were recently eating at a restaurant and two ladies came up and asked the couple, "Are you planning on doing that to your baby when she gets older?" At first, they just looked at the ladies confused, because they had no idea what they were talking about. Finally it dawned on them, that the strangers were referencing their arm sleeves, and they asked them forthright, "Do you honestly think we would go out and get our child tattooed because we are?" They looked at the ladies, aghast in shock, and finally gave a firm reply to get them away from their dinner table, "No. If she decides when she gets older that she wants them, we will recommend a good artist. If she doesn't, we will still love her."

Lola and Liam met in California. His family is from Scotland. They left Scotland due to the religious persecution of the Protestants, and they first settled in Canada (where he was born), then moved to the states. His family rarely went to church though, since the strife they had endured "really turned them off from organized religion." Lola's Catholic family essentially raised her with an awareness of their god, but church was reserved for baptisms, and quinceañeras. *[Quinceañeras are a formal and elaborate celebration in Latin cultures of a girl turning fifteen, filled with ritual and symbolism, feasting and dancing. The historical purpose was to prepare the girl for marriage and announce her availability to suitors; the modern context however has evolved, and varies regionally, but now focuses both on her future goals, and suitable match-making, again varying based on the specific locale and its needs/standards. I attended several as pre-teen growing up in Oak Cliff, and was so jealous of my friends who got to have this big, spectacular party. I wanted one! It was like Cinderella's ball. And the North Texas American celebrations I attended were really lavish birthday parties, with no marriage match-making for kids between parents.]* Since they both grew up in semi-religious households, they redefined a spiritual connection to god for their children that is both open and casual. This is right in line with their overall world view, and acceptance of people and diversity.

"My family is Catholic, but they really left it up to me, if I wanted to be or not; same with my brother, and were pretty much doing the same thing with our kids. Everything has its place and purpose. And if you chose to worship a god, or something, or whatever, that's fine too. I've always told Ian I believe in a higher power, but I don't believe in giving someone one-hundred-percent of my income, to go to a certain place to worship. They tell you he's everywhere, so if I want to worship while sitting on a toilet taking a shit, so be it. But you know that's my feeling. But we don't put people down for their beliefs, or push ours down their throats, we just ask for the same. Don't do it."

Lola feels that moms don't get much support, and parents deemed 'different' certainly get even less. As a mom she knows the suffering can be two-fold. She recalls a crucifying event one mom went through while traveling:

"I was on a flight and a woman had a crying and screaming child who was upset the whole flight. And you could tell people were getting frustrated with her. I felt so bad for her. All these assholes were just staring at her like she should die—as if it was her fault that the poor kid was probably scared and hurting with popping ears! No one offered to lend a hand."

She acknowledged if she had to the opportunity to do it over again, she would help her, especially in such a hateful and tense environment. Empathy and compassion are values she attempts to model and incorporate into her household, but this encounter taught her the need to be able to articulate it, and act upon it, when out-and-about in society. She has felt the stigma herself of the perfect mother and perfect child fairytale [coined as 'powerless responsibility' by amazing Poet and Academic Adrienne Rich], and can relate to many moms who fall within this damnation circle. She is determined that the next time she will step-up to the plate for a mom-in-need that is being scorned.

The most frightening aspect of motherhood came when Ian was just a baby. He almost died due to being diabetic. Once his illness was discovered, and his recovery was assured, the hardest part was just keeping up with him as he got older; to ensure he was taking his medication. There was no room for mistakes. That's a huge responsibility for an adult to bear, much less a child; so far, so good. She emphasizes that you never know what life is going to hold, good or bad, and it's generally a mixed bag. So don't let it hold you back from your dreams or from wanting to be a parent, if it's your calling, or if it's in your blood.

Before motherhood, Lola was just enjoying life each day with Liam, working hard and having fun. She thinks in retrospect that she was still figuring out her angle on life. Then life shifted.

> "I didn't have a lot of direction, but then you have a baby, and good-god! You suddenly want to give that person, the moon, the stars, the planets, and the whole damn solar system! How do you that? Goal-setting! Having Ian really helped me think about that. What do I want to pursue being a hairdresser? I wanted to work in a really posh salon and specialize in something, and I did that over the years. But once we had Hannah, it just got to be too much, and we could now afford for me to stay home, so I did."

Lola reflects and concludes that she has it all. She's got a family that she adores, a scene that she digs, and she's fulfilled her career ambitions—while putting her family first. And her husband has done the same. What more could a woman want?

Damn Straight!

The Ink Slingers and Piercers

Meet daring women who raise kids and are shamans of modern rituals in this chapter. They help women reclaim their bodies through tattoo art and body piercing. They redefine empowered motherhood.

In this chapter you will be introduced to the gatekeepers of the otherworld of working moms who specialize in something truly unique: the empowerment of women through the symbolic body decoration they provide. You have to make time for fun things in life though, says one mom, besides tattooing and owning your own business. Like skateboarding, rock climbing and going to shows with your teenage daughter (and helping her make good decisions). She's proof of how strong and courageous working class moms are, and that teen moms can persevere. Another mom knew what she wanted to do for a living and went from one coast to another to get her body modification training. She will also give you a shoulder to lean on, if you're going through a divorce. She's been there. You will meet a mom whose love affair with hot rods, thanks to helping her dad under the hood, led her into the world of tattooing. She will also show you the Orient, the world of Wicca, and the tools to start your own business concepts. Another really cool mom will show you the ropes when you first crossover from without baby, to with baby. She will also help you jam out to classic rock, and tell you about the world of piercing, and surviving childhood abuse. Our mom who closes the chapter comes from a family of artists, who have been tattooing for generations and host the world's biggest ball in the industry. She's a scientist in the making, a working stay-at-home mom, and real Hollywood.

Get ready to rev your engines when you dive into the world of the Ink Slingers and Piercers.

"I am what I am, and I make no apologies for that."

Momma Roxy
Fighter
Skater
Rock-Climber
Gorgeous Graphic Design Artist
Tattooist
Owner of Diversity Studios
Toronto, Canada.

Momma Roxy is an amazing woman of character, power and strength. She owns Diversity Studio, a tattoo shop, piercing studio, hair salon and clothing boutique all-in-one. She is one hell of a renegade momma.

The studio is pink with three main rules: No racial slurs, no Nazi tattoos, and no tattoos of the names of lovers. (She has encountered way too many individuals who have needed cover-ups because of break-ups.) She however, will tattoo symbolic memorial tattoos for deceased loved ones (that was the start of her daughter Aimee's tattoos—in memory of her aunt and her grandfather), as well as portraitures of children.

Roxy has given Aimee several piercings and bought Aimee's first tattoo at sixteen. Aimee got two sparrows, one on each hip, which Roxy drew. Aimee's second set of tattoos consisted of traditional roses with skulls coming out of the buds and banners underneath that say, 'Friends' and 'Family'. Both Aimee and Roxy believe the body is a canvas—their own.

At the time of this writing Roxy is thirty-five, and her daughter Aimee is eighteen. They have experienced: tattooing, music, shops, road-trips and growing up alongside one another.

Roxy was a fifteen-year-old teenager when she had an unexpected pregnancy. Motherhood and life has sent her traveling down many roads before her current accomplishment as an owner of a successful studio. She is a triumphant single parent against all odds. Beforehand, she was the typical teenager: on the phone a lot, going out, experimenting and seeing the world. She was an honor roll student who left school after 11th grade, entered rehab, and then became a mom. Before adolescence and unplanned parenting—all she could dream of was being a rock star or a vet.

Roxy was sixteen when she had Aimee. Initially, she kept her out of spite for her parents, but deep down she knew and believed that no matter what, "Motherhood was a gift and no matter what anyone else said or did, the only people that mattered were her and I." Roxy knew everything she did would be setting an example for little Aimee. This motivated her to keep on going clear and strong; and to avoid traps that catch young adults cyclically like: unsavory relationships, drugs and alcohol. She had already dealt with that before becoming teenage mom.

Roxy is fully aware firsthand of how difficult it is to raise a child, and even harder when you are a child yourself. All the lessons of living and learning have made both Roxy and Aimee strong people today, who are both confident and happy.

Roxy did what most single moms, of working class origins, have to do when having to support a family: she danced. She worked as an adult/exotic dancer and danced for five years to make ends meet, while she went to school for graphic design part-time. This training has helped her take the leap from having cool ideas in her head to being able to execute them into inked tattoos.

As a dancer, she met strong women who were fabulous dancers and moms. You can ask any mom who has had to strip; working for a club gives you the kind of flexibility you need as a parent. Dancers have one of the few jobs where you can miss work if your kid is sick and not worry about getting fired, and the pay is much better than entry level corporate jobs as well. These are critical supports, especially, if you are a single parent.

On the other hand though, the demands of the job suck, and there are dangerous elements that have to be reckoned with, especially in the more seedy/unsavory places (abuse, forced prostitution, illegal human trafficking, and forced drug addiction). Roxy as a rule avoided the places on the lower end of the food-chain, since she was a mom, and a smart one. Even in the more legit, and best of environments, if you are not a strong person the availability of drugs and alcohol in that environment can still suck you in voluntarily. By the time Roxy quit stripping, she hated men. While she was working in strip clubs she saw how disgusting some of them can be and how little they think of women.

Rebel Mom Roxy did what most single moms, of working class origins, have to do when having to support a family: she danced. Dancers have one of the few jobs where you can miss work if your kid is sick and not worry about getting fired, and the pay is much better than entry level corporate jobs as well. These are critical supports, especially, if you are a single parent. On the other hand though, the demands of the job suck.

She observed there were two types of women in this

field, those for whom it is their job, and those who make it their life. For Roxy, it was a job and nothing more. She has seen that industry wreck a lot of good people and wouldn't suggest that line of work for too many. It is hard on the faint of heart. I share with Roxy, during our interview, a funny story of when I was eighteen. I worked one night in a strip club as a shot girl. I was so sick of working fifty-to-sixty hours a week and making next to nothing and my friends were killing it at the clubs. I refused to sit in men's laps, or throw myself at them, which I didn't realize was required as a shot girl. Soon after, I started telling one guy about my mom. When that happened I knew this wasn't the place for me. I lasted two hours and made no sells. I ripped my blonde wig off (my head was shaved then) and left. I never looked back. Roxy almost fell out of the chair on the other line from all the laughter.

Eventually, Roxy got into the field of piercing and moved into that direction as she wrapped up school. She did that in addition to contract work for graphic design and layout productions. From this she transitioned into tattooing (and moving across the border from the NE U.S.) and eventually opening her own studio in Canada.

Roxy does feel that sometimes people jump into the trend of tattooing without knowing what they are really getting into. This is why Diversity is a custom shop, and in general does not do flash. She has seen many bad tattoos come in the door from teenagers getting work on them, or young adults letting their friends do it (mostly to save money), instead of going to a professional. She wishes people thought about the long-term of their tattoo art instead of the short-term. They also short-change themselves on health when they do this. Diversity uses a steam sterilizer and also does monthly spore samples that are sent to be tested to ensure the cells are being killed by the sterilizer. (Dentists and doctors generally do the same thing for their tools as well.)

One of the few regrets Roxy has is for far too long she tried to be the stereotypical mother … but now Aimee and Roxy have a very open relationship and are best friends—all it took was Roxy throwing out stereotypical momma, and making herself and motherhood her own. Aimee could now tell Roxy anything and knows Roxy could handle it.

Roxy's concern while raising Aimee was that she was bringing a decent person into the world. Her parenting philosophy was: honesty. Honesty was an important value and Roxy led by example, always being truthful with her daughter, no matter what. Also, Roxy encouraged her daughter to be whoever she wanted to be:

> "My role to her was to show her no matter who told you that you couldn't do something, you could always prove them wrong. That there were no barriers for her and that the world could be anything she wanted and her place in it her own."

Roxy would always give Aimee choices and would point out the good and bad in all avenues, and let her choose for herself. Roxy wanted Aimee to surpass all stereotypical 'women' roles and be who she truly was, no matter what.

Who is Roxy herself? She loves skateboarding, rock-climbing and weekend trips. She will tell you she is too honest for her own good sometimes. She will go out of her way to prove someone wrong. This is especially true if someone tells her she can't do something. So, she's a little headstrong, she needed to be to make it. She will never stop learning. She will never settle for less than what she wants. She is a passionate, free-spirited person who can't stay in one spot to long. Roxy wears her heart on her sleeve and has no fear,

> **"I am not defined by tattoos, piercing, clothing, job, [a] man, child, vehicle—I am beyond definition. Since I lived the past seventeen years mostly for her (Aimee) and working on growing up … I believe the next era for me is to experience all that I have dreamed of and make it happen for myself."**

Rock on.

"When I pierced her nipples she cried. It wasn't from pain. She told me it was her rite of passage that her body finally belonged to HER. I had goose bumps and almost cried with her. Instead, I just hugged her. It was beautiful."

Picture by Stacey Potter at StaceyPotter.com

Pamela
Professional Piercer
Sexy Suspension Queen
Former Scooter Racer
Mexican Art Collector
Dallas, Texas.

Pamela has been a professional piercer for over eleven years now. She loves suspension, which is hanging from hooks and flying around. She is a huge fan of Day of the Dead Art and collects the statues. She's a fan of Vespa and Lambretta motor-scooters and used to race them until she had a bad accident. David Eddings is an author she loves. He writes fiction and according to Pamela, "He has a great imagination that will suck you in."

Pamela is silly, fun, and she's a die-hard romantic. She loves being in love. She loves all of her friends and is a very understanding person as well. She would give anything for people close to her. She is very open-minded. She is short on patience, but seeks to develop it.

She likes rhythm and blues music, which is what she grew up with, and punk rock which she has been listening to since she was twelve-years-old. Traveling and being outdoors gets her real excited, and hot rod cars as well. Pamela emphasizes though, "I am just a total girl too, because I love shopping!"

Rebel Mom Pam's checklist if you want to become a pro-piercer!

- ✓ **Read Elayne Angel's awesome book: *The Piercing Bible.***
- ✓ **Get online and read *BME Zine* (Body Modification E-zine) BMEZine.com.**
- ✓ **Go to an A.P.P. (The Association of Professional Piercers) conference and take all the classes you can.**
- ✓ **Find a respectable, educated piercer and apprentice!**

Her house looks like a fun room from Beetlejuice the movie. She has pink walls, monster dolls, and masks and posters are hung up everywhere. Her daughter Lilly gets to dress the way she wants, and decorates her bedroom with the same liberty.

Oliver Peck, a well known tattoo artist, is one of Pamela's favorites. She herself has over eleven tattoos, plus two partial 3/4 arm sleeves. Her favorite pieces thus far are: the demon snake lady on her thigh, the Day of the Dead Skulls on her booty cheeks, and the tattoo on her chest which is a picture of her daughter's face with wings around it. Her earlobes are stretched to 5/8 of an inch. As far as her tattoo and piercing lifestyles she adds, "I love tattoos and how individual and unique they can make a person. It's a real commitment."

Pamela's inspiration to get into piercing was her first experience with getting her tongue pierced by a woman named Faschia at Obscurities Studio. She really liked Faschia's persona and vibe. She felt really comfortable with her and how smooth she made the experience for Pamela. She was also impressed that Faschia was a mother. She knew right then and there that this is what she wanted to do for a living.

A short time later she was dating a tattoo artist (whom she later married, had a daughter with (Lilly), and divorced) and they were working at Cyber Graphx. The studio didn't have a piercer and she couldn't find anyone to apprentice under. Pamela decided to take control of her destiny and went to learning seminars in San Francisco, California. She also attended the Gauntlet school in L.A. (In fact, very recently, a master certified piercer from that school/studio, Elayne Angel, just put out an awesome book: *The Piercing Bible.*)

For the first few years she did novice piercing. She kept everything simple and was honest with her clients about her experience. She slowly advanced. She made most of her money from selling the jewelry, "which is almost always overpriced at the studios." Her piercing experience expanded significantly once she had her own shop in the studio Suffer City that she and her now ex-husband had opened. It was a critical leap in her development, before she left and started working at other studios. She acknowledges that some of the hardest moments and the most rewarding ones in her career so far have been,

"Well everyone has a bad day and makes mistakes. When I screw something up it really gets to me. It makes me want to quit. Sometimes working for certain people can be really upsetting. Feeling like I'm not as advanced as I should be can be very frustrating, especially when you want to advance. Sometimes your atmosphere and your other co-workers make it impossible. But I love what I do.

I love inner ear piercing; they seem a little more tactical at times. I love women genital piercings because they trust you to take proper care of them as a client. It's very emotional for them and they will never forget you. My favorite experience was piercing one lady. She wanted her nipples pierced and she had a lot of hidden issues sexually. When I pierced her nipples she cried. It wasn't from pain. She told me it was her rite of passage that her body finally belonged to HER. I had goose bumps and almost cried with her. Instead I just hugged her. It was beautiful. My favorite piercing to do on a regular basis is the eyebrow. It's just so easy and I can freehand it. A lot of piercers can freehand everything, but I'm not comfortable with it yet."

For prospective clients looking for a professional, she does suggest that you always look at their portfolio and then talk to them; make sure they are "the right one." They should always have very cleans stations too. For those who want to get into the profession she suggests,

> "Get online and read *BME Zine* (*Body Modification Ezine*/BMEzine.com), as much as possible. Learn all you can online and talk to a lot of people in the business. Find a few seminars and go to them all. Go to an A.P.P. (The Association of Professional Piercers) conference and take all the classes you can. Find a respectable, educated piercer and apprentice. Learn as much as you can from as many piercers as you can. No one way is the right way. There is a lot of good and bad out there, so take your time, and learn right."

Pamela is very happy she stuck with her career choice and has made it work, even through the hard times of personal change and financial up and downs when business would slow; and that she can still provide for her child doing what she loves.

Pamela is now thirty and her daughter Lilly is eight. Some of Pamela's core philosophies about parenting are that she aspires to be the best and most understanding mother she can be without passing judgments on her child's choices as she grows up. Her role as a guardian is to keep her safe, healthy, and to help her understand the world is made up of a lot of different people. Pamela hopes Lilly will be a good judge of right and wrong, as she is now, and respect others for their way of life. Lilly's education is a primary focus for her as well and she combines humanitarian values with teaching primary subjects, and sees every opportunity in life as a potential for a lesson. Pamela believes that not everyone that has a child should be a parent though.

> "I see lots of abusive mothers and fathers out there and sometimes I wish I could just take their kid away. I hate seeing people take family for granted and talking down to their children. That there are people brave enough to give their children up for adoption for their child's own good, well in my book, they are wonderful people and I salute them."

One area as a parent she is still working on is to always put her child's needs before her own, but she is human too, and wants to greatly improve in this area.

One rule Pamela has is not letting Lilly talk to people she doesn't know. She always tells Lilly to be nice and respectful, but to always keep her distance. She never forces Lilly to say hello to strangers, or to people that aren't close to the family. She does explain to her why some people are different, if they are handicapped, or homeless. Lilly is not allowed to judge people by the way they look. She does however, let Lilly trust her own intuition about someone. (And let's her do what is best—warmly greet the person under mom's eye, or completely retreat and make mom aware of the intuitive danger.)

At the time Lilly was born she was happily married to her Cyber Graphx beau, and they had planned on having a baby. She describes the situation like this:

> "I was one of the lucky few. I was married and actually planned to have my child. She has a great dad that I am divorced from now. He helps with her on a regular basis. I don't get, nor do I ask for, child support. He takes care of her one-hundred percent on the days he has her, as do I.
>
> We rented a nice house, had a large scooter collection and owned a tattoo shop at the time. We dedicated one of the rooms just for her as a play room so she could go to work with us, and when we divorced we kept it hers. She has never gone to daycare and always has been with one of us either at work or at home."

When Lilly was an infant she had a mini-crib set up in her parent's office at the studio. Once Lilly became older they converted the nursery into a play room. It was known as the Hello Kitty Coloring Book Shop. In Lilly's shop there was TV-DVD player, a sit-n-spin toy, a tricycle, tons of toys, educational material, and decorations.

The other artists that worked for them were very supportive of Lilly being there and often dropped into *her shop* to color and play with her. Pamela describes the whole experience as being part of a tribe and everyone helping each other out, and loving the kids.

The customers also respected them for making this work and having their kid with them in the studio. It made the shop feel real home-like and comfortable. Having that kind of environment can be really soothing since clients can be nervous, especially if they have never had tattoo or needlework before.

One rule Pamela has is not letting Lilly talk to people she doesn't know. She always tells Lilly to be nice and respectful, but to always keep her distance. She never forces Lilly to say hello to strangers, or to people that aren't close to the family. She does explain to her why some people are different, if they are handicapped, or homeless. Lilly is not allowed to judge people by the way they look.

She does however, let Lilly trust her own intuition about someone. (And let's her do what is best—warmly greet the person under mom's eye, or completely retreat and make mom aware of the intuitive danger.)

Pamela's hopes were like many when they married. She hoped to have a great kid, husband and family, but things don't always work out that way. She was sad about the divorce, but knew it was the right choice. She was fortunate that her ex-husband is an awesome person and a great dad, but realized she had married her best friend, not her soul mate. People grow apart for different reasons. It was really hard for her to leave her husband, but she felt more alone living with him than living actually living by herself. Losing her family life was intensely frightening. For her, it was scary coming out into the world and hoping she would find whatever it is she was looking for, without screwing up too much. She describes one of the darkest moments of the separation,

"He told me one night it would be a good idea that I moved out. That night I had the worst panic attack ever. I remember sitting on my hardwood floor with blankets around me. Lilly was asleep on our bed. I was shaking, crying and losing my mind. He had to comfort me and I felt like I was going to be put in a hospital. Then one day I had to tell him I wasn't in love with him and I wasn't sure I had ever been 'in love' with him. I basically married my best friend hoping romance would follow eventually, it never did.

My fears were more that her daddy wouldn't be able to raise her when he had her alone, but he proved me wrong—he is the best dad. Since then my fears are that I'm not as independent as I thought. I'm a very stubborn and proud mom. I don't like help and when I ask for it, it is because I'm out of other plans. I don't ask for or get government assistance, but sometimes I want to break down and seek it anyway."

One reason Pamela was afraid initially that her ex-husband wouldn't be able to raise Lilly was because when they were married, "He didn't seem to do much in terms of child rearing, if I was around to do it for him." Once they were each on their own she saw they were both capable of doing a lot for themselves and Lilly. One of the bleakest moments as a newly divorced mom was:

"I'm generally a physically weak person, meaning I can't normally carry more than four bags of groceries. One night in my apartment I was having a really BAD feeling … from my parking lot I carried ten bags of groceries on my arms, my sleeping girl in my arms, my keys in one hand and my knife in the other. I was scared of something unseen, but I knew I could kill anything that threatened my child. After we made it into the apartment, I was able to put all the groceries down and put her into bed safely. I realized just how much strength I had, because NONE of it seemed heavy at the time. Life is more precious than I ever realized, that keeping myself safe and alive all the sudden mattered for someone other than me. That I had more strength and power than I knew possible when it came to the safety of my child."

Words of advice Pamela has for women in a similar situation, who are asking the same questions about possibly leaving a marriage, or staying in one are, "Have faith in yourself! You can do anything as long as love is in your heart."

Pamela and her ex share equal custody. Lilly has a room of her own at both of her parent's houses. They often have blended family and friends outings together as well. Pamela defines her relationship with her ex as great and she is very fond of his new wife as well. Lilly is one of the most loved children and receives lots of care and attention from her parents, and their friends.

Pamela only knows a few moms like herself, and they get funny looks like, "What is the weird lil' person doing with a child? Oh my god!"

Pamela believes though that they (sub and counter-culture moms) are more loving and giving than the traditional mothers who stare at them in disbelief. Pamela doesn't expect to force Lilly to live up to unrealistic expectations (such as mastering dance and foreign languages in order to get into an exclusive prep school, etc.). What Pamela would like traditional moms to ask themselves is: "Why is this so important? Is it for my child's well-being, or is it for my social standing? Why do you judge me as a mother?" What makes her circle of counterculture moms unique? Pamela views it this way,

> "We wear what we want whether it's for looks or comfort. It's not to make someone else happy, a boss, or a family member. We speak our minds because it's what we feel without the care of other people's judgments or opinions. I believe we have more faith and love, more honesty and realism. We are not afraid of looks, opinions or loss for our beliefs."

Pamela was attracted to the subculture scene when she was twelve-years-old. She was at the Irving Mall in Texas and met a group of young punk kids there. They were so different from the people in her junior high school. They liked her without worrying about what she was wearing or what she said. The lifestyle attracted her so much that she has never gone back.

Before becoming a mother she drank more, had fist-fights here and there when confrontations happened, went out a lot, and worked hard. She has become much more cautious in her approach to people and confrontations. She rarely ever has to have a fist-fight now with someone unless it's strictly in self-defense. She is just as immersed in the punk and skin/oi scene as before and goes to shows by herself when her ex has Lilly. Although more laid back now, she still goes to BBQs, she still does suspension, sees bands play, and hangs out with her friends.

Pamela had always wanted a baby and seeing Lilly look into her eyes was one of the happiest moments of her life. Watching Lilly laugh in her sleep still makes Pamela smile. There is nothing that makes Pamela more proud of herself than being an awesome mom to Lilly.

Her future plans include continuing to develop her career, doing more suspensions, scooting, going to shows, spending quality time with her kiddo and showing her the world when she is old enough to handle the long flights to Europe. She also hopes to find her soul mate who will be an amazing man that is proud of her, Lilly and whatever family and life they may build later. But if this doesn't happen, she has found out that by standing on her own two feet, she can be happy alone.

**Since this interview: She has found the love of her life, and they have had a beautiful baby girl named Chloe together. Also, after fifteen years working as a piercer, her employer let her go, right before the holidays, and a few months before she gave birth to Chloe. She thinks sexism was clearly involved: the male piercer stayed on, and they canned her, citing the economy. Other options could have been made if she was valued, such as both piercers sharing a full-time position. She is now committed to helping women find a better economical business model through the world's coolest make-up line, Mary Kay! Make-up that gives working moms real options! It's PETA backed and good for your skin! Check out Pam's site at: MaryKay.com/PamelaSpector.*

"I love tattooing and putting artwork on people, but the business is hard. It's still very much a man's world."

Syren
Wickedly Cool
Tattoo Artist
Accessories Designer
Business Owner
Wiccan
Phoenix, Arizona.

Syren takes her name from Greek mythology. She fancies it because sirens have been known to be savers of guests, and they have a bad history of making men crazy while luring them to their deaths with their enchanting voices.

Some of her favorite things to do are: riding around town in her vintage black hearse, drinking rum and vanilla smoothies, thrift shopping, wearing high heels, and hanging out in her living room coffin.

She is a tattoo artist and a store owner. Tattooing has been a family affair; her brother is a tattoo artist too. She loves hot rods and working on them. She credits her father with this since he was always under the hood with her by his side. He called her Duce II and the name has stuck with her. When Syren gave birth to a son she continued the family tradition by naming him Duce.

It's her father's rearing that gave her the thick skin she needed when she professionally entered the world of tattooing. He taught her to work on cars, and to take care of herself. Her father raised her with this motto, "Do it for yourself; don't rely on a man to do it."

She got into tattooing as an artist by the guy who had been tattooing her. They wanted a girl in the shop to attract more business. Her mentor felt she had great drawing skill and could do it. Syren apprenticed for several years at that studio, and mostly under him. Initially, she worked managing a vintage clothing store during the day and worked in the shop at night assisting, cleaning, selling merchandise, making appointments, drawing and practicing tattooing on oranges. She gradually progressed from fruits to people, and eventually this evolved to full-time work and she was tattooing in the studio twelve-hours a day, six-days a week.

It was grueling work as mom of a pre-teen too. Luckily, she had her second husband and friends and family to help out. When she was pregnant with her second child she worked until the day he was born. But some customers were uncomfortable with the idea of a woman tattooing them, especially a visibly pregnant one. She ran into frequent encounters with men who did not want her belly touching them while getting inked, as if the condition was contagious.

She took her son Duce to work with her the first few months. All the guys at the shop were very supportive, but she needed to be with her son more. As the one always closing the shop, she was always afraid deep down of being robbed or raped, since she's so small. Syren is 5'3 and weighs 125 lbs.

She and her second husband decided to open their own merchandise store specializing in tattoo art accessories. Their store's success has allowed them to now include designing and making furniture. In fact, she not only has much more time with her family, but makes enough to live on that she just strictly tattoos on the side now, for pleasure.

For anyone wanting to get into that field she does recommend going to as many tattoo shows and related events as you can like: Viva Las Vegas and Bulletproof. She adds:

"Be persistent. Pursue tour art because you never know what's going to happen. It is still very much a man's profession, so you have to be persistent and network. It's a man's business and you have to fight."

Check out Rebel Mom Syren's awesome online store Lucky-11.com! She makes and sells hand-painted purses, tattoo-covered suitcases, and custom skull, coffin, bat, and spider fashioned jewelry.

Read about her line in rad mags like *Old Skool Hot Rod* and *International Tattoo Magazine.*

Syren and her second husband are both covered head-to-toe in tattoos, but she points out this irony:

"We will be out together, but I am the one who gets weird looks and questions from strangers, because women aren't suppose to have tattoos. My husband has never gotten this even though he is covered from neck-to-hands."

The accessories she makes and sells at the store include hand-painted purses, tattoo-covered suitcases, and custom skull, coffin, bat, and spider influenced jewelry. You can also order some of their cool merchandise online at Lucky-11.com. Recently, she has had articles and promotions in *Old Skool Hot Rod* and *International Tattoo Magazine.*

She also has a beautiful daughter Ravona from her first marriage. Ravona's father hasn't been part of her life since she was two or so. Syren's second husband has legally adopted her.

Her first husband was a punk rock guy with a mohawk who joined the Marines to treat his drug problems before they married. He had a lot of personal conflicts and problems beyond drug addiction, which ultimately weren't treatable by the Marines or marriage. He is gay and tried unsuccessfully riding himself of his sexual nature by jumping into the overtly masculine Marine life and traditional heterosexual marriage.

Syren looks back and is happy her ex-husband has come out of the closet, since she feels fighting that (and trying to avoid the persecution that comes with being homosexual in society) was the source of his drug problems, but she can't let her daughter be around his drug addiction, or the chaotic and dangerous behaviors it provokes from him. She doesn't regret the marriage, because it helped form who is she is today, and her life would be incomplete without Ravona.

Even though Rebel Mom Syren's family is obviously different on the outside with their tattoos and mohawks, she has learned that physical differences are perceived as less of a threat to others than what's on the inside. Like different values, or religious beliefs. If you look at humanity's history with all the ethnic or religious 'cleansing', the crusades and witch-hunts (or woman-hunts) and trials, the modern day conflicts in the Middle East, Eastern Europe and Africa, and the battles for dominance in the United States by right-wing 'Christians', she is right. Her family is semi-guarded about what they will let outsiders know about them, including that they are Wiccans.

While she was married to Ravona's biological father, they traveled the Orient with the military. She views the Japanese culture in particular as beautiful and spiritual. She cites that their culture has an awareness of life and death and they live reverently in between. She loves the ancient temples, and religious celebrations. She feels many (but not all) U.S. Americans are void of ancient spiritualism and that is why materialism and dogma-based religious zest are such a binding and hindering problem here (in the social and political realms).

Syren believes this lack of spiritualism and focus on materialism contributes to people's negative attitudes and fear of things unknown to them, or different from them. Syren recalls an encounter with a stranger at the store when she was pregnant with Duce. A woman made a snide side comment to her friend, "Is the baby going to have tattoos too?" Her daughter Ravona replied, "No, you get them."

Even though her family is obviously different on the outside with their tattoos and mohawks, she has learned that physical differences are perceived as less of a threat to others than what's on the inside. Like different values, or religious beliefs. If you look at humanity's history with all the ethnic or religious 'cleansing', the crusades and witch-hunts (or woman-hunts) and trials, the modern day conflicts in the Middle East, Eastern Europe and Africa, and the battles for dominance in the United States by right-wing 'Christians', she is right. Her family is semi-guarded about what they will let outsiders know about them.

> "My family is Wiccan. We embellish spiritual discipline into our family living through deep respect for animals, and a reverence for nature. Our children are raised in a very warm and accepting environment that is open to including others regardless of the individual's choice of religious preference. We have a lot of active discussions in our house about this. My family does keep it on the down-low though about our spiritualism, because of the prejudice against Wiccans and other Earth religions in society. We have to keep this guard up some because of the way we look, with the children's school. Our children don't generally discuss the family's spiritual religion with their friends because of potential parental backlash, or misunderstanding. We have taught our children to be accepting of the world itself, but be cautious because it is a very close-minded, judgmental place."

Wicca is a loosely structured universal religion that is the antithesis to organized religion. It is said to have evolved from ancient pagan forms of Earth-worship and the witchcraft of early Europe. Primarily, Wiccans celebrate through festivals designed around full moon Esbats and the eight Sabbats. There is use of spells, herbs, and a worshipping of either a pantheon of ancient gods/goddesses, or a focus on one.

However, it is clearly understood among Wiccans that any use of magic is limited to good purposes only. There is a code of ethics outlined for general purpose, even though are various forms of Wicca. You can learn more at Wicca.org.

Syren wants to keep focusing on her two businesses—the storefront and the online store, while spending time with family and friends. Her husband, in addition to his role in the family and the businesses, is a musician who plays in two bands: a punk one and a psychobilly band. Their plans are to keep having have fun and exploring the world together as a family living on the edge.

Awesome!

**Since this interview: Syren and her family just bought their first home and moved to California. In addition, they were a guest family on the show Wife-Swap.*

"I am an extremist and a survivor. I had a rough start and then chose a rough path, but it has motivated me to strive for happiness. Now the most important thing that I am is a mother and I think my past will only feed my desire to be a good one."

Syndea
Pretty Piercer
Stoic Survivor
Head-strong Healer
Classic Rock Momma
Waitress/Server
Ellensburg, Washington.

Syndea is a new mom who loves reading true crimes and psychological thriller books. She has a big personality and is not afraid of change, and is always doing something new. She is a working stay-at-home mom currently, but has worked as both a body piercer and a server. [Most artisans have to have a day job to support their night job or vice versa.]

She has turned to writers and artists all of her life for the inspiration to keep going and survive the hard times, which has been plenty for this twenty-four-year-old. She cites Emily Dickenson and Edgar Allen Poe as two of the big reasons why she made it through the teenage years. She loves classic rock, and music has been her lifeline, especially in the darkest of times. She has dreamt of being a singer since she was five-years-old and has been writing songs just as long. Her favorite musicians are: Bob Dylan, Janis Joplin, Judy Collins, Angelic Upstarts, Pinkerton Thugs, Ducky Boys and Jimmy Cliff. Her son was born to another one of her favorite artists as well: Bob Marley. Syndea is very new to the world of mothering. Her son Cade is only two-months-old. Motherhood is where her life has taken her, and that is her primary focus right now, "Everything he does seems new and it thrills me to watch his little milestones." She wants to ensure she provides a better life for him, and not make the mistakes that her birth mom or later adoptive parents made. Her current family is the one she has made with Cade.

She grew up mostly in Napa Valley, but life was far from idyllic. She had been molested and was later raped by her father. She reached out for help and turned him in when she was only four years of age. Even with her testimony in court, he just got a slap on the hand. Instead of it making her life better, it just

Society can easily identify children of abuse by the symptoms of behavior. Routinely, authority figures and institutions make problems worse by essentially blaming the victims, and punishing them for 'behavior problems', or very early criminal acts of mischief. They typically fail to address the cause of the problems. Of course to do this, society would have to take a hard look in the mirror and how it contributes to predatory exploitations and crimes against people, including children. Society would also have to take more responsibility for how it conducts itself and its values as a whole from child-rearing to big business.

put her in more sexually abusive situations. The state seized custody of her and she endured years of abuse in foster care. She was molested, physically beaten, and suffered extreme physiological torture. She had a slight reprieve when she was adopted, but by then (as do most abused children) she had what society calls 'behavioral problems' and was placed back in foster care, relinquished by her adoptive family. *[Society can easily identify children of abuse by the symptoms of behavior. Routinely, authority figures and institutions make problems worse by essentially blaming the victims, and punishing them for 'behavior problems', or very early criminal acts of mischief. They typically fail to address the cause of the problems. Of course to do this, society would have to take a hard look in the mirror and how it contributes to predatory exploitations and crimes against people, including children. Society would also have to take more responsibility for how it conducts itself and its values as a whole from child-rearing to big business.]*

By the time she was eighteen, she had an eating disorder, and a drug problem. She was shooting drugs for a year-and-a-half, and there was a time when she couldn't "ever imagine not shooting up." There were some people intermittently that came into her life who helped her,

> "Getting clean was a major one for me. I am lucky enough to have met key people through my life that have helped me stay strong, or become strong again, when its been rough. I have been fortunate enough to be loved by these people and I may not be so well adjusted now if not for having them show me [that] people can be good.
>
> I have come through a lot of challenges since birth that I could have let break me, but I feel like have bested those experiences and become a happy person with a good heart and mind. I feel like I have done well and come out of it all unscathed. I think I am actually stronger for it and this makes me proud. Now I can't imagine ever shooting up again."

She thinks to deal with any major life problem, from depression to drug abuse, besides having the love and support of others to help you, it is also important that you love yourself, "I'm human and I've made mistakes. I can forgive myself those mistakes, because I have kept trying. I have achieved better than I, or anyone, once thought I would." The experiences of her youth have fundamentally shaped her outlook on life as well …

> "I try not to regret anything that has happened in my life that I have done, or that was done to me, because our experiences are what make us, and I shouldn't regret me. Life is all about perspective. If all you see is shit, that's all you will carry with you. Everything has a positive and a negative. No matter what happens we have a series of choices—so I am never powerless in the outcome."

The addiction she overcame and the physical abuse she endured was her segway into the body modification world, "There are people that see it as mutilation whereas we might view it as self-realization, taking ownership of ourselves and our bodies." She herself had gotten several piercings and tattoos by the time she knew she wanted do this professionally. She wanted to help people face their fears and conquer them. Just two weeks after she made this decision an opportunity opened up.

> "I responded to the word on the street that a place needed a piercer. I trained heavily for two weeks, and then became the only piercer in the store. I learned how to order and use medical supplies and jewelry. I was able to become a better piercer and I improved the quality of our shop through my own research and study. I felt like I had risen to the occasion."

It allowed her to express herself in a way that was nurturing and therapeutic for her spirit and her body. Since Syndea had confided so much to me, to help other women by being in this book, I shared my story with her of the sexual abuse and the violence I endured growing up. Reclaiming my body, and myself, had everything to do with tattooing and piercings. She was not alone. She in turn shared with me the fact that being heavily involved in the world of body alteration has also helped her stay clean by focusing on a discipline. [Most clean ex-addicts who were addicted to uppers become dare devils and get physically defying, or challenging, jobs and/or hobbies like: sky-diving, rock-climbing, stunt work on movie-sets, personal fitness, etc. It gives them a rush—but a healthy one. Downer addicts, who are clean, may focus on relaxing, thoughtful work, such as: counseling, landscaping, etc.] As she healed, she became an avid body-modificationist.

"I had over seventy-two different piercings—some more exotic; though I usually had only twenty-five to thirty at any given time. I would get an urge and decide to get a corset piercing or some face project done, and just do it, which is convenient when you work at a tattoo/piercing shop. I even got a big 10 gauge circular barbell implanted into my skin. What I really loved about it was getting more and more extreme with the piercings or the number I got at each sitting and controlling the pain rather than having the pain control me."

She was abruptly let go from her studio after four years there when she had a falling out with her boss. Instead of it getting her down, she saw it as an opportunity to make a life-change and moved to a small town in Washington that she had briefly lived in when she was a teen. She needed some time to reflect and build a new life. She took out all of her visible piercings so that she could find work. She took a job waiting tables, and was figuring out her plan when she ran into a friend from high school. They started dating.

"I always knew I was meant to be a mother. I hadn't planned it to be with the person it was with, however. Beer was involved. I was living with him, and we had been together only three months. I was afraid to tell him I was pregnant because our relationship was very rough, angry, and a spiteful one. I finally did and he freaked out and told me, 'I had to get an abortion' and otherwise flipped. I am pro-choice, but it wasn't the choice for me. So I told him he wasn't necessary for me to raise this child. He chose to stick by me. I did move into a motel for a month to think things through. I wasn't sure 'we' wanted to be together."

She moved back in with him and they decided to try to work things out. She hoped she would have the wisdom to make the right choices, one day at a time. She knew however, before their baby was born they had to get out of "the crappy trailer" they were in. It was one thing as a crash pad for them, but entirely another to try to turn it into a home. It was just to run down and small. Syndea got a bank account and started saving her checks so that they could get an apartment. She also hoped a new place would give them a new chance at happiness together. He had been verbally abusive and she hoped this new beginning would induce better treatment from him for their newly forming threesome.

Because of her own dismal childhood she was fraught with fear that she wouldn't be "a good enough mom, or know how to be a mom." She had common mother-to-be anxieties like fears of dropping him on the stairs, etc. She was surprised by the unexpected support she got from her biological mom and adoptive mom. Her boyfriend's parents were also great and helped them get essential items for the baby.

The restaurant she worked at went out of business when she was five months pregnant and she got laid off. Her boyfriend cleaned up his act significantly and not only worked full-time, but also worked extra graveyard shifts so that she could stay home, rest, and get ready for the baby. His extra help and effort is what is allowing her to stay-at-home with their son Cade now, since they wouldn't be able to make it on one income without significant overtime hours and pay. She is grateful for this time to be with her child:

> "Being a parent is wonderful. At first I was too tired to really feel anything, or take it in. I was induced for three days before I had him, but once it set in, it was awesome. I am still new to the whole thing, but I really love how I feel so connected to him. I feel like we know each other better than I ever known anyone in my life. I love him more than I love anyone in the world. Being a mom is more natural and easy than I had thought. Of course, the new sleep schedule and crying was, and sometimes is, a bit frustrating, but I can't imagine not having him here. Sometimes I feel like he shows me a great amount of patience."

Syndea hopes Cade will be honest, kind, self-assured, independent, unafraid, adventurous, and full of love for life. She thinks the only way to teach him these traits is to have them herself, "I guess I need to know in my heart, as I raise him, that these are the things that he can have, if I allow it." She wants to be vigilant in her awareness of her new role as a mother, "He is the most important and blessed thing I will ever have in my life. It's up to me to keep him balanced while he is young, so he will be able to do it for himself when he is on his own." Ultimately, she thinks …

> "It's my job to make sure that my son Cade gets a well rounded, diverse experience in his childhood so he can hopefully go into the world as an open-minded adult that doesn't feel bound by social 'norms' or judge others based on their differences from him. Most importantly, he needs to feel secure, loved, and free of shame so he can become the most secure and strong person possible. I also hope he leaves home with a strong sense of self and faith in his own ability to face life and whatever it brings him."

She doesn't feel she has a stigma attached to her as a mom, because of her professional piercing background, but acknowledges this may very well be due not to the world becoming a better place, but the fact that she's "pretty tame looking" now. She does think though that the world has become more desensitized to tattoos and body mods, and hopes it is becoming more acceptable of diversity but,

> "It's hard to gauge how people will peg me as a mother at this point, with no obvious piercings. I'm sure there are those that think me exposing my child to tats and piercings warrant CPS (Child 'Protective' Services) involvement. I really hope that mindset is diminishing. In all honesty though when I didn't have a kid and I was all pierced up people would give me dirty looks and ask me if I 'worshipped satan' …
>
> So, yeah, I guess that body modification is still a definite stigma in relation to parenting. And actually, now that I think of it, a lot of people without tattoos have asked me what my children will think of mine, or what I will tell them. I always (kind of) laugh. My kid won't think it's strange."

Syndea thinks too many parents force their fears and shortcomings on their children, and that parents have a bad habit of justifying their actions by referencing what their own parents did. She feels most parents would be better parents if they didn't define their own, or their kids, success in strictly terms of money and status, but personal accomplishments and a healthy, flexible value system. She sees kids that are weighed down from a young age with, "The expectation to carry on their parents beliefs and customs and don't always encourage their children to form their own." For Cade she plans to,

> "Be fair and honest, I want to allow for a relationship that enables Cade to come to me with anything. I plan to expose him to a lot of different people and lifestyles so he can learn and be aware of all the choices he has in life. I never want to be overbearing or affect our relationship in a negative way. I want to be a good role-model and a strong woman so he can learn to respect and love women."

"If our kids grow up seeing us as different maybe it will take the fear out of other peoples differences. Maybe it will encourage them to be more vocal or unafraid in regards to what makes them different. I hope that it makes them less prone to prejudice."

She doesn't know many moms in town with the level of body modification she has done, but she does think the subject would be too taboo for many people, so it never comes up. Plus with a new baby at home, it's the last thing on her mind. What she needs right now is advice, sleep, and help, "Its nerve-wracking being a new mom and having no previous experience to draw from. I think a lot of moms relate to me no matter what their background. They all remember what it's like to be a new mom." She cites that there seems to be an underlying kindred feeling. [I remember that feeling as well, and it is very compassionate and unifying—and seems to cross all boundaries. It also fades like breast milk though, when the kids grow and crossover from the infancy stage to the toddler stage, and we become a different type of busy, and back to ourselves—including prejudgments and prejudices. We, women, need to make a mental note to bring it back when we interact with each other from different walks of life.]

She has one close friend who is a mom that she looks up to. She's an "untraditional hippie-type mom" that is one of the strongest women she knows. She has three children, and lost one of her sons whom drowned while being watched by a friend. Syndea hopes to never know that pain, but her friend had to find the strength and serenity to keep going for her family.

She doesn't think of herself as counter or subculture, just that "I don't want to live my life in fear of the unknown and I like to test my own boundaries of what mainstream society finds acceptable."

Syndea feels people look for excuses to be "just cruel and mean-spirited" and even if they have had bad lives, it's no excuse and it upsets her. She detests people that enjoy hurting others and feels this is rampant in our culture at large. We may say we value kindness and consideration, but it is not modeled and it's what we see every day in how people treat one another in public; and in organized religion, government, business and politics—there's lots of foul actions right under handshakes and smiles. She summarizes her take on things:

> "Politics are geared towards helping only certain people and when Bush was elected [prior] it only validated my belief that the system is flawed. As for religion, if being a good person isn't good enough, I don't need it."

She does think general society needs a more fearless approach to life,

> "If our kids grow up seeing us as different maybe it will take the fear out of other peoples differences. Maybe it will encourage them to be more vocal or unafraid in regards to what makes them different. I hope that it makes them less prone to prejudice. I do think it takes all kinds to make up the world, and as long as we aren't hurting anyone we all have the right to live our lives however we feel is right. Anyone different from me has something of value to share, and I will value it, whatever it may be. Sometimes I suspect the mainstream is just a world full of people that hide their unique traits and fetishes better.
>
> The world has a lot of beauty in it, and a lot of ugliness, and it's our responsibility to face both full on, even when it's not easy. Sometimes changing the world is as small as voicing an opinion, even when it's not the easy thing to do, or the most popular with those around you. If you can say something that triggers a new thought process

to occur in someone's mind, even if they never agree with you, then you have in fact made a difference in someone's world."

One mantra she lives by that helps her stay level headed and confident is a quote of Dolly Parton's that she thinks can help all of us, *"Find out who you are and do it on purpose."* Purpose has been on her mind since she was able to get clean, and she hopes once Cade is older she will be able to open a piercing and tattoo studio of her own. She was planning to apprentice for tattooing when she learned of her pregnancy, and was taking a few courses on human anatomy at the community college to further her skill as a practitioner. But for the moment mommy-hood beckons,

"I have only been a mom for two months now, but it's been a big life change and spiritual experience. I feel like I have to make things happen quicker in my life, like the clock is actually ticking and I can't waste a moment. I want more out of life because I want more for my son."

**Since this interview: Syndea and her boyfriend did finally call it quits. And she is now a mom of two awesome boys! She had to take dependable, good paying corporate work to put food on the table, but hasn't forgotten about her dreams and where they may lead her someday when she has more time and resources on her hands. She also started a blog helping victims of childhood sexual abuse.*

Sadly, after our last update for the book, Syndea and her boys were killed in a tragic late night house fire.

My heart, her family, and her friends mourn.
She was a modern hero for us all …
An advocate for healing for childhood abuse survivors,
and a wonderful woman, mother, and human being.

We love you Syndea.

In memory of Syndea Smith and her sons Cade and Trevor, whom passed away on April 16th, 2011.

If there was anything Syndea could share now, I'm sure it would be stay strong, live happy, love your kids and friends, and please always do your monthly check on your smoke detector batteries. And she would lovingly chide you while telling you this, with her big, hearty smile bringing her dimples out, and you would finally comply and get with it, living that is.

"A parent's personal experience is what is important when it comes to educating your own child. And the tattoo world, being a family affiliated world, has offered my family, myself, and my children, a very international life. And that is cool."

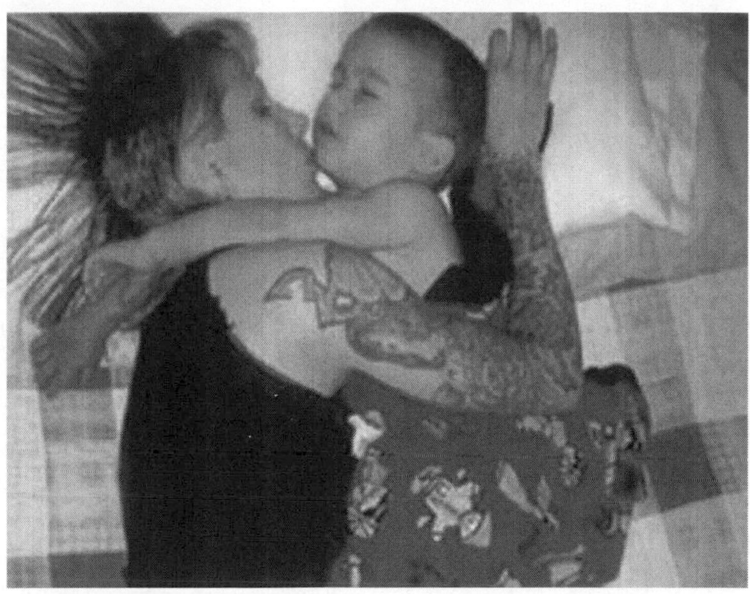

Sheila Rose Montie
Homemaker
Inked Inventor
Foxy Family Historian
Cosmetology Tattooist
San Diego, California.

Sheila Rose is a rocking mom who lives in San Diego, but grew up on the road. She loves getting tattooed, giving tattoos, hanging out in the sun, horse-back riding, and chilling with her boys. She grew up in the infamous generational tattoo family, the Montie's. She loves dabbling in science and working on inventions. She can't live without sweet iced tea, science, math and music. Music is as essential to her diet as the food pyramid; she needs to hear heavy metal, punk, and gangster rap each and every day.

The roles that mean the most to her are her roles as: mother, wife, daughter, and sister. However, don't be fooled into thinking she is meek and quiet. On the contrary she is extraordinary. She's "Punk Rock, real Hollywood, a righteous friend, and a heavily tattooed woman." She is working as a full-time stay-at-home mom, but apprenticing under her mom for cosmetic tattooing. She's getting ready for her future for when she has one foot in the home, and one foot out. Her priority right now though is her family.

At the time of this interview Sheila was in her late twenties and her two sons, Mohawk Vinni and Mohawk Charlie, were ages three and five. She met her husband Tycho (who is an internationally acclaimed artist from Amsterdam) on the tattoo show circuit. It was a smoldering infatuation at first glance. They fell in love, got married and had babies. Sheila's goal is to raise her children the old-fashioned way, just like she and her brother Shane were.

★★★★★★★★

"I always wanted to be a mother. I have an amazing mother too. She set the bar for me—love living up to her. They came from me, and it is my job to raise them. Stay-at-home, play, love them … that's the deal."

★★★★★★★★

> "I always wanted to be a mother. I have an amazing mother too. She set the bar for me—love living up to her. They came from me, and it is my job to raise them. Stay at home, play, love them … that's the deal."

Sheila grew up around artists and feels very fortunate to have been born into the family she has. Her closest relatives are artists: her mother Cathy Montie, her father Gill Montie, her brother Shane Montie, her uncle Tyler Burbank, and husband Tycho Veldhoen. Her family traveled every summer and fall, with friends and family, and making additional income from tattooing at festivals, shows and conventions. During non-travel seasons they would go back to their home-base in Hollywood, California, and Cathy would focus on home-schooling, and Gill would work as a guest at a studio. As the kids got older, they also owned numerous tattoo shops in California and Texas.

Sheila fondly remembers the summer BBQs on the road, and what a magical, amazing time it was for them as a family. She even recalls as far back as four-years-of-age, when the family lived on a school bus and traveled up the East Coast, with mom and dad tattooing at special events. Through her parents nurturing and values, Sheila is a very confident and independent woman. She lives with spirit, honor and heart. Her childhood was very loving, warm, and safe. It saddens her to know that so many kids are discarded by their parents in today's world. She counts her blessings daily.

> "How I was raised, I am proud to be raising my children that way also. I look back myself, and both my parents being tattooed from head-to-toe, I never knew, or thought any different; loved them just the way that they are. I also believe that my children will love their family just the way we are. I know for outsiders, they think that we're crazy looking, but beyond their eyes, we are a huge family in a small world. For my children growing up in the tattoo business makes them third generation. How proud of that I am—Aaaargh, tattoos, the only life for me and my family."

Sheila as a teenager got to help her dad start and run the infamous Inkslingers Ball. It started out over a decade ago in Hollywood. It grew in both notoriety and popularity over the years, attracting numerous fans. Some of who have been to the party are: Drew Barrymore, Johnny Depp, Billy Idol, the Stray Cats, Social Distortion, Cher, Motley Crue, and so on. It has given her a head for business, and a lasting passion for the wild side. When we were done interviewing Shelia very kindly invited me out to Hollywood to attend the then 13th Inkslingers Ball. Much to my dismay, I had to decline. [Not because I don't love good tunes, good times, and cool ink—but as a struggling mom, student, and worker, I just couldn't take a trip. But damn, I wanted to!]

She grew up well-guided by her parents and plans on doing the same for her boys. They supported her becoming a cheerleader. She loved cheering and did it with discipline and enthusiasm, and was starting to carve out her role in it professionally. It wasn't until she knew she was going to be a mother, that she closed that chapter of her life. Her parents always supported her and loved her no matter what path she has traveled on. They were quite excited though when she embraced the family business and tradition, and when they became grandparents!

When she learned she was going to be a mom, she had unparalleled support and encouragement from not only her family, but her new husband. They decided she would stay-at-home, since he had to travel for work internationally, and as their children got older, she and the kids would join him on the road. Sheila didn't have any fears of becoming a mom, nor big ideas for would happen afterwards. She doesn't think that way about life. Her philosophy is, "I live my life for today."

She is very proud of her children, and her main focus is simply "to love them, give them life experience and stability." She wants her children to have the finer things in life and to get the best education in every aspect possible. She tries to make the right decisions and hopes they see that, so that when they are adults they can reflect on their childhood, and be guided in the choices they make as she herself was.

Sheila, as a member of tattooed family, has had more than her fair share of discrimination at the hands of mainstream society. She's very happy in her niche, and keeps her distance from those she doesn't know now as a result of. Especially, now that she is a mom and has two young boys to protect. When it comes to society, her mantra is, "Fuck Society. They don't want none [of me]. People are very cruel and I am a pirate." She won't take your shit, so just leave her alone, if you've got nothing good or nice to say.

She thinks most people can do the job of raising kids since, "It doesn't take a genius and we all have been one, a child, and we can remember what it's like if we try." The problem she sees is not an issue of ability, but of choice … "Most people don't know how to raise their kids because they don't care too." She thinks society is too concerned about superficial things and chasing those, rather than doing what's right for their kids and families. She doesn't get it, "It doesn't take that much effort to be with your kids; to remember what being a kid is about."

She knows a few moms like herself, mainly through the family business, tattoo and show circuits.

She's certain if she hadn't been born into the lifestyle she would have chosen it cause, "The people are so damn good." She also knows firsthand the world her family offered, beats the world that the world offers hands-down. There were no daycare issues because of a job, abuse issues, or stifling super-authoritarian issues. Her parents created the type of life they wanted, and incorporated their kids and parental needs into it. They created work that would support their family, and not just financially. She and Tycho plan on doing the same … "Straight real, wouldn't have it any other way."

Sheila is currently working on her families memoirs and is reflecting on all the life lessons her parents and grandparents have handed down to her. When her grandmother Marcia passed away she was appointed to be the new family historian. She wants the book that she writes to capture the paths her family has paved in the tattoo business as well as to show what wonderful people they are. They went after the American dream, did it their way, and built a great life and a great family.

She is very proud of what she has achieved thus far, and what she has been able to fulfill in her life such as being an educated woman, a caring and involved mother and wife. If there is one thing she wants us to walk away with from her story, it is to hold on to life, and cherish it. She has lost too many good people to death, and we never know when it's coming, so make every day count. And to always remember the special bond you have with your babies and don't take that for granted. The closing thought she wants to share is, "I made it this far, it has not been easy, but in the best of company. And damn, it's been fun."

The Performers and Warriors

Have you ever dreamt of pin-up modeling? Or putting out fires? Or starring in movies? Boxing? Roller derby? Saving the world? Well, dream no more …

You are about to meet moms whose intrepidity and prowess invite you to go where wolves hunt and mate, and eagles dare and soar! And where they crash, heal, and get back up again.

Women are made to feel ashamed of their bodies, and this is even more so as we age and/or give birth. One mom rejected this notion and honored American tradition by becoming a Suicide Girl. Another mom went from stripper to fire-fighter while earning multiple degrees and starting an eco-friendly cleaning business. But first she helped Native Americans and inner-city moms, with AmeriCorps. Oh yeah, she battles in skates too. Our young blue-collar mom from the Midwest shows you how tough it is working in a man's world as a printer and roller in the Newspaper industry. She also shows you how fulfilling it is to become a boxer and stand up for yourself and your kid. To go with all the strength these women will help you develop, you need to add some flexibility training. Welcome our very awesome and independent Yogini mother and accomplished circus performer. She teaches the kids how to find their yoga core and push through, and she will help you too. She will also help you work up the nerve to make momentous, yet essential, life changes. Endurance and hope is what our last mom gives you. She tells her story through poetry and acting. She had to let a cool t-shirt business go, save her girls, go through a horrible divorce, all while finishing college and working. She wasn't even twenty-five yet. She didn't lose faith and neither should you.

Get ready to make your dreams come true with the Performers and Warriors!

"I am proud of my photo sets with Suicide Girls and have no regrets. A woman's body is a beautiful creation, and it's great to show that it is nothing to be ashamed of."

Stasia
Professional Tattoo & Pin-Up Model
Musician
Rockin' Rapper
Awesome Actress
Sinfully Sexy Spiritualist
Hollywood, California.

Stasia is a hardworking momma who acts, sings, plays, and models. She loves every single form of music and views it all as an expression of our minds and feelings. She has dedicated herself to this line of work and doesn't limit herself to any genres, or styles, that can compromise both talent and content.

She prides herself on listening to her heart, and is rewarded by the comfort and simplistic self-love of just truly living. She feels she deserves this in life, and that all of us do. She takes nothing for granted and is grateful for everyday she is alive.

Her friends and children tell her she reminds them of an anime character: witty, honest, and always doing something that both amuses and inspires others. She sings and dances everywhere she goes, no matter who is watching. She has been this way ever since she was a young kid. She has the heart of a healer and the demeanor of a child.

Through art, music, and acting she hopes to spread her message of truth (living with heart and honesty) with a positive attitude—no matter what, or who, she may encounter on this big crazy planet of ours. She describes herself as, "I am free, like a butterfly, yet tough as a warrior. I work hard for what I want, but I never lose my compassion in the process."

> ***Check out Rebel Mom Stasia's gorgeous sets at: SuicideGirls.com.***
>
> **"I am proud of my photo sets and have no regrets. A woman's body is a beautiful creation and it's great to show that. It's nothing to be ashamed of, and it's not dirty. We were all born naked, so why cover it up? I feel confident showing my curves. I mean, I am not perfect. I have stretch marks, and fat, just like most women, and I am not ashamed of it anymore, thanks to the site. I express myself without feeling insecure. Unfortunately, some people get the wrong idea, and think I'm being promiscuous … and that's just sad."**

As a child she was heavily involved in drama and dancing. She trained professionally for elementary acting as a young adult at Mesa College, and has a fifteen year background in choreography and dance training. She describes her special skills as a dancer who can do: tap, ballet, modern, jazz, hip-hop and burlesque.

To help support herself and her family throughout her many artistic endeavors she has worked as a yoga teacher, waitress, computer tech, nurse and a secretary. Her professional resume though is broad and accomplished; which is what she has worked hard for. She has been in numerous films including: *Herbie Fully Loaded*, *Constantine*, and *Demon Hunter*. The TV shows to her credit include: *Jack & Bobby*, *Charmed*, *Las Vegas*, *Malcolm in the Middle*, and *Grey's Anatomy*. She has also been in countless music videos, some of which have aired on MTV, for bands like: KRS One, Black Label Society, and Trust Company. She has modeled too. She was a lead model in London Underground's Spring Fashion show in 2005. Some of her favorite modeling though has been the pin-up modeling that she has done most recently with Suicide Girls. She speaks of the experience as:

"It was something I came across through word of mouth. I have had a fascination with pin-up photography. The women of our history have mapped out a true symbol of beauty and I am happy to continue with this celebration of women in the modern day. My photos are always classy, a celebration of what women are all about. Some people get the wrong idea about the site, or my intentions, but they have to realize that we all do it for different reasons, and that you can't compare any of us to each other. As individuals, we are all different. I am proud of my photo sets and have no regrets. A woman's body is a beautiful creation and it's great to show that. It's nothing to be ashamed of, and it's not dirty. We were all born naked, so why cover it up?

I hadn't done any pin-up modeling prior to this and I always believed that you had to be tall and skinny. Thanks to Missy, who is the founder of Suicide Girls, I feel confident showing my curves. I mean, I am not perfect. I have stretch marks, and fat, just like most women, and I am not ashamed of it anymore, thanks to the site. I express myself without feeling insecure. Unfortunately, some people get the wrong idea, and think I'm being promiscuous … and that's just sad.

I have done sets with two of my closet friends Michelle and Sarah. I am totally comfortable with them. I don't know how I would feel about working with a man, and I don't even know if I'll ever pose again. It was something I wanted to see if I could do it. I did and it was successful."

You can check out Suicide Girls (and Stasia's gorgeous sets) at: SuicideGirls.com. She has also done tattoo modeling for *Skin & Ink* magazine. Stasia herself has over sixteen different pieces and they are all symbolic and sentimental.

"I love them all. They are all meaningful. They have all been done at the right time and moments in my life; times of struggles, times of healing, and times of redemption. They are like symbols or reflections of my life and what I have learned and experienced. I would never get anything that didn't mean something to me. It's not about trends, or style. It's about peeling layers of my skin off and revealing the true me underneath."

Music is her dominant passion and excitement (besides her children). One artist that has had a huge influence on her is Bjork,

"She is so full of expression and true raw emotion. It baffles me that someone can express themselves with such honesty and then share it with the entire world. That is courage. I really admire that. So to Bjork ... thank you."

The very first band Stasia was in was StretchMarxxx. It was an all-girl punk band in which she was the lead singer. She came up with the name because she thought it was the most punk rock thing about women, since we all have them, and our bodies go through a lot to get them. Her second band was a three-person experimental electronica band, Sterile Eden. She was the female vocalist for the act. It is with this band she learned how to use software to make beats. After that band she focused on mostly solo projects and strengthened her production skills. She explains her musical experience:

"I never thought I was capable of making music, because I never had the patience to learn an instrument, ha! I was wrong! Thank god for computers! After a couple of years of doing solo stuff I started another electronic project with a producer friend of mine. We were called D'Junk. Like all the projects thus far it was short lived but sometimes it's better to let stuff fade away.

This brings me back to where I am now, and where I feel most comfortable, which is working on my own solo projects. I do enjoy working with others on music, but it is much more rewarding to be performing and working on songs that mean a lot to me. I use music as a healing mechanism for myself and hopefully for others. If I can relate to it, I hope that other people can as well. Until I have completed an amazing album that completely describes and expresses myself and my true purpose/message I will continue to work alone. Someday I do hope to work on other duo projects though, but it's very important to work with people that can relate to your emotions, otherwise it becomes an attention struggle. That is not what music is about for me."

★★★★★★★★

"You can create music, pose nude, tattoo your skin, color your hair, etc. You can be as creative as you like, and in that expression of natural beauty in 'being yourself' you can spread that confidence to other mothers who may find themselves compromising how they would like to currently express themselves simply because they are mothers. It seems as though any mother who doesn't fit 'society's mold' is looked down upon.

★★★★★★★★

It is demanding for Stasia to balance work, art, music, love, children and the world. One thing that helps keep her focused and keeps her on her feet is her drive to never give up, as well as being spiritually and philosophically focused. Stasia studies all forms of religions and mysticisms, and has taken something special from every single one. She would never claim one religion, or philosophy, one-hundred percent—because she would leave something out, or would be cutting something out, and to her that would be ignorance. This helps her stay focused on her heart and doing this helps her stay happy.

It saddens her to see so many people walking around unhappy. She feels it's because many people choose to live with their head and not their heart; when they neglect their heart to make important life decisions it affects them and those around them. She feels this particular kind of sickness is evident all over the world, and in how our leaders and politicians run government and business.

Her two children give her life profound meaning and enable her to live freely with passion. Before having kids she was very self-involved, but yet still nurturing and caring as an individual towards others. She has realized how fragile and delicate children are, and therefore life itself. She makes sure that every decision she makes reflects that sensitivity to life and others. Loving two children without limits has humbled her, and without her role as mother she feels she would now be lost and lonely.

One unique advantage she has is: as a mother she has lived both in the United States and in various European countries, including Ireland. She tells us that,

> "There is a huge cultural difference between here and Europe. It is really based on the beliefs and upbringing of the two continents. I wouldn't call it ignorance, but people in Europe are much more conservative, since it's a very religious region. I'd say there is more fear in Europe: fear of expression, fear of truth basically, but I do respect that, because it's different from my upbringing. I learned a lot from Europe, as we all can. Maybe we are all a little lax here, because of the lack of boundaries, and some American parents take it too far, like taking their kids on the *Jerry Springer Show* for example and the kind of stories you get from that. In European parenting, respect and honor comes before anything else, before selfishness."

She has sadly recently divorced. When her Irish ex-husband and she married, they both wanted children so badly—they couldn't wait to get started. Their families on both continents were completely supportive. Stasia is now thirty and her children are nine and eleven. They wanted to create a beautiful life out of the energy of their combined love for one another, no plans and no fears. It was tough at first, but as with anything you learn as you go and anything worth having isn't easy.

Her basic belief about parenting is to continue to spread her love and creativity with her children, which is a tenet of human values that she feels all children should be shown, given, and nurtured with, so that as adults they are caring and giving to one another in society. She also expands upon this message of salvation/redemption through poetic exploration of love and creativity through her music, and this is her gift to the rest of the world. To be able to do what she loves and share that with the children she has created, is like a dream coming true. The principles she lives by (and shares with her children) are:

"I expect to live my life 100% completely as my true-self. To never compromise my beliefs for someone else's benefit. Hopefully, doing this will show my children that it's okay to speak your truths and live from your heart. My belief is that you give your children unconditional love and respect, if you give them that respect, you will earn the respect of your children. You will also form an unbreakable bond of trust. There is much more going on in the world that is invisible, rather than visible. If we can remember that, and take time to enjoy every minute, you can never go wrong. I am on a mission to spread love, truth, and strength to all that I can. My hopes for my children are that they live a positive and fulfilling life. That they learn as much as they can, and teach us as much as they can, but most importantly that they share their light with the world. Life's too short! Enjoy!"

Stasia doesn't know a lot of moms like herself, but she knows that they are out there, and they, like life, are always changing and evolving. [Stasia and I met online for example, and we live hundreds of miles from each other.] She does try to relate to any mother she encounters. She frequently laughs, talks, and smiles with children in general. She always concludes any interaction with other people's children by adding, "I have two of my own." The other parents are normally shocked, but she is used to that. She is always pushing the envelope and she shows people that mothers are being redefined every single moment,

"That you can create music, pose nude, tattoo your skin, color your hair, etc. You can be as creative as you like, and in that expression of natural beauty in 'being yourself' you can spread that confidence to other mothers who may find themselves compromising how they would like to currently express themselves simply because they are mothers. It seems as though any mother who doesn't fit 'society's mold' is looked down upon.

I have lived in Europe, and while I believe the children have a more stable, positive upbringing there, I was shocked to see the reactions that a mother, like me, would get when I was collecting my children from school. Children need to be taught that all people are equal and beautiful, regardless of their appearance, or lifestyle. I think that in America and Europe there are a lot of pre-conceived notions about what a mother should be like. I find this very disturbing. I think there is an open-mindedness (among subculture moms) that the mainstream lacks, and would benefit from. There is also an extreme lack of creativity in the mainstream that makes me ill, where loosening up with some freedom and heart would be healthy."

There was nothing specific that attracted her to a subculture way of life. She has always just been herself in spite of butting society as a consequence. She continues to do this as a woman, mother, artist, and as an individual. If being herself means not fitting in the world, and being rejected by it, because of, then so be it. If being herself makes her part of a subculture, then she's proud to be a member.

She has struggled with many things in life such as body-image, divorce, etc., but that is what has made her the confident and brilliant woman she is today. Her only plans now are to continue loving, working, raising her children, and hopefully getting signed to a major label this year. In conclusion she states: "I believe that we do have something more to offer. I mean everyone is capable of it, but so many people are afraid to just be themselves. Stand up and take a risk, and do it with LOVE! That's what it is all about!"

"It totally takes a village to make a roller derby baby!"

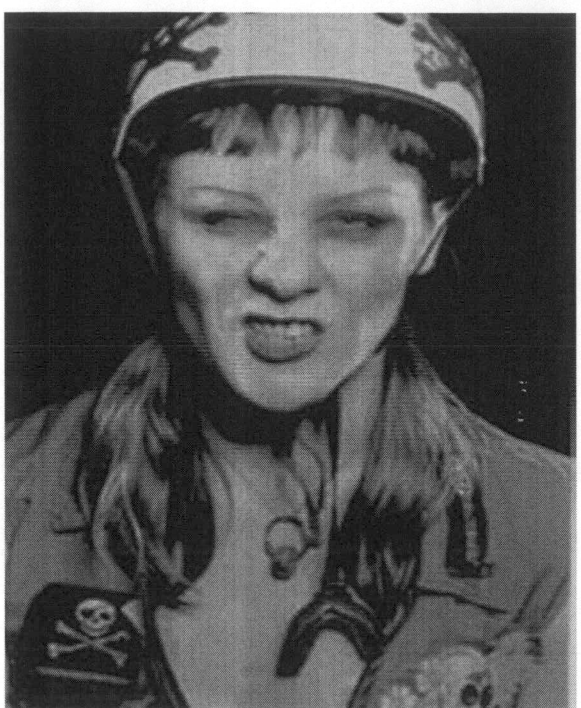

Picture by Frank Blau at FrankBlauPhotography.com

Momma Cherry
Roller Derby Queen
Firefighter
Business Owner
Pretty Peace Corps Hero
Performance Artist
Wicked Writer
Seattle, Washington.

Momma Cherry is a feng shui space-loving-woman with multiple degrees in liberal arts and sociology. She loves writing poetry and doing performance art. She puts out fires (literally), and makes eco-friendly house care products, and battles in skates.

Roller derby is her community and her life. She gets to see her best friends all the time and their derby team trains three times a week. A normal training session includes going over strategies, planning the events, and community care. The Rat City Roller Girls spend about twenty-to-thirty hours a week working on their craft. The group is made up of sixty women who are feminists, artists, musicians, Ph.D.'s, housewives, bartenders, tattoo artists, etc.

The Rat City Roller Girls chip in and help their community on a project-by-project basis. They had recently adopted a section of roadwork and cleaned it up. For Xmas, they normally have a huge annual fundraiser party for the Homeless Youth Center in Seattle, Washington, helping kids in need of mentors and basic necessities. The center provides clothing, education, and showers to the areas homeless kids. They also cook and clean for the center on a regular basis. The group has also participated in the local Gay Pride Parade and donated money to a local AIDS group. They received an honorable mention award from the organization for their work. An independent film was made about them as well titled *Blood at the Flat Track … The Rise of the Rat City Roller Girls*. You check them out at: RatCityRollergirls.com.

Check out Rebel Mom Momma Cherry's awesome derby team movie *Blood at the Flat Track … The Rise of the Rat City Roller Girls*. See more action at: RatCityRollergirls.com.

Momma Cherry got into derby about five years ago. The Godmothers of this generation's derby are the Texas Lone Star Roller Girls & Texas Roller Girls, which branched off and did flat track instead of the older oval track. When Momma Cherry saw them she knew she wanted to get involved with this sport. As a kid she skated in the skate rinks, but this was seeing empowered women doing what they love—and making the rules—which was so different from anything she had ever seen before. She read everything she could on the LA Thunderbolts, and the Bay City Bombers which are some of the oldest derby teams.

Momma Cherry then got involved with the local roller derby action and joined.

Since becoming a derby queen, she has broken her tailbone, and sprained, or twisted just about everything else, but exclaims, "I broke my ass doing something I love!"

Injuries are just part of the game just like any sport. One girl she knows has pins in both of her legs. It's not a good show if you don't earn some bruises on the way. She describes her derby like this,

> "It feels a void that opened up after I stopped stripping. I loved performance art and being a stripper on stage. However, for derby I don't have to be super thin. I just have to be bad-ass on skates and I have the freedom to be myself!
>
> Girls are being sexy, hurting each other, and it's on their own terms. We have a really good time and have good shows. It's incredible to be part of that. The first bout I was in sold out in one day! It was on the local news, 'Teams Revolutionaries and Paper Dolls' ..."

Her daughter Althea, who is six-years-old, loves hanging out with all these cool women and is exposed to incredible debate, and strong opinions. Momma Cherry has thought about quitting before, because the hours are so grueling, and it has resulted in numerous one-minute tardy slips from her daughter's school. But Althea always convinces her mom to stick with it.

Her daughter Althea, who is six-years-old, loves hanging out with all these cool women and is exposed to incredible debate, and strong opinions. Momma Cherry has thought about quitting derby before, because the hours are so grueling, and it has resulted in numerous one-minute tardy slips from her daughter's school. But Althea always convinces her mom to stick with it.

Momma Cherry's work load is intense, but her day job makes it a lot easier for her and her partner Scott. She is a firefighter with the perfect schedule: twenty-four hours on duty and forty-eight hours off duty. It gives her enough time to spend with her family and do derby. She works a person's average work week in two days. She became a firefighter for the hours, pay, and benefits.

On the side she still makes eco-friendly house cleaning products that used to be a full-time home business and house cleaning business. She developed her lines of cleaners after having Althea, because she didn't want chemicals in her house that could harm her daughter. They are generally made with baking soda, vinegar, a variety of herbs, and natural citrus. During the interview I imagine her long wavy red hair pinned up as her kitchen becomes a chemistry lab and she starts making all these great smelling cleaning potions. I can fondly imagine the smell the lemon and lavender now!

When Althea was much younger Momma Cherry's line of thinking developed in several ways: eco-friendly home, eco-friendly cleaners, eco-friendly parenting, and eco-friendly job. She scheduled all of her cleaning jobs around her daughter's daily schedule and took her daughter with her everywhere. This was her daily routine as far as childcare and work was concerned until Althea started school. Before her home business took off she did social work, which is great, but normally you're overworked and under paid.

When Althea was about two-years-old Momma Cherry worked for AmeriCorps after being a working stay-at-home mom. The reason for the change was a divorce from her husband. They had an ad in the paper that promised: benefits, and they would help you pay off student loans, and you get to help your community. It sounded like the perfect job, and in many ways it was, and in many ways it wasn't. Momma Cherry learned she was not a "desk-girl" at all while working for them. Her best memories were of the work she did out in the field:

"The worst part of the day was the early hours behind the desk, but the best part was getting out and meeting these really amazing people. I worked on the Headstart program as a special advocate for the family. I also helped with local Native American Tribes, and worked on their reservations doing all kinds of things: repainting their recreation center, and working with the schools. We also had a big group of volunteers that went out there once every six weeks to do a big project with the tribe.

One stigma I ran into at AmeriCorps was the 'welfare mom kind-of-thing, and the troubled kid.' A lot of AmeriCorps volunteers and employees lived in the suburbs and brought this stigma in with them. A lot of the moms who needed our help just w179anted the same things we did. We want our kids to be happy and healthy.

I felt a lot of guilt about going home and being so comfortable, and being very aware of all the different circumstances. Eventually, I went through an identity crisis and realized I don't belong at AmeriCorps as well as I thought I did. I didn't fit in anymore, so I left."

When Momma Cherry and her ex-husband met they were both twenty-years-old. Before they met, she had already left home at eighteen and had traveled all over the country selling products door-to-door. She settled down in Houston, Texas for awhile and started stripping for her income. The money was great and she enjoyed being onstage, but eventually she got into the darker side of it, and became strung out on drugs. She moved back home to California to get cleaned up.

Her ex was raised in a loving and strict household. She on the other hand was raised in a very abusive one. She was the average kid who grew up listening to Metallica and Pantera. She never fit in with 'normal' people, and eventually this is why she thinks she got into drug use to escape from that feeling; in addition to the underlying issues with parental abuse.

She got off drugs and worked as a stripper in a small town. She met her ex there. They weren't high school sweethearts or anything like that. He was friends with the bouncer and she eventually got to know everyone there. Her ex and she had an awful on-and-off again relationship for a year. He joined the Navy and his Sea Captain convinced him he should marry her to *keep* her, since he was going to be traveling all over the world. They got married for all the wrong reasons. He did it to make sure she stayed, and she did it for the medical and dental insurance. They resettled in Seattle, and loved each other the best they could, but went through many separations along the way.

Eventually, Althea came along. They had been married for six years at this point, and tried to make another go of it, but it just wasn't working. Althea is the best thing that came out of their marriage. Their divorce was a very amicable one, but it was a little messy, emotionally, for all three of them. However, they made an effort to make it work as parents and friends, and her ex is a great father and is very involved with Althea; and has been since the split four-years ago. Parenting is mutually their first priority.

Momma Cherry has since developed a life with another partner, and Althea is lucky, because in essence she has two dads. Her partner Scott is very involved in Althea's life and frequently the whole gang gets together for blended family events.

One thing that is hard for them is that Althea does occasionally wish that "mommy and daddy lived together again," but Momma Cherry understands her daughter's feelings and Althea is free to express them. She raises her daughter without boundaries or fear.

Prior to becoming a mom, Momma Cherry developed a liking of feminist literature and read everything she could. This knowledge has been the core of her parenting beliefs.

When she learned she was pregnant she found an online group of expectant moms on AOL and every time she opened her mouth, they judged her. These moms even went so far to alienate her by calling her insulting names. This infuriated her and she decided to form her own email group called Freaky Parents. It was for parents who didn't fit in and were from varied backgrounds. In fact, it's that variety that makes the group cohesive, and they stuck together.

She later went on to discover *Hip Mama* and the *Mamaphonic* web magazines and online communities. She took a writing class that *Mamaphonic* offered. She would later write and publish pieces through the group including poetry and essays. You can learn more by visiting *Mamaphonic.com*.

From there she got into freeform chopping, a loose style of poetry and performance art, and worked up the nerve to start reading at coffee shops in Seattle. She was later joined by friends that played bass and produced graphic design and they named their performance art trio, Project Three. They went on to do shows, opening for a variety of bands, and opened numerous festivals including: *Hip Mama's* tenth year anniversary festival. They would later open for roller derby events. This is what opened the door to roller derby for her and the rest is history.

Her future plans are to complete her master's degree in psychology, and start a burlesque show based on the history of prostitution in Seattle. Considering that prostitution is the only age-old profession in which many women had to work in, be it through wage-earning, or as a wife, she feels it is very important to the history of feminism. Momma Cherry, considering her background in stripping, has a soft-spot for the sex industry and understands its impact not only on women, but the economy. She would like to see more rights for sex workers and more acknowledgement of it as a legitimate profession, in addition to its historical background. We (women) didn't create patriarchy, or sexism, but we have to live in it and make a living as well.

**Since this interview: Momma Cherry has now moved to Sacramento, California and has joined the Sacred City Derby Girls.*

"I wasn't the greatest of people to be around before I got pregnant. I didn't care about my life. I was on the road to falling. When the doctor told me I was pregnant, I decided this was the one thing in my life I shouldn't fuck up."

Qui Qui
Ballsy Boxer
Printing Pressman
Ink Roller
Cute Crafter
Fantasy Writer
Rude Girl
Evansville, Indiana.

Qui Qui is a twenty-four-year-old hard-working mom in the printing industry, raising a young boy on her own. She chills out by boxing, singing, crafting, and making clothes. She also enjoys writing fantasy stories for kids, and checking out poetry and pastel paintings by some of her closest friends, Amber Scales and Jamey Colbert. Alex Grey, whose work is focused on metaphysical anatomy, is another favorite artist of hers; as is Max Brooks whom she considers to be "an undead genius!"

Qui Qui also has a love for music, especially Oi!, and reggae; and she can pogo like nobody's business! She adores Billie Holiday, Frank Sinatra, and Madonna, who are frequently featured on her turn-table. And she just could not live without Toots and the Maytals, Blitz, and Lower Class Brats. She was singing for the band Hog Luv Dog and the Gas Guzzlers, when they first formed in 2004, but ended up getting cut loose since, as a full-time mom and worker, she couldn't commit to more than one weekly band practice. She eventually replaced being in a band with boxing, because as a strong woman with many demands placed on her she needed an aggressive, but positive way, to "get it all out."

She boxes weekly and trains at a local downtown boxing gym. Qui Qui has even been toying with the idea of going pro, but she wants to further her training and development first. She plans to do so by competing in local matches and becoming part of the competitive amateur circuit for at least a few years. It will be easier for her to incorporate a grueling career as a professional athlete when Lavel, her four-year-old son, is older. You can check out all the latest news on boxing at WomensBoxing.com and USABoxing.org. For now, her work in the labor field pays the bills and her back-up plan is to work her way up at the printing press.

Qui Qui has even been toying with the idea of going pro, but she wants to further her training and development first. It will be easier for her to incorporate a grueling career as a professional athlete when Lavel is older. Get all the latest news on knocking someone out at: WomensBoxing. com & USABoxing.org!

"Well, as of now I am a printing pressman, but my work consists of more than just that. It's a man's world, but who says that I can't work just as hard. Hopefully, one day, I will be the 'big dog' at the newspaper. The goal I hold highest, though, is to raise my son."

She grew up in a diverse, but hardened, ruffian blue-collar neighborhood. She's the proud daughter of a "mod mom and greaser dad." Qui Qui is a working class traditional (non-racist and apolitical) skin-head fashioned after the 1950s dancehall rocksteady influence of Kingston, Jamaica and the United Kingdom's rude girl culture that later evolved from it. Before long, she found herself immersed in street life, drinking and fighting, but having a damn good time and defining who she is.

"I am a very stand-up kinda gal. I speak my mind, not to force my beliefs on others, but to get them off my chest, more so. I will listen to what others have to say, just as long as they are willing to do the same. I don't take bullshit, and I can't stand people who lie to me. I'm very head and heart strong. Don't try to force your political or moral views down my throat. Don't fuck with my family, or try to hurt anyone I love. If you do, you're fucking with me. I may be just a girl, but this girl got tricks and is tough-as-nails. Ask anyone that knows me, and they will tell you the same. I have been through too much crap in my life to wanna deal with anyone who tries to fuck with my family or my life. I won't hesitate for even a sec to cripple someone if they try to wrong me, or my loved ones."

Her view on life, she says, can best be described by the Hudson Falcons song *Working Woman*. She credits Lavel for forcing her to make something out of her life and turning it around. Before having him, the fighting and partying was getting out of control and taking her down with it. Lavel was her saving grace. She feels that having him was something "that needed to be," and she was blessed with the opportunity to be his mom. This awakening made her determined to be the best parent she could be because she was scared to death of "fucking up." She is adamant that:

"If it hadn't been for me boy, I wouldn't be here right now telling my story. Your life changes so drastically when becoming a mother; it's almost overwhelming. It is something I needed. Life is still hard, but I will keep on standing strong and standing proud."

She had wonderful support from her mom who has been there for her though thick and thin, and she credits her mom as: "The strongest human being I know, and I am fortunate that she is my mother. She has fought breast cancer, two horrible divorces and me. Oi! to you mum, you've been the best! I love you lady!" She was betrayed by Lavel's father who refused to get cleaned up for their son. She can't understand how drugs and alcohol could be more important than one's own child ... she had no choice, but to cut his father out of the picture,

> "I was a single mom from the get-go. I had some delusions that the father would clean up his act, but I waited and waited ... and by the end of my pregnancy I decided it was pointless to wait any longer. There are only so many chances you can give someone, especially when it pertains to taking care of a human being. It wasn't that he left—I did. I refuse to have a low-life drunk piece of drug abusing shit be any influence in my boys life."

Her message to all the moms out there whose children were sired by losers is: get rid of them! If they can't be a positive role-model, and thus a good father, or even contribute to your family's household, you are not only inviting disaster and hardship, but possibly abuse for you and your children. If they get it together later on in life and want to be a father, so be it, but know that it is unlikely, or at least unlikely to last. When we touched on this subject I shared with her some of the stories of the struggles single mothers I know have gone through, and Qui Qui agreed undoubtedly that it is hard at first. It was much more challenging than she had initially thought it would be, but she can assure you that it just takes time to get the hang of motherhood.

> "It might be a rocky road, but remain strong and hold your head high; and feel privileged that you have someone who will look up to you for the rest of your life, and the rest of theirs as well. All you and your children need is each other—my son and I couldn't be happier. You can't stop what life throws in your path. You just have to stand ready, accept and fight ... But you can do it."

She emphasizes, however, that motherhood, single or not, is more about love than struggle:

> "Being a mother is fucking fantastic! If it hadn't been for that little turd, I would've lost my life. Having to be the mother and the father doesn't affect him in any way. I enjoy the snuggles and the kisses we share. Disciplining him sucks, but it's a must. It makes me giggle when we are sitting there at the dinner table and he can hold an adult conversation. I have worked hard with him on reading, colors, numbers, and now writing."

Her main parenting focus is to teach Lavel and to instill an ongoing appreciation of the importance of an education. She hopes he will grow to be his own person and fight for his beliefs. She lives by example and hopes he will know that his "mummy is a strong woman," and that he in turn can be a strong man when he is older. Her parenting philosophy is straightforward: just do your best. She feels that, "If you live life with your heart filled with love and keep on fighting the good fight, you can't go wrong." She lives by those words and they have helped her transition from a reckless teen to a dynamic and powerful woman—not to mention an awesome mother!

She, like all moms, needs a break from time-to-time from the stressful roles of parenting and working. She has a few friends who are also moms that she makes time to kick-it with, and they occasionally go to a party or a show. They all put their children first, and any breaks come second. Their alliance to one another is a deep bond, and she feels all moms should get in on empowering each other and supporting one another—and making time for fun, both kid-centric, and adult-oriented!

She also sees society for what it is, and won't stand for others telling her how to raise or not raise her son. It annoys her to no end when other moms who have nothing in common with her, or can't relate to her world at all, attempt to demean her and speak as a higher authority (feeling entitled from an elevated station?). She thinks it's more or less them reacting to her fringe hairstyle, Doc Martens, and tight blue jeans than her actual parenting skills, but she asserts nonetheless:

"I am a blue collar working class woman and I am proud to be part of it. I bust my ass trying to support my son. If I have a question about something, I'll ask. Otherwise, don't tell me I am doing it all wrong. Because I know for a fact, that I am doing my best, and am raising him to the best of my capabilities, and there aren't too many dedicated moms out there like me. I will raise my boy the way I see fit, and if society doesn't like it, I will tell them where to stick it."

Qui Qui doesn't see much of a difference between the mainstream world and that of subcultures. The underlying values may differ some, but overall she sees us as sharing similar issues and hardships, especially with alcoholism, drug addiction, abuse, exploitative employers, intolerance, and a need for adequate and shared resources. She thinks we have a more honest dialogue about these problems, more realistic expectations, and a more constructive way of handling them than regular mainstream society—and maybe that's the benefit of. She says being a rebel simply runs in her bloodline. She jokingly questions, "What else could you be when mother was a mod and father was a greaser?" The most important statement she feels she, or anyone, can really make is, "Live your life the way you see fit, just as long as you're not hurting yourself, or others around you."

She is looking forward to the rest of her life, which is not how she felt before becoming a mom. Her dream is not to die disappointed and wondering what could have been, because she knows there is still so much for her to see and do. On that list is the hope for a future love affair with Vin Diesel. She's pretty enthusiastic about that one! But mostly she just wants to share the facts of her story, the good and the bad, with other moms who may need some support. She bids us farewell with, "Just about every turn in my life has been an obstacle, but jump back because nothing can get me down!"

Right on!

"There is no absolute truth, find your own. This is what my experience has taught me. I would want my experience to tell of all my scandal, and all of my goodness, because I wouldn't be one without the other."

Lucid
Dreamy Dancer
Circus Performer
Gallery Owner
Actress/Model
Rocker/Singer
Fashion Designer
Yoga & Drama Teacher
Spiritualist
San Francisco, California.

Lucid is in her late thirties and she's a performer who still loves shocking people. Part of her plan in doing this is to make the world a more colorful place, filled with joyful people who get righteously angry and inspired to revolt. She wants less rules and more celebration out of life.

Her entire life journey has been one of rebirth, ®evolution, and the co-creation of beauty. She describes herself as loud, bold, dramatic, sexy, and a giver. She has finally accepted all the things that make her who she is while accepting it's okay to be an "outgoing freak," while being an introverted suburban mother. She describes herself as:

> "Okay, so I'm a rebel-in-conflict as I find motherhood softening my edges just a bit. But I am still a circus-freak, rocker, and a sexual deviant who breaks rules to recreate them. I must go against the grain. I'm not happy in this bleached white bread hypocrisy … I'm interested in openness and honesty, which is not what the general culture offers—everyone hiding in their 'safe' secular little worlds. I dress crazy, perform in the street on stilts, in the air I dare. I play with fire. I want change, revolution. I will not accept the status quo. I think it would be great if complete deconstruction would occur, no matter how painful, so that we can build it up again, better and new. All my friends are freaks too and we love life, and hate the government who gives us nothing but cheese."

Her musical muses are P.J. Harvey, Jeff Buckley, Nina Simone, Eenor, Tool, the Cure, Bob Marley, Roots, XXX Action Marching Band, Mark Growden, and the White Stripes. Her favorite genres are deep country, blues, and reggae. She loves torch singers and anything that compels her to sing. She just needs to rock-out really loud and hard.

One of her favorite artists is Alex Grey, "For all his levels and his incredible visual articulation of these layers of human experience …" Rumi is one of her most beloved poets because, "He was so drunk with life and wasn't afraid of being crude, or of death."

Lucid loves sewing, studying works on sensuality, healing, and spiritualism. She also likes scary stuff and horror films. She has lived in New York City, Los Angeles, San Francisco, and Boston. Her fashion design career started in Boston.

When she was a kid she was always reading, writing, and drawing. She attended a vocational high school for fashion design which set her on that path. Because her work was challenging, dramatic, and involved unique use of shapes, it gathered much attention and affirmation of her skill. She later graduated with a two-year-degree with honors from the college in Boston.

She then moved to New York City to be closer to the fashion world. Eventually, after a few years of working in the industry, she opened her own gallery on the Lower East Side; which involved custom designing and bringing together a great community of artists and performers.

Her introduction into performing began with a band called Tongue. It ended up being mostly musical jams with spoken word. This compelled her to start auditioning with an agency and getting regular paid work performing in addition to her income from her gallery.

During this time she also had one of her first romantic relationships which was intense, scary, and overtly controlling in nature. She was trying to distance herself from the relationship, and the cold winters in New York, by moving to warm and sunny California.

She wanted to give West Hollywood a try. Her ex followed her though, and they had "some issues to thrash through." They had two unplanned pregnancies that she terminated through herbal and medical means. She knew this was not the right relationship to bring a child into, but for some reason he really wanted her to have his child. She felt a lot of guilt, neediness and sadness, and she didn't want to pass this on to a child, nor be attached to this controlling and abusive person forever. She finally ended the turbulent on-and-off again relationship once he kicked down the door to her apartment.

Her career seemed to be picking up speed in L.A. Within two weeks of living there she landed a contract as a model and actress for a national funky sportswear company. She also had a guest role in a TV pilot program. She stayed in Hollywood for four years and sums up her experience as:

> "At one point I remember going to an audition and was seriously wondering if I should have blonde hair and fake big boobs too. For a long time I had been told I was a breath of fresh air, but after so many hopeful callbacks that ended in the big-boobied-blonde getting the part, it kept me wondering if I was an unnatural absurdity with my red hair and small chest. I thought to myself I have to get outta here."

She took off to a Burning Man Festival. The festival generally attracts over 25,000 people a year to a remote desert location called Black Rock City. They gather in an ancient lake bed called the playa. The community that revolves around the Burning Man Festival is best described as an experimental, earth-conscious art-based following. Each attendee is a valued contributor and participant. Their main rule is: there are none. Every year has a different art theme so the artists work can all co-relate. You can learn more this universal art party at: BurningMan.com.

It was at the playa that she met the love of her life who swept her off her feet—literally. We chatted on instant messenger during the interview process, and Lucid told me all the great details. Playful eye contact and coming close, backing-off, waiting to meet. Finally, the moment came and the next thing she knew, she was in his arms and swinging her legs up in excitement. They were inseparable. They were side-by-side for the rest of the festival and drove back to L.A together. She rode naked in the car just for kicks.

She met many great people in L.A that actually lived in San Francisco, and she moved again. This time it was to a place that finally felt like home. She quickly made new friends there, and this was her gateway into circus, ritual performance, and storytelling. She learned new skills like acrobatics and fire-eating. She discovered her true circus passion when she saw a tissu artist. (They specialize in aerial performance with fabrics and silks.) Lucid has always had a fetish for flying and fabrics, so this was a perfect fit and she started training. One thing she loves about the circus is that there is a wardrobe for every element and the circus is endlessly fun and comic.

Her circus group is called the Mystic Family. They have opened on countless occasions for Cirque De Soleil, and have hosted their after-parties. Her greatest achievement in circus performance was a show she produced, directed, and co-choreographed, called *Of Light*. It played at the Xenodome for three nights and it consisted of: six tango dancers, three tissu artists, a fire and a moon dancer. All the music for the show was created and sung by Lucid and her love/life-partner.

Lucid explained the meaning of the show and the name, "It symbolizes rebirth, and then everyone lifting each other up. It's about how we can rise above nonsense by empowering each other." Lucid has worked in various dramatic backgrounds from music, acting, and performing. Her words of advice for anyone who wants to make a career of it are:

> "It is absolutely all about confidence. The careless, cocky confidence of youth works well. Relying on someone else to stroke your confidence does not work, because eventually everyone will go away. You have to be able to sustain yourself. The youthful confidence can be a good starter, but it can also be your downfall if you do not follow through with practice and professionalism. It's very important to be good at what you do and to be able to trust your own ability. The funny thing about learning sometimes is that it can make you realize that you don't know very much. This is where your confidence can be cultivated, the kind that cannot be shaken because it is in your bones. You know it; you have practiced this thing over and over again.
>
> I always think it would be great if I could focus on one thing, instead of being pretty good at a lot of things. So I would say if you can, choose a focus and never stop learning it. Keep accounts, pictures, etc., for your portfolio. It might not seem like a big deal now, but it will become more valuable with time. Everything you do is a big deal, and they are all stepping stones to be learned from. Keep learning diligently."

She has had some negative experiences with bands, but she keeps working at it, musically. Her take on bands are:

> "Damn, bands are hard to do (especially when the boys are drinkers or stoners). If they don't really like each other, or have big egos, it can cause a lot of malcontent to deal with. I also have had the experience of singing with a woman who blasted so well, that I thought I should just shut up. My experience has mostly been wishing everyone would shut up, or feeling like I should. My best luck has been singing solo or singing with a group of women choir-style with set songs, parts, and intentions."

She does enjoy working on musical projects with her partner. They have produced amazing music for their circus acts and solo acts. Her partner is super-professional and formally trained, where she is, "totally raw and emotional, a from-the-heart singer." She feels their opposing musical temperaments make it a struggle to collaborate, but they bear some amazing fruit.

It was during the beginning of their circus performing that the pregnancy occurred. It was the middle of winter, December 4th to be exact, that the conception occurred. They had spent the night out dancing and eating sushi. They were living in a motor home in front of an artist's warehouse in Oakland. They spent the entire night making love over and over again. An earthquake occurred during the last orgasm. It felt like six men were just vigorously shaking the motor home, there was a loud thud, and time stopped. All movement was suspended. Then there was a sudden and sharp bird call. Lucid heard it resonate throughout her head, "I'm here." She knew she had a little girl with her. It was too shocking so they went to sleep and didn't speak of it for two weeks.

They had only been dating for three months. Lucid confirmed the pregnancy with an official test. They were both panicked and terrified, so they bought herbs for an abortion and plane tickets to Maui. When she was making the herbal brew late one night, she stared at the night sky, and was hoping to be lifted from her confusing circumstances. Instead of comfort, or solace, it seemed Sirius (the galaxy star—the scorcher) in his brightness screamed at her for what she was about to do, and she let the brew smash onto the ground. Her partner was freaking out about it, and Lucid decided it was time to contact fate. She pulled a tarot card and it was fire and spirals. It seemed to be telling them, "Just you wait … she can't wait to get here." Lucid realized she needed her and the signs were so clear beneath all the overwhelming fear of having a child.

They faced their fears and decided to continue the pregnancy; right after they boarded for Maui. Upon arrival, it seemed angels were directing them to a perfect and symbolic spot on the beach. They named their daughter *Olai Mahu Mele* which means Earthquake Singing Bird.

Lucid hoped her "rock star darling" would be able to be strong, and be both a supportive partner and a budding father, but if not she devised a back-up plan (like all smart women) to be an independent momma. If he fell through, she was going to move back to New York to be with friends and family.

In the first trimester of her pregnancy, and even post-Maui, her partner did freak-out and he lost control. She distanced herself from him and moved back to L.A. to work, and to see if he would come around or not. He started trying to pull himself together (and eventually he did come through for her), and she returned to San Francisco. She was welcomed back by her circus, the Mystic Family. She was given, "PWP: Pregnant Woman Priority," by her group and she always got good seats to shows, body massages, and her naked growing belly received lots of love and kisses. She was the first one in their circus family to ever be pregnant, so she was treated like a goddess. Although, she received tremendous support from them … she still felt alone and isolated.

> "No one really understood how hard it was for me to keep up sometimes, or to be alone so often, in this strange new place with a man who had other girlfriends three months prior. He was out rocking while I was on my hilltop with no care, gestated. The only thing I could do was read to my baby [in utero], and stare at my belly with hope."

Things finally worked out. They moved back in together into a barn house apartment in the suburbs. Her partner got a contracted musical position that would last three years, adding new financial stability for them. They combined circus performing and parenting, and took the time to learn and attend to their child's needs and signals. It was a shock at first though,

> "Everyone went on about doing their own thing, going-out, etc … and there I was alone at home. I felt without community, or even a friend so often that I went to Trader Joe's and smiled hopefully at other mothers. Really wanting to ask, will you be my friend, can we hang out? I have a baby too. The isolation was intense. I look back in wonderment, it doesn't really happen so fast after all. The days were long."

In retrospect, she realizes there is a real magic that comes from being pregnant, if you allow yourself to be submersed into it. From the growing womb anything can grow and be possible. Lucid is thankful (looking back over the past seven years) that the universe has completely taken care of them. She fully appreciates the value of their life together and how incredible it is for them. Children are amazing and it hurts her to see so many children already "ruined by the archaic and limiting infrastructure."

Lucid knows that motherhood is the ultimate gift and the ultimate challenge. Her role is to redefine it; to challenge the role as it was set forth by her mother, and grandmother, and so on. At the same time she thanks them for the lessons she got passed on to her, while cutting out the limitations. Her role to her daughter Lali is to provide support and encouragement without passing judgments. Her daughter has the freedom to have her own growth experiences. Lali will initiate it and Lucid will watch, care, and follow through with Lali … so that she blossoms into, "the most incredible little human" that she has ever known. Lucid sees the limited infrastructure and how it affects kids all the time:

"Rules, rules, and rules! You shouldn't have that baby here, you can't bring the baby to that, or she's gonna do this, be that, and on and on. Everyone has all these rules and not enough people are finding ways to make things new, or accept others harmless ways of being. People have dragged their kids away from us at snotty far East Bay parks. They have glared at me appalled by the 'things I let her get away with.' Children in this society are not given the freedom and respect they need to find out who they are. There is so much generalizing and constraint. Too many kids are trained from a very young age to be afraid and to be like 'everyone else.' This might make some things easier, but it makes a lot of things harder for the kids in the future, for human evolution, and for the kids, as kids, to be their own brilliant selves.

Lali has always been 'ahead' of the other kids and I don't think it's because she came in 'special', but because we allowed her to be. She initiates and we enable. It's our job. Saying no is bad, saying 'you're going to hurt yourself' or 'you are not … whatever' is so damaging. I hope for my child to always know, and to be, this incredible, creative, buoyant life-force that she is; to share it healthfully with others and sustain herself in this world. To be able to ask for, and create what she needs, respectfully of others and the earth. I try to instill this by being it myself and giving her the experience of other good healthy people. I also hope she learns discipline and skill. I do this by practicing hard myself and exposing her to others as such."

Her philosophy is that she has to provide her daughter with a safe, comfortable environment, so that Lali can discover the world and herself, and what it means to be a good, thoughtful, and caring person. Lucid provides nurturing foods, and learning experiences that are varied, as well as a multi-cultural. She highlights life's complexities, so that Lali knows the various options that are there to choose from. Lucid expects herself to be her daughter's friend, as well as the first one to teach her the importance of limitations and structure, but in perspective and balance. Structure shouldn't choke the life out of you, but be a strong springboard that supports your weight as you fly upward and out.

Lucid feels we can learn some about the importance of routine and structure from mainstream moms, because kids do need to feel secure and protected—which can only come from structure and routine. [Strong foundations will lend to flexibility as well providing options for parents that will make sense to kids too.] She feels they can learn from us a thing or two about freedom and acceptance—and getting past the limitations of the status quo.

She feels too many kids get caught in the web of social standing/status quo pressure by their parents, authorities, and later their peers. Kids should be themselves, to be different, and dare to question authority and to know that all is possible—with the safe guard of knowing their parents are there to guide them. If we don't question things around us, and challenge what we don't like, then we just accept things as they are, from poverty, exploitation, hatred and war. She feels society's fear of questioning things [from the most elementary level, like child-targeted marketing (vendors in schools like McDonalds, etc.), to highly critical things like questioning the leadership of our country.] impedes one's growth. Lucid knows finding balance and being open-minded are key.

"Do some yoga and other shared spiritual disciplines. Doing things for personal growth are awesome. It's fun to take your kids to shows, going dancing together. You can still go out at night. Your dreams have not come to an end. Abolish the classic parent/child roles and co-create together. Take action in your community, be a voice for the people. Have the world you really want for your children. Suppression breeds perversion."

Before becoming a parent Lucid describes herself as impulsive, non-committal, and overconfident. She still considers herself a person in recovery, recovery from a violent system that brought her into a dysfunctional family. She survived the drug-addicted, suicidal teenage years to blossom into an artist, performer, and a wonderful person.

She had severe repressed anger against her family for "fucking her up" and towards men for years. She always felt trapped in this sexual role for girls: expected to be sluts, yet without being sluttish? [And our society reinforcing that girls and women have no value, other than sexuality, and not teaching boys/men to respect us.] She always felt society blamed her somehow—for their own expectations and roles that they (society) themselves had created. It took her a long time to claim for herself her own value as a person, and to command respect from others, especially men. She is insuring she instills this self-respect and worth in her daughter. Lucid struggled for years to find her voice after being told she didn't have one, or the right one, for so long. But she kept fighting for it and she has found it,

> "To be able to love everyone and share what I want and let others share what they want, and feel alright about what I do or don't have to be, and be empowered to change that. To know when to be quiet and when to scream, sing, or state my peace. Getting over addictive, abusive relationships, learning how to love openly, and not to run, or kill, when things get to close. I've never really killed anyone, but letting go of that kind of thinking and moving into tolerance, acceptance, and having the strength to keep moving forward. To surround myself with people and environments that are inspiring, and do not hold me down."

In her early twenties, she searched and found other people who were trying to make themselves and the world a better place, instead of merely surviving in it. When you find others with that same passion, or spark, it helps you understand how wonderful our potential is, especially later when you have a child. The things that attracted her to a sub-culture way of life was the need to connect to others, and the need to embrace living that breaks away from the "damaging, patriarchal, sexually-exploited, repressed and insidiously dishonest infrastructure," that is our mainstream culture.

As a parent herself now, she realizes what a good job her mom did as an eighteen-year-old single and unsupported mom, though the parenting is questionable. Lucid spent most of her youth in misery, so she feels she has moved very far away from where she came from. Her focus the last fifteen years is questioning everything she was taught, and not succumbing to depression, or anger. She is doing the internal and external work of "rebirth, ®evolution, and co-creation of life." It's a never ending process. She likens herself "to a screw" and she has been screwed over a lot, but like a screw she "sure can hold things together." She is constantly letting go of, "selfish needs and finding places where I can serve the greater needs of humanity."

She feels life is a spiritual journey wherein the body can have a lot of fun and do amazing things along the way. It's a spiral we ascend, repeating the same things in different forms until we have reached a higher level of perfection. She adds about the world at large, "Were just babies, man, were just babies."

Lali is now almost nine-years-old. Lucid is one of the few families she knows that is not a 'split' family (the parents are separated) and that makes her really happy that they, as a trio, have been able to hold it together for so long …

"My life has been so blessed since becoming a momma. I still live in a barn in the suburbs, but I feel so blessed because I truly embrace and cherish this life and my chances, which are many, to make a difference every day. I've not slowed down too much, but I have to admit my aspirations have become a little less grand. I used to think I'd be a rock-star living this wild life. Now I can only do that part-time, but I do. I have lots of fun, maybe on a smaller scale, but I am happy. I've also realized how much work everything is from birth, to watching Lali learn to crawl, to talk, to teaching myself about music, or how to keep it all together: the relationship, career, work, deviant behavior, and responsible, nurturing mothering. It's all about doing things over and over again, with patience and practice, diligence and willingness to change. Then it all turns out okay. I'm blessed with a wonderful partner who is a great dad and an adventurous friend/lover and he's a rocking musician too! So yes, having it all is possible! My prince did come, yet still there is so much work to be done.

Sometimes I think it might be nice to have a split family, just so I could have every other week off, but for those moments when Lali comes and grabs us both for a family hug, it washes it all away. She beams when she squeezes us. We all love each other so much. It's incredible, and I'm still just hoping it's all really possible, because I have never known love like I do now. Motherhood has blessed me with this gift, this workload, this profound growth which has caused this leap in the evolutionary actions of my lineage. I'm grateful for being so messed up so young, and being aware of it, because it has given me a different way to live, and to mother my child in a way that is raw and powerful."

Lucid is now teaching yoga to Lali and her classmates at school. She has been doing this for a few years, and it all started when Lali's pre-school teacher approached her and asked if she would teach a summer camp, and put on a kids circus show. The kids did yoga for warm-ups. It was so successful the school asked if she would offer yoga classes to the kids in the afterschool program twice a week and incorporate it with theatre games. The class now even does summer dance programs and they put on annual shows.

"It's such an amazing thing to see an automatic return for effort. The little ones, age's three-to-five, LOVE it! What amazing tools we are offering them when we give them constructive and fun ways to release their tension/anger/fear etc., through breathing, sound, and movement. How rewarding it is for them (and you) when the child says, 'I can't do that' and then you give them assistance, show them again, and they do it. There is nothing like that smile that comes from deep inside where a child's self confidence grows. Someone believing in them, in that moment, and the very next they blossom for it. So much of it is about relaxing and releasing self-doubt. It's awesome to give them that experience that they can recreate over and over throughout their lives.

The kids laugh a lot during some of the routines, especially when they are doing animal sounds and the fun games that engage them in yoga. It's very different from an adult's class. Sometimes they will initiate new poses or games on their own. Yoga gives the kids the tool of paying attention to breathing and the effect it has on the body and the mind. It's a great thing to help them calm down. I had a little boy, a very angry little boy, who stayed (surprisingly) through a whole class once and then at the end one of the teachers told me that he was upset because he couldn't do a fish pose. I stayed with him privately, got him to change his breathing from crying and try it again with me. For him finding the pose was about pushing through his heart center and when he did there was a smile and what a gift to see him go from that mad/sad place to beaming with joy and confidence. There are kids in my class, age's seven-through-eleven, who already have so much pain and tightness in their bodies; it's unbelievable. I've had kids saying ouch, ouch, I can't do it, it hurts my back, etc … All these learned things, these bad postures, worries, etc … breathing and stretching can easily take them away, especially when kids are still so close to their natural, flexible, vibrant truth. Some more than others, but kids are all closer to this state than adults."

Through the yoga class Lucid has met other moms at her daughter's school. Initially, the interactions were very cordial, but tense, and they never asked, "What's your story?" Most of the other moms seemed very nervous around her. They just smiled cautiously at Lucid and put space between themselves and her. Even though Lucid has water-downed her appearance significantly in order to teach the class (and their kids) she senses they feel somehow that she is different from them.

A few have opened up to her over the years since she has been teaching the class and their confessions have been quite surprising, "I used to do this," or "I like this, but never thought I could do it." They look to Lucid for validation for having feelings, likes, or aspirations that fall outside the Working Mother, or Gerber Ad mom-periphery. They seek validation from Lucid and assurance that this is okay and normal. Most of her student's moms though are very reserved, have at least two kids, and are settled into their routines. Lucid finds this both, "very lovely, and very frightening." Lucid questions if having the big house is worth the personal sacrifice in order to be accepted. Lucid resists settling into roles. She does realize it takes effort and insight to move beyond it, so she is cautious and discreet when engaging with moms in her neighborhood, or at Lali's school; those who open up to her however, she will share some of her vision with and her version of living and motherhood.

She has met a few moms like herself and they are all performers. The common ground they have is: trying to balance it all, needing sisters, feeling isolated, and wondering if the struggle to "do it all" is really worth it. She is the only "long-termer" she knows, as far as staying with her partner. It's sad because they have no alternative family to look up to, or to turn to when times are tough. It is hard and tricky to maintain a relationship, but Lucid is very content that they've done it thus far. Lucid does feel that many moms, subculture and mainstream alike, have a lot to offer, share, and learn from one another. And that we all should get together, take turns listening to each other, and keep on trying new things out, and making changes until things work for the good of the whole—including for our children.

Lucid has started designing again and making custom creations and costumes for the circus and weddings. She also specializes in recycled custom fashions, and yoga wear. You can reach her and her design team at her webstore: Lucidawn.com. She loves the art of creation and shares this,

"Do some yoga and other shared spiritual disciplines. Doing things for personal growth are awesome. It's fun to take your kids to shows, going dancing together. You can still go out at night. Your dreams have not come to an end. Abolish the classic parent/child roles and co-create together. Take action in your community, be a voice for the people. Have the world you really want for your children. Suppression breeds perversion."

Get more of Rebel Mom Lucid at Lucidawn.com!

"My favorite one so far has been for my first bride who is a dear friend. She wanted a whole cowgirl themed wedding and wanted a corset and bustle look. She got it. It was my toughest job to date that I carried through without a teacher and that set me up for a return to that focus as a profession after being distracted by performance, and only making things off the cuff for years. I've finished my sixth wedding and the last one was a dozy. I made a remake of an 18th century men's costume; cutaway coat, waistcoat and pantaloons. All true tailored and made from pattern to buttonholes by me. I'm on a roll now and ready to dress all the lovers and hire a team to sew each summer, create the big show each winter, and have it premier each spring. All while being a most fantastic momma."

Her occupations are all still combined and complimentary. On any given week she is: a circus performer, yoga teacher, fashion designer, musician and momma. Her next plans are to start a burlesque dance/rock band and a Pink Floyd influenced Cirque Du Soliel-like Burning Man movie with organic interactive performance. About life and living she concludes,

"It's all about the THE BIG SHOW! Ta-da! Look at what we can do together. Allow experience to change your life, allow your life to change the world! To see people getting better, to learn new things, busting out! To experience someone opening up and revealing who they are, their hope, their joy, their sadness, their desire, and their humanness! Whatever means of expression, I like it big and loud! I want to hear you! I want to feel alive and help you to feel alive and that is why I am here. I love music, dancing, poetry, sex, food, experimentation, adventure, travel, learning ... living!"

"I knew it wasn't working, but I was so committed. I promised, and I just had these kids and they aren't going to spend half their lives being traded off between divorced parents."

Jenn
Emerging Actress
Musing Poet
Lovely Naturalist
Ad Location Director
Sexy Stars & Dots Clothing Co. Creator
Dallas, Texas.

Jenn is an amazing mother mending a broken heart after a recent divorce. She is the very first mom I interviewed for this book. The day I decided this book needed to be written, I saw her and her two radiant girls playing at the Hollywood Hills Park and recruited her right then and there. If moms ever find themselves needing a light in this world so that they can find a way to reemerge after a dark storm, Jenn's story is that light.

Jenn's passion for music, stanzas, and art are the backdrop to her love story which led to a breath-taking romantic interlude and the painful, crushing end of it. Her personal world is expressed through the sounds and lyrics of bands like Sonic Youth, A Tribe Called Quest, Sleigh Bells, and Panda Bear. Her hands seek out texture to place her poetry on. Her eyes take in color like light to find its way into her artistic creations, and her body yearns to be pulled into drama. That is Jenn and her captivating essence. Her ex-husband Thomas became her first love and her writing muse.

They met while she was in a magnet high school for performing and visual arts. He tried to convince her to marry him on their second date, she said, "No, no, no!" He was barely out of his teens and she was almost eighteen. They had an intense love affair for the next nine months, and he proposed again after her graduation. This time she yelled, "Yes, yes, yes!" They had a wonderful ceremony, and then she started school again at a local community college. It wasn't long before they were making plans, getting tattoos, and making babies. She wrote some of her most poignant poetry during this time period in her life. It went from sweet to cutting as motherhood merged with Plath-like tears. The passion was short-lived due to Thomas's then unknown growing drug addiction and his neglect of his wife and lover once she became the mother of his children.

Both of their daughters were planned and conceived in the first few years of their short marriage. Eden was born first, and followed shortly thereafter by Lola. Jenn was still breastfeeding Eden when she resumed college, but this time she was taking courses at the University of North Texas, when she learned she was pregnant again. Although they were trying, she didn't expect their second conception to happen quite so quickly, because her gynecologist indicated that there would be fertilization issues. [And ladies, I have heard this story from many moms who had gotten foreboding, but proven incorrect, news from their doctor. My conclusion is that if you are trying to get pregnant, just relax and have a good time. It will happen sooner or later, and tends to be sooner, ha-ha. And if you're not, use protection. I also know many moms who were told they couldn't medically get pregnant and they did when they least expected it—myself included.] She winces at recalling the juggling:

> "Breastfeeding and going to school was really frustrating. And I was puking in the bathrooms from morning sickness! I already knew by then that my relationship with Thomas was over, but I knew I wanted two kids, so ... I was so young, but I knew. Lola was born the day before my graduation. I was going to school full-time, working part-time, and started a company at the time with my husband and some friends called Stars and Dots, which was my idea. The job I got when Stars and Dots couldn't support us anymore."

Stars and Dots was her other baby, and when she started it in the late 1990s it was her first entrepreneurial exploration. [I received several of their very cute t-shirts at my baby shower for my son Corben. My little tiger looked adorable running around town in them. I showered Jenn with adulations after I found out that she was the creator!] She came up with the artistic and business concept, her husband's friend Oliver drew the traditional Sailor-Jerry tattoo art that were featured on the clothes, and her husband was the sales power house behind it. Stars and Dots was one of the first indie tattoo art clothing lines for kids to emerge onto the scene. Despite that fact, and the very promising start, the company ended up floundering. Many years later, indie kids clothing lines have since followed in its footsteps, influenced by the original—whether they know it or not. Many were started by moms as well as very small businesses from home. [Several moms I know who wanted to be stay-at-home moms, yet needed an outlet, and an income, have successfully combined clothes-designing, housecleaning, consulting, craft-making, etc. My aim with my writing's/book's was the same intent, to put something good for the world out there, and to make enough money to be able to stay-at-home. But it didn't pan out.]

Jenn sold her share of the company to her soon-to-be ex and Oliver once it became evident her marriage wasn't going to work, and they started divorce proceedings. The timing for her sell was ironic; she was the only one who'd made a profit from the company. She shares with us what home was like right before the end of the marriage …

"He was on the road for weeks at a time promoting Stars and Dots on the trade show circuit. I was unhappy. I knew it wasn't working, but I was so committed. I promised, and I just had these kids and they aren't going to spend half their lives being traded off between divorced parents. I had thought a lot about divorce, but not real seriously, I mean I had considered it seriously, but wasn't going to do it. Then he came home from the trade show and he asked me for a divorce! I was stunned, shocked. Seriously, you want to divorce me? You're the one that sucks! It was pretty awful. But I think since I'm the one who really wanted it, it was perfect. I was still getting out of it, and my karma was clean. I wasn't bailing on him."

Jenn at this time was astonished to learn that her husband was a drug addict:

"Lola was a year old when we split up, and he was using pretty heavily throughout our relationship, but I seriously didn't know. He was on-and-off again [with using] opiates, vicodin, and his habit increased dramatically right at the end of our relationship. He took me to court for the kids, and he was fooling everyone at first. He even got all of our friends to stand up against me—and then it came out he had been using heroin, but had been clean, and he didn't need rehab [he asserted], and then he didn't have any friends. They were all pissed at him for lying. Then he started using again, and was in-and-out of rehab."

Jenn did receive custody in light of the heroin addiction. It took some time, but Thomas was able to get clean, and has been trying to rebuild his life for his girls and to be a good father. It's been roughly two years now, as of this interview, that he has been clean and managing his addiction with prescribed methadone, clinical and group therapeutic sessions, as well as the support of his parents. He is almost at the point in his treatment that he will be completely weaned off methadone. Jenn has a hard time understanding nihilistic and destructive patterns and addictions:

"I'm not straight-edge by any means, but I've never been heavily into anything. I think I smoked pot maybe five times in my life with friends, and got drunk a couple of times, but it just holds very little appeal for me. Now I see so clearly. I find that when I'm hurting, which the divorce had been very hurtful, and I don't want to hurt anymore, my first inclination is to just stop the feeling and drink. But I usually then just have one drink and that's it, I stop. I never get to that point of abandon, or absurdity. I don't have room in my life to drink, or smoke pot heavily—everyday, or once a week, or even once a month! I don't mind so much when it's safe, and in a safe environment in which it is okay, I don't object to that. But it's so hard finding people that can do that. It seems all or nothing for everybody! I don't understand why there aren't more people like me, do it sometimes, have fun, but don't let it rule you. It just makes me want to go the opposite way, 'Fine, I just can't be with you, or know you if you do any of it'."

Right now she is still "emotionally a wreck," but she is talking to her ex-husband and the past two years of them being apart has given her some time for space to articulate how she feels. She wrote a sharp, bittersweet, decaying chapbook of poetry aptly titled *Cesarean Storefront* during this time … here's a poem from:

all of the warriors dressed like trees
to surprise

and so I run while dressing

feet materialize to just splash silly
puddles of blood and semen

why don't you tell me what you wonder?

a sweet asphyxiation to suffocate sleepily
by a marshmallow in the throat

the whole knowing of the thing is the black
handbag clutched by the white-gloved old one
in a pastel suit

and so I run while dressing

This is where she was metaphysically when we met and spoke. She was struggling in life's turmoil while trying her best to be a good, patient, loving, and *single* mom, a full-time worker (her income is indispensable) and a confessional wordsmith by emotional necessity. Although the end of the brief life they had built was tragic and painful, she has managed to become friends with her ex-husband, and finally reached out to him … "You have to help me." They worked out an arrangement where every other weekend he would take the kids, so she could work on herself and rest. She knew her limit and knew she couldn't take care of them how they deserved to be taken care of, unless she had some space and reprieve. It also gave him a chance to gradually resume some responsibility, safely, while developing a bond with his daughters. She feels, "He is a great dad. He's just got his problems."

Eden is five, and Lola is almost three. Jenn feels relieved to be half way through the waste management phase [Thanks Suzy Riddle for the great term!] of child-rearing. Eden still occasionally has accidents, and Lola is in the middle of her boot-camp training. She is mesmerized by her daughters and how similar, yet different they are.

> "My five-year-old Eden is such a girl through and through. She loves dolls, big dolls, and frilly dresses. And she is very beautiful, extremely intelligent, and intense. Lola though is a scrapper, very loud, expressive and not quaint at all. She is going to piss a lot of people off, ha-ha. Lola tries to imitate her older sister, but it's very awkward for her. She's very masculine and strong."

Jenn is struggling as a single mom, as most parents do with strained financial resources, and feels overwhelmed. She has help with their schooling, courtesy of their grandparents whom started an education fund for them, which pays for their private school. But even then, after she pays rent, her car payment, and the part-time wage for a nanny, that leaves little left to cover basics, food, and utilities …

> "I'm not wealthy. I don't have the financial struggles of most single moms, but even as it is I still find it difficult. If their grandparents didn't pay their schooling, I

don't know how I would do it. I wouldn't have enough, and I really don't know how I could anyway. There wouldn't be enough money, I don't have extra. I don't buy stuff for myself, and I don't go over the top for my kids. I don't know how single moms who make less than me and have to pay for daycare do it … How do they do it?"

Jenn makes a median income, mid-thirties, isn't an executive, and doesn't live in the suburbs. Nannies are generally considered by many a status symbol of the upper class, think of the movie and book, *The Nanny Diaries*; but as moms we need to shatter that myth and make it a workable option for the majority of us. Jenn's resourceful experience is a case-in-point. She doesn't know many moms like herself, and was amongst the first of her close friends to have children so she had no one really to turn to for advice, or for help. Daycare was too expensive, and she just wanted someone who could pick up her girls from school and hang-out with them at the house until she got home from work. Her job was inflexible, so leaving early was out of the question; however she was fortunate nonetheless to have a nine-to-five schedule Monday-Friday, freeing up more time to spend with her kids. She didn't have many options so she sought out a nanny amongst students. She was looking for someone who just wanted part-time work (true part-time) and was reliable and good with kids. Her advice on locating an affordable nanny is to do what she did. She put a flyer up at the university near her, interviewed individuals after running candidates through the

★★★★★★★★★

"I'm not wealthy. I don't have the financial struggles of most single moms, but even as it is I still find it difficult. If their grandparents didn't pay their schooling, I don't know how I would do it. I wouldn't have enough, and I really don't know how I could anyway. There wouldn't be enough money, I don't have extra. I don't buy stuff for myself, and I don't go over the top for my kids. I don't know how single moms who make less than me and have to pay for daycare do it … How do they do it?"

★★★★★★★★★

local school system database (background checks, sex offender, and criminal checks) and verified multiple personal and professional references, and then from there she trusted her intuition. She found the perfect full-time student at Southern Methodist University who would pick up the girls from school and hang out with them until she got home at around 5:30 pm each day. She paid her nanny twelve dollars an hour for approximately two-and-a-half hours of work each day, for around one hundred and twenty-five dollars a week; which was less than even the least desirable daycares she looked into. With the nanny, the kids get picked up from the school and are comfy at home. It was ideal for mom, the student, and the kids—a win-win, and this could be more of a win-win for many moms if we look in to it. Most of us just presumed it was never an affordable option.

Rebel Mom Jenn enjoys performing, as much as she does writing, and sculpting. She has most recently performed a dramatic role in Eve Ensler's *The Vagina Monologues* at the Latino Cultural Center. You can check out the monologues and the cool work of Ms. Ensler herself, and other contributors encouraged/motivated by Eve, at VDay.org.

Jenn is working as a location director for an Ad Agency called Independent Artists. The company has been around for about ten years. The locations she seeks are cool, funky gems tucked away in the city for commercial photo shoots. She's grateful that she does get to make a living while doing something semi-artistic and fun, but nods and confides that advertising isn't really her bag. However, she is betting on the unique position she is in for networking to pay off and open doorways into acting. She enjoys performing, as much as she does writing, and sculpting. She has most recently performed a dramatic role in Eve Ensler's *The Vagina Monologues* at the Latino Cultural Center. You can check out the monologues and the cool work of Ms.

Ensler herself, and other contributors encouraged/motivated by Eve, at VDay.org.

She is keeping her eyes and her ears open for any roles that would compliment her current journey back to herself and wholeness. Although she loves writing, it is not an at-will art form for her. She needs a catalyst, or a muse, to be inspired. Her former husband spurned her to writing daily, lost in love and longing, then recovering in despair. Her dream is to be inspired daily; so that she can write more. For now, she wants to put her past relationship behind her and figure out what direction she wants to move in … "I don't think I've paid attention to myself in a long time. So I think the next couple of months will be about that, about me figuring out what I want."

**Since the interview: Jenn has found love again, and started her own company Sisterbrother Management and they specialize in representing artists. You can check them out and see their work at: SisterbrotherMgmt.com.*

The Writers and Teachers

Let me introduce you to the scribes and heroes of modern motherhood. They are our storytellers, teachers, and bloggers.

They are the moms that help you 'read' parenthood. They are the poets who capture our most surreal emotions and put it back on a carving board for us, bloody, milky, and defined. They are the archaic composers woken in the middle of the night for whiff of words fleeting and needful children. They are the ones who teach us life, and teach our children the alphabet.

Our first mom is an acclaimed and celebrated author and teacher. But she started from the trenches of teenage motherhood and welfare. She will help guide you. She is the Hip Mama. Our poet laureate's work has been read by the Queen of the Damned herself, Anne Rice. Her story covers diapers, dishes, and hardship, but has a silver lining, as will yours. She's a Riot Grrrl—we wouldn't expect anything less than triumph. Our aspiring novelist has traveled all over the Americas and she has chronicled the punk life. At age thirty-two she suddenly wanted a baby. She happily had said baby, and now has a house full of: toys, books, reptiles and bondage belts. Our next mom started off as a working class hero, who suddenly found herself on her own and pregnant. She got a job at a daycare nurturing and teaching young children, so that she could pay the bills and raise her son hands-on. The chapter closes with one of my favorite writers. She has earned multiple degrees and has produced an award winning college newspaper. But she traded in her New York Times dream to put food on the table. She is a great role-model for her daughter and for all of us. Her feminist writing kicks ass, and her mothering does too!

Get ready to find your voice, in the world of the Writers and Teachers!

"I loved my daughter deeply, but it was important to me to see myself as a woman first, as an individual first. Feminism taught us to be very careful about the roles we allow to consume us."

Ariel Gore
Zinester
Tartly Teacher
Rockin' Radical Preacher
***Hip Mama* Zine Creator**
Published Author
Portland, Oregon.

Ariel Gore was the first widely published mother-writer who gave a voice back to the urban poor mother, the welfare mother, the lesbian mother, the working class mom, the teen mother, the single mother, the activist mom, and to the mother who didn't 'fit-in' with the rest. She is the epitome of a Rebel Mom and a mentor to many of us who have succeeded her in redefining our terms of womanhood and motherhood combined. As well as trying to make work 'work' for mothers and kids. Ariel Gore describes herself as: "Queer, writer, radical, preacher, crazy, teacher, crunchy, white girl, Indy publishing powerhouse, dangerous housewife … all those are fine. But I am a mother."

When asked what her life has been like since being a mother, she replied honestly with a laugh, "lots of schooling." Ariel now has a master's degree in journalism, and teaches creative writing in high school; in addition to still running a variety of projects: the award winning *Hip Mama Magazine* (she just recently passed the torch on to a new editor), and has published numerous works such as *Atlas of the Human Heart* (An account of her life as a world traveling squatter-teenager.), *The Mother Trip* (A collection of emotion-filled tales and experiences of mothers who broke the mold and told us about it.) and the book that started it all: *The Hip Mama Survival Guide.*

When you read the type of anthologies Ariel has worked on, the real true voice of marginalized women and mothers comes out loud and clear. Their voices contrast the images of what mothers/women are supposed to be, think, do, or feel according to mainstream magazines and culture. It was the images being shoved down her throat that compelled her to start the *Hip Mama* zine, which opened the door to the books she has written since then …

Check out the musings and work of our favorite Rebel Mom writer Ariel Gore at: ArielGore.com!

Don't forget HipMama.com HipMamaZine.com and SealPress.com!

"The pressure to be a really specific Prozac-prescribed mom, super-mom, is really intense when they [children] are younger; a 1950s sitcom mom, with a contemporary mom, partly Christian, and a commercialized minivan mom."

It was this pseudo image forced upon her that she struggled against, and the welfare/single mom stereotype, not motherhood itself. Motherhood itself was a totally different reality both internally, and externally, from the polished mom we see in ads. (The wonder-woman-mom who has twenty jobs while driving the kids back and forth between their twenty engagements—and who looks perfect). Thus *Hip Mama* was born. She started the magazine with a thousand dollar school loan and used her college's newspaper room for resources. Her first issue sold out at five-hundred copies, and it kept growing from there each month.

With the launch of *Hip Mama*, she suddenly found herself in a few local newspapers, and then became the target for a local L.A. 'conservative' disk jockey [I have always found it ironic that the worst behavior tends to emit from the self-preaching saviors of society type.] who crucified her for being, "*A Welfare mom who puts out a leftist-commie-lesbian mom zine, who has student loans, and sleeps around.*" Even Newt Gingrich (He's a Republican and a former speaker of the house during the Clinton era.) got in on the act during his zealous welfare mom reform PR. [There lacked an equal 'dead-beat-dad-reform' both then and now.]

Ariel was sick of being degraded by these public personalities and politician types, and she accepted an offer by MTV to debate Newt Gingrich. She did it for herself—and the millions of mothers lumped into the same oppressive (un)status in society, and walked away feeling very empowered. *Hip Mama* took off even more after the exposure.

If you look around many of the moms in our society seem to be slaves to their roles, whether they want to be or not. Be it the role as wife, mother, whore, virgin, employee, and so forth. Ariel Gore's approach was anti-Prozac and anti-fitting in. She chose to enjoy motherhood and her kid. This approach was natural for her coming from a feminist background. She decided she was doing this for herself and it was fun. This approach confronted everything that defined motherhood in our society. Ariel felt compelled to offer some different ideas and stories. This inadvertently led to the breakthrough of some of those walls. In contrast to this image she states:

> "However with the whole notion of subculture, if you are a parent, you get flacked at. People are accepting and ignore you and your lifestyle, but once you have a kid you are expected to clean up. Better be sure of who I really am and what I am doing, because there is a tunnel of truth of what I am doing and what I am doing is right on, a level of confidence."

When she first started school it was a complete culture shock. There were no moms there. She was just a weird girl with a baby. No support system whatsoever. There was no magical system in which everyone helped watch each other's kids, while everyone did homework. She never walked into a co-op, she helped create one. She transferred schools and started reaching out to others. She put up flyers. You never know if your next door neighbor is in the same position or not. Reach out and use your head she says. Spawn co-ops and create action and support.

Not everyone needs to be of the same sub-culture. Ariel was living in Oakland, California for most of this time. Most of the mothers involved in this, in Oakland, did not have much in common as far as varied subcultures go. But they did have some basic commonalities including: everybody is starting in the same place. When she became a mom, she didn't really have a lot of cultural beliefs, and out of necessity, she had to peel back the nuclear family protocol, and step out of the isolation (that the nuclear family entails). The nuclear family stays secluded in its own walls and roles, and Ariel had no family. It was just her and her daughter Maia. This led her to reach out to as many moms as possible, for survival. She built her own kind of new local family, and a local community evolved. This also gave birth to her writings and her unique voice, and that became a central platform of ideas and input that grew into a national and international community.

Ariel was not a born/natural writer; in fact she didn't find her vocation, or calling, until after she started college as a new mother. It was writing that saved her life, and it was a natural outlet—for suddenly she had a lot to say. Prior to the voice building and developing, she was knee-deep in loneliness and commercial mom magazines, that didn't help her at all, "All the stupid magazines said, put a smile on your face and buy a mini-van." This ultimately led to the creation of both her voice and her magazine. (*Hip Mama* was immediately diverse because it was for a targeted urban poor/struggling/single/gay or hetero, mom audience, whose core is really subculture in contrast to the images on television and in the media.)

Ariel didn't sleep much during the making of *Hip Mama*, or the first few years of parenting—she was battling the right-wing all the while attending school full-time. She barely got by on welfare. She stayed up all night on many occasions working on the magazine and finishing school assignments. She knew deep down that she had no intention of getting a straight job, which is not easy to pull off. So she worked double hard. She loved what she was doing and it was doing a great thing for women and mothers. [It was work that didn't drain you, or destroy your soul, so she was able to do a lot of it.] During this time she also wrote her first book *The Hip Mama Survival Guide*.

All of her hard work paid off when she un-expectantly got a book deal from the very first publisher she submitted to. She was shocked when she got her first advance check for one-hundred thousand dollars! It came with a contract offer from Seal Press in the mail. (Seal Press is an awesome feminist press housed in CA—and one of my favorites. You can check them out at SealPress.com.) During our phone interview, I sensed the utter relief and joy she must have felt at the moment, as she relived it with me, holding that contract in her hand. [I'm a writer with small successes and I had been burning the candle at both ends myself {50 hour work weeks, part-time school, parenting, loving, living, protests, writing projects, and cleaning}.You always dream of that contract.] Once she had the Seal contract she felt secure. She could stop burning the candle at both ends (as much anyway) and stop worrying about having to serve beans for dinner yet again.

"Work with your teenager with love, not against them, avoid power bouts. They still need you, be prepared to be honest. The teenage years are a lot like infancy—taking it one day at a time, and thanking the stars for survival."

Ariel is now in her late thirties and her daughter at the time of this interview is sixteen. The teenage years have led to a new philosophy for her, "Live in the present and take it day-by-day." Ariel was a single mom for most of her daughter's life and didn't have to deal with any internalized structure in the house. The father of her child faded from the picture almost as abruptly as he had entered Ariel's life. He was twice the age of Ariel when she meet him at age nineteen in Italy. There was a brief attempt in the beginning to be involved and he occasionally would send fifty dollars to help out.

Ariel realized some years ago that she was attracted to women on every level: spiritually, intellectually, mentally; emotionally, and sexually. She has now has been with her life-partner, an acupuncturist, for a few years and they recently bought a house in Portland, Oregon. With her daughter being a teenager now the rules of motherhood have loosened. In the wake of 'teenage-dom', and Ariel's relationship with her partner, all three of them have had to work out and break away from the typical male/female and mother/daughter roles. They are learning how to live and love together while figuring out work and home-sharing and gender issues. The biggest gem she could offer up for navigating the teenage years is: "Work with your teenager with love, not against them, avoid power bouts. They still need you, be prepared to be honest. The teenage years are a lot like infancy—taking it one day at a time, and thanking the stars for survival."

Ariel (and her family) has support in the local DIY/ Anarcho Punk and L.G.B.T. (Lesbian/Gay/Bisexual/Transgender) communities in her new hometown. She has also found the perfect high school to teach creative writing at. She occasionally gets cautionary words for topics that may be deemed as obscene, or questionable, simply because the mainstream has not approved it yet. But overall, the school is accepting and she loves what she is doing, and the parents are very supportive. In Portland, she has also found a thriving culture of artists and has been very successful in offering a variety of writing workshops that range from outdoor excursions lasting several days, to class-styled workshops at a non-corporate coffeehouse. Her teachings range from the memoir to literary star training coffee-camps. You can check out her awesome site and all the offerings at: ArielGore.com.

Ariel also enjoys a side of spiritual activism that we don't get to hear about too often, preaching. She preaches at Big Momma's on the weekends. It is an eclectic worship house where people get to talk about their previous experiences with organized religion and spirituality. Everything gets discussed from what you need to do if you're going to be a draft-dodger, doing political work, or just further developing your moral compass. It's a positive and politically charged powerhouse where you can also reach out for TLC, and ask for some prayers if you need them.

You need patience and prayers as a woman and as a mother—it takes a strong core to make it work, and to raise happy kids who care and are concerned about their neighbor and the world. The "little mommy culture," Ariel acknowledged is hard when the kids are young. She's observed that, "People are very vocal and in your face and can't get past the wealthy-prozac'ed-married-heterosexual-mom-minivan stereotype, and the mainstream doesn't tend to get off your back until children are past the primary ages." Ariel pointed out an interesting contrast about mainstream parents being more accepting of subculture parents once all the kids are teenagers. What's the reason for this phenomenon?

> "All the teenagers are raising hell. It's weird that the straightest of mothers are compelled to confess things to me all the time, like 'My oldest son is jail' ... and so on. Half the stuff they're leaning on me for—I have no idea about. Love your son? Go see him? They sometimes presume I must know, or have been there."

Before becoming a mother, Ariel was a self-described vagabond squatter, high school dropout, homeless teenager and international bag lady. Before she was seventeen, she had traveled to numerous countries including China, England, and Italy. Her travels started with savings from a summer job and her I-Ching book. It was in Italy, her final destination before she came back home, that she fell in love and became pregnant. Maia was born in a small village town in Italy. (Ariel lived in a farmer's barn.)

She feels her identity is much more lucid and flowing now, than when she was both a younger woman and a very young parent. She said, "There is no more divides. There is no individual woman/writer/teacher/mother. I simply am." What are her plans now? More work and more love. That sounds like an awesome plan!

**Since this interview: Ariel's latest book is a spiritual and journal-ling look at women and happiness, and our concepts of, called Bluebird. In addition, she put out a cool anthology, published by Microcosm publishing, titled Portland Queer: Tales of the Rose City. She and her life-partner now have had a beautiful son named Max. They have happily joined the ranks of parents with a baby and a teen at home.*

"I do not think I fit the 'standard' in any sort of way. I'm a single mother. I am a feminist. I don't think women need men. I am not subservient and I will think and do exactly as I damn please."

Heather
Smashing Writer
Poignant Poet
Animal Lover
Foxy Feminist
Student
Dallas, Texas.

Heather is a single mom. She is bipolar. She has never wanted to define herself by one subculture, because she has always been interested in so many of them! Her roots are largely punk rock/riot grrrl and "gothy stuff" with a little bit of psychobilly and rockabilly thrown in just for kicks. She participates in all these different scenes, but always holds her own.

Heather has always been attracted to more complex schools of thought, including music, and rejected the 90s shallow trimmings of pop music and popular thought that ignored the realities of philosophy, soul, life-experience, and real social issues. In middle school she just dived into music and wrote all the time. She knew what she believed in and it all stemmed from there. It wasn't anything she set out to do, or to necessarily become, it just was. She just likes tattoos, piercings, and blue hair. She thinks they're gorgeous.

> "I have never 'fit-in'. I was never part of the crowd, even when I was a cheerleader. There's just something about ME that is slightly out of joint with the rest of the world. I suppose it's just how I am."

Heather doesn't do things just because everyone else is. Often her opinion is not popular, nor her humor well received. When she was younger she made attempts to be 'normal'. [What the media portrays as normal and thus acceptable anyway. Normally (all pun intended) also reinforced by schools/churches and authority figures, including parents-in-the-box.] She was just trying to fit-in, but who she was attempting to be, wasn't her. She doesn't see herself as a sheep, but views the mainstream that way. Heather feels that if we don't, or if we fail to look deeper, we leave people out. And we then leave out necessary experiences and realities that are critical to our species evolution, as well as to have a healthy and safe community to raise our children in. She feels until the mainstream gets with it, it will continue to be elitist and borderline fascist and it will continue to poison its own kids and communities. [It goes back to the 'why' question that we have probed, pondered, kicked, and thrown about all along in our Rebel Mom discussions/book.]

She is extremely intelligent and a free thinker. She is a devout feminist and refuses to back-down from anything, or bow-down to anyone. She is compassionate, kind, loyal, and would do anything for anyone in need, friend or foe. She is very empathetic and loves animals. She is also a very sexual and sensual being and honors this part of herself with love, tenderness and enjoyment—which is contrary to society's expectations of women. (Women are to be sexually available and desirable, but not their own masters of and seekers in. All of these elements of her life and personality are reflected in her analytical writings and her gripping and poignant poetry.) She thinks of herself as mostly happy, but worries she may come off as depressive as she wrestles with the life she has both been given and struggles to create.

She is a self-described Agnostic Atheist and disdains Christianity and the harm she sees that the religion [Not so much harm by the famed Jesus Christ himself, but the religion has served as a mock reason or scapegoat by those in power to justify war, oppression, exploitation, etc.] has caused in the world since the early Middle Ages to current injustices in the name of. She rejects god and religion and the violence embraced by dogmas. Although, she doesn't believe in god, she does believe in luck, fate and karma. She is a "fucking liberal" and definitely "pro-choice without fucking apology, for any reason." Heather believes, "There should not have to be a 'reason' that a woman wants an abortion. It should be her fucking right regardless."

She initially never imagined she would become a mother. She never thought she would have a role within it despite how much she secretly wanted to. Prior to becoming a mom, she thought that being a mom meant diminishing her femininity—basically it was synonymous with frumpy. She has realized now though that motherhood is "totally hot."

One thing she has embraced about herself since becoming a mother is her own beauty. Between the cultural obsession with Barbie and Ken Doll type superstars, and all the magazines in the United States selling nothing but an image of women and men super-slim/sexed-up and photoshopped to perfection/ death, one has to fight for their self-esteem. Heather has finally found her own strength and beauty, "I'm fat and while I am not always 'proud' of that, I try to be positive about it and support fat-positive schools of thought."

Heather's favorite writers include: Anne Rice, Anne Sexton, Sylvia Plath, Pablo Neruda, and Ariel Gore, "She is so fucking right on." She also loves the Bronte Sisters, Dylan Thomas, Oscar Wilde, and Poppy Z. Brite. Heather is a passionate reader who is fond of morbid horror genres. She finds the courage to live creatively, and boldly, through the art works of Matisse, Frida Kahlo, Michael Parks, and Salvador Dali. She is also inspired by the work of David Kirk, a children's book illustrator and writer.

She has sent her writings and poetry to her two favorite writers: Ariel Gore and Anne Rice. Ariel Gore told her that her work was good. Anne Rice once told her a poem she wrote was beautiful. She has pieces published and has published her own zines as well.

Musically, she loves Cocteau Twins, Weezer, Tori Amos, Siouxsie and the Banshees, Depeche Mode, the Cure, the Pixies, the Breeders, Operation Ivy, Rev. Horton Heat, Tiger Army, Kim Lenz and the Jaguars, Morrissey, the Smiths, the Cranes, Beastie Boys, Eminem, White Stripes, Ramones, and Screeching Weasel. The list could go on forever. Heather knows her music, and loves her music!

Heather would have sold her soul to have lived in the Northwest during the 1990s, the heyday of the Riot Grrrl movement. Bands like Bratmobile, Sleater-Kinney, Tribe 8, 7 Year Bitch, Team Dresch, and the Lunachicks, defined the movement musically and politically. Kathleen Hanna from the band Bikini Kill, Courtney Love from Hole, and Kate

Need a fun rocker-feminist starting point?

Then check out: Planned Parenthood, NARAL, American Civil Liberties Union, N.O.W. (National Organization for Women), Black Women's Health Imperative, Feminist Majority, National Latina Institute for Reproductive Health, and mags like *Ms. Magazine, BUST* and *Bitch*.

And jam out to the classics by:
Bikini Kill,
Bratmobile,
Sleater-Kinney,
Tribe 8,
the Gits,
7 Year Bitch,
Team Dresch,
Lunachicks,
Babes in Toyland,
and Hole!

Bjelland from Babes in Toyland were her idols. It impressed her because …

> "Hearing females play hard, loud punk rock was SOOOOOO empowering. A big FUCK YOU to the music establishment in general. I thought they were way more *Punk Rock* than say, the Sex Pistols. I also love Madonna and think she is VERY fucking punk rock in her own right, even though she may not be a punk rock musician. Most music I like has lyrical content that is either extremely political or emotional."

Heather gets real excited about women's (and inadvertently children's politics) and knowing that people are out there in the world working for change, and that her and her son Ian can be part of it. She really wanted to go to the March on Washington for Choice in D.C. 2004, but she lacked the financial resources needed for travel. [I was in the same boat.] It drew more than five-hundred thousand supporters from the United States and was promoted by many organizations such as: Planned Parenthood, NARAL Pro-Choice America, the American Civil Liberties Union, N.O.W. (National Organization for Women), the Black Women's Health Imperative, the Feminist Majority, the National Latina Institute for Reproductive Health, and *Ms. Magazine*.

Heather's day-to-day life can be summed up as fun, fun, fun! She loves chocolate milk and wishes there was a milk bar she could go to and hang out at sometimes. She can switch back and forth between listening to Britney Spears and Screeching Weasel without batting an eye. She loves hanging out with other moms, and her sister. She visits the park and playground frequently with both her son and her dog. She and Ian also enjoy playing with their cats and hedgehogs. They frequent bookstores and shows too.

Heather takes needed breaks throughout the day by daydreaming about: getting all the tattoos she wants, pretending she is rich, dining on interesting and exotic cuisine, and finding a boyfriend that is her equal. Her house looks like a Halloween haunted house and the walls are adorned with posters and the rooms are filled with loud music.

Heather's expectations of herself as a parent are to raise Ian as a socially conscious, kind, compassionate, intelligent, and open-minded individual. Her hopes are that he doesn't go to prison due to poverty, or because of really bad choices. She loves her son and nurtures him. She shows him right from wrong, but she is determined to let him find his own path instead of her directing him in any certain type of way,

> "I think society generally is pretty kid-friendly and kid-centric, but I think society in general is terrible. I want my son to be open-minded and to love, and I think society often looks for a scapegoat to blame its problems on, and they will always pick the underdog. I don't want him to be part of the social norm if that's what it amounts to. I think society tries to mold people to be a certain way, and I see it as my job to make sure my son does not fit that mold.
>
> I think boys should wear pink and girls can wear blue. I think boys can play with dolls and they can cry. I think girls should be encouraged to be just as rough and tumble as boys are. I think they should be told they can be/do anything they want, not that if they do A, B, and C they will be socially 'perfect'."

Her philosophy is that there is no reason why boys and girls shouldn't both be able to be: strong, opinionated, free, and emotionally sensitive and aware. [We are all human after all and blurring the gender lines can free us or unclog us as people, versus putting us in a box we either die in or fight to escape from and get stigmatized for it. This can be true for any identity definitions in society that can be narrowing and limiting.] When she was much younger, she didn't understand hippies at all, but she gets it now. She also understands that the popular notion of hippies, which was negative, came from mainstream society. Once she became a parent it clicked—she gets the general philosophy now and meaning of the lifestyle, "I think that everyone should love another and be kind to one another. Sadly, the reality is so much different." For her son she hopes:

> "I want my son to be a feminist. I want to teach him to respect women. (And all people, really.) I will consistently show him that women can do everything that men can do and then some, by example. And of course, he can listen to some Bikini Kill

with me too, if he wants. Ha-ha! I want him to love animals, to love in general, to not be susceptible to apathy. I will teach him to care. I will take him to political events/rallies. I will take him everywhere I possibly can to show him different points of view, but to also instill that just because people may disagree, does not make anyone better than another.

I want him to finish school, because I did not. (I got my GED in 11th grade. I then enrolled in college within the same hour of withdrawing from high school, because I just knew there had to be something better academically.) I want him to go to college and be successful, of course. I want him to be the one to help pave the way for future generations of compassionate, caring, and socially-conscious individuals. I want him to have good taste in music!"

Her overall parenting belief is to show him love and lots of it. It's imperative that Ian knows that without a doubt, because it's something Heather says she never knew as a child herself. She likes many of the ideas around attachment parenting like co-sleeping. She simply takes her cues from her child about his needs. Reading is an important value in their home. Every day they read, and every day they learn. Heather believes there is nothing more powerful than the written word. She knows our kids aren't lemmings, and she can show Ian to think outside of the box, and that not everyone has to do the same thing. It's okay to be different. In Heather's opinion, it's people who do not follow everyone else that are often more intelligent. She feels promoting intelligence and education are very good things and not following the crowd builds that.

His education is one of her biggest goals. This is a substantial challenge for a parent and child living in poverty, especially a single parent household such as Ian and Heather's. It's an additional struggle, to prioritize educational enrichment, when that single parent living in poverty has to work away from the home at least forty hours a week, typically (if not more). She hopes to be able to send him to a Montessori school because she shares a similar philosophy about teaching and children. It's basically a child-driven educational format that also includes self-paced work and creative play. If she can't financially afford that eventually, she at least wants a safer apartment environment and a really good public school.

Heather has always struggled with being consistent with goals and work because of the severity of her bi-polar disorder. She has worked in coffee shops, pet stores, art stores, natural grocery stores, and as a computer technician. She now has permanent disability for her medical condition, but she knows that on a state income she won't be able to provide some of the additional environmental changes she wants for Ian. But it has enabled her to be with her son and raise him from infancy onward versus an uncertain daycare environment. It is for Ian that she has been able to get through life and not be apathetic with her disorder. For Ian she has to care, she has to get up, she has to be responsible and meet all of his needs and enrich his life. She adds: "I think motherhood is the most fucking awesome job ever. I think there should be a payroll for mommas. Oh yeah, is it called welfare?"

The ideal situation for her would be to find a roommate that is a single mother, which would enable a little more financial freedom for both parties while having a co-parent in the house and they could lean on each other for support. She hasn't yet met a mom that would be right. She feels she doesn't have much in common with other moms, "No husband to come home to and no mini-van to drive." She does share the love of children though that most moms have, but she can't relate at all to the nuclear family.

For the time being, she has to deal with the frustration of poverty and single parenting. Below is a journal entry she wrote:

"I feel so much younger than I am. I can't believe I will be 28 on my next birthday. It is a highly depressing thought. Depressing, that I am still totally alone and almost 30. This is such bullshit. I know that's just some sort of sick social pressure ringing in my ears that I need to be married or some bullshit. Right??? Yeah. I mean, I would like to be. I think it's fucking amazing when I hear about people being married more than twice. It's like, holy shit; I can't even find one to marry me once!

I am sick of eating spaghetti. I hate having no gas in my car. I hate that my tire went flat tonight and now I'm driving on a spare. I hate that Ian has 5 diapers left. I hate that I have a food-stamp appointment to go to on Thursday and no fucking gas to get to it. I hate that. Even if I got a job, it wouldn't pay me enough to put Ian in daycare, and if it did, all of my money would go to daycare and I wouldn't have more money than I have now, so what would be the fucking point.

I hate that I live in this ghetto-ass apartment where people with guns stand around outside, pit bulls are everywhere, blah, blah. I just wonder if there will ever be an end to this. Actually, this is the way it is all the time and I just generally don't really bitch about it. I get paid next week, and then all the shit will disappear temporarily. Sometimes bein' all ghetto fabulous just ain't that fabulous."

Her philosophy about herself though is that no matter what she will always come out on top. She has experienced many struggles and ordeals, but she always make it through and often for the better.

She didn't originally envision she would be a single mom. She had her son with her best friend of many years. He worked at a tattoo shop and they were roommates. They did everything together from cooking to taking their dogs to the park. Their friendship had lasted almost a decade and was also very sexual—as best friends they experienced many sexual firsts together, as well as life in all its variances and ups and downs.

When Heather found out she was pregnant she did imagine him being supportive and wanting to be there, and he wasn't. Since they had shared life together so well, and so long, and so happily, she actually thought he would be excited. She was not prepared at all for his cold and harsh rejection that he slapped her with—her best friend did not want to be her boyfriend, or even live in the same house anymore, child on the way or not. It upset her that he didn't want to be in a familial unit. She never expected this from him, but couldn't fathom not having their child. (Which let her down, but more importantly according to Heather, he also later neglected his adult responsibilities and became an almost absolutely absent and indifferent father, letting Ian down both then and now.) She was terrified about how she going to do it all alone and everything seemed bleak. Because of the pregnancy she had to stop taking her bi-polar medication and she was miserable. But she preserved and made it …

"Parenting is 200,000 times better than I could have ever imagined! Don't get me wrong, it was tough as fuck, but I know that I am perfectly fucking capable of parenting alone, and perfectly capable of doing a GREAT JOB. I guess in some ways it isn't as bad as I thought it would be."

Her family and friends doubted her ability to parent because of her bi-polar disorder and her own past which was riddled with sadness. Her father abandoned her and her sister after their parents divorced when she was just five. They lived in poverty thereafter and her mother suffered from mental illness which is borderline personality disorder with psychotic features.

Her mother was emotionally, verbally, and mentally abusive. Her own mother did not know how to parent, or even how to show love. Heather became the caregiver in the house and raised her little sister. She understands her mother's illness and doesn't even necessarily blame her for everything ... because she also understands her own. Unlike her mother as a parent though, Heather has fought hard every day of her life to be a good person, a good parent, and to stay in control.

Prior to Ian, she struggled with being bi-polar and having suicidal tendencies, but now successfully manages it with medicine, determination, positive thinking, love of herself, and love of her child. She rejects the notion that once a woman becomes a mother she has to be perfect and in perfect circumstances:

"Well I think that society thinks that in order to have children, you have to be Susie Homemaker, that you have to be 100% mentally sound, that you have to be rich, or well-off, and that every household should have two parents. This is just not the case. In fact, if anything, I think it is the minority. No one is perfect.

Mothers are held in this Madonna/Whore sort of place, the Madonna place. We can be whores too! Ha-ha! No seriously, mothers can be just as diverse as anyone else. We don't have to live by a certain standard. We can still raise productive, intelligent human beings if we aren't the 'standard'."

One thing that has helped to sustain her over the last six years of being a single mom is that she resumed going to college on a part-time basis and has been a kick-ass and a great mother despite the lack of support—from Ian's dad, or society.

Her future plans are eventually to get a double major in journalism and creative writing and write tons of books. She hopes to someday live in New York City or Los Angeles. These two cities seem to thrive with artists and she wants to be part of that creative culture. She also wants to buy a Mini Cooper. As far as life in general this is what she has to say, "I guess it's simplistic, but my overall philosophy is to take lemons and make lemonade. Shit might not be perfect, but it can always be worse. I generally feel very lucky."

**Since this interview: Heather has completed Cosmetology school and life is rocking and rolling! And she has moved into a better apartment and safer neighborhood, with a good public school!*

"I think Punk and Christianity have a lot more in common than you would think. They both involve rebelling against the world and how it is. They both can be sanctuaries for those who have had darkness in their lives."

Debbey
Memoir Writer
Fiction Novelist
Gorgeous Working Stay-at-Home Mom
Catalyst Christian
Fort Worth, Texas.

The things that excite Debbey about living are: her family, good books, movies, traveling, and experiences that remind her how big the world is. Her hobbies include herpetology (The study of reptiles and amphibians.), photography, and writing.

She loves Frida Kahlo's artwork. She likes how her paintings show painful and broken experiences, while conveying wholeness and hope despite misery.

Her favorite comic book series of all time is *Love and Rockets.* The comic book was launched in the eighties via self-publishing by Gilbert and Jamie Hernandez. It's had numerous series including one that has been described as a commentary on the Chicano/Latino Los Angeles Punk Scene in the eighties, and one in a fictional village in Central America. (One of the main characters Maggie is beloved by many comic book fans. She grows from a young teenage girl into a woman who as she ages grows more rubenesque in her figure. Despite pressure from male fans of the comic, Maggie keeps her attitude and her curves.) You can learn more about this amazing and fun comic at: FantaGraphics.com/artist/losbros/losbros.html.

Debbey's favorite books are semi-autobiographical stories written by women whose experiences are subtlety told through the stories. She has not yet been disappointed by an Oprah recommended book.

Punk music has been part of Debbey's identity for over twenty years now. Her favorite bands include Chaos U.K., the Boys, the Pogues, Some Chicken, the Stooges, the Clash, Patti Smith, the Electric Chairs, and X-Ray Spex. She adds, "Mainly, I like the music I like because I can put it on and get excited about life. You know, either remember good memories, or be inspired by the energy."

She defines herself as, "I'm a Christian-Punk-Rock-Mom in my mid-thirties and being a weird outcast is what I am all about!"

Debbey has just recently become a Christian. She is adamant though that it is a spiritual and philosophical way of living for her. For most people religion is used as a straitjacket with rules and authoritarian dogma. This is what repelled Debbey for a long time from any form of organized religion. She feels just because this is what religion means for most, that ultimately that did not stop her from embarking on a deeper spiritual quest as her need for spiritual enlightenment grew …

"Well the Christian thing is still fairly new to me and I haven't really talked about it with a lot of old friends and I haven't met enough people to see what the reaction thing is. I think it might give some people a shock because of a lot of things associated with religion, but it is more of a spiritual thing than a right-wing political thing for me. I think Punk and Christianity have a lot more in common than you would think. They both involve rebelling against the world and how it is. They can both be sanctuaries for those who have had a lot of darkness in their lives.

As far as being active in the ministry I'm still looking for a church I'm a comfortable in. I've only been to one in my life, as a Christian, not as a guest, and it was a good church, but not for me."

One thing that led her down the path to motherhood, as well as Christianity, is that she had spent the past few years getting her life together. She had quit drinking, stopped doing drugs, and was working on building her self-esteem. She stopped getting involved in unhealthy relationships and drama, which she seemed to find plenty of in her punk circles. She wanted to develop a strong mental state. She stopped looking at life as, "A big pile of poop, but as a wonderful thing full of surprises and wonder." She feels you can choose to view life, or the world, as full of things to fear or a place of excitement.

This new belief system and focus helps keep her strong after years of sadness, losing friends to death, and enduring personal betrayal by those she has loved. In the past, whenever she had an inkling of chaos on the horizon she would have "flipped out," but not anymore.

Her husband has also grown as a person, and in essence they have grown together as a couple, which is what opened the door to parenthood. How they initially met though is … well, interesting.

Years ago, Debbey's ex-boyfriend kept trying to set her up with his friend Jared who also had a recent ex as well. Her ex's motivation behind this is was simply sneaky. He wanted to hook up with his friend's ex and this was his way of trying to keep karma.

Debbey and Jared did eventually hook up in the midst of drunken chaos. Eventually, each newly matched couple did marry and have children; before that though during the years of each couple's dating there was a weird unspoken rivalry and jealousy by Debbey's ex-boyfriend who initiated fate.

As Debbey shares this story with me, my mouth is hanging wide open. She and I simultaneously burst out in laughter—although we are communicating online. Smiley faces dash across the screens, coffee chilling on our desks on a Saturday morning, as the kids fly by with dads in tow. I share my story of how Jason and I hooked up, which is not quite as dramatic as hers and only semi-funny. He was just my new found good buddy, and well one night of whiskey, he got ballsy. I liked teddy bears with attitudes. I sweetly told Jason we have another punk rock drunk-love story as Debbey typed updates for me.

Debbey and Jared's first few years of dating became a bizarre on and off again thing. Eventually she got sick of the scene in Portland, Oregon and moved—across the nation. Jared followed. He didn't want to be without his girl; now that is punk rock love.

They have been together ever since and finally ended up in Fort Worth, Texas. They got married in the most defiant state in the union and they had a kid; which brings us to where we are now in her story. Debbey is thirty-eight-years-old at the time of this interview and their son is three-years-old. Her current career goals as a working stay-at-home mother are toilet training and getting their son to sleep in his own bed.

Debbey had never considered having kids or gave motherhood much thought. She had never even held a baby before her own. At thirty-two years of age a strange thing occurred and she started crying at baby commercials, and peeking in at little angel faces hidden in strollers. She couldn't rationalize it, and it was frankly unexpected.

Debbey was in the middle of writing a novel when she got pregnant, and she thought she would easily resume it after giving birth. Three years later she is still trying to finish that damn novel! [She wasn't prepared for the reality of trying to write and care for a newborn and later a toddler. Yes, we are all this naive with the first child. I innocently thought I would be writing on a laptop at coffee shops as my darling watched and cooed snugly from the stroller, happy and content.] Debbey has written all of her life and as a younger adult she made money writing fetish stories for low budget porn magazines. Fifteen years ago, she had written her first novel about some punks in a small town. She has over seventeen life journals written that eventually she plans on developing into semi-fictional stories and publishing.

Her current novel started when she began the spiritual and mental journey to recovery and self-realization. The novel is autobiographical and is inspired by her life in Portland and the time she spent in a very toxic relationship.

During this time she had become very agoraphobic and couldn't leave the house, and she had to work this out through writing. The novel is about characters who hit rock-bottom in their life and then go back to their past to see how events may have contributed to it. They start picking up the pieces with clarity from there and moving on. She also wanted to write about all of the interesting people she met while living there. Of course they are the inspiration. Through writing the novel she is taking unpleasant memories and transforming them into valuable life fables with pseudo names.

The novel which is half-way completed has had to be put on hold until her son is a little older and can at least partially entertain himself. Right now, she doesn't have an hour to herself that is not consumed by being a mom.

Before becoming a mother she didn't realize its importance to society (regardless if society itself doesn't get that) and the shaping of how people develop and grow.

Debbey knows now how many aspects of everyone's life goes back to how they were *or were not* nurtured as a child. Good qualities and bad qualities can be developed from this time. She feels her role as a mother is to lay a good foundation for her son to build on. She hopes he will have a full life with everything she missed out on, and that he also experiences everything she did enjoy too while growing up.

When she had "the little guy hanging out in her uterus" she worried constantly if he was physically and mentally okay. She was plagued with fears. She calmed herself by knowing if he can make it out alive everything will be alright.

She had strong support and care from her family and her in-laws. She was startled by the unexpected support during her pregnancy that she had from people she met on the street, women she worked with, and her nurse and mid-wives. The care just poured out of the woodwork from everywhere. She felt very blessed with all the help, advice, and the encouragement she received. It was a completely new experience for her. It was an amazing community she never even knew existed.

Debbey grew up in New Hampshire and never went outside of New England until she was twenty-two. She felt alone and rejected most of her life. Her first experience with any kind of seminal community happened as a teenager:

> "I was fifteen and awkward, ugly, with no friends when I discovered Punk Rock through the media. I lived in a very backwards state. It was energizing, exciting, and best of all, I could continue being a freak—but I was in control. People thought I was weird because of my bizarre clothes not because of my awkwardness. Then I moved to San Francisco, California and talk about culture shock! It was great."

She became more heavily involved in the punk scene in San Francisco and her first true experience of community. This scene led her to explore different cities while meeting more people. It even led her south to Mexico for awhile and took her north to Canada. But also being a confused young woman she took a lot of childhood baggage with her that took her down the self-destructive paths she was on until she decided to change the course of her life in her early thirties.

Of course the travel experience she has had is significant in shaping who she has become. She hopes her son gets to see many parts of the world as well. She thinks that anywhere in the world is good to see because everyplace is different in its own special way. She sees lots of educational travel in their future … from playing in the snow up north, to seeing sea animals in the ocean. She also hopes her son takes after them and loves reptiles and will want to study them as they do. Parenting has surprised her in many ways …

> "I didn't think he would be sooooo loud. He had colic from six-weeks to four months, not just crying in the evening, but all day long. Now even as a toddler he has tantrums that you can hear from one end of a large supermarket to the other. He screams when upset, yells when happy, hollers when bored, and wails when sad. I was quiet as a kid and so was my husband. I guess I just assumed he would be too.

I also was so completely positive he was a girl that it took a week or two to get used to that after the ultrasound.

I always kind of perceived society as a threat like a bunch of predators that will reject me and make my life miserable if I don't completely conform. I'm getting over that and mainly because having a child is making me try to be more positive.

I have been pleasantly surprised at how much kinder society seems when you have a child. Babies seem to bring out the best in everyone. I walk down the street and people who might have once sneered at me are asking me about my baby. Motherhood has been a wonderful common ground for me, people who once would have judged me (and vice versa) I'm having conversations with.

All in all though, I think society can have a detrimental effect on a child. I see mothers yelling at their toddler sons for playing with dolls, or families encouraging their children to look down on people who are different. Making fun of retarded people on TV is an example that pains me to remember. I think society can and will suppress the best qualities in children. My husband and I have discussed this in length, and how we need to be vigilant about this and how we will deal with it when it comes."

Debbey always hopes to be fair and remembers what it's like to be a child and to see things from her child's perspective. She wants to keep the conservation lines open and to always be someone he can approach with any problem. She hopes in doing this she will always be a big part in his life as well.

She feels the highest quality he can have is empathy towards others and being a compassionate human being. Already, she is conveying to him how his actions affect others, for example hitting mommy with toys hurts and makes mommy sad, or not saying hello to grandma hurts her feelings. Through their childrearing she hopes to instill enough faith in him that it will guide him through the inevitable dark times. Even if he rejects their teachings later, it will always be a part of him.

They hope he will love animals, swimming, and music like they do, but they will always make time to pursue his specific interests as well. Right now, their son loves lions ... so they take him to the zoo frequently and have watched Lion King over forty times, literally, and read countless books about the cat that rules the jungle. She adds:

"In a nutshell, I love my son unconditionally and will always be there. Everything else I just take as it comes. I don't think there is really any way to completely shield him from what we would consider negative ideas and such, at least not without it backfiring on us. Our plans seem to be to talk about everything and answer any questions asked, or anticipated, so he'll have an open view of things and be able to make his own decisions."

Debbey is not part of any punk social scene anymore, but she still very much feels a punk. Her unique experiences give her a unique perspective. The same goes for her value system. She already plans on stressing individuality rather than popularity, once her son starts school.

She doesn't know any moms like herself, but the ones she does run into she can relate to amazingly well. There are sometimes differences but she can overlook them to get good advice, and senses they can do the same.

She knew a few punk moms in Oregon, but they were much younger than her and had little relative life experience before they had their babies. She noted also the difference in age, because they all still managed to party pretty hard and still be good mothers, which is something she doesn't have the endurance for.

Debbey does want to compensate somehow though for how shockingly domestic her life has become. She used to have thrilling adventures, and emphasizes that her new adventures with her child are fabulous, but she would like a little more balance between the two.

She doesn't view punk or subculture different from the mainstream anymore, even though she thinks there are still people who are more genuine out there and understand the real scene. She does believe that when you are part of a subculture you do check yourself more in regards to how you're living and why, that your values and behaviors are more thought-out, rather than just going through life doing what you were never meant to do. She feels the mainstream could benefit from a little more self-examination and that pondering motivations for what you're doing and why is good for everyone.

When Debbey was a child her mother struggled in understanding Debbey's choices and motivations which further fueled her rebellion. Debbey knows that there isn't much her son can do and be in life that she will not support. She knows that children of rebellious mothers are shown more and given more options in life. On the other hand, in her own experience, she has seen that mainstream moms seem to be given more resources and approval by society, making the labor of parenting more endurable.

Her plans now are to finish her novel and start her publishing adventures, but her boy is her top priority:

> **"My little man is the source of my pride, as cliché as that sounds. The fact that I went through so much pain to have him, well I'm proud of that. I'm not sure if his confidence, optimism and enthusiasm are because of me, but they make me swell with pride."**

"I believe society would love to just sweep me and women like me under the rug, along with our offspring—out of sight, out of mind. As if they have to 'put up with' or 'deal' with us. We are considered a blemish on American culture."

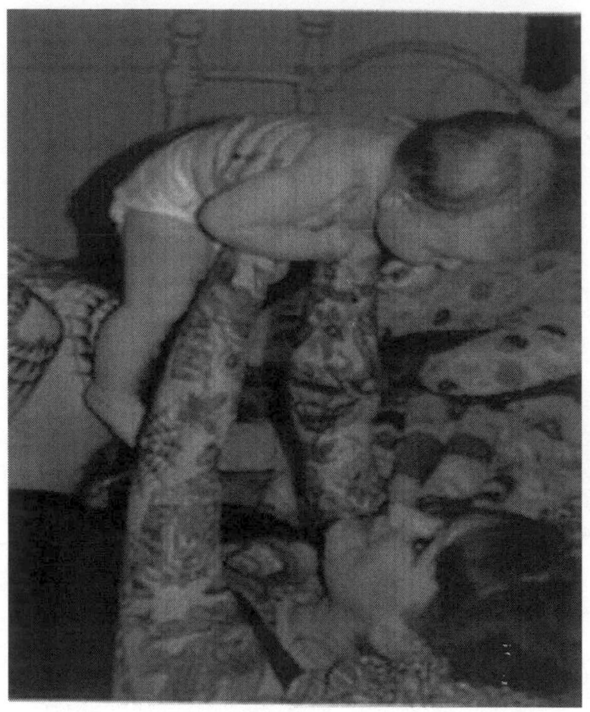

Stacey
Pretty Pre-K Teacher
Oi! Skinhead
Rat Rod Enthusiast
Photo Frame Crafter
Music Student
Sacramento, California.

Stacey is a single mom in her late twenties working hard to make life happen for her and her son. She has worked as a Pre-K teacher at a day care for the last ten years while raising her son at work. She made the impossible happen when everything seemed stacked against her. She relaxes by focusing on crafting cool tattoo inspired picture frames, and dreaming about building and having hot rods. Her other baby is her 1964 Ford Galaxie. The three things that really get her excited about life and in this exact order are: her son, music and tattoos.

Music was her life before motherhood and she digs mostly Oi!, street punk, ska and reggae. She can't live without her favorite musicians though: Corey Parks, another righteous Rebel Mom in this book, and her husband Duane Peters. (Stacey's favorite bands that they have been in, and not necessarily together, are: Nashville Pussy, Chelsea Girls, Die Hunns, Charley Horse, and the U.S. Bombs.) She also digs Lars Frederiksen (Rancid, the Bastards), and Kenny Beasley. She is studying bass guitar right now, and eventually hopes to play in a band. Her favorite tattoo artists are: Jack Rudy, Scott Sylvia, and Brent Patten. She has many more, and she loves them all equally! They all are Cali artists that call San Fran and L.A. home.

She grew up in California with a good, loving family. For her, family and friends is everything. She is loyal, loving, and caring towards those in her life. She stands up for what she believes in and she refuses to be taken advantage of, "I don't use the word homegirl/homeboy lightly. If you are 'down' for me, I will be 'down' for you." She prides herself on being a mother, daughter, sister, auntie, prankster, and all round rad chick.

When she started working in a daycare as a teacher, she had no foresight that it would later be essential to her survival when she became a mom for the first time,

> "It was totally a fluke. I had been laid-off because the place I worked at was going bankrupt. Mind you, I had NEVER worked with children before and had NO experience at all. (Scary thought isn't it? Think about that one next time you think of putting your child in daycare/pre-school!) I was twenty-years-old and straight up had the shaved head, a fringe on a 3' guard. The only reason why I could walk up to a place like that and get hired is because I was friends with the boss. I've always stuck with my jobs and usually didn't leave unless a better opportunity came up, or something happened, like bankruptcy. Well … I got my preschool teacher qualifications, which isn't much, and stayed put. After being there for a few years, I got pregnant and really thought it was best that I stayed there."

She was a working class (anti-racist) skinhead girl working hard and having fun, when she became pregnant. She was with someone she loved, and the father-to-be freaked out and split. She was scared, but knew she was, "A strong person, an adult. I know about the birds and the bees, so now I must be responsible for my actions." She planned to do the best she could even if it meant she would be on her own. She was frightened to bring a child into a world like ours, with poverty, crime and hate, but knew she could be a great mom, and would fight like hell to both protect and provide for her kid.

She didn't have much support as she faced her pregnancy. She moved back home briefly, because the rent she paid her mom was less than rent for a place of her own. She had no help from the government (except for medical), by her choice, and it was grueling. This experience she feels has made her stronger, and made the bond with her son unbreakable. The biological father eventually came around, sort of, "His priorities are still not in order," but he makes an occasional attempt to contribute to the cost of taking care of a child, and being involved with his son. Since motherhood introduced itself to Stacey life has been quiet …

> "I hardly ever go out compared to before. I have less friends, but not on purpose. After I grew my hair out some considered me a 'sell-out'; while some came around, and realized that way of thinking was fucking stupid, others didn't or whatever. Not too sure, and at this point, don't really care. My priorities are in order. My son always comes first as it should be."

What she wants for her son is,

> "I hope for my child to be happy and to have the kind of relationship with me that will last forever. I want him to be comfortable enough to come to me for anything and about anything. I want him to love life and be happy—whatever he ends up doing. I want him to know that I am behind him one hundred percent. I don't want him to have trust for everyone though, and to be cautious of the 'snakes' in this world. I want for him to know that his mama has 'got his back'. I am real with him and try to be truthful and honest with him about life and people in it (within reason and age-appropriateness)."

Stacey loves motherhood even though she feels it is hands-down the hardest job in the world. She believes in just one basic principle, which is treating others as you would want to be treated. She strives to be there for him and to make the right decisions—including the choice to be happy. She views this as essential to raising happy kids who will later be well-adjusted. In her line of work she sees this negligence and negativity all too frequently with parents and their children. She wishes other parents had this discipline,

> "I expect myself to be the best mother possible. I can be. This is not a part-time job and it does not end at the age of eighteen! It's twenty-four seven, three hundred and sixty five days a year! For life! Get used to it!
>
> You are responsible for your child and need to be there to nurture and raise this individual with love, care, and respect. Do not pass this responsibility off because you don't want it, or can't 'deal' with it. Don't have kids if you can't handle it!"

She works for everything she has, and credits her parents for this, "I was brought up with a very strong work ethic. Therefore, I am a very tired woman." She feels too many people use or rely on welfare as a cop-out for not getting the job done or not trying too. It's hard for her to relate, since she faced huge obstacles and found a way to support her son by finding work that allowed her to have him with her, and just cutting through the bullshit. She understands with the high amount of dead-beat dads, herself included in that statistic, it's more of a challenge for single moms, and some assistance should be provided to compensate for the lack of help, but she feels it is too often an excuse to do nothing, or the bare minimum, when we all can do more to make our society and our children's circumstances better. She's clear on the record here that she sees parents whose childcare is paid for by the state and taxes and that they drop their kids off to her, but they don't have a job or school they are going to, which is the basis of her opinion. It perplexes her to no end,

> "I personally always wanted to be a stay-at-home home and wanted so badly to be, but that was just not an option. Sure, I could have gotten on welfare for about

two years and stayed home, but that's not the road I wanted to travel. So what most of the women I work with did was get a job at a daycare or pre-school. Some don't charge their employees to have their children there, some do, but it is much less than what you would pay normally. Some of the mothers that did get welfare are also eligible to also have their child care expenses paid for. So they don't have to pay at all because the government does. I on the other hand have to pay to bring my child to work, and I get be with him all day as I earn money. I make sure we have all that we need, and even some things we want. This is how I was able to stay out of the system, with the exception of health care."

It was a bit of a tender subject for me when we originally interviewed, because I—like her, wanted to make a better life for my son and be a stay-at-home mom, but it was not an option for me either. I had no resources except of my own making, just like Stacey. I wanted to scale back work to part-time, and increase my classes from two a semester to four. All I was asking for was help with child care assistance while I was at school and work. Long story short, the State of Texas said I didn't qualify because I made a dollar too much an hour, and would have to quit work completely … just to be initially considered for the program. (And how would I pay rent? Put food on the table?) The message I was getting was that I would have to be completely dependent on the state in order to get any help, which seemed an oxymoron to all the recent welfare 'reforms'. The fact that I had been a contributing full-time worker and tax payer for over ten years didn't matter either. It was quite transparent what the true motive was: control and degradation of mothers, working class mothers specifically. I continued working full-time and made every minute with my son count, and took a class or two when I could afford it. Did I mention many years later, I am still a part-time student? (But I'm also still a righteous mom who has given my son an incredible life, and I've worked extremely hard to do so. And I have continued to support my community through activist and volunteer work regardless of strapped or changing resources—while being a full-time worker and tax payer.)

The point however that Stacey is making, is that we as a culture need to work a little smarter, and try to put in some good old-fashioned elbow grease before just calling it quits. Don't just take the easy way out, simply because it may be there. Don't take the easy way out in parenting, at work, at school, in your community, or in life. [Don't let business and government get off the hook either for bad behavior and exploitation, especially of the working-class and poor. Both of which has resulted in universal starvation, the world's largest killer, and also creates the need for welfare.] She hopes we as a society come to realize that we need to: a) value children more b) value moms more c) value ourselves more by becoming self-respecting and investing in ourselves and our kids, as well as appreciating hard work for what is, hard work. She thinks to get us moving in the right direction we should fight being complacent, "Treat others as you would want to be treated. Give back, don't just take. Get off your ass and be productive. Pick up the slack."

She sees this lack of value for what she does and the lack of return for hard work in the low wages she makes (and no health care from her employer):

"Yes, our wages suck. This is a very touchy subject with me because I am baffled about how low our wages are and what our job is. We have what should be considered the most precious possession in our responsibility and we are paid the same, if not LESS than, the people that handle the latest releases at the nearest Blockbuster! This is not an exaggeration and it's unbelievable in my opinion. It's very sad."

Has it been easy balancing work and motherhood? Absolutely not!

"My personal struggle has been being able to work and be with him every day since he was born. I stayed with him until he was four-months-old. [The legal amount of time in California for job protected maternity leave. California is very progressive and pro-family unlike the majority of the states in the Union.] When I returned, I was in the infant room with him and breastfed him until he was fourteen-months-old. I moved up as his teacher every year. I am blessed to have been with him. But do you know who made that happen? Me. I was determined to not be on welfare, raise him, and make money to support my child and me at the same time. It was not easy, let me tell you, but I forced my way through whether people I worked for liked it or not. I made it a reality for me."

★★★★★★★★
"I love children, especially young children. It's amazing how sweet, and innocent, and non-judgmental they are before their parents start filling their heads with conformity and prejudice."
★★★★★★★★

As a pre-k teacher, Stacey gets an up-close view of behind-the-scenes family life for the general American. It saddens her, what eventually happens to most children, "I love children, especially young children. It's amazing how sweet, and innocent, and non-judgmental they are before their parents start filling their heads with conformity and prejudice."

Stacey also feels children are placed "so low on the totem pole of life," by society. She thinks if society really wanted to make the world a better place, they would (and could), but are too selfish. She asserts that selfishness is the reason why we as a nation, and as a people, have the problems we have today in our world and communities. She hopes we can work at getting it right. A good place to start she says, is allowing children to be seen, and allowing children to be heard.

Stacey has noticed since becoming a mom, how bad you're treated and looked down upon by others if you are a working class mom:

> "I already knew how differently people with and without money get treated, but it was more noticeable now that I had a baby. In fact, everything became more noticeable. Before I stuck with my own underground society, but now that I had a child I was forced to be in places I might not have been before."

Stacey thinks this alienation (in addition to being judged for not being wealthy, or marginally wealthy) is compounded further because other moms tend to prejudge her character (based on her tattoos and Oi! skin girl life) and fear that she would be a bad influence on their children. It sucks, because those moms are missing out big-time. They are missing out on meeting a remarkable and gallant person, who would be a better influence for their child than most adults or popular culture! She's a vibrant, gentle, considerate, and incorruptible woman who has a huge heart of gold for kids. Their stereotype would be simply shattered if they knew not only does she rock, but she specializes in teaching and caring for young children, including theirs. Because of pre-conceived notions and judgments, Stacey does have to cover up all of her body art when working. She has to cover every inch of her skin from neck to toe. [I have to do the same thing. It sucks, especially in Texas summer time heat! But you do what you have to do to get by, and to still be the awesome person you are!] Stacey has some pretty well balanced thoughts on the subject though,

> "I have to wear long sleeves and pants every day. I wish sometimes that I had the drive to become a lawyer and specifically handle (discrimination) cases like mine. I do not think I should have to, but at the same time I do understand because it's not something most people see everyday and they are shocked. I didn't say it was right—I just said I do put myself in other people's shoes. I've been at my center for so long everyone I work with knows me and I am the 'token' tattooed girl at work, and in their lives, actually. Also, many of the parents know about my tattoos and they are cool about them too. Some people say that they would never cover up or compromise who they are, but I do this for my son. I work like this because I want to be with my son and raise him, and give him things that he deserves. For him, I will do anything.

Many people have argued that this is a life we chose, and because we aren't born with tattoos etc., it's not discrimination, unlike people that suffer from indignities like racism or sexism; who are born as a girl/boy or black/white/brown/yellow/and so on., and had no choice in the matter, biologically speaking. And I get that, so does Stacey. However, it's more complicated and frankly it's not that simple. The closest analogy I could compare it to, is something that just is, but unseen, for example sexuality. Is a gay man, less gay since it's not as pronounced and easily identifiable? And is his right to a safe and healthy/

happy existence less than that of others? It's still a biological determination and should warrant the same consideration and respect. I don't see ours as any different. We also know that so much of our human chemistry and biology is influenced by environment as well; so not all paths lead to the same destination. I think, that's a good thing though and I am actually quite awed by the amazing diversity of the human race and our cultures. Stacey's thoughts on the subject are:

> "It's not something you are 'attracted' too. You are born with it. It is you. It's a way of life for you from the get-go. It's not 'cool' or something you 'wanna be someday'. It is how it is. There is no option."

Stacey does have a close group of moms that she hangs out with that help counter all the negativity she gets from society. They do fun things together liking taking their families to tattoo conventions, and sometimes even to see bands play. It just depends on the band, the age of the child, and the circumstances. She thinks it's becoming more common now to see us out and about since, "The 'misfits' are growing up and having children of our own. We are the outcast, and we have formed a bond and our numbers are growing." One thing she knows for sure though,

> "I do not 'fit-in' to the mainstream, nor do I intend to. I don't fit the image forced down your throat in the magazines or on Oprah. You will never see a person like me in a commercial for the latest laundry detergent."

She fights the urge to be reactive to the biasness she encounters, more often than not, from the mainstream world by recalling that:

> "Something to remember though, and I have to remind myself of, is that not all society is negative, hates us, or is 'out to get us'. I have been surprised I will admit. I'm not one to trust; sometimes I am even guilty of prejudging people that are 'normal' and just thinking they are automatically going to be against me. This is not always the case."

She thinks if there is one cornerstone that society can help remodel itself after, for a better world for our kids and ourselves, it is the love of children and of our children—which most moms have regardless of their obvious differences. That cornerstone is a great meeting and starting place.

Stacey works hard, loves her son, and dreams of a job where she didn't have to pretend to be someone else. Her dream is to work in the tattoo or music industry. Her final closing thoughts are, "Everything is give and take. The things that make you so happy sometimes in life will also make you very sad. You can't have one without the other." Ain't that the truth.

**Since this interview: Stacey has found and married the love of her life! They have had a beautiful little girl! She also finally gets to be a stay-at-home mom to her babies! In addition, the family has opened a very cool All-American sandwich shop called Dads. Check it out, DadsSandwiches.com. And if you're ever in Sacramento, swing by and tell them* Rebel Moms *sent ya!*

"I was editor-in-chief of my college newspaper. I had this vision that I was going to go on to a much bigger university, graduate, and go work as a hard news reporter for the New York Times. I was still getting my feet wet as an adult in some ways."

Katy
Journalist
Writer & Editor
Bid Specialist
Retail Manager
Sassy Single Mom
Spiritualist
Foxy Feminist
Richardson, Texas.

Katy is an academic journalist who dove into love and motherhood while earning double associate degrees. Her writings are sharp, her commentary adroit. Her observations are keen, frank, and objective. She is passionate and likes life on the sarcastic side, and she will play devil's advocate to anyone's stance. She is loyal to, and a fierce protector of, those that are part of her tribe. She has many shoes to fi woman, writer, lover, mother, sister, daughter, and worker. Her current muse is law—she dreams of being an attorney, and is going to chip away at it gradually. Going to school is in her blood, and she has been attending colleges and lectures both full-time and part-time since she left high school. Her motto is, why stop learning?

She loves music and especially female vocals with a piano thrown in. You can always hear Blondie, No Doubt, or Lily Allen, serenading guests when you walk in the door. When she's in the mood to simply rock, she puts on MIA, Them Crooked Vultures, Blanks 77, or the Clash. You can also catch her checking out her favorite movie Blade Runner, or her daughter Anna's favorite series Monty Python, on the weekends. When she needs some TLC she simply curls up with books, journals or magazines printed by her favorite publisher, McSweeney's, which is an aesthetically quirky press in the Bay Area that specializes in mainstream houses rejects. In other words, their shit rocks! Their titles range from the charmingly outlandish, such as Lisa Brown's baby board books, that are just as interesting for the caregiver as they are for the baby, such as *Baby Mix Me a Drink*, and more brutally sobering works such as Peter Orner's *Underground America: Narratives of Undocumented Lives.* You can check out this very cool press at: Store.McSweeneys.net.

Katy recently was promoted to a bid specialist for a retail Fortune 100 company, from regional general manager. Her journalism career suddenly became dissolutive as the world of literary media print shrank enormously, and writers, as we romantically and classically knew them to be, became an endangered species. Becoming a blogger was not her thing so she works on the side doing editorial and creative projects, while focusing on the tangibles needed to build a life, right now, for herself and her daughter Anna. Anna is nine, and Katy has been a single mom since she was four-years-old.

"My goal was never to be a retail slave, but after the market fell out on what I got my degree in, I had to take a job with a company that paid well, had good benefits, and would work with me as a single mom. I have so many personal goals; it is hard to list them all. I tend to constantly evaluate where I am in life and where I want to be. I am starting up an editing business and hope to have it solid by the end of the year. My true love is writing and editing. Unfortunately, it cannot pay the bills presently, so I work for 'the man'; in the meantime I am milking it for all I can.

I am working on becoming more financially secure and Anna is pretty self-sufficient, so I am able to focus more on the future than worrying if I am going to make rent this month. I want to buy a house. I want to go back to school. I want to travel and expose her to many different situations and people. I want to save money so that when she goes to college, she has it easier than I did. I want to enjoy life and the people I have in it, instead of just struggling to survive."

Katy grew up the oldest of five kids, and knew what it would be like, to an extent, to be a struggling mom. When her dad and mom were married, they had it all. Or really, he did. When her parents divorced, he kept everything, and his family was left to make ends meet in near-poverty. She grew up in an upper middle class home, went to private school, where children had nannies, and her parents drove brand new Volvos. She didn't know what it was like to not be able to get something, because it was unaffordable. It was a foreign concept. Then when her parents divorced, mom got the kids and just the clothes on their backs pretty much. Suddenly, Katy found herself around the age of twelve or thirteen, living in a small apartment with their large family and they had no car, and her mom had to rely on food stamps to feed Katy and her siblings. The income her mom made from work, even with some meager child support added to the budget, wasn't enough to pay the bills and put food on the table. Although both parents loved her deeply, it was clearly evident that priorities had shifted for dad once the kids were living under a different roof—less monetary support, and less fathering.

Most divorced or single moms see less and less equitable financial support for their children from the fathers, hence the *Dead-Beat-Dad* epidemic, and the feminization of poverty in the U.S. Regardless of the crude catapult in Katy's adolescent family life, which led her to punk and Riot Grrrl ideology, she stayed on point. She had big plans for her future,

"I was a twenty-year-old college student. I was still trying to hang on to my identity as a punk, but realizing that my goals had changed from when I was fifteen. I couldn't go out to shows all the time, I had to study! I was working on my A.A. in journalism. I was writing and editing like crazy. I edited the Humor Magazine. Also, I was editor-in-chief of my college newspaper. I had this vision that I was going to go on to a much bigger university, graduate, and go work as a hard news reporter for the New York Times. I was still getting my feet wet as an adult in some ways."

★★★★★★★★★

I am beginning to realize this 'working mother' thing is a myth, I cannot work all day, then come home and just give, give, give. Because you will give to the point of having nothing left. There are days where the most I am going to be able to do is take care of my child's basic needs and my own, and I am not going to feel guilty about that."

★★★★★★★★★

During this time, Katy had her real first boyfriend, and she moved out on her own. She was young, idealistic, independent, and working on her goals one savory accomplishment at a time. Then the bomb was dropped. She learned she was pregnant.

"It was unplanned. I had always wanted kids, but I had figured it would be later, around thirty. There was a lot of pressure from my father to put her up for adoption, a decision I could never make. I had thought about abortion, but it came down to me just not wanting one. I wanted this baby even though it was a far from ideal situation. I think I had these naive ideas that we were going to build this family and this life together. I thought that maybe if I just worked really hard I could make it all happen. It was what I had been doing all my life. I was twenty-one when I had her. I had been with her father for a year-and-a-half. I worked at school and he did not have a job. We had no car. Looking back, I can see why everyone was freaking out!"

She was optimistic, and knew everything would work out fine. She planned on continuing school (which she did and eventually earned two degrees), marrying Anna's dad (which she did not) and being a successful journalist (she tried, but despite her successes and credentials, she could not find paying work, so she had to move on). Eventually, both families came around and were happy for her, and helpful. Looking back she feels lucky to have had so much support from relatives and friends, "I had this little community that had always been there for me, but it was in this much deeper capacity. I am so blessed that most of these same people are still there for me."

She tried to make things work with Anna's father for four years, but there seemed to be issues with motivation, and sustainability. She decided it best to end the relationship, because she felt that it was only going to hold her back in life. She found herself being a single mom, something she had never anticipated. At first, Anna's dad tried to stay involved, but he eventually ended up meeting someone else, and shortly thereafter he created a new family and moved out of the state. His support as a father, both to Anna interpersonally, but also financially, has been fleeting.

The first few years of single motherhood Katy was determined to keep Anna out of daycare.

> "I have no judgment against anyone who has children in daycare; it just didn't feel right for me. So I hustled and took jobs that allowed me to stay-at-home with her. I wasn't making as much money as I could sometimes, but I was always there for my child."

This is an option that has worked out well for several moms I've known. They worked from home, so that they could parent actively, which they felt was most crucial to their children's well-being (and theirs too). Some of the legitimate at home work you can find, that most of the time pays at least comparable starting wages to a call center, ranges from customer service, adult chat, physic readings, insurance counseling, and sales. This type of job helps you earn an income while being at home with your kids. It is tricky … and it's challenging. It takes self-discipline and a committed routine. With the exception of self-created consulting work which can pay what is considered appropriate for that field, there are few legitimate work-from-home companies (and any company that asks you to pay them to find out about the job I would caution you against). You just have to dig around online. When I lived in Denver, I was a supervisor for a company that essentially ran a virtual call center 'onshore-outsourcing' throughout the U.S., providing customer service, tech support, and sales, for various household named companies. I managed a group of thirty competent, confident, and knowledgeable, customer service reps who all worked from home across the nation. It was cool and fun! Now, I didn't get to work from home—with the exception of an occasional mountain blizzard. Despite the hardships Katy appreciates what motherhood has given her …

"It gave me the impetus to become a better person. I have talked to other moms and a few dads about how being a parent changed us, and it is amazing to look back and see how much more you will push yourself for your child. I think, though, that there are very unrealistic expectations placed upon mothers. I am beginning to realize this 'working mother' thing is a myth, I cannot work all day, then come home and just give, give, give. Because you will give to the point of having nothing left. There are days where the most I am going to be able to do is take care of my child's basic needs and my own, and I am not going to feel guilty about that. I lost myself as a person in those first few years because of who I thought I had to be. I realized that I am a better mom and a better example for my daughter when I take time to develop myself."

Katy wants to be the best person she can be in this world and by doing so she knows she will inadvertently be the best mother as well. She has chosen a spiritual path that places a high value on self-reliance and accountability for your own actions. Katy hopes that her daughter will be open-minded and non-judgmental. She wants Anna to grow into a strong, confident, independent, smart, and capable young woman who respects herself and stays true to her own core values.

"I place the expectation upon myself to give my daughter the tools necessary for her to grow into the best person she can be, not who I want her to be. I instill this by trying to set an example. I am very honest with Anna about the mistakes I have made in my life. If she questions something, I explain why I made that decision to the best of my ability. Anna is one of the most important things in my life, but she is not my entire life. I think by continuing to develop myself, set my own goals and achieve them—I show her that anything is possible. She knows that I have struggled and that we struggle. But she also knows that I work hard to make our life better."

Katy defines her core parenting philosophy for us:

"My role as a parent is not to break her spirit and will, and force her to conform to what I want her to be. I respect her individuality. I support what she wants to do, even sometimes when it is at odds with who I am. If it is something I am adamantly opposed to and just cannot live with, then I explain why. An example would be Bratz dolls. I think those dolls perpetuate a stereotype of women as sex objects and I think it places that in little girl's heads way too early. I know that women are sexual beings and I respect that, but I also want to have my daughter learn about sex in a healthy way. When some of the women in her dad's side of the family wanted to buy her the toys, I told them no. I then explained to Anna, that those dolls weren't meant for little girls, they were at best meant for teenagers (or at least modeled after them). Because I have so few restrictions on Anna, to their credit, my in-laws respected my decision.

Anna happens to be part Puerto Rican, amongst other cultures. I want her to know about that side of her family. I don't feel the need to Anglicize her, and I think that can happen especially when the child is raised by the parent who is not of that culture. I want her to value diversity and multiculturalism as much as I do.

My philosophy is to try to expose her, and give her access to, as many experiences as I can and out of that she can discover the richness of life. There is a quote from Nietzsche, "*The unresolved dissonances in the relation of the character and sentiments of the parents survive in the nature of the child and make up the history of it inner sufferings.*" And to me that expresses itself as our unrealized hopes and dreams, and our past prejudices. I try to not let my past affect how I parent Anna."

One area that influences her parenting is her feminist view on life, and she concludes she will "raise Anna and any future children (regardless of gender) the same way." One thing she has observed recently that frustrates her is the backlash against stay-at-home working moms—from feminists and/or career women. She finds that, "Holier-than-thou feminists seem to take the stance that women, who choose to stay home to raise their kids head-on and hands-on, must not be educated or are submitting to the patriarchy." She feels that today's situation is altogether different from the 1950s after women were forced to leave their high-paying work (when WWII ended) as mechanics, engineers, factory workers, etc., for the only other available role then: subservient motherhood. Many parents now simply want to be more actively involved. Sometimes this means staying-at-home as the primary caregiver, or two parents sharing one full-time job, or just trying to balance things out, even if it means leaving work behind for a while, so to speak. However, another dynamic that this dividing and argumentative debate between women and parents neglects is the false assumption that employers are, and will be, flexible and accommodating to parents. For the average worker they are not, and this often results in severe conflicts of interest between the two separate obligations as a worker and a parent. Katy thinks that,

> "Now that women would *gasp* possibly choose to fulfill these roles willingly, we are going to malign them? That is hypocritical! We shouldn't be judging women's choices, as long as they are just that, choices. I once had a teacher tell me that when you go too far right or too far left politically, no matter the views and opinions, it almost becomes one in the same sense because of the level of fanaticism."

One thing we know for sure, is that moms need bigger helping hands, regardless of if they have a job outside the home or not. And that is one area that feminists of all creeds should be able to agree on. Katy has spent her whole life observing the treatment of women, and children, and concludes …

> "I think Western society does not respect motherhood, or value parenthood. And furthermore children are not seen as vital either. There is this attitude that I find when I venture outside of my core community, that children are not people. I realized from the moment I could feel my daughter kick, even though she was an extension of me, and dependent on my very body to live, she was still an individual and a person. I think some parents do not begin to realize how much of an individual their child is until they are toddlers, and begin to physically exert themselves upon their environments. Children are sentient beings. I do not think children should be seen and not heard. I think all children should have a voice.
>
> It breaks my heart that Americans spend all this time and money villianizing the right of women to choose; all the while taking away anything that would enable a

less privileged mother to succeed. Let's cut Planned Parenthood, and Food Stamps. Let's not enable families to earn a living wage. Let's make it so that women are working just so they can pay for daycare. Let's blame the single mothers, instead of the deadbeat-dads. I feel women with lesser means and lesser access are railroaded.

I have seen what it is like to have and seen what it is like to not have. However, because I do not fit the societal stereotype of what people perceive as a poor mom, people tend to think I will agree with about how wrong welfare is. It really pisses me off to hear people say that women are living the high life off of welfare. What they give a family for Food Stamps and TANF is not much [and generally it subsidizes absent fathers who aren't paying child support and jobs that do not pay livable wages]. Section 8 housing these days for those not already in the system is non-existent."

Katy does believe that children are an important part of society, a "fabric of the world," and that there has been some positive progression in the Western societal normative in how children are parented. Things such as corporal punishment is taboo, not being a present parent is taboo (regardless of the lack of employers who fail to help enable parents to meet this obligation), however she does feel the middle and upper class suburban pendulum has swung a little too far. She thinks the environments that these kids are being raised in lacks the experience of struggle or conflict:

"When everyone's child is a special snowflake, what happens to the regular snowflakes? These parents tend to advocate for their children to the point where they handicap them. Every child is unique and different, but children also have to learn to deal with some adversity such as children they do not get along with, difficult teachers, not getting picked first for team sports. That shit gets on my nerves."

Katy applauds her parents, especially her mom, for how they raised her, and encouraged her to be who she was. In her childhood, fitting in and being normal was not a goal, nor was *not being normal* per se. They did teach her about society and how to navigate it, so if she needed to fit-in or achieve something that was essential or important (like work or avoiding bullying, etc.) she could navigate accordingly. Katy strives to be a person who has her own set of morals and values, which may or may not be reflective of the norm; that honest self-dialogue and scrutiny is what initially attracted her to the punk-feminist movement, but her concepts of identity have evolved.

"I often feel like I am playing a game. I'm not normal, but sometimes I pass for it. I want my child to be exposed to a range of people and experiences. And I am not a complete iconoclast like I was in my teen years where I rejected the norm, just because it was the norm. These days I am not so quick to throw the baby out with the bathwater. If I have a strong opinion on something, I examine why. Is this a gut reaction based completely on an emotional response?

I started out as more of a punk rock mom/riot grrrl. As I have evolved as a person, while I still enjoy that subculture, I do not identify with it as strongly. I identify more with my spirituality, which is metaphysical and non-Christian. Anna has been raised to be knowledgeable, with a respect for Christianity and the Abrahamic religions. And if she chooses to be in an organized religion I will respect that choice. She will have to come to that decision after being presented with all of her options and not because it was the religion her parents chose for her. I still present the ethos of punk rock and the riot grrrl culture to Anna just by virtue of the fact that whether or not I still go to shows, or wear combat boots, or read zines, those things are still a part of me. I still believe in DIY. I question authority. I am pro-choice. I am a feminist. And the funny thing is that punk rock is more pervasive in our culture these days and even though I do not steer Anna towards something because it is punk rock, she often comes to like it and discover it all on her own. Her new favorite artist is Joan Jett. She loves the Runaways.

I am hard-working and responsible. I think that passion is important. And I try not to judge other peoples lives. As long as someone's actions are not hurting me or the ones that I love, it is their business. I don't think that Western Culture is this horrible thing that I have to constantly change. I have my issues and I explain my viewpoints to my daughter. I think that any society has its problems, but the grass is not always greener on the other side."

Katy is an evolving feminist who takes direct action and subtle action through her daily parenting and running of her household. She does not feel the need to stigmatize herself or alienate others; that teen angst brought a lot of enlightenment that has transitioned well into a happy, hard-working, and subversive adulthood for her.

She was the first of her immediate circle to become a mom, but she had a few friends who had children shortly thereafter which gave both her, and her daughter, an opportunity to be around like-minded people. As she has grown out of the punk rock community and has become very involved in her spiritual one, she has found additional parents and children for them to bond with. It has helped her to parent more constructively with taking into consideration all of the different paths, trials, tribulations, and experiences that other moms and dads have shared with her. Katy does feel that parenting is a bridge, and that the intersecting similarity she generally has with other parents, even affluent or conservative ones, is "always our children, and then we find our own commonalities beyond that." Initially, when Anna did start school Katy was worried about how this would play out,

> "I was a very young single mom. I just threw myself into volunteering at the school and kind of proved to them that I wasn't some fuck-up. That, yes, we were a different kind of family. But I had the same end goal that they did. We all wanted to raise happy, healthy kids. And I think that is how I relate to other parents, through our children."

Katy is just glad that she is finally at a point, where she does have substantial support from her inner community and from the parents she has bonded with, and Anna is doing well, and is content. With her new promotion, she anticipates being able to buy her house soon, and her new corporate gig actually frees up her time some, since she will not be managing the retail outlets anymore, to launch her writing and editing consultation business—allowing her to get back to what she is passionate about. And law school? She is still contemplating it, but I bet it won't be long before she holds that degree in her hand too. I can see her future now and she's rocking and rolling while combining justice, writing, and politics into a multi-level grassroots career.

**Since this interview: Katy is accepting offers of work and proposals for her writing, and editorial services. In fact, she was the copy editor for* Rebel Moms *and is a special project editor for* Rebellion Press. *Feel free to reach out to her at* KatyKrisak@RebellionPress.com.

The Students and Shakers

Are you still looking for your niche in life? Or are you in the throes of diaper changing and school work? Have you been juggling it all and feeling alone in your struggles?

Well you're not. In this final chapter you will meet outstanding women in all stages of life, work, and school. Our first mom went from writing about mayhem to turning the art of demolition into a paying business. Our second mom is completing school (again) to become a teacher, who focuses on international politics—and is definitely slated for being a U.S. President! If you think your dream is out of reach, then check out her story! One mom is just starting out with a young family after successfully overcoming addiction. She is blending work as a fast food cook while going to school for her dream job! There is nothing she can't do! Are you in need of some redemption? Our E.R. nurse wasn't always saving lives. She had a reckless teenage taste of danger, and then turned her life around hard and fast. Next on her to do list is: becoming a M.D. Have you ever dated the boyfriend from hell? Worse, had a baby by him? This mom did and she had to go to jail to get him away from her! Now she's a co-parenting co-op mom with big, fashionable plans for the future, while raising her daughter in an atmosphere of love and respect. Are you just taking it one day-at-a-time? If so, our Cali mom is just for you. She wants to become financially stable as a bookkeeper with tattoos, while getting used to single momma-hood. We close with a new mom starting out and over. She's figuring out her footing and her future. All she knows is that she wants the best for her son. And we have all been there.

Welcome to the world of the Students and Shakers! They will show you how to hope, salvage, restart, rebuild, and to go for it!

"I do a lot of volunteer work at my daughter's school, despite the 'odd-parent' feeling."

April
Demolition Queen
Camper
Hot Hostess
Headbanger
Former Punk Club Owner
Business Manager and Co-Owner
Fort Worth, Texas.

April is an out-spoken, stylish, metalhead momma with a huge heart. She is a tenacious woman who has taken a turbulent life and steered it in the direction she wanted it to go. She has been with her life-partner Brad for over fifteen years; since high school. They have two incredible kids, Sydney, their charming and popular pre-teen daughter, and Zachary their Tonka-truck-loving son who is almost five-years-old. They have raised their children within a core community of rockers and punkers, while also showing them that you can be true to your "who you are," and be yourself, while still being successful, happy, and providing a good and loving family home. They also love blowing things up and playing with dynamite, hence their demolition company; which evolved from the tear-down work they did as contracted homebuilders for her father-in-law's company. Her motto in life is, "Family first, then shoes."

April enjoys going to see bands play, jamming out, having margaritas, studying law and sociology, reading and writing. She works an average of fifty hours a week and volunteers at Sydney's school frequently, so she treats herself to a well deserved Queen treatment at the spa at least once a month. Afterwards, she meets her girls for a night out in her chains and black leather heels. Right now though, she is spending her weekends fixing up a large farm house they just purchased in the country, and looks forward to throwing huge family BBQs under the stars, and putting on occasional weekend shows with touring bands taking center stage.

She is frequently awed by her two favorite artists, whom have mesmerized her since adolescence, such as M.C. Escher's metaphysically dynamic woodcuts and sketches, and Picasso's bigger than life and sensual abstracts. April likes work that lingers in your head long after you have walked away from it. Like Escher, she believes life is fascinating and wondrous. That penchant for reality weighted down with ironic exaggeration, is what attracted her to the works of her favorite writers: Charles Bukowski, Mark Twain, Hermann Hesse, Jack Kerouac, William S. Burroughs, C.S. Lewis, J.R.R. Tolkien, and renegade-surrealist French writer Georges Bataille.

Poetry is her muse, but music is her rock. The louder and faster it is, the more she digs it, "I pretty much like it all, with the exception of boy-bands, Britney-bands, and shit like that. Mainly, I like metal and punk." Her favorite bands are Testament, Motley Crue, Iron Maiden, Judas Priest, Megadeth, Street Dogs, No Means No, the Architects, and her life-partner's bands: Spazm 151 and Damage Case. Brad is her favorite rocker and drummer, hands-down.

They met in their home state of Arkansas, and quickly became best friends. Teenage love-sparks soon followed. He was proud to be with the coolest and hottest girl in their school. They have been together ever since. Like most couples in a long-term relationship, they have had their share of hardships and triumphs.

They had only been dating a few months when tragedy struck. April's brother was killed in a gruesome and horrible car accident. After her world fell out from under her, she leaned heavily on the one person she considered family, Brad. Although, they have had bare-knuckled love-and-hate brawls and tire-screeching fights, followed by occasional and brief periods of separation, in the end they always have had each other's backs and would find their way home to one another. There was however, a lot of growing up and living to be done in-between their high school romance, and the successful, affectionate, and mature couple that they have become today.

Their first pregnancy was unplanned, and both of them were in their early twenties. They had moved to Dallas, and were living the daily life of thrill-seeking rockers, dabbling in this and that, and lived in a punk house with travelers and bands coming through. The loss of her brother left a hole she filled with seeking out and meeting people, and with excessive partying. She derived manic inspiration from the characters she met daily in a mix of parties, bars, and shows, for her dramatic writing. She had big dreams of becoming the next iconic and martyred working class poet. Then she learned she was going to be a mom.

Suddenly, she found herself isolated and alone, and she knew no parents. They were amongst the first in their circle of friends to have a pregnancy. Brad didn't take the news well, and he was in denial the whole time. April had to change her way of life, and fast. She had only one person she could count on during that time, which was her neighbor Lisa … who was "a saint, a god-send, and her confidant." [Ironically, I've known kick-ass Lisa since I was thirteen and she taught me how to drive!] Of all her friends, at that time, Lisa was the only one with significant responsibility, as a Montessori school teacher, and she offered the understanding and support that April needed for the life transition she was unexpectedly going through.

"When I became pregnant, Brad and I had decided to do the adoption thing. It was a very difficult decision. Once Sydney was born, I could not part with her. The weird thing is that when I made that decision, I still had not even seen her. I had chosen the most perfect parents to adopt her and I am sure they hate me to this day. I regret nothing. I could not imagine my life without Sydney."

Eventually, Brad adjusted to fatherhood, and not only accepted his responsibilities, but embraced them. It took an act of tough love on April's part though. When Sydney was still a toddler, she finally left him, got her own place, and took work as an account manager. He still had some wild oats to sow, and after a few months of life without April and his daughter, he realized that it was no life at all. They reconciled and gradually merged a rockers life with that of caring and mature parenting. Within a matter of a few years, they built a side business of homebuilding through the work and resources they obtained through familial contacts in the builders industry. From there, they gained knowledge and experience in tear-downs, and eventually evolved from homes, to big business complexes, and then launched their own demolition company. April handles most of the sales, project bids, and occasionally gets to play with the explosives or the wrecking ball.

They were hitting the road in a large RV, going on summer band tours while Sydney enjoyed visiting her grandparents, when she learned she was pregnant again. Sydney was about eight or nine-years-old by this time. Although, this pregnancy took them by surprise too, they were in a much better place as a couple and as individuals to handle it. Most of their friends had become parents by now, so April was surrounded by loving friends throughout her pregnancy. They were excited when they learned they were having a boy, and looked forward to being older, but wiser, this time around. April had forgotten how rough the first year of baby care can be, "Motherhood is not a role to be taken lightly. It is most definitely a full-time job that will test your every strength." On child-rearing she adds, "I expected parenthood to be a lot easier. It is hard to compromise so many situations."

When April first became a mom she struggled trying to be the perfect mother, but has since realized there is no such thing, and she just needs to be a good mother who loves her kids, takes care of them, and raises them well. She works extremely hard to ensure they not only have everything that they need, but some things they want too. She wants her kids to look at her as their best friend, their model, their protector, and their teacher. So that they can then grow up and be the same for their kids.

She teaches her children to be kind, and forgiving of themselves and others, since … "We all make mistakes, but mistakes make us wiser." She also advises her children that it's okay to be confident and act on your beliefs, if you feel that strongly about them. April is a champion of education and frequently challenges her kids to try something new, learn something that they don't know, and engages them in roundtable discussions about what is going on in the world, and their own neighborhood. She feels that life does indeed suck sometimes, but you just got to take the bad with the good, but challenge that which must be challenged, to make things right. She also wishes

She also wishes that society would take kids seriously, instead of disregarding their feedback and perception on matters. "Kids are very honest and people tend to brush that off." April doesn't harbor any hidden agendas, nor mislead her children into thinking that all is perfect in the world. She's pretty straight-forward with them when they ask her about what's happening in life. Their home is secure and strong, and that gives them the anchor and the love they need in which to navigate the world's twists and turns.

that society would take kids seriously, instead of disregarding their feedback and perception on matters. "Kids are very honest and people tend to brush that off." April doesn't harbor any hidden agendas, nor mislead her children into thinking that all is perfect in the world. She's pretty straight-forward with them when they ask her about what's happening in life. Their home is secure and strong, and that gives them the anchor and the love they need in which to navigate the world's twists and turns.

It was this forthcoming realism and honesty that attracted her to the subculture way of life. Yes, the music is a blast, but she suddenly found a home for her way of thinking that made sense, and that could be articulated. As a young adult that translated into writing, adventure and music, and as an experienced mom and business-partner that led to her taking over a beloved Deep Ellum punk club that was otherwise on its way out.

When April and Brad bought the Red Blood Club, in order to keep the only remaining punk club in Dallas from closing its doors in 2005, it was their dream come true. They didn't fathom the amount of work they just added to their roster. In an attempt to convert it into their dream punk club, with a sleek pink and faux diamond girl's bathroom and edgy red and black gentlemen's bathroom, it would become an absolute money pit. What was essentially supposed to be only aesthetic remodeling, unearthed hidden plumping and structural problems—that had to be fixed; soon after another hurdle was thrown their way.

City Hall was taking a move through legislation to get all the punk bars and clubs out, in an attempt to convert the historically working class downtown arts and music sector into an upgraded, posh, commercial Petri-dish. As bar owners this made it extremely difficult for them, especially with the rezoning and licenses. April found herself working seventy hours a week trying to save the club that they just invested over thirty thousand dollars into. Ultimately, city hall got its way, and the club closed as well as several others. Red Blood Club hosted some amazing shows during its time like legends: MDC, the Exploited, Conflict, Defiance and Naked Aggression.

April looks back and doesn't know how she managed all this, other than raw determination. Her son Zachary was maybe two-years-old. There was a lot of juggling and lost sleep for sure. April does feel that although subculture women specifically have totally different ways of thinking, different morals and ideas, and may appear different in regards to our physical appearance, that one thing is certain for all moms:

> "We all want to provide the best we can for our children. I believe that all moms have something to offer to their children, and I don't think that has anything to do with whether or not they are mainstream or counterculture. We all have things that make us unique or different from each other, whether you are labeled as subculture or mainstream. I believe all moms by natural instinct have a lot to offer their children. Although it may not always be apparent, we all simply want the best for our children."

April has worked hard at Sydney's school to overcome barriers and make a connection with other moms, although she doesn't relate to them at all. She's in it for the kids, and some of the moms have come around, some remain stand-offish, but she doesn't let it get to her. She will continue to strive to do the best she can for kids, and that includes making their school more successful so that her kids can be too.

What's next for April? They have recovered from the huge expenditure into the punk club, and have grown their demolition business significantly. Other than hosting awesome baby showers for future rocker parents, she just plans on blowing shit up occasionally.

Rock on!

"The world presents us with exactly what we need when we need it. We may not always want what is presented, but it's exactly what we need at any given moment."

April
Tartly Teaching Student
Political Visionary
Administrative Assistant
Knock-Out Knitter
Yoga Practitioner
Future President of the U.S.
Austin, Texas.

April is a sharply intelligent, disciplined, creative, and loving single mom to an amazing ten-year-old daughter named Echo. April embraces the moment and the journey of life daily through focused awareness. She makes her home in the capitol of Texas, and can hold her whole body up on just one arm! She enjoys listening to downtempo and drum and bass music, which is nice and mellow, and that helps balance her temperament which is gets enflamed by her passion for politics.

April is into trail-blazers and as such her favorite artists are: Dali, Kahlo, Picasso, and Van Gogh. She likes the fact that their personal lives are "slightly crazy" and their works are "extremely creative." Her favorite musical artist is Madonna whom she admires for "taking life on her own terms."

The writers whose works she enjoys most are Jeffrey Eugenides who authored *Middlesex* and *The Virgin Suicides*, and also Yann Martel who wrote the enchanting fable the *Life of Pi*. She likes work that is "fun reading, good reading, and profound and interesting." If you layer all of these interesting dynamics of life, art and work, with mighty pieces of astute political involvement, anchored on a peace-inducing Buddhist mentality, you, my friends, have conjured up April in the flesh. And she is all-awesome.

She grew up in the Texas Panhandle, explored her teenage years in Irving (a suburb of DFW), and graduated college in 2004 majoring in international studies with a focus on diplomacy. She realized later she wanted to teach, and currently she is one class away from her teaching certification. She plans to teach government, which is her main interest, while hotly debating politics. She considers herself "pretty opinionated and in-your-face about things." She does take other peoples feeling and thought into consideration, but she has found it normally just solidifies her own beliefs. "I am really fed-up with the crap that's going on in the world these days. I am trying to change it by getting people to vote and take part in the political system."

It frustrates her [and me] that according to the U.S. Census Bureau's last national election data issued in 2006 (for 2004) by Kristy Holder titled *Current Population Reports*, of 216 million voting-age citizens, only an estimated 126 million voted, approximately 58%, and of that amount 25% had voted for then president Bush. Which to her and I just seems moronic if you are considering the health and vibrancy of our nation, our communities, and our people. It's ironic that most people who voted for him (and those didn't vote at all) in the first and second election would later suffer stiff financial consequences, that would impale their families and communities, because of his elitist policies in business, American family life, and international diplomacy. She and I both sighed back-and-forth several times bewildered at our nations own partial consent to its destruction (partial because more Americans actually did not vote for him, but more states had), during our interview for the book.

April had wanted to go to work with the State Department after the events of 9/11 and the invasion of Iraq. She wants to "be a fly on the wall of the United Nations, Congress and the White House." She yearns to know the reasons behind all the decisions that don't make sense to her, especially since she has studied politics, government, and diplomacy in depth. She postponed her career ambitions though due to her daughter's needs, since Echo doesn't like traveling and moving. She has already formulated how she would help facilitate some international conversations and resolutions, both in a political leadership role as a future government employee and as a teacher. More ambitiously if she was our president,

"I wouldn't support a troop surge. Of course, I wouldn't have started a completely useless war because daddy wanted me to either. So I probably wouldn't be faced with that decision. I would go back to working with the international community, eat some crow, and try to establish more stability in Iraq. Saddam wasn't a great guy to begin with, but he managed to establish stability in an extremely unstable country. I'd try like hell to get key people, the Muftis and Maliki into a meeting, and work out a mutually beneficial plan (one exists, I know it does) for the future of Iraq. It was a HUGE mistake to invade Iraq! Afghanistan didn't have a fighting chance without intervention of some sort to establish a government beyond what amounts to feudal law and repression under the Taliban.

Then I'd work on establishing a Palestinian state and Israeli state. There's a lot of animosity within that entire region (if that wasn't obvious) and all interested parties are chipping at it with jackhammers.

Then I'd get Kim Jong II, Mahmoud Ahmadinejad, and Chavez (North Korea, Iran, and Venezuela) and work out the issues with them. They want legitimacy and transparency, and some amount of attention from the Western World. I don't agree with Ahmadinejad's politics, or worldview. I think he's very limited, but that doesn't mean he's stupid. In fact, I think he's very intelligent, just ignorant. I think the same can be said of all politicians. They aren't very enlightened, as far as education about alternative world views.

Domestic policy: education reform, education reform, education reform! Instead of this horrible *No Child Left Behind* nonsense, where failing schools would lose funding, I'd go into the 'failing' schools and put into place, as much as I could, socialization programs. These programs would stress education, staying in school, and successes within those realms, mentoring programs, partnering with business owners, and community involvement. Being in one of the best school districts I have learned a lot about how much community involvement makes a difference in the school and learning environment. I think this speaks to how much we undervalue parenthood and our children's lives."

As I try to sell her on running for public office, taking a direct action more-legislative role, versus a behind-the-scenes supportive-role, she confides that one of her favorite presidents was as sexist as they come …

"The one founding father I have a certain degree of respect for is Thomas Jefferson. He read the Koran, he studied other languages, and he felt it was important to learn about other cultures and beliefs, even if they didn't coincide with his own. And he was a Unitarian Universalist, which is more or less what I subscribe to. Of course, he also thought that women would never be able to understand such profound and intellectual pursuits, so I'd have to backhand him to the 18th century."

April does plan on fully pursuing this career path once Echo is in college, which will be in approximately seven years. For now, she is going to step into the world of teaching locally, gain some experience, and advance, then transition to teaching internationally which will then position herself for a career in politics and diplomacy. She eventually wants to teach in the Middle East region and the former Soviet Bloc countries. She feels that,

"In teaching you actually learn more than you share with other people. I like the aspect of being able to share in other people's life experiences, rather than just thinking that my way is the best way and everybody should follow that. The other part is the very altruistic side of me that has this overly romantic idea of helping youth realize their fullest potential and all of the worldwide peace stuff."

For now, April is content in getting her feet wet since her primary work role is still supporting her daughter, and developing Echo's leadership and critical thinking skills, and a humanitarian mindset. April pays the bills by working for a home healthcare company as an administrative assistant. She was nineteen when she became a mom, and asserts that, "If I had not had her then, I wouldn't be here now." In retrospect, she admits, that then, she was still just a child herself and didn't have any real goals other than a vague notion of going to school, but "didn't really have the drive to accomplish that goal." Like most nineteen-year-olds, she didn't really know what she wanted yet out of life. "At that point in my life, life was just kind of happening to me, rather than me happening to it. I was not planning on being a mom. I wasn't actively trying nor actively *not* trying." When she learned she was pregnant, there was no doubt that she was going to do this though she didn't know how she would. She contemplated joining the military so that she could somehow afford to be a parent, and get funding at the same time for college, but she quickly changed her mind, after she learned she would have to wait until after delivery. (You cannot enlist and be pregnant or under legal obligation of supporting a child, according to Military.com.) The military lost a star since April ended up having plenty of time to think about it, and once she had Echo she realized that as a single mom, it would not work, because who

★★★★★★★★

"The one founding father I have a certain degree of respect for is Thomas Jefferson. He read the Koran, he studied other languages, and he felt it was important to learn about other cultures and beliefs, even if they didn't coincide with his own. Of course, he also thought that women would never be able to understand such profound and intellectual pursuits, so I'd have to backhand him to the 18th century."

★★★★★★★★

would be there to raise her? She had never really been around small children, and the one time she took care of her best friend's baby, she rolled off the couch, and April felt certain that her baby would be doomed. Luckily, that did not happen! She did learn how to care for her, and she became more confident as a new mom, and Echo, as a baby was pretty laid-back and happy, which definitely isn't always the case. That ensured a more successful transition for April. Her pregnancy though was very traumatic:

"When the word finally got out, my parents freaked. My dad told me to get married or have an abortion, because mine and my child's lives were going to be extremely difficult without being married. My mom almost kicked me out and the father didn't talk to me for about nine months. About halfway through the pregnancy my mom came around and helped me get all the stuff for the baby. My dad pretty much disowned me, but this really didn't change much because he wasn't really all that active in my life. (My parents got divorced when I was three, and I don't think my dad ever really got to know me, or bonded with me, and our relationship was strained.) Eventually, Echo's father came around and really stepped up to the plate. He's active in her life. We later tried to have the whole relationship thing, but we are not very good for each other."

April is grateful that Echo's father, his parents, and her mom, came through and made an absolute difference in what type of life Echo would have, and that April could provide. Without their help she would have been seemingly stuck in the hand-to-mouth poverty cycle, with no assistance except what meager offerings, if any, she could have gotten from the state, to help her feed her child, and provide some sort of daycare while she worked a low-paying job. Because of their help she was able to have hope for their future since they contributed time, love, and resources, in supporting her in the day-to-day survival of young motherhood.

"I have since made goals, achieved them, and made even more goals. I graduated college in 2004, which I did with the support of my family. If I had not had the support of Echo's grandparents, her dad, and my mom—I would definitely not have gotten to go to, much less graduated from college. Her dad's parents paid for the first couple of semesters of community college. I lived then with my mom, which kind of drove us both crazy, but we worked it out. Her dad would take her on non-visitation days so I could study, write papers, and that kind of thing."

April adds that this beginning was a launching pad for her, which later led to a four-year university degree and good paying work so that she could meet her daughter's needs, and later move her to the most ideal environment, with one of the best school districts in the state, to raise her in: Austin, Texas. Her story demonstrates that moms need support, kids need support, and because of the positive and responsible choices of the father, and the grandparents, we not only have two people who will make the world a better place, but April is going to have a profound impact on the lives of students, and ultimately international relations, and the safety of Americans. The moral of the story is what would have happened in an anti-welfare state if April didn't have the support of her family? Her and Echo would have been thrown to the wolves and most likely eaten. And we as a nation wouldn't benefit from their contributions and April's efforts and ideas. That is in essence the problem with not supporting mothers and children, it not only undermines their lives, but it also undermines ours.

Since becoming a mom she has had numerous trials and tribulations, and every time she thinks she has learned a lesson, Echo blatantly points out to her when she hasn't. April is thankful though that "children definitely reflect ourselves back to us," because it keeps her developing and being self-aware—which is critical in effective parenting. Her upbringing has shaped her identity and her parenting style, and although she loves her parents, it was hard growing up under their separate, but equal roofs.

"My upbringing definitely had the most profound effect. Having been through an abusive childhood, being treated like crap by my dad and his wife, and having my mom be the person she is, has definitely taught me to be who I am. That may sound stupid and very intuitive but the fact that my parents are so completely, unabashedly conservative, and tried to enforce their way of life on me, to my little kid-self, they sucked. Their way of life sucked, who they were as people sucked. I knew I didn't want to suck, so I rebelled and went in the exactly opposite direction."

April hopes her daughter will be creative, and confident enough to follow her own aspirations, be it becoming a paleontologist, writer, artist, etc. April knows that Echo "deserves to be able to live up to her potential without inhibiting that potential." The main thing that could get in Echo's way, besides her own choices, is the world and its negativity and the compulsive need to contain people into modes of 'you can't do this'. April is also very cautious of this in her own actions and word-choices as a mom (since these are generally learned behaviors we got from our parents, which are reinforced by society). As such, April tries to follow *Positive Discipline* by Jane Nelsen:

"It's based on the idea that children will make good decisions for themselves, but you are a model of the behavior you want. Children are capable of making good decisions if given the appropriate information. You can instill your values to a certain degree, but how do you know if those values exist if they are never tested?"

April leans more towards a natural child-rearing approach and attachment parenting. She also is appalled by overt authoritarian parenting styles,

"I don't like being told what to do, why would I do that to somebody else? If given the appropriate opportunity Echo will make the best decision and is quite capable of working out her own issues. Dr. Greene, the author of *The Explosive Child*, calls it 'Plan B'. It's a collaborative problem-solving process. I don't think punishment for punishment's sake works. Most things in life have their own consequences. If you skip breakfast, you're hungry, if you don't want to wear a coat, you're cold. I don't push either issue, and if she complains I don't jump her case. I generally say something like, 'you're hungry', or 'your cold', and let her come to the conclusion that she needs to eat and put her coat on. She reacts very well when she's allowed to exercise her creativity to solve problems. I've also found that being pro-active with her, telling her what my expectations are in certain situation, helps ease the way. I used to joke with other parents in certain situations that usually are stressful that I lock her in the closet. The truth is we both know what to expect from the other."

April found herself putting her philosophy into practice, including some trial and error runs, after they moved from Dallas to Austin a few years ago. There was the stress of making new friends, and adapting, and additional financial burdens were placed on them. She learned after the fact that Echo doesn't transition well, and was surprised when her daughters anger came bubbling up at her new school.

"Some of it can be attributed to just plain anger, and not knowing a better way to handle it. Some of it is hard-wired to an extent. Echo's very intelligent, but she doesn't put things together like everybody else does, and this can lead to friction in a classroom setting, especially with teachers that expect a higher level of conformity. Echo's definitely got her own ideas about the way the world should work, and sometimes they don't coincide with how adults think the world should work, and that causes a great deal of stress.

She's had violent outbursts, hitting, destruction of property; she yelled at a character in a math program on the computer and started shaking the monitor out of frustration. She's been suspended for a total of nine days, and sent to another school for five days, in third grade. I think she wasn't being listened to, her complaints weren't allowed to come out all the way, and her process was interrupted. I definitely lost track of my own philosophy and started taking a harder line in an effort to steer her back. What ultimately ended up happening was I ended up pushing her further to the edge. The school wasn't helping in this situation, because they were trying to bully her back into submission. She's a lot like me in that respect, she doesn't submit to anybody's will.

Her individuality is a good thing and a bad thing. I encourage her to define herself on her own terms, the unfortunate side effect of that, for now, is that a lot of people don't allow kids to do their own thing. They are somehow afraid that children will automatically make bad decisions, and it's a reflection of you as a person. In a way, it's kind of true that children are a reflection of ourselves, our strengths and weaknesses, but at the same time, were not completely responsible for the decisions our children make. We're responsible to our children, to provide shelter, a safe home, clothes and food, but as far as their decisions, we can't make those for them. I think it's a serious folly on parents to try to control and inhibit their children from growing up 'too fast' or trying to make decisions for them. It generally ends up backfiring in some way, generally as kids grow up to be teens, or even into adulthood.

That doesn't mean that you should just allow children to do whatever they want, just because they want, you do have influence over their decisions. The way I look at it, she can go through this now at ten, or later when she's a teenager, or bottle it all in and go through it in her adult years, but eventually she's going to have to figure out who she is as a person; better for her to get some of it worked out as a kid than as an adult."

Another element of April's parental awareness is paying attention to her daughter's moods (as well as her own) and having a sense of emotional intelligence:

"A lot of people have this idea that being in touch with one's emotions means you're going to cry or have violent outbursts, but the fact of the matter is, if you can assess how you're feeling in any given situation, you won't need to have outbursts. It's far more acceptable to say, 'I really don't like this, I don't feel …' than cussing someone out and screaming 'I hate you' and beating up on people. That's very much the environment I was raised in. If I didn't agree with my parents, or my sister, or anybody, I didn't have a good way of expressing myself because of what was modeled to me. For a really long time I had two conflicting emotions: happy and angry."

April has re-raised herself into the person she wants to be, and what type of role-model and mom she wants to be. She feels her biggest obstacle was overcoming herself, and her own short-comings, and ego. "I have a tendency to jump to conclusions, and end up burning bridges with people that I need to have on my side." She finally found a cause to believe in and followed it—being a mom. Her journey of self-growth

Need parenting help? Rebel Mom April suggests these books:

Positive Discipline **by Jane Nelsen**

The Explosive Child **by Ross W. Greene, Ph.D.**

Getting Past No **by William Ury**

Getting to Yes **by William Ury and Roger Fisher**

How to Talk so Kids will Listen and Listen so Kids will Talk **by Adele Faber and Elaine Mazlish.**

And don't forget her favorite read *Hip Tranquil Chick* by Kimberly Wilson!

has empowered her as an individual and as a mother. Some additional books she cites critical to this development are: *Getting Past No* by William Ury. It's a challenging read on how to stand up for yourself without being confrontational, but cooperative. She also read *Getting to Yes* by William Ury and Roger Fisher, an art of negotiation self-guidance book, and *How to Talk so Kids will Listen and Listen so Kids will Talk* by Adele Faber and Elaine Mazlish. This book is a step-by-step toolkit for parents who need, or want to improve communication with their kids and family. It's based on their hugely successful and beneficial workshops. Lastly, she read *Hip Tranquil Chick* by Kimberly Wilson which places emphasis on living a life in balance, with yoga at the core, but with flair. [I googled it today, and wow, the book seems incredibly fun and would be an awesome rare indulgent treat in the tub! It also has an appealing and cute website titled after the book too.]

April has been a practicing yogic enthusiast, who has delved deeper in Buddhism, for over ten years now. She credits this spiritual discipline in helping her develop the flexibility to sustain the constantly changing winds and storms of parenthood, as well as adulthood:

> "It can be a deeply spiritual practice. It can get your ass in shape, but if you dig deeper into it, you can find so much more there. Beyond the Gucci yoga mat with matching bag and expensive yoga clothes, it has a lot to teach about balancing modern life. I like that more people are coming to their mats. Maybe they'll take that practice off the mat and find a greater meaning.

"It can be a deeply spiritual practice. It can get your ass in shape, but if you dig deeper into it, you can find so much more there. Beyond the Gucci yoga mat with matching bag and expensive yoga clothes, it has a lot to teach about balancing modern life. I like that more people are coming to their mats. Maybe they'll take that practice off the mat and find a greater meaning."

We live in a world of gross-over consumption. Americans are the fattest people; we consume more resources than any other country on the planet, including China and India (which have the highest populations). That fact alone is pretty daunting. It's time to realize that the world is completely incapable of supporting six billion people. I crack up whenever I see those bumper stickers that say something about the human fetus being an endangered species. My reaction is, 'Are you paying attention?' If something can awaken the interdependence we have with the world yoga is definitely at the top of that list. So if more people jump onto the 'fad' of yoga, the merrier.

It's definitely a practice that very young, very old, and in between people can do on a daily basis. Much more so than pumping iron at the gym, and doing extreme sports of whichever variety. It's also something that's existed longer than Western religion. It doesn't negate any of them; if anything, it deepens religious practice, because you're trying to attain a higher form of yourself. It's non-dogmatic, and it doesn't judge if you fall off a little bit to the side. It's not about becoming like God, or anything close to the sort, it's about being mindful in your decisions."

As we reflected back on our individual eclipses, and struggles, as older teens, [That's when we first met. We shared a mutual best friend and used to BBQ at the park with our then-boyfriends and drink Olde English and Mickey's.] moms, and students, one word emerges: breathe. Breathing deep is a core technique in yoga exercise, and also in defraying the stress of school, work, motherhood, and life as it became full for us both. April shares her tricks of the trade:

"I had to be able to balance all of it. I had to take days just to go to the park. I tended to be in class every day, and I tried to work my school schedule around Echo's school schedule, and then purposefully schedule 'free' time where it was just me and her, no books, school, or work involved. The biggest stress-buster secret I have is you must take time to de-compress. I'm not a structured, super scheduled person. When I was in actual college, not community college, I went to UNT in Denton and lived in Irving, a forty-five minute commute one-way. I regretted that I couldn't squeeze study time in there, because I really wanted my time home to be the time with my daughter, but I took time to listen to music as loud as I wanted, to scream, yell, work things out in my head. The drive time was probably the best time to just leave all the stress of everything behind and work out plans for dealing with all of it."

April feels that children are incredibly undervalued and that we expect them to 'do', but in reality they're just figuring out what we already know. "They know what we end up covering with all the crap of socialization. I know my daughter makes a whole lot more sense about life, than adults do. She's very astute." April is certain that the present is the only thing that really exists and to an extent we should live and let live. She thinks you do not, or should not have to compromise your talents, strengths, interests, and personality to make it in the world … but relents that the way we have built the world, or rather the way it is designed to contain us, prohibits this natural essence of being who we truly are. She is determined to provide Echo options to help her navigate the sea of the human landscape in how it should be, naturally is, and both within and outside of its artificial containments. She admits though that for her, life and parenting is a simply a work in progress.

April doesn't know many moms she can relate to, but she feels this attributes more to the fact that she doesn't talk a lot about who she is with people and she doesn't have a lot of identifiers about what she is into, so people just don't approach her. She also acknowledges that she is also somewhat timid about approaching others out of fear of rejection. Some of that stems from when she was younger and first became involved in the punk music scene which was filled with teenagers emitting a 'holier/punker-than-thou attitude'. [Cliques have always been cliques, and they infest every social circle, even self-proclaimed radical ones. It's just seemingly human nature to both want to be part of a group, but to also have a compelling need to ostracize others to better your perceived social ranking.] She is thankful for some of the teenage animosity since it has enabled her to live beyond labels. She did later feel more associated with the subculture world through her more eastern lifestyle and philosophies, but now that …"Everybody and their dog is getting into the yoga thing, a two-thousand-year-old fad in the making, I'm not so sure anymore."

For the first time she feels rather normal, now that the choices she made early in life and the direction she took, are suddenly being mirrored back from the mainstream world. She does know that all isn't as it seems and that people are still too repressed here, especially when compared to other societies, despite yogic philosophies making a slight dent in it. She thinks that creativity and freedom have much to offer everybody, and that is something we should pass down to our own children instead of repression. Repression and fierce competition tend to converge, and carry over to how the general world works and how other parents perceive her.

"Most people my age are just getting married and starting their families. I have more or less had mine established for ten years. The parents that have children the same age as Echo are older, and see me as the less experienced kid sister. Her friends see me as the cool young mom. I think people see me being really over lenient, and letting my daughter walk over me. I don't think that's the case, but then I'm not the one on the outside looking in.

I think a lot of people think I'm her older sister more than her mother. I've gotten a lot of surprised looks when she calls me 'mom'. I live in a pretty upper middle class, upper class area. Most of the moms in this area are in their thirties and forties and they kind of look at me as this little kid that doesn't fit their mold. There's definitely the element of competition between the moms to see who can be the most involved in their kids schools, and whose kid has earned the highest honors. My daughter was in the advanced language arts class. To get into that class, she had to write an essay. Of all the kids in her grade, she was the only one that got a four out of four possible. Two parents were questioning why their precocious and brilliant child didn't make it into said class. The school used my daughter's writing sample as an example. I know parenting is a competitive sport for some, but not for me."

April continues to be scrutinized by her neighbors, and while their antics amuse her, she does hope the enlightenment that underlies the yoga discipline does take root and has a positive effect on them and their kids, and thus the little part of the world she and Echo live in. She's gearing up for teaching and getting ready for the next stage of parenting: the teenage years. She is definitely confident that with the environment and principles their home is made of, that they will be much better positioned for the years to come than most households. Love, yoga and respect are what it's all about … "Motherhood is definitely a spiritual growth process. Having my daughter has taught me more about myself, who I am, and who I want to be, how those things are the same, and they differ."

"Having a child really has given my life meaning and it's given me the motivation to do something with my life other than be content with the fast food, waitressing, factory life."

Kaisea
Cosmetology Student
Sexy Seamstress
Cool Crafter
Fast Food Worker
Recovering Addict
Lebanon, Missouri.

Kaisea is a bold, spirited, opinionated mom in her late twenties from Chicago who raises eyebrows in her new small town that's big on trout fishing, camping, and gun expos. She spends her downtime creating computer animations and illustrations, writing, and making her own custom clothing. She went from "hitting rock bottom to being on cloud nine" after less than two years of committing to a more stable drug-and-alcohol-free life.

Some of her favorite artists have battled similar problems. She likes poet Jim Carroll because, "He comes from a hard life and has had to work hard to recover from addiction and make a life for himself. I can relate." She also relates to the musician and poet Tim Armstrong from Rancid for similar reasons and finds herself getting lost in a trance and literally conversing with his music. She's also attracted to the "twisted and amazing" work of Clive Barker. She now finds happiness in the simplicity and beauty of everyday life,

> "Hearing a song I can dance to. I get excited about the little things all the time, spending time with my family, seeing my son smile or getting him to laugh, getting to see my friends, getting a night off from work. And hugs; hugs are some of the bestest things ever!"

Kaisea loves "being girlie and playing dress up" and is going to be very proud of herself when she is done with school; she wants her family to be proud of her too. Her son Seth is only five-months-old and she knows that in order to have a better tomorrow for him, she needs to make a better today for herself. Completing cosmetology school will be the first step of many she will take on her path to success, as she hopes to open her own salon within five years. She wants it to have a mellow and comfortable atmosphere, and plans to include a coffee shop inside—so that people can come right in and feel at home. She intends to learn a variety of techniques between now and then so that she may offer anything from unusual styles to mainstream cuts.

She and her husband just bought their first house, and Seth was conceived on their wedding night. But before she got to this chapter in her life, she had to rewrite her own story; one which had gone horribly wrong. Kaisea started drinking when she was only fourteen-years-old and started doing drugs at age fifteen. The two led to an addiction right away, and she didn't stop completely until she was twenty-seven. At first it was alcohol, marijuana and pills, and soon included cocaine and L.S.D. (Lysergic acid diethylamide); by the time she left home at twenty-one she was doing meth, which lasted six months.

"I got real bad on that stuff really quick, so I realized I needed to stop or lose my sanity. I stopped doing all drugs when I was twenty-two, except for the occasional joint here and there until I was twenty-seven. I've been sober ever since, but in all honesty I still get cravings once in a while."

The problems that led to such an early addiction in life were complex. She didn't feel comfortable with herself and felt out of place. She also suffered from depression, which had been undiagnosed. She remembers how the adults in her life dealt with their issues:

"I was looking to belong somewhere in life. I started drinking because I knew some older kids who did it, and I didn't have any friends so I was trying to be cool. Besides, I don't ever remember being told that drinking was bad and I saw my step-dad do it. God, how cliché is that? I was a depressed kid though, and getting drunk seemed to make things better. Plus, having people to hang out with made me feel like I belonged somewhere. So yeah, I was learning how to self-medicate at an early age. That's how I dealt with any bad things that came my way for a long time."

It wasn't something at the age of fourteen she had imagined her life would consist of—addiction and destruction. Generally, it sneaks up on you when you least expect it. Kaisea doesn't remember much about her life between fourteen and twenty-seven. She describes her twenties as particularly damaging:

"There really are a lot of things that are hazy. There were a lot of drunken nights at bars, driving home when I shouldn't have. There were one-night stands and casual flings. Spontaneously moving across the country to Las Vegas to live with some asshole I couldn't stand, and then when I was twenty-five getting into a chaotic relationship with a guy who was gorgeous, but completely bad for me. We fought, we screamed, he hated that I was punk and wanted to change me into a preppy lil' flower. Then there was the guy from Florida … So, to sum things up, drama. My life was a soap opera because I couldn't get enough drama. I created bad situations so I could live in chaos. But needless to say I never had a dull moment, ha-ha."

It was when she "drank herself homeless" that she knew something had to be done—she moved back in with her parents and she put herself through rehab. She was taking life a day-at-a-time and focusing on sobriety. She was toying with the idea of going back to school when she met the man who would become her husband. She has realized since then that she is a strong person; before she got clean she thought she was weak. She asserts, "I'm nowhere near the person I was two years ago. I was a fucked-up gal, but cleaned myself up before having a family." Part of getting clean meant she had to address the underlying mental health issues.

> "I'm a self-destructive person. I'm also bi-polar with an anxiety disorder and a borderline personality disorder. Plus, I'm an addict. I've had to learn to live with mental instability and to quit self-medicating myself. Accepting the fact that I'm gonna be sick in the head for the rest of my life was hard to do, but I'm really okay with it. I do know that I need to take medication or I'm unbearable to be around. But with help, I've learned to deal and I function well, mostly. My husband is a saint for putting up with me.
>
> I'm proud of overcoming addiction. I still deal with it, but it's not as hard. I know the rough patch is over and I'm proud of picking myself up out of the gutter and becoming who I am today. And in a year I will be proud of finishing school too."

Her advice for anyone who needs help is to reach out to loved ones for support and be prepared to distance yourself from anyone who is in the same boat. Although this may be hard, it is absolutely essential until you get past the rough patch and sobriety becomes a way of life. And when you find yourself in an environment where temptation is present, be strong. If you find yourself wavering, leave. She also suggests defining your own recovery mantra:

"I'm proud of overcoming addiction. I still deal with it, but it's not as hard. I know the rough patch is over and I'm proud of picking myself up out of the gutter and becoming who I am today. And in a year I will be proud of finishing school too."

"With the drinking I used to always say: 'I'll never drink again', until I actually quit. To this day I refuse to say I'll never have another drink because that puts pressure on me. If I leave myself open to the option of having a drink, I want it less. It's what works for me."

She met her husband Pat a few months after she had sobered up. They'd been running in the same social circles for years, but had never met (even though there is video footage of them standing next to each other). They were finally introduced by members of a band called the Overdogs from Lebanon that they are both friends with. She thought he was a "typical, angry, punk rock guy with his nose pierced and his studded leather jacket," but she was surprised to find that he was real soft-spoken and shy. He was attracted to her new perspective on life and her foot-tall emerald green mohawk. She knew she liked him, but wanted to take a different approach with him and "made him work" to get her phone number. She told him that if he wanted to call her he could get her number from their mutual friend, Rob. Two days later he called and they made plans to meet that night.

She got butterflies when he walked in, and they ended up holding hands. Later that week she went to his house for a New Year's Eve party. He saw that she wasn't drinking and he choose not to either; that night they talked until dawn …

"We ended up talking on the couch forever. I really hardly remember anyone else being there. But that was the night we had our first kiss and I swear I knew I was going to marry this guy. He was just so different than anyone else I had met. We hung out every night from that point on. I moved in with him about two months later, we got engaged a month after that and got married in September. It happened really fast, but we just knew we were supposed to be together."

She feels lucky to have met her soul-mate and to have had a baby together. She describes her husband's parenting as:

"He's just the proudest daddy ever! He works really hard to be a good provider. He said he feels more pressure to make sure that everything's done for us … like having a house. And he's working really hard to get us a heating system in here. We're just using space heaters right now. He just really puts us first and I really think he would do just about anything to keep us happy and comfortable. I think Pat was made to be a father; he's just so good at it!"

Motherhood wasn't something she chose, it just sort of chose her. When they got married, it just happened. They "sometimes used condoms," but she wasn't sure she could even get pregnant "due to having irregular periods and how much abuse" she had put her body through previously. When Kaisea learned she was pregnant, it was a complete shock for her, and it took her a couple of months to stop freaking out. It's not that she didn't want to be a mom, she was just extremely worried that she would be bad at it and wasn't ready for it.

"I was scared I wouldn't be a good mother. I wasn't sure if I'd have the patience for the job. I worried a little about people's opinions of me as a parent. Once the initial shock wore off though, I was planning on being a stay-at-home mom and letting my husband work. I wanted to be there for every little moment of my baby's life. I was really hoping it was a girl. Thinking back though, I don't know why; my lil' boy is so much fun!"

They had tons of support from her family and his, and from their friends. They spent the rest of the pregnancy preparing, working, saving, and celebrating the transition. She was only able to stay-at-home for the first few months of Seth's life, due to financial needs. Then she resumed working full-time at the fast food restaurant; Pat and her split work times, and taking care of Seth, and she just eased into motherhood. She had worried she wouldn't have motherly instincts and was pleasantly surprised that parenting seemed to come quite naturally to her and that it was easier than she'd feared. She acknowledges that it is hard work, but she thought she would never get a minute to herself, and she still does. She'd also expected her social life to die, "Well, that part really did happen! We've only gone out twice since he was born, but I don't mind it!" Luckily, some of her friends still come by to say hi and visit, since they understand her life has changed and the dynamics are different.

"I've never been so happy! I've never been so busy either! My life is just so full of love. I never knew a person could love someone so much until I gave birth, it's just so intense. I live my life in constant amazement now. I'm stunned that I made something so completely beautiful and wonderful. I mean that came out of me!!! I've never been so proud of anything either! I'm definitely on a schedule now too which is new to me. I have to do everything on his time. Like now, he's sleeping so I can finally do the interview and fill this thing out!"

Once Kaisea is done with school and she has transitioned into her new career, they want to have another baby, before Seth gets too old, so probably before he starts kindergarten. Considering Seth is still a baby, and she just started school, after layering paid work back into the mix, her life has become very vigorous, but satisfying.

"Having a child really has given my life meaning and it's given me the motivation to do something with my life other than be content with the fast food, waitressing, and factory life. It's hard. I don't know how I do it half the time. The only thing I can think of is drink lots of coffee and get as many naps in as possible to preserve your sanity. And try to have people around who can help you. And always make sure that you have plenty of time to spend with your child and family because being a parent is the most important job a person will have. Your family should always come first."

Kasiea recognizes how difficult this balance can be, and tries to live by that principle. For now, she is supplementing sleep with naps and extra coffee, but she knows she can't do that for the long-term, just the short-term while she is getting her cosmetology schooling. She doesn't really know what to expect as a mom, she just knows she is going to do the best she can, and hopes everything turns out all right. She does however expect her son to, "Grow up with manners and respect. Knowing he's the child and I am the parent, but at the same time learning to be his own person." She wants him to be a leader and not a follower, and to have a strong inner-confidence and belief-in-himself. She hopes this will develop his core self-esteem, and deter him from going down the path she did. She also hopes he is kind, open-minded, and non-judgmental of others. She thinks the only way she can instill this in him is for her to live her life in the same manner. She is a firm believer that "Children are going to imitate us to an extent. After all, we are their first teachers." She also thinks too many parents forget this and end up acting more like baby-sitters than parents.

"I think the way most people are raising their children now is really crappy! I see all these little kids yelling at their parents and disrespecting everything ... What the hell happened to discipline and learning to respect others? Parents nowadays literally seem like they just don't care. They're lazy about their jobs as parents! And when the hell did it become okay to have an obese eight-year-old? It seems like too many parents just give their child some junk food and sit them in front of the TV to keep 'em quiet. How is this okay? Kids are supposed to be outside playing and not being lazy coach potatoes!!! I am constantly getting mad about the way people are raising their children. I can't stand to see these misbehaving lil' fat kids getting away with murder ... oh, it pisses me off! I really think most parents don't spend enough time with their kids either. I know everyone has to work, I have to do it too, but when I'm home I'm mostly playing with my baby cause, well, it's what parents are supposed to do. And I just can't get enough of him.

I also think in today's society we put too much emphasis on being rich, or having expensive things. I think people have really forgotten how to enjoy the little things. Remember, a kid can have as much fun with a box and sticks as an expensive toy. We're taught to be materialistic ... and we lose out on imagination when we become like that. We lose out too on being involved with our kids, and we lose out on exercise."

As a mom with vividly colored hair and tattoos, she does encounter some serious close-mindedness and rudeness when she ventures out.

"I do know that there are people who probably think people like me shouldn't breed. I still get comments like, 'If I had been your parent then I would have locked you in a closest until you could look like a normal person.' I am in the very middle of the Bible Belt now though, and I know things are a little different here than the rest of the country."

Kasiea feels that too many kids, especially in the Bible Belt, suffer a double-whammy from either parental neglect or the baby-sitter parent syndrome combined with a casual enforcement of going along with the majority (even when it's inherently detrimental to the community and the individual). She feels that somewhere along the lines consumerism has been confused with identity. She adheres to the school of thought that parents are supposed to teach their children to grow into great adults, providing them with enriching life experiences and allowing them to form their own opinions, so that they might develop into their own persons rather than conforming to shallow social standards of identity tied up in monetary value. She concludes that if you want great people you must nurture great kids and embrace open-mindedness, do things differently and talk through different experiences—from the norm to the aberrant—and find varying outcomes for those experiences in life. In essence, spend time with your kids, be a role model, set the example, and be flexible even in your own ideas and opinions. She doesn't think you can go wrong with that parenting formula.

"I also think in today's society we put too much emphasis on being rich, or having expensive things. I think people have really forgotten how to enjoy the little things. Remember, a kid can have as much fun with a box and sticks as an expensive toy. We're taught to be materialistic ... and we lose out on imagination when we become like that. We lose out too on being involved with our kids, and we lose out on exercise."

Kasiea always strives to be happy and believes happiness is something kids need to see more of. She sees way too much violence going on in the world and attributes it to there being "too many conservatives, and conservatives suck!" She thinks conservatives are always provoking people to fight each other by being hateful and judgmental. She's okay with the fact that most conservatives don't like her since she doesn't fit the norm, isn't mean, and doesn't care about the Gap, or labels, or what people think about her in general. She thinks the issue with the world is that not enough people try to be good people, and maybe they don't know how to due to incompetent or mean child-rearing. She advises me that if anyone gets anything from her story, she would want it to be that all anyone ever needs to do is try their best to be a good person. That is the basis of her life, and her parenting, and she concludes it is essential for our collective future.

Kaisea remembers being attracted to the counterculture way of life at a very young age:

> "I still remember the first time I saw a mohawk. I was seven-years-old and on a class field trip to the museum, and there was a punk guy and his girlfriend. They just looked so amazing to me, I was fascinated. I was sent to Catholic school in fourth grade and I was immediately picked on. Cliques had already formed and I was an outsider, and no matter what I did, I just couldn't be accepted. I was beat-up and constantly degraded and I just couldn't figure out why. So I became more and more drawn to punk rock and heavy metal and non-conformists. I figured out if they were gonna hate me and make fun of me I would give them a reason, or more like I would give myself an explanation. By the time I was in high school, I was dying my hair and had piercings. I got my first tattoo when I was fifteen.
>
> I've never fit in with most people and once I started expressing myself through my appearance I instantly felt better; more comfortable. And it didn't matter to me what other people said because I learned how to be happy with me."

The way Kaisea sees it, people are people, and each and every person has a reason for being who they are—be it the classroom bully, the cruel and violent school girl cliques, or the boy with no supposed future in the leather jacket—and mostly they are all taught stereotypes and have learned ways of being mean or cruel to mask their insecurities. However, at the core of each of these basic personality profiles there are elements of truth for who that person is and will be. How those traits are magnified really depends on the household in which they are raised and the immediate social culture of which they are a part of, basically society is this way by its own doing. If we ask why, we can start to scratch at the surface and see a better way of living and being together in a society. On a more intimate note, she thinks there are actually people who would love to have a mohawk like she does, but lack the courage. There are also, "people who think that people like us are freaks, but those types are close-minded anyway so it doesn't really matter." She adds:

> "I try not to judge people, but when it comes to the mainstream letting ten-year old girls wear make-up and dress slutty like Britney, that's pretty sick. And the fact that the country collectively has become idiots politically bothers me. But other than that, to each their own."

Kasiea likes punk music because she feels you can't really label it,

> "It can be political, fast, and angry. It's a music made for working class folks who don't fit-in with the rest of society. It comes with its own class of people and when it comes down to it, there's so many different ways to describe it. I don't even know why I'm trying. So I like it because it speaks directly to me."

Kasiea has Rancid's … *And Out Come the Wolves* album cover tattooed on her thigh as a tribute. It was her first professionally done tattoo. The rest of her tattoos, including a NIN logo, are self-done just like her piercings. [I did my own nostril at seventeen and about ten rings in each ear cartridge with the piercing gun from work. But I didn't know anything about the role and function, or placement of my nerve endings. If you hit the nerve you can cause nerve damage and loss of sensation, or area-death. Luckily, that didn't happen to Kaisea, or me, for that matter.]

She doesn't know any moms like herself where she lives, but she has a few friends online. She thinks all moms can relate to wanting to keep their children safe and sharing a profound love for their children, but have little in common outside of those emotions because they live in very different worlds. However, she thinks our world can help the mainstream world become a much better place to live if our love of freedom of expression, respect for children and people, and open-minded living are adopted authentically. The mainstream culture has already widely began to adopt sub/countercultures varying fashions, some philosophical and political ideas (animal rights, green living, bohemianism, etc) so why not? Changing the core of a sick society is a way to make it healthy, which is a good thing for our kids. Kasiea's final thoughts are, "I know I can overcome obstacles and I've been through a lot of things most people never will. My life experiences made me; from being homeless to being fearless, and being reckless at times, from battling addiction to being two-years sober." Amen.

**Since this interview: Kaisea and Pat divorced a few years afterwards, and Seth now has a beautiful little baby sister named Scarlet that Kaisea recently had with her current partner.*

"I am a mother, first and foremost. I am a Christian who also studies Buddhist practices. I am a single mother of two young children. I am a friend. I am an activist against child abuse. I am an ER nurse. I save lives. I am proud of who I have become."

Picture by Maria Hibbs at SquaresvilleStudios.com

Blaire
Optimist
Pragmatic Realist
Pin-up Poker Player
Emergency Room Nurse
Future Medical Doctor
Legal Nurse Consultant
Photographer
Dallas, Texas.

Blaire is a sprightly, brilliant, and daring woman who saves lives for a living, and helps those who are suffering. She has a heart of gold, and a light way of lifting those up around her, courtesy of her clever and caring nature. She loves baking, watching baseball games, and playing Nintendo. She has a wicked poker hand and a hearty laugh. She enlivens a room with a jolt of energy, humor, and positivity. It is no wonder she has two wondrously happy and keenly intelligent children, Jude and Presley, who are a reflection of her great mothering and the home environment they are raised in. She has two side businesses to help her make enough money for a comfortable lifestyle, and freeing her up to be a stay-at-home mom per se with a full-time job. She literally works when the kids are asleep at night. She thanks the stars every day that she has an incredible energy level that lets her keep this up.

She loves reading, and sometimes the ER is slow at night, so she gets to catch up on some of her favorite works, such as *Diseases and Disorders: A Nursing Therapeutics Manual* by Marilyn Sawyer Sommers, *The Hobbit* by J.R.R. Tolkien, *A Clockwork Orange* by Anthony Burgess, cartoonist Nicole Hollander's amusing rants in her epic book *Ma, Can I Be A Feminist and Still Like Men? Lyrics from Life*. She frequently is shuffling her iPod back-and-forth between her favorite bands and musicians like Gogol Bordello, Concrete Blonde, Ray Charles, Bad Brains, Dwight Yoakam and Bob Marley.

Besides great books and artists, she loves movies that really speak to her inner being's organic, wild child side such as *Edward Scissorhands*, *True Romance*, *Urban Cowboy* and the movie *Frida*. That inner child led to some frightening detours though before she became a nurse, and later a wife and mother.

Her teen years were spent being your "run of the mill punk rock chick," and her weekends were reserved for going to shows, partying, and drinking. She is very grateful that somehow during this time as a hell-raiser she managed to graduate from high school. It was her growing and stretching period, but she is frank, that she "didn't contribute anything worthy of mentioning." She feels that she wasn't being the person she knew she needed to be, but that's in retrospect.

"I was blessed with a very strict, very loving dad and maybe not so blessed with my vivacious, larger-than-life mother, who was brought down by alcohol, psych problems, and issues of codependency. I say blessed with a strict dad, as I needed that. I was already going with my very untamed nature, and putting them through hell, but I felt their hearts hurting for me. I always knew that there was a difference with me; I knew bigger and better things were awaiting me; I just had to settle down and let them happen. I was living for the present with no attempt being made to be a contributing member of society."

During this time, she ended up leaving Texas to go explore the U.S. with her best friend Kim, and some squatters they had just met. She learned after they had left, that one of the young men they were traveling with had recently committed some horrific crimes, which soon after landed him on death row …

"I flipped my shit, of course! And I had to plan a way out—a way out from there and a way out from that mess of a life. I thought how did I get to be where I thought I was bulletproof? It was really a surprise, that I was even still alive. So I got back to Dallas, moved away from everyone, and began to build my life. I went to court on a docket, had my warrants dismissed, enrolled in college, and quit squandering away a brain that was meant for being used."

She isn't proud of the choices she made during this time in her life as a young adolescent. If she could change some of her past choices, she would in a heartbeat—as long as it still led her to where she is now, as a successful nurse, mother, and a children's advocate. Her path to healing was through symbolic and soulful purging and creation; her path to nursing was both chance and genealogy.

"I left what I knew was my life and headed for the local community college, where I took several years of basics and tons of art classes. I needed this. I needed to remember that I was a smart girl, though I was not sure where I was headed. I ran into a girl at school that I went to high school with and she told me she was going to go for nursing. This was so foreign to me at that time, but I became interested. It was only after I had been accepted to nursing school that I realized that this was right up my alley. I had been a special-ed aide in the high school I went to and worked at an adult daycare as a young teenager. My grandmother was a nurse in the military, and I thought this was special and we could bond through [it].

It was funny when I first got accepted; I do believe I may have been the only student ever that started nursing school with blue hair. I was a bit different from the rest of the students, but it was there that I met one of my very best friends in the world, Annette. She was popular and sweet, with her brilliant red hair and beaming smile. She saw that I was alone, and was not even about to let someone be isolated and she walked straight up to invite me to her study group. She then went on to be there for the birth of my babies. We joke now that we are identical on the inside and completely opposite on the outside. She's my sister."

It was also chance that she had met a good and sweet man, before she had left on what she thought, naively, would be a traveling adventure. She found herself in a dark place very far from home, faced with the gruesome realities of the worst human malevolence. She came running home, literally, running for her life. She reached out to that sweet man with the benevolent aura she had briefly known before her departure, and he rescued her. She stayed with him, and he nurtured her through this grieving period. She was still frightened, and he was soothing, loving and caring, the antithesis to the traveling partner she fled. She knew his heart was pure and good. As her strength solidified and she became whole again, and life started flowing through her veins once more, she married that sweet man, who brought her "chocolate covered gummy bears all the time." Before long, they found themselves following 'the plan': marriage, buying a house, being happy, and then having babies. Life for them was good.

They had been married five years when they had their first child Jude. She figured out fast "what you have planned may as well be thrown out the window. Babies don't really follow our set of guidelines." But life as a mother agreed with her, and she thinks motherhood is "inspiring and humbling and hard!" It took her a little while to get used to the fact that it's a job that the clock never stops ticking on. That is a culture-shock for most moms, and so is the additional higher dimension of life and love that suddenly engulfs you, filling a void that you never knew was missing in the first place. Blaire fell head-over-heels and found her calling: parenting. Jude was still a toddler when she and her husband had their second child, a daughter, named Presley. Blaire's thoughts on the subject are:

"Motherhood … What the hell was the purpose of my life before this? I ask myself this often. What was I doing that really mattered in this world? And then there was them, these tiny little people that changed everything! Everything! I then wanted to be the best person/caretaker/role-model for my children that ever existed and believed that they deserved no less than that. Being a mother means everything to me. They are my world! I will never understand how people can take this monumental role so lightly sometimes. It breaks my heart to hear of a child who has suffered at the hands of a selfish, evil person. It is our jobs, as mothers, and members of humanity, to speak out about this and prevent these things from occurring! I know when I observe my children, who show me every day their magnificent compassion, unconditional love, budding brilliance, blissful demeanors, perfect affection towards me, each other, and the people they know … I know that I have done something right in this world and what better to get right than our children."

Overall, the young couple felt isolated though as people and parents.

"We were really alone on this one! There were no offerings of support, no village, just us. Shortly after, it became just me. Ninety percent of the help I had was hired. This has taught me everything about how to be autonomous and self-sufficient, so for that, I suppose, I am thankful."

By the time she had Presley, their marriage was on its last leg. The overwhelming demand of parenting and responsibility, which largely fell on Blaire's shoulders, took its toll. They decided their marriage wasn't savable and filed for divorce. Blaire was heart-broken.

"I became a single mom when Presley was just a neonate. I was devastated and sacred, and was faced with being alone for the first time in my life, all while having a boob in a mouth what seemed like twenty-four hours a day. I joked that I could have stood up, let go of the child, and my son Jude would have been able to hang on to me with that latch! But things got real scary, real fast. One day I was living what I saw as my perfect life and the next it was gone. I never cried in front of my children, and my son was confused enough. I remember talking to a very great guy friend of mine, saying how I just did not know what I was going to do, how I was going to get through this. His reply was inspiring! He told me, 'Blaire you are the strongest woman I have ever met, you are even stronger than me, you got this!' And I realized I did! Though I was married, I was still on my own. I put my big girl panties back on and crowd-rushed head-first into my new life."

Today she feels much more confident, and secure in who she is as a woman, and a mom, than she did on those first few distressing nights when reality set in. For anyone facing a separation or divorce, her words of solace are:

"It was hard, but my only advice would be to allow yourself to cry (only as many times as years you were together), pray (to something or someone, regardless of what you believe, there is a spiritual ear listening), and look at those kids as often as you can, and see what wonderfulness came out of it ultimately. I don't regret any of that, because I have him to thank for these two wonderful beings. Presley was too young to really get it, but my son, was confused. I just talked as plainly as I could and answered everything, even when I didn't want to talk about why daddy was gone. I never said an ill word about their dad, not to this day, in front of them. That was very important to me as I remember my folks just downright degrading each other in front of me as a small child, and I hated it."

A couple of years have passed since they divorced, and Blaire has realized a few

★★★★★★★★

One day I was living what I saw as my perfect life and the next it was gone. I remember talking to a very great guy friend of mine, saying how I just did not know what I was going to do, how I was going to get through this. His reply was inspiring! He told me, 'Blaire you are the strongest woman I have ever met, you are even stronger than me, you got this!' And I realized I did! Though I was married, I was still on my own. I put my big girl panties back on and crowd-rushed head-first into my new life."

★★★★★★★★

things about herself, as well as about her ex. She thinks that she subconsciously chose a sweet, gentle, but passive partner, because of her Type A personality, and the circumstances she was in at that time. And although she loved him with all her heart, she looks back and thinks ultimately with or without parenting stresses, their marriage would have eventually ended.

> "I was in charge of everything: bills, appointments, children, and kept up my own lawn. He was, and is, a very good dad fortunately. Sometimes I would joke (tongue-in-cheek) that I had three children. I chose this type of man long ago, so that is the repercussion of that decision. As a side note, I now tend to date very strong-willed, opinionated, contributing men. I want my thoughts to be challenged and my opinions to be explored. I need more of a mental companion as well as a physical companion."

It took a few months after the divorce before her ex came back around, and resumed his role as father. Blaire knows that he loves their children "with all his heart, no doubt about it." They co-parent pretty well, and are now friends too. Jude and Presley are very lucky to have two loving and dedicated parents. He has the children every third day of the week, based on his paramedic rotation schedule. When they divorced, they amicably agreed for her to keep the house since she could afford it on her salary, and he couldn't, and it would help provide a sense of security for the kids. She is the primary provider for their children, and she still finds herself helping him out financially on occasion: from child support not being paid, or helping him pay his utilities. However, she does this to make their family work, and he was there for her when she needed him in the beginning, so although unusual, it's kind of karmic. She knows they will never be intimate or close again, but she does know that she can count on him as a dad and a friend, even if he still has a little more growing up to do.

She does advise that being open-minded, respectful, and courteous is critical if you are going to co-parent successfully together, and to remember, "Co-parenting is better when you choose your words carefully, and realize that you cannot control everything. So if something is not affecting their health or safety, let dad parent his own way. He is learning too."

The most important task she feels she has is to raise her children to be smart, funny, witty, and loving kids who will grow up to be respectful adults with confidence and "ironclad self-esteem." She wants her children to have goals, and wishes, and the drive to make this happen. She thinks the most integrally critical component in a childhood environment besides love, is conversation—having an open and ongoing dialogue. She and her kids talk all the time about everything, and she wants them to know "one hundred percent deep down in their heart" that she is on their side. She encourages them to try new things, especially when they take the lead with expressing an interest or curiosity in a subject.

Love, trust, and dialogue—it is what it's all about, and I know this firsthand too from raising my son Corben. He comes to me freely about any topic, including what some people consider taboo, or age inappropriate, and he lets me know when he has learned enough. I also feel free to address my concerns about this world, and discuss them with him, so he can be aware of any dangers, like drugs, predators, etc. I also balance my concerns by also bringing his attention to the good things in the world, including recognizing acts of others that demonstrate wisdom, care, bravery and valor.

Blaire knows in her heart this is the right way to parent, and she is strongly opposed to the idea of parents withholding love as a form of punishment and she finds it be very cruel.

> "I am a strict mother who provides love regardless of their actions. I just want them to feel overwhelmed with love. I know I am doing a good job at that when I hear my children randomly state, 'I love you, mommy' in the middle of play-time, or run all the way across the playground to kiss me! I believe that you have to be strict in order for children to learn what is expected from them and never falter. Love and consistency, I believe is key."

She is leading by example to ensure she is modeling the behavior she wants to see from her children, and hopefully from others in the world, which is to be a loving, kind, patient person, who is there for her kids. She feels there is no slack on this, and that she didn't "take on this role to be a passenger." She adds that,

"I think people are generally good for the sake of being good. I think that motherhood is taken with way too much of a laissez-faire attitude, and people take for granted the precious lives they hold in their hands. I think that everyone we meet, from the homeless man to the CEO of my hospital, has something to give us, and some role that they were brought into our lives for. I teach my children to value others opinions and to respect others. I realize that everything will play into my children's development into thoughtful, curious, culturally competent beings."

She explains this parenting concept in a broader context …

"One of my favorite quotes states, *'The chief obstacle to the progress of the human race is the human race.'* [Quote by U.S. Humorist Don Marquis] I think this is hilarious and true. Our lack of being able to work for the greater good of people or ability to expand our views limits the progress we could make. We have to help each other out, people. How can one feel right by themselves, if they live an egocentric life?"

She has realized single motherhood is admittedly the hardest thing she has ever done, and making it work, makes her very proud. She had some somber moments initially.

"I really have just learned to depend only on myself, so when someone does offer help it is a pleasant surprise. I was just upsetting myself and getting negative at first thinking about how it was just myself, but then I realized this happened for a reason. I needed to know I could do this on my own and God was always with us anyhow, and he really has not given us anything we could not handle. The more I meditate and am able to express myself though art, the more peaceful I find myself, the less I am concerned with being lonely and in a rut."

As a single mom working the third shift in the ER, and on a strained budget, she had to figure out two solutions: childcare, and how to increase her income without sacrificing time with her kids. She tackled them head on.

"Good help on a budget, this one got kind of tricky without family or friends being available. I work overnights (7 PM to 7 AM) and this is not obviously your standard daycare hours. I put the word out to friends and church folks, and found a college student that I let live with me for free in exchange for three nights a week of childcare when I needed to work. It was a good set-up, and my children and I grew to love her. Since then, I just tried to find stay-at-home moms to watch the kids overnight when I worked so that they could earn some extra money for the family and I paid a per-night fee, not a per-hour fee.

Though nursing pays well, it is still hard to support the type of life I wanted on a singular income. I needed something to do that would not take more time away from my children. I started the legal consultation/summarization business and would do it when the kids were asleep. I worked with one lawyer and when I got that down, added another, until I had a full boat. The photography business was started a little easier. I offered to shoot events for free until I had built up a portfolio that I could be proud of and show to potential customers. Both of these, I only put in money that I had already made to improve the business. For example, I had a relatively nice SLR [single lens reflex] camera to begin with that I shot with. After several paying gigs, I then bought a nicer camera, and other lenses I wanted; the same thing with the side nursing business. I actually started that with a busted laptop, the screen was not even attached to the keyboard. I had to place the computer against the wall, just to prop the screen up to see what I was typing. After many paid jobs, I had enough to buy a decent computer. If the attorneys actually saw that junky thing I was typing on, they would have died laughing. But I never had the money to just spend outright, so everything that improved my businesses has been earned.

I am always busy. There is rarely any down-time, but I believe this is where I thrive! I did cut back on the amount of photography jobs I would accept because it got to the point where I was earning more than I actually needed to live. I did all this to stay afloat, while maximizing kid time and that was really my goal. I will have many years when my children are grown to work for the sake of money. My little family is first and always will be."

Blaire shares some starter tips for building your own income: start with something you love and something your great at, and devise a plan to offer that expertise to the world with the resources you already have. Take one idea and run with it, and if it takes seed, use your earnings to develop it professionally, while meeting your family needs. When she started offering her services as a legal nurse consultant to attorneys, she pitched directly to them from her laptop and operated the whole business online and communication was through email. Nursing was what she already did for a living, and she could offer her knowledge and medical expertise for attorneys who have a medical element of their case to run past her. She invoices them through the mail afterwards. Have faith and take it one-step-at-a-time. And specifically for the mom with tattoos, she advises, "I've had my share of having to dress-up for jobs, and all I can say is high-cut shirts and long sleeves, pants, and hair down over the ears. It's annoying, but you gotta do what you gotta do."

She still does occasional photography jobs since she immensely enjoys using her old enlarger and using alternative developing and printing techniques. You can take a sneak peak of her vibrant work at: ADifferentAnglePhotography.com.

Her final encouraging thoughts she shares if you're a struggling, or single mom, are … just remember to live in the moment, and have fun! You can't control everything, so just stop battling with that and let it go; work on the things within your means and things beyond your control—release them. And never forget "how damn lucky you are to have amazing kids and know in your heart that things are going to be just fine, and be at peace with that."

The two main things she sees herself doing, in the next five-to-ten years, is having more babies, and then starting medical school:

> "I just want to keep-on keeping-on, really. I have big plans for school and life and traveling with and without my kiddos. I want to be married eventually and have more children. I feel at least two more in my ovaries! And I have to adopt! I believe God places particular burdens on people's hearts because that is what they are supposed to change. My heart bleeds for all the non-parented children and I want to have as many of them as I can. I used to want to adopt from Africa, being the largest population of abandoned children, related to HIV, but then after an adoption seminar I visited, I realized there are so many here in the U.S., the state, and even my own city, that do not have the love of a parent. I can help this! I can do something about this! I am a good parent, and there is too much love in this heart to not give it away.

I want to be a MD one day, though I am not in a terrible hurry. I really just want to do this to show myself that I can. I realize how much time it would take away from my children to be in medical school, and I am not willing to make that time sacrifice when they are so young. I am doing fine financially; I will wait until they are older. I will still have to intern, unfortunately.

I used to be against holistic medicine, because sometimes it failed to prove the medical pathophysiology that other practices I had learned about had. It is only recently that I see that there is so much more to this. People can heal themselves sometimes and who really wants all this artificial junk in their body when you can choose something pure and created by the Earth to treat their ailments. I do need to state though that people still need to do their research first, before treating yourself. For example, one may try potassium in an attempt to cure leg pain. Too much potassium can cause cardiac dysrthymias, so we still need to be educated.

However, I am one hundred percent for immunizing children. This is a must! I believe it's neglect to not protect your children in this studied and proven, easy method."

Blaire is able to work hard, and dream big. She loves parenting her kids, because she is a smart mom who knows her limits. She also knows that she needs to fit-in fun adult time, being it playing poker with the girls, going to a show, hitting the gym, or just enjoying a whiskey on the rocks occasionally, or greeting the sun in the morning with fresh donuts and a smile.

"I am responsible to the T and have to 'schedule' time-off just for me. And that's when the fun Blaire comes out to play, and dances, daydreams, giggles, and snorts. Sometimes I forget to remember that I am not a kid. I am told I have my own language and colorful view of the world around me. I get myself in some very silly predicaments up to par with Lucy's shenanigans.

I want to redo a European trip that I took when I was fifteen. I went to Italy, Germany, and Switzerland and utilized my teenager like brain to drive that trip. I was concerned with meeting people, going to cool shows, and not really absorbing much of what that land has to offer. I want to redo that trip.

More currently, I am working on planning a trip to a beach where I can make my own Corona commercial. I want nothing more than to see my feet, the water, and a nice cold adult beverage for miles. This is a bit of conflict, as I have never been away from my children for more than two days, but I am working on it. I feel that I physically ache in my chest when they are not around."

So, yes adult time is essential for any mom—Blaire's strategy is every other week, try to get at least a few hours out and about, or to yourself. She reminds us don't forget our friends and don't forget the women we were before motherhood, who had interests, other than children. If we do, we start feeling burn-out. So throw out the mother martyr guilt, and responsibly indulge or kick your feet up, every once in a while, it's good for the soul. And what's good for momma, is good for her kids.

Blaire see's her role as a mom, and a nurse, as an opportunity to get people to think outside that box when it comes to stereotyping and labeling in general,

"Some may say that it does not matter what others think, this is true sometimes, but I tend to take a stance on the way society sees me physically, a tattooed lady with two children in tow. I use this opportunity to bridge the gap, as much as I can, and help people see that just because we look different does not necessarily mean we do not have the same goals or outlooks on life. I like that I can be who I am, truly, and represent a large demographic of alterna-moms who put their children first. I am the one at all the sports, the gym class, the drama class, the park, the pool, story-time, church, enjoying my time just as much as other moms. I want to show people there doesn't have to be segregation between people with the same common goal."

Blaire takes peoples sometimes shocking disbelief that a rowdy, fun loving rocker can be a serious and astute nurse—and a great mom—and lets it roll off her back like water.

"I am a poker-playing, tattooed, neon-headed, pierced-up mama that you might have seen at the Adicts show the other night, but I'm also the one who lives in the suburbs, goes to HOA meetings and saves your life when you show up to the hospital half-dead. I like the oxymoron of myself. I like surprising people. Too often, I hear ... 'Would you ever imagine she's an ER nurse?' They do not realize it's condescending, but I am used to dealing with the unintelligent by now. I was also told once, 'Blaire, you are the weirdest looking, completely normal person I've ever met.' I liked that one! Ha-ha."

As a Rebel Mom, she is just going to keep rockin' and rollin' by saving lives, loving her kids and holding them close, and blowing people's minds who think moms have to be this way or that, or that people do for that matter. Someday soon she will also be your doctor, in addition to your HOA leader, and neighborhood activist fighting for children abused and neglected by their parents. Until your path crosses with hers, she reminds you mommas out there, that you can do it, and do it with heart and passion, "Just love. Love a lot. Love until it runs out. Things will work out the way they are supposed to."

Sweet!

"I think there are a lot of benefits of being a single mother. She sees me not making compromises for a man and maybe she won't make the mistakes I did."

Taylore
Single Mom
Smokin' Seamstress
Hot Home Improvement Queen
Fashion Design Major
Domestic Violence Survivor
Richardson, Texas.

Taylore is an intelligent, disciplined, "compulsive neat-freak" who lives by the golden rule of treating others as you wish to be treated. She co-parents as a single mom in a blended friend and family household with her best friend and her best friend's husband. They both have kids, and help support each other with child-rearing, housework, and college homework. They split kid-duty so that everyone can go to school and work. Their parent model is an ideal one for the modern age.

Taylore dreams of wall paint and trim, and stylish clothes that are: functional, fashionable, and affordable. Her goal is to bring this to the masses, and then buy a house in Austin that she can fix-up with her home improvement background. The art world, house frames, her daughter Averill, and music are her muses.

She loves the eighties, and the bold freedom that defined the fashion and the music of that era. There was a cultural openness in the eighties that seemed to dissipate under the over-achieving and stricter nineties. She is also attracted to the 1970s punk and music scene with its frankness, toughness, and grit. She does have a sweet spot though for old-world country and is fond of Roger Miller and Merle Haggard.

She looks to her favorite fashion designers for career aspirations. She loves what Thierry Mugler does with vinyl and latex, and how he ubiquitously, yet slyly, places things like "Chevy emblems on breasts and ignition things on hips." She embraces the low-brow art scene where she gets to mingle, interact, and get inspired. She enjoys big art with lots of patterns, details, and information.

Her favorite book is *Soaring Solo* by Wendy Keller. It helped her embrace life as a single mother and the book empowers you to feel good about yourself, while giving you ideas on how to manage the responsibilities of single parenthood harmoniously and fearlessly. The book also enabled Taylore to put things in perspective when it came to her body image, "I was stressing out about my body after child-birth; yes my body is different, but it's all in your head really, and it's a change for the better." Life as a single mom happened almost simultaneously as she ended a turbulent early adulthood romance that had become vicious and angry.

Averill's biological father and Taylore met in New Orleans on Valentine's Day, and they were seduced by the decadence, spirit, and charm of the Big Easy. After her trip, she abruptly went home with him to Atlanta. Like most domestic violence situations, the abuse wasn't immediate, but gradually and subtly introduced itself like a virus, that makes you sicker, and sicker, as it spreads and becomes stronger. Her romeo, over the course of a couple of years, had become the devil himself. When the pushing and shoving and name calling escalated to hitting and punching, and the cycles of love/forgiveness followed by cycles of abuse/threats, became more frequent and were escalating Taylore knew she had to get out and get back home to Texas.

She did just that with the help of her mom. She quickly found work at one of the largest home improvement stores, and within a few months she had her own place again. She felt free, good, and happy. She was making great money and had the inside learning track on general household repairs and interior design. Her apartment was quickly transformed into a living blueprint. Her working vacation from hell would soon end though. She made the mistake of talking to her ex when he got a hold of her through mutual friends.

"I ended up letting him move here, believing all his promises of change, and that this time would be better. We resumed our relationship, and I resumed supporting him somehow, and it started back up again in a couple of months. Ultimately, one night my mom called and heard him threatening to kill me. She called the cops, and the cops that came were the cops I knew from the store in Garland that I worked at. They took me to jail because I had a warrant, and I wouldn't press charges against him."

Reach out for help at TheHotline.org or call 1-800-799-SAFE. The National Domestic Violence Hotline is staffed by advocates for victims; many of them abuse survivors as well.

The time she spent in jail, gave her some time to think, and she got him out of her life for good this time. She evicted him and sent him back to Atlanta under the ultimatum of: if he didn't leave she would press charges. He didn't want to go to jail, so he left. Most domestic violence victims aren't that lucky. Most victims who are tormented by their spouses share the same local geography and/or have no fear of jail. For anyone who ever finds themselves in this situation, courtesy to the legislation authored and supported by Senators Joseph Biden (now our vice-president), and Orrin G. Hatch, we now have a federal bill, the Violence Against Women Act, and a national crisis hotline and website. You can reach out for help at TheHotline.org or call 1-800-799-SAFE. The National Domestic Violence Hotline is staffed by advocates for victims; many of them abuse survivors as well. They will help connect victims with local authorities, crisis centers, and life-saving resources. They also track statistics, studies, and keep an eye on the law. Their motto is a good relationship is one that is based on dignity, respect, and love. Once Taylore got away from him, she swore to herself, never again.

She was in shock when she learned she was pregnant a few weeks later. She knew she wanted to have the child, albeit it would be a challenge. She kept the news of pregnancy confined to herself, her mother, and close friends. She did not want it to be leverage for her abuser to use to try to control her, or to force his way back into her life. Now that Averill is almost two-years-old, he now knows about his daughter but makes no attempt to be a dad, but in this unique situation that's good news for Taylore and Averill. Most batterers also beat their children. She has specific views on life as a single mom:

> "People, (more so than I thought, though less than what used to be), expect you to be married, and feel sorry for you if you are not married, even if you are not sorry for yourself. They expect me to want to be married. I don't necessarily want to be. I think there are a lot of benefits of being a single mother. She sees me not make compromises for a man, and maybe she won't make the mistakes I did. When it's a positive parenting situation with a mother and father it's a good thing, but when it is not, it's just not. Single parenthood is looked upon as a problem and I really don't see it that way. I see it as somewhat of an obstacle, but that's just temporary. I could get married if I wanted too, but why? I'm thankful that I get to do things my way. I know that the decisions you make when they are young, affect who they are later. I still want to do it the way I believe it should be done, and I am thankful that I don't have to argue with anybody about it."

Her view on parenting thus far is that she always knew you only get one shot at life, but it didn't really hit home until she had Averill. Taylore doesn't believe in reincarnation, so it is important to her that she lives each day with no worries, and lives it like her last, enjoys her time with her daughter, and does not stress about things. She strives to make each day constructive and optimistic, and to end it that way, no matter what occurs in-between. She has accepted that life is a struggle and she is not going to let that distract her from living in the moment with her daughter. Nor will she infuse their home with unproductive (and reactive) fear and worry. The world is what it is, work is what it is, and she is going to focus on what she can control while trying to balance the necessary responsibilities while being an involved parent. She is creating the environment her daughter will grow up in, by design.

> "You have to create the family when you are a single mom. I'm definitely missing his half of the family history. Her father was adopted. I don't even really know what races my daughter really is. So I can make our family be whatever I want it to be. It's a very liberating feeling and like I said, I like doing things my own way."

She does feel that children need a sense of security and family, and that trumps even the most dynamic and positive environment otherwise. She co-parents with her best friend and her best friend's husband and there are definite benefits including: a sibling type relationship or bond that is developing between their toddler-aged daughters, sharing the bills and responsibilities, built in co-op childcare and each person gets a little more 'me' time than they would otherwise. Taylore also thinks that it is a healthier setting for kids to grow up and know that they can also trust people that they are not necessarily related to. Taylore insists, though, that the friendship and support, is the best thing, only second to the 'me' time, and shared child-care.

In fact, during his interview she was getting ready to go to work, at a local grocery store, and she went from drinking coffee and putting up dishes, to putting on her make-up and uniform. Of course, the other half of this interview was spent with me chasing my son Corben, who was chasing the cat, and the babies were chasing him. [He was then almost three-years-old; I quickly learned trying to combine family and creative work wasn't going very well. I soon devised a work-from-home plan, and focused on internet and phone interviews, and I split my days off between Corben and family life, and the project.] Taylore shared with me her opinions on their unique family model:

"We're all different. We have different ways to do things, and Averill knows things are not just one way. There's built-in flexibility and different solutions and outcomes. Co-parenting amongst friends and family, I think, would be an ideal model for single parents. If I was living by myself, I wouldn't have anybody to hand her too—even for just ten seconds! And that's something I could not live without. That is one area that's really great about co-parenting."

There is a wonderful non-profit that specifically matches up single moms with other single moms, called CoAdobe.org. They specialize in single mothers home-sharing. Their motto is, *"Two single moms raising children together can achieve more than one struggling alone."*

And don't forget Rebel Mom Taylore's favorite book: *Soaring Solo* by Wendy Keller!

For Taylore, who has a punk background, it was a natural progression in her concept of family and ideals of community. Although, that line of thinking may be out of the box for some, if you are a single mom and this sounds like a model that could work for you, there is a wonderful non-profit that specifically matches up single moms with other single moms, called CoAdobe.org. They specialize in single mothers home-sharing. Their motto is, *"Two single moms raising children together can achieve more than one struggling alone."* Taylore doesn't like the bad rep that's forced upon single moms such as: they do a bad job, or do not do as good of a job as a married mom. She adds:

"I sympathize with other single mothers—I know it's hard. Being married and parenting just seems so much harder to me. I sympathize more with married mothers because they have two people to care for. I'm not trying to say stop complaining, single parenthood is not easy. And I know I have it really, really good. My struggling has been minimized by family and good friends."

Taylore feels her life has redirection, and that's a good thing. She acknowledges she would never put herself through some of the things she did before, including an abusive relationship, or self-destructive habits and demeaning choices. Motherhood has cultivated a keen sense of self-respect that she never knew before, "You can say some things are okay for yourself, but you cannot say it is okay for your child. If it's not okay for your child, then it is not okay for you, as her mother."

It's been an adjustment for her, getting used to the idea of not being able to just get up and go, like she had before. When she was younger she deliberately avoided getting tied down, "I would freak out as a kid if I couldn't just get up and go! I would keep everything cleared out so I could avoid responsibility. Well responsibility is here now." She views it as trade-off in an evolution of maturity.

She wants to resume her study of fashion design, and schooling, once Averill is past the toddler phase. Once her daughter is older she will gradually immerse herself post-graduation into the fashion world, which does require travel and some flexibility, as well as spontaneity. She does plan on rewriting the rules as needed to fulfill her ambitions both as a designer and a mom. She's thinking when Averill starts first grade, then that should be a good time to get restarted.

Very cool!

**Since this interview: Taylore changed course when Averill started first grade. She moved to Portland, Oregon instead of Austin, Texas, and took a great job with a large insurance company helping people with their medical needs. She also fell in love, married, and created a blended family. She is now a proud mom of four!*

"I'd hoped my best friend, son, and I could be a happy family, but that didn't happen. I really think moms have it harder than dads. My ex and I both work full-time, but I've always felt like a full-time mom as well. It's tough."

Leah
Diva Dreamer
Clothes-maker
Foxy Fun Lover
Accounts Payable Clerk
Screen Printing Consultant
Santa Ana, California.

Leah is a fun, trustworthy, and generous twenty-year-old who lives each day with enthusiasm, and like it's her last. Her philosophy is that "you never know when you won't wake up, so … be patient, loving, and enjoy your day!" She loves making clothes, doing make-up and hair, playing her with her young son Gregory, and taking long car rides with no particular destination.

She grew up on the Beatles, the Talking Heads, Devo, and David Bowie, which brings back happy childhood memories when she plays their music. She loves the Stooges and Exene Cervenka. Her favorite writer is Jack Kerouac, and she is frequently inspired by his book *On the Road*, which was his ode to living profoundly (and profusely), one thrilling destination after another. Her brother, Greg, however is the artist that claims her heart. He's a fantastic comic book and storyboard illustrator. You can check out his cool work at Rankinstein.com.

Right now Leah is a new mom trying to find her footing after a devastating family loss. She works full-time at Felon Clothing Company and Lucky 13 Apparel as a sort of Jill of all trades. She does reception work, bookkeeping, and designs some the screen prints for clients. She would eventually like to work as a designer with her own line of products and clothes, or travel the world leisurely; either would be great and a-okay with her. But for the more immediate future, she just wants to be stable financially and emotionally.

Leah reflects on how lucky she was growing up, and hopes she turns out to be "even half-as-good" at parenting as her mom and dad were. Leah grew up in a family of five kids, and she was the youngest and also the only girl. Her dad was a blue collar self-employed working man, and her mom was a working stay-at-home caregiver to the family. She smiles nostalgically as she recalls the warmth, security, love, and confidence that filled the house she grew up in. "They taught me so well. We went through struggles, but we appreciated each other and loved each other so much. I hope I can give that love to my son."

Her dad died right before she turned eighteen, and her world collapsed. She is still struggling with losing him so unexpectedly, and it's been a difficult time for her entire family. She reminds us how important it is that men be both good fathers and role models. "He was the best dad you could ever imagine. He was supportive in every way, loving in every way.

I'm still coping with losing him." Having her son filled some of the void left by her father's death, but it's still a very grievous time for her family. She hopes her son gives them all more hope for the future and eases some of the pain. Leah, however, never planned on being a mom, and at such a young age.

> "A year prior to becoming pregnant I lost my dad, and that was huge to me—he was my world. After that I really woke up from my carelessness and realized to make it—I'd have to become more self-sufficient. After he died, I had no choice but to grow up. I found out I was pregnant when I turned nineteen. I knew I couldn't put myself through anymore loss in my life. My son was born just five days after my dad's birthday. I named him Gregory, just like my father. I would not change a thing!"

She had been having a sexual relationship with her best friend, and thought the unplanned pregnancy would be well-received and everything would work out, but her best friend had different ideas. Fast forward a year-and-a-half later, she's a full-time single mom with an involved part-time dad. She hadn't expected this, "I'd hoped my best friend, son, and I could be a happy family but that didn't happen. I really think moms have it harder than dads. Both me and my ex work full-time, but I've always felt like a full-time mom as well. It's tough."

Her now former best friend made his intentions clear from the beginning of the pregnancy that there wouldn't be a family in the traditional sense, like hers. She faced a frightening transition from being a teenager to becoming a mother solo. She never imagined how lonely and isolating her pregnancy would be. Leah went from having no goals to having to think about not only her future, but her new child's future too. She started off with many friends, friends that she thought she would be friends with forever, to almost none overnight as she bowed out of partying and going to shows, and her pregnancy became known. She worried about her son not turning out right, which is a common pregnancy fear, and overall she was extremely overwhelmed.

She, however, was very fortunate that she had an amazing family to lean on for support and is eternally grateful; since she knows some moms go through all of the above during pregnancy and have no family to lean on. They stood by her from the very beginning and did what they could to give her moral and emotional support, and they chip in to help her. Her mom watches Gregory while she works and Leah knows without a doubt that he is being loved and well cared for; which gives her absolute peace of mind. This is a luxury many working moms do not have, and they worry about their child's care while earning the income necessary to provide for them. She never fathomed motherhood being as demanding as it actually is, "Mommies got it hard!!! So many moms are taken advantage of and it's sexist. It's true." Nor could she have possibly dreamt of how rewarding it would be, "I find myself crying tears of joy when my son smiles at me. And it's so awesome!"

She hopes Gregory turns out confident and honest, but she is learning by trial and error like most parents. She thinks the most important thing parents can do, besides love their kids and provide for them, is to "let kids be kids." In an over-scheduled and over-stimulated world that is a strong, and very much needed, statement. Her son isn't even one yet, but she has already observed what most new moms, and dads, pick up on early: gender programming.

"It's manipulative that boys gotta wear clothes in shades of blue and red with footballs on them. I know some parents who freak out if their son wants to play with a doll, and they punish them for it! I think that just confuses them more. I think it's totally natural for boys and girls to explore, and if my son wants to play with a Barbie, I'm gonna let him! It doesn't mean he's confused!"

★★★★★★★★

"It's manipulative that boys gotta wear clothes in shades of blue and red with footballs on them. I know some parents who freak out if their son wants to play with a doll, and they punish them for it! I think that just confuses them more. I think it's totally natural for boys and girls to explore, and if my son wants to play with a Barbie, I'm gonna let him! It doesn't mean he's confused!"

★★★★★★★★

She enjoys her son's laughter and giggles, immensely, and his "enthusiasm for life is contagious" and it makes her "so happy to be alive." But as a young mom she has faced ridicule and judgment in ways that she never anticipated:

"Society is very close-minded when it comes to moms and children. I'm sure a lot of people take one look at me and think I stole this baby or something. I've been to the pharmacy to pick up a prescription for my son and the pharmacist demanded for me to show my ID three times, and kept asking me if I was really his mother! I said, 'No. I'm just trying to get drugged up on this medication for my son's thrush on his tongue! Ha-ha."

Leah knows some moms casually in her neighborhood and they relate to each other as parents, talking about normal baby things like, teething, how to help them sleep well when colicky, but she feels pretty disconnected from them otherwise. She senses that their lives are so different from hers. They are much more financially stable, and because she lives in the suburbs, they are mostly much older and established women who either have powerful and/or wealthy careers of their own, or their husbands do. She doesn't know any moms like herself, moms into bands, the eighties, kitsch fun, or retro flair. She feels very out of place in an overtly picturesque neighborhood. She now knows how her dad must have felt as the blue collar worker amongst mostly white collar neighbors. She credits her upbringing as the reason why she is such a good person, but she also felt empowered to choose the path that felt appropriate for her:

"I think it started when I was a teenager. You know everyone defines it as 'acting out', by being defiant. My whole life I've been different from the 'norm'. My parents were not ashamed of us wanting to be different, because they themselves didn't care what the snobby neighbors thought. My dad would walk around in Levi's and a white tee shirt covered in dirt from selling wheels all day. He'd come home everyday happier than ever. He had this confidence in him; there were never any fears when he was around. He didn't care what people said or thought about him. He'd smile and be polite to everyone even when they were pricks to him because he wasn't wearing a tie or something!

So it started when I was really young. You don't have to relate to the whole entire world, and you don't have to dress a certain way to feel accepted. Because if you're not happy yourself, conforming to what they [the mainstream or subculture for that matter] define as normal, will not make you happier even for a second."

Leah views mainstream life as very over-bearing, very 'one-way.' She wants people to branch out, stretch their comfort zones, and get over this dead-end mentality that we all must be the same. We need to put to an end to thoughts like … *You're a loser because you're this or that, or I'm better than you because I have more money, or I view my work as important and yours degrading or meaningless, etc.* She thinks the world needs to value the lost art of self-respect and treating others with respect, and raise our kids that way. She feels how we live our life, regardless of our circumstances, has to do with the temperament we are raised with, "The world can be cruel and it can be awesome. You can be happy as long as you want to be."

She reflects on her life before her dads passing and her son's birth, and concludes wistfully, "I'm not crazy and irresponsible anymore. Having a baby got my life on track and gave me hope for the future. It's scary, but being a mom really makes you wanna be the best you can be in all aspects of your life." Her plans now are to just take it one-day-at-a-time and have a blast with her son. Sounds awesome to me!

**Since this interview: Gregory just went to his first day of school! And Leah is still kicking butt as a mom and woman!*

"People, even subculture people, get into vicious arguments about parenting. Don't judge me just because I won't carry my baby in a sling till their five, or nurse till their seventeen. If it works for you fine, but don't judge me."

Lindsay
Dog Lover
Insurance Underwriter
Business Grad
Former Hairstylist
Lovely LP Collector
Vixen Vintage Car Fan
Rockabilly Momma
Richardson, Texas.

Lindsay is a smart, fantastic, Southern Baptist woman who gets a kick out of watching the antics of people bickering over religious differences, musical differences, or parenting differences. It affirms for her that absurdity is moronic. She wishes everyone would just sit down, enjoy a good hummus plate with some samosas from Cosmic Café and chill out. She grew up in Atlanta, Georgia and recently moved with her sweetheart to Texas. The move was inspired by fun, friendship, and home-ownership.

Lindsay and her husband Adam, now both in their thirties, are new parents that formerly spent the weekends traveling the United States, going to their favorite Rockabilly and car shows. Their daughter, Dixie, is the apple of their eye, and suddenly the appeal of Viva Las Vegas pales in comparison to a weekend at home with her. They are both dog enthusiasts and have a Chihuahua, a Dachshund (commonly referred to in the U.S., as Doxons), and a Great Dane. Their household is filled with snapshots of Dixie cooing and being adorable, and the dogs striking a pose.

They were initially living in Austin, when they first moved to Texas, but felt that the scene was isolating, and cliquish. This wedge was driven in further when they became parents. They reached out for support via a rockabilly parents message board, and bonded with Lola (another Rebel Mom whose story was featured earlier in the book) and her family. Pretty soon, the two families were inseparable. Lindsay and Adam moved about two-hundred and thirty miles north to Richardson, and bought a house neighboring Lola's family. They needed the support as new parents and found it.

Lindsay currently works for a small insurance company, and evaluates the risks of their accounts. She initially worked as a hairdresser straight out of high school, but she grew tired of hair and make-up, and she was always great with numbers, statistics, and predicting probability. She also knew she wanted a nine-to-five office job with weekends off so that she could be free to pursue her other passion: music. She did hair for eight years to support herself while going to school part-time, and earned her bachelor's degree in business. It was during this time she met Adam, and they married after a couple years of dating. Their path to parenting was planned.

"For me, it was different. I was twenty-nine, and about to turn thirty. So I already had all the partying out of me, and I put myself through college. Adam and I were going out on weekends, to shows and to Vegas, but it was different too—not reckless partying. And then we had her. And even though we could, we suddenly didn't want to go to out. We didn't want to leave her."

Lindsay grew up in a loving, and supportive home, and has a very close relationship with her mom and dad. She was taught to take pride in herself, work for and be involved in her community, and that we all have a responsibility to our country to participate in the political system, and working for positive change in the world. She fondly remembers Saturday morning political debates around pancakes. Her parents questioned things, and raised her to have the same backbone.

"I'm a Southern Baptist tattooed woman who goes to church to get what I want out of it. But a lot of my friends believe in this or that, and between all of us who are close, you would think there would be this big conflict between us, because of different belief systems, but there's not. We all respect each other's beliefs, and even ask each other questions. Like one friend had asked me, 'How can you still believe in God after 9/11?' But we can have these types of open conversations, and all maintain our love for each other."

"My parents were Baptist, but raised me to think for myself. They taught me to like what I liked, even if they didn't, and not to just accept what they liked either and take it for myself. They told me often just because they like it, doesn't mean I have to. They wanted me to think on my own and challenge authority. I used to beg my parents to tell me who they voted for, and they would never tell me. They also told me that who they voted for was none of my business, ha-ha. And that I needed to figure out who I would vote for and why. But also, despite the stereotype of Baptists, my parents taught me to be loving and non-judgmental, especially, if I haven't walked in that person's shoes. My brother and I have carried over that mentality as adults. We just don't judge people or whatever you like (if you're not hurting anyone or children)."

She describes the open communication and respect that is frequently demonstrated amongst her and her friends:

> "I'm a Southern Baptist tattooed woman who goes to church to get what I want out of it. But a lot of my friends believe in this or that, and between all of us who are close, you would think there would be this big conflict between us, because of different belief systems, but there's not. We all respect each other's beliefs, and even ask each other questions. Like one friend had asked me, 'How can you still believe in God after 9/11?' But we can have these types of open conversations, and all maintain our love for each other. You don't find that in organized religion, where people get into vicious arguments."

That open-mindedness is what attracted her to a rockabilly way of life. But she was surprised to experience ridicule for not parenting the same as others, and for expressing her opinions. She concluded that it seems like the minute anyone has a kid that open-mindedness turns into iron-clad right or wrong concepts of child-rearing, "People, even subculture and counterculture people, get into vicious arguments about parenting. Don't judge me just because I won't carry my baby in a sling till their five, or nurse till their seventeen. If it works for you fine, but don't judge me." Lindsay resents the way some moms seem to go into super-snob mode when it comes to their way of parenting not aligning exactly with others,

> "I see a lot of parents like us who are so vocal about being different and being judged then they seem to do exactly the same thing they're so against. I know as moms we run into that all the time. To be this type of mom, you have to do this, you have to do that, or you kid will be all screwed up or be a serial killer. We're so not like that, if that works for you great, but don't criticize us if we're not."

She also thinks it's important for parents to filter out not only the harsh or unasked for opinions of others, but also the advice, perhaps well intentioned, that's given if it doesn't make sense for you and your family. She references an encounter she had with a woman who was a babysitter, whom insisted that she should leave Dixie in her diaper all day, without changing it, in order to potty-train her. Lindsay's response was, "What part of negative reinforcement and making her suffer would help my child become potty-trained?" Lindsay says she gets stuff like that all the time from people.

Now that Dixie is almost two-years-old, Lindsay and Adam plan on taking their cues from her and progressing from here, while raising her in an aware, secure, and warm home. They share the care-giving work and housework since they both have full-time jobs.

> "Adam and I do split-shift parenting. He has Dixie during the day, and then I have her at night, and he works. He plays Misfits to her and just enjoys being a dad. He's a very involved dad. Adam is different, than most dads whose interest and involvement really don't pick up with their kids until five or six, according to our pediatrician. This is because he was raised by a single mom, so he has a maternal leaning towards loving, helping, and parenting."

The scariest moment they have faced as parents was just learning that Dixie is blind in one eye and will need occupational therapy when she is older. They are struggling to catch her up developmentally as well, since the partial disability has caused her to fall behind in some milestones. She just started walking which is huge relief. But it was this delay that prompted a close friend, who's a pediatrician, to figure out what was the cause. Lindsay feels guilt and shame, and like most moms we're raised to believe we caused it somehow, especially if we work outside of the home, due to financial necessity or another need. This is a guilt that is not intrinsic to men who become fathers. Rationally, Lindsay knows that she did everything she could to take good care of her daughter, and responded appropriately when Dixie first started showing signs that something could be wrong, but she doesn't feel that rational explanation deep down, "I work, and felt responsible, that somehow it was my fault. I'm the baby's mom; I'm supposed to be there." One thing that's helping her work through that is the awesome feeling of love she has for her daughter …

> "My dad said to me when I had Dixie, 'Now you know how much your mom and I love you. You can never know that until you have one of your own.' It's like

taking all the love for every person you've ever known and loved, and then you can begin to fathom. The first week we couldn't even look at her without crying, we loved her so much."

They were slightly taken aback however, when they were first sent home from the hospital with her. They asked unabashedly, "What do we do? What if we kill her?" The staff assured them they would do fine, and sent them on their way. Of course, they got the hang of it and were pros after a week. But this raised some deeper concerns for Lindsay. She asserts that:

"I've known a couple who adopted, and he and his partner had to go through so much, from classes, to tests, to even privacy questions, like: what beds do they sleep in? And do they plan on her sleeping with the child? If everybody had to go through the stringent and trying process of adoption, even to give birth to their own child, there would be a lot less children getting abused or murdered by their parents. I think this screening should be required."

She also feels that children should be heard, not just seen. When we silence children, it denies them their rightful place in the world as people, and you just cannot contain them, nor should we suppress them with threats. She views this as entirely different from teaching a child care and consideration, and thus good manners, but even then you have to be aware of a child's development stages for it to even be age-appropriate. She asserts that contrary to public disbelief, a toddler isn't an adult. She cringes when she thinks of the way parents use spanking as a means to discipline, teaching their child only fear and pain.

Although Lindsay and her mom are close, close enough for her mom to openly ask Lindsay what if her daughter just wants to be normal, say a cheerleader instead of a tattooed rockabilly girl? Lindsay assured her mom, she will support Dixie's interests and talents, even if it's something she's not into. She also informed her mom, that hypothetically, if Dixie did want to be cheerleader, she would also ensure that she is a nice one who is caring, not condescending, to her schoolmates—which is contrary to the popular cheerleader stereotype.

Lindsay is looking forward to the new adventures she will have as a mom, and possibly even the poop murals she has heard so much about from friends. She chuckles as we end our interview, knowing what the future holds—an awesome mom, going through the next phase of parenting: potty-training.

"I'm no angel, but I try to do the right thing in most situations. We all have had our moments from time-to-time."

Jennifer S.
EBay Seller
Job Hunter
Sexy Song Writer
Gutsy Guitar Player
Sweet Seamstress
Shawnee, Oklahoma.

Jennifer is a sweet, good-hearted, fun-natured, twenty-three-year-old mom who is on the cusp of figuring out what her dreams are and how to make them a reality. She is a new mom starting out fresh after a hard crash course and detour in: life, love, and young adulthood.

She enjoys sewing and dancing around her kitchen to the Cramps and Wanda Jackson with her three-year-old son Elijah, and hanging out with her fiancé Adam. She likes all types of music from ska, new wave, industrial, punk, rhythm and blues, billy, country, and that she "could take up the whole book just talking about music!" She is "absolutely obsessed" with the 1940s and 1950s genre and proudly has a thing for hot rods and classic cars, but motherhood and music are her bread and butter—they give her life meaning, purpose, and a new found drive. She secretly dreams of being in a band someday, and practices guitar and writes songs for that very purpose.

She credits herself with having a great sense of humor and that by nature's design she is very nice, and that her "heart is way too big and there is a little bit of everyone in there that consumes it." This has resulted in her being taken advantage of, but she asserts she wouldn't change that part of her, because she feels that her trusting and loving nature, in essence is the best part of, and quality about humanity. She also, by trial-and-error, has learned some life-lessons that are important: take care of others when they need you, don't take anything for granted, avoid dramatic situations (she adds they are nothing but big time and spirit wasters), and just try the best you can each day.

She has overcome serious obstacles including: teenage homelessness and abuse, and severe anxiety. In line with her disposition she shrugs off the grave reality of her past hurdles, with a laugh and a smile, "What can you do but move on?" One artist that has helped her go through these life transitions is Exene Cervenka from the band X. She looks up to her as a writer, performer, artist, poet, and a mother. She met her recently and concluded that, "She has such a beautiful disposition and is just cute as hell. Her words make a lot of sense to me. She seems to give a shit and that goes over well with me." She helps us put it in perspective by sharing her favorite Exene quote,

'Having a child makes you less selfish, of course you try to save the world for your children. I had a dream once, in it a person asked me 'What do you think the future is going to be like?'

I answered, 'There isn't going to be one.' I hope that's the wrong answer. What do you think the future is going to be like?"

She admires John Doe, also of the band X, and thinks he is the best songwriter and singer in the whole world, except for Elvis! But she likes that his writing gets in her head and makes her think. Also, notably, he is a proud husband and father—and that is a character strength that more men need to develop [and we as a society need to place serious value on] and that means a lot in her book.

Motherhood and life-goals have been on her mind lately, and she's trying to figure out which way is the best way for her. She loves being a mom, but is caught in the crossfire of needing to meet his needs (and her own as a parent) while providing for him. She has been looking for good-paying work with benefits but hasn't been able to find a job. She has been resourceful and is eking out a living from selling vintage and thrift finds on EBay, but it doesn't lend the type of financial stability she wants. She has always wanted to own her own business, but until now wasn't sure what type of business that would be. She has narrowed it down to:

> "I want to design and make my own line of clothing, and co-own a business with my fiancé making reproduction vintage furniture. I have many dreams and I believe I can make them happen if I just push myself to finish the things I start and work hard at making them a reality."

EBay gives her the perfect platform to launch her own vintage clothing reproduction line. She has the experience in selling on EBay, and what she needs to know now to make her own business come true is: more textile experience, and figuring out how to get the drawing off the pad and onto a body for fashion, and to connect with manufacturers and wood makers for the furniture line and thus bring her, and her fiancés, visions to life. Those both can be the anchor of both online businesses, and vintage themed small items can lend to the bottom line in term of sales, which can help them raise capital to fund the bigger, more visionary, but overall less profitable, core of their businesses which will be custom pieces. Through this cycle repeated, eventually they can save to open a storefront, the largest obstacle outside of networking, building knowledge and skill-sets, will be getting enough money together for the furniture manufacturing and ordering; unless they do the wood work themselves.

Having a dream is a tough road to pursue, as many entrepreneurs and artists will tell you (especially ones without resources, or family, that can help out). It takes tenacity, high hopes, and tons of work, and even then it may not pan-out. But Jennifer sees now the future she wants and she refuses to let it just pass her by. She will make the clothing line fruitful, since that will be the least challenging start-up, and least expensive, doing it one ordered piece at-a-time from home, and then they will gradually work on starting the other and they will blend it. Until then, she needs a job, so they can pay the bills, all of them, so her hunt will continue. But before this stage in her evolution, she was plotting on how to get out of Oklahoma …

> "Before I became a mom, I was definitely a lot more active, more outgoing, I wasn't scared of much, but I was still quite a confused little girl. I think I just lived for the moment then and it got me into trouble quite a few times. All I had plans for was moving out of Oklahoma and owning a business. Other than that my plans were pretty scattered here and there. My best friend almost got me to join the National Guard once, just to make it easier to get out of Oklahoma. I really didn't want to. I am so glad I didn't join! My best friend did join the Coast Guard though, and is a wonderful wife and mother herself."

Jennifer's only family are her friends, fiancé, and her son. Her biological dad passed away years ago and her mom had remarried a hostile man. Although, she has been vulnerable and weak at times, she has always been strong enough to pull herself back up again. She has done things in the past that she never was able to explain, and regrets that she can't go back to tell her side of the story, but she has cared deeply for everybody that has ever been a part of her life, both the good and the bad. She explains a little more about her circumstances:

"My home life was ripped apart at a young age, and watching my mother cry made me very sad. And shortly later, I was being treated differently by my step parents, feeling like I wasn't wanted.

It all started when I was very young. My mother and I were taken away by a terrible man that was obsessed with her. He took us to some place in Texas, and I cannot really remember the time I was there, but I know I was not happy. The man came back for us after we escaped and tried to kill my father and take my mother back. He didn't succeed, but the next thing I knew my parents were divorced and I lived with my mother. I continued to live with her until she married my step-dad, then I lived with my father until he married my step-mom.

From then on it was back-and-forth between the two. Finally, I knew my place was with my mother. My step-father however, had become an abusive born-again preacher and started beating me, and then I started drinking and doing drugs at thirteen, and my step-dad kicked me out. I was eating out of dumpsters and living in my car by the time I was seventeen."

At this point in her life she had started getting involved in dead-end relationships and felt she was an "easy target for people who liked to play minds games" and she was brought down to a pretty desperate and low emotional and mental state. She lost control and felt hopeless:

"I struggled with many people treating me like shit, then me doing the same back, and dumb meaningless relationships and friendships, and lots of drug use. I decided at age fifteen to stop the drugs because it was just stupid. I won that battle without a problem. But time flies with more nonsense and a long term relationship with a shit head who was threatening and crazy—first real boyfriend. Then I started dating Elijah's father."

Their relationship was tumultuous and frequently on-and-off again for years, from the age of seventeen through twenty-two. He would leave her in one state or another, and she would fall apart, then he would come back and get her. This created a cruel cycle of codependence that affected both of them. Although, he treated her very badly, she blames herself (as most victims of abuse do). "I still came around for it, so maybe I asked for it." His friends treated her just as meanly and talked down to her, and because she had lost contact with her friends, all she had at this point in her life was the reflection of herself as they portrayed her. Her self-worth plummeted gradually over years of cyclical patterns of love, control, demeaning mental abuse, followed by make-ups, then break-ups. Despite all of this, they wanted to have a baby together …

"We were together, and I visited a doctor for a physical check-up and the test results came back that I might have cervical cancer. I was scared I would never have kids so before my biopsy we decided to try to have a baby. It didn't take too much work. I had my biopsy and everything was okay. Next thing I knew I was pregnant and we were both happy about it."

It took her a long time to free herself of this web that they had weaved, but she earnestly wanted to have a happy family for her son and him. Her immediate fears were put to rest when Elijah was born healthy, and she seemingly had the support of his family and their friends during the pregnancy. But after the first few months of parenthood, life soon started reverting back to the way things were before.

"There were many problems in the relationship between Elijah's dad and I; the relationship was full of jealousy, accusations, no trust what so ever, and a lot of controlling behavior. A few years pass with more accusations and I didn't leave the house much. I was lucky to get out once a month. All of my friends were slowly driven away by him, and before I knew it, they really were all gone, except for the few he approved of, which coincidentally were friends with him before I came into the picture. I dealt with it and we went on. Time passes, and we decide to go to Vegas and get married. We didn't make it, and a few months later he left me for a friend. He was with her for a weekend, and then wanted me back.

We got back together and then came more jealousy, accusations, and so on from him. He met a girl at our work (who had befriended me). A couple months pass by, he tells me we are breaking it off in a month, and I have to live with the repeat situation of before, and that he and that girl were together. Elijah and I were on our own. After he was gone I went through a grieving period, but in a sense I was relieved that the biggest ball and chain of my life was gone."

She took some time to heal, and to pick up all the pieces of her life that had been shattered. She gradually started making new friends, and some of her old ones came back around, and for the first time in years, she realized there wasn't anything wrong with her. She felt peacefully happy for the first time since she was a small child.

During this time she and her good friend Adam became close, and he had been there for her, and at times he was the only one she could lean on for advice and help. Eventually, their friendship turned into romantic love and they knew they complimented each other well and wanted to be together. He had been a great friend to her and Elijah, and a good role model for her son. He also treated her very well, they way she deserved to be treated, and they fully trusted each other. Their relationship is built on confidence, passion, friendship, and respect. They recently announced and celebrated their engagement, and have articulated their future plans (beyond just starting a business) for a long life of being together, being happy, traveling, kissing, and raising Elijah.

"I am getting married to one of my best friends since high school, Adam, and we hope to open our own business some day. Moving out of Oklahoma isn't an option anymore due to family, but I'll make the best of it where I am at. I am starting to get back into meeting new people and want to be as outgoing as I used to be. My main goal is to raise my son to be a very smart mature young man who will not be afraid to be who he is."

Now that Jennifer has had time to reflect on what motherhood is like, she feels that ...

"Becoming a mother is in itself rewarding and exciting. The day I saw my little monster in person was the best day of my life. I wish I could say the rest of it was peaches and cream, but it wasn't that at all! Not any fault of my sons, I was just in a bad situation as far as relationships go. My relationship with my son's father deteriorated over the past three years of Elijah's life. Due to relationship problems I suffered what I believe was a slight case of agoraphobia and social anxiety problems. I have battled them without being wacked out on drugs and antidepressants. My relationship with Elijah was, and is, always strong. When I was going through the hardest of times with his dad, he was always there and made me smile. We started the off again, on again scenario in hope that my son would be able to grow up in a happy environment with both parents. Things just got worse and worse from then on. After the last break up between his father and me, I decided it really was the last.

Everything now is a lot better. Although, I enjoyed being a mother before, I can fully enjoy it now without worry. I think Elijah is able to calm down and enjoy things as well. His father and I get along a lot better apart, and I think that this is more healthy for Elijah, as opposed to the typical fighting parents that despise each other and bring the child up in that environment.

It is a lot harder to participate in everything, such as going out to a show or a party, but I have worked out ways around that. Anyone that is a parent knows that you learn that quickly. I try to include Elijah in a lot of things I do, as long as it is a safe environment for him. I will probably take him to shows when he is a little older."

When she learned she was pregnant, the reality of being a mom was immediate, but she didn't know what to expect outside of a looming sense of bigger, yet different, and unknown responsibilities. When Elijah was born, she gazed upon him with doe eyes and her heart sang; this little man was hers. It clicked then that any and every action she takes will affect his life too.

Parenting has become more challenging since keeping up with a toddler definitely requires a diet high in protein, lots of outside time, zeal and zest. As Jennifer tells me the rigors of chasing Elijah, I remember my days of running marathons after Corben, my blazing lion with long golden locks, at the park, parties (he even streaked at a BBQ!), and the store. [Corben has since grown into his energy. When Elijah's body grows and encompasses more of him, he will become calmer and centered too. Then Jennifer will have a chance to recover from the sheer exhaustion of the chase-the-kid work-out's, and suddenly she will find herself missing those high-spirited days full of laughter and sprint-running, like I am doing right now.] She adds:

"I think motherhood is wonderful, yet hard and stressful at times. When I look at my son, I honestly couldn't tell you where I would be right now. I wouldn't change having him for the world. I have gone through many rough times in life and he has been the one to pull me through them. He may be small, but he's stronger than I am. He makes me stronger. Everything I do in life includes him and always will. I try to teach him not to judge people and keep an open mind, and will continue to teach him that."

Jennifer expects herself to be the best mom she can be, period. She will always put Elijah first, and he will be the first to know of any major changes in their life that she may be contemplating, so she can get his input on it, and consider his wishes in the decision making, especially as he becomes older. This is an important parenting principle, because kids need to feel like a valued part of the family and that their wishes/needs/opinions are considered too, instead of just feeling like they don't matter—which is the fuel for teen angst in any strictly authoritarian household. [When we as a family made the decision to move to Denver, Corben had a vested say-so in the matter, he wanted to move too. And as such the transition for him was very smooth, and he had a great time the year we lived there. He also had a vested say-so in the decision for us to move back to Dallas—he missed his uncle, aunts, grandmas, and friends. And so it was time to head back home.]

Jennifer plans on always talking to Elijah, and hearing what he has got to say. She is already bracing herself for when he is older and more sharply blunt, but she is determined to stand by him through anything, and anything he may say, no matter how opinionated, or contrary to her feelings it may be. She knows the relationship she builds now, and the dialogue she creates, will make life's later transitions easier for them to navigate together. She hopes that nothing but good things happen to and for him, but she realizes how unlikely that may be when considering forces beyond her control:

"Some things are out of my power and some things I can try my best to make happen. I wish the current situation with how the world is—wasn't the way it is. It seems as though our country, the world, and everything in it is going downhill. I am afraid of the wars and all of the fighting. I don't want my son to grow up in this kind of situation. I want my son to have every opportunity that I had when I was growing up and more.

I know that just about every generation has a war, but it's looked at in a different perspective when you are a parent. I hope that he grows up to be just a good human being that will take advantage of every positive opportunity that comes to him. I want him to be open-minded and not scared to learn new things. I want him to know that hitting people and violence is stupidity, and the people that act way all of the time are people who aren't smart enough to come up with something clever to say. I will do everything in my power to teach him these things. If all of us could teach our kids this—maybe every generation wouldn't have a war."

Jennifer overall is concerned with the state of affairs in the world today and how that will affect our children. She thinks there is way too much violence popularized in the media, and in the decisions of our leaders, and in the actions of the community. It all just reeks of aggression. She doesn't think society is setting the type of examples that our kids should learn from. On the flip side, she points out that …

"I think people are teaching their kids to be more-close minded and focusing too much attention on how violent their child's cartoon might be. What I would like to tell them is that is only a cartoon, which we know is fake, and tell your child that! Believe it or not, kids will listen. They need to take a good look at real life where you see these commercials, with people shooting Middle Eastern people, while telling you to join the Army and saying things like 'defeat the enemy' and such. I can't look at my son and say that is fake."

Jennifer thinks we unnecessarily sugar coat the truth, while focusing on the irrelevant, as exampled above. That may have more to do with living in an aggression-based, *fear and rape culture*, than a peaceful-based, *everyone is important culture*. Actions speak louder than words, and yes, you can judge a society by how it acts. Children model the behaviors, and absorb the opinions and messages, that both parents and society demonstrates. Children need their parents (just like populations need their leaders) to give them the real-deal, but to also act with compassion, integrity, and insight.

How can we ever expect our society to improve and our children to become empathetic, fair and ethical leaders, if it's all about the newest toy and cartoon violence? And not about the reality of real people being hurt because of the decisions and choices of others? Jennifer thinks that if the world leaders just sat down and stewed on this epiphany a bit, they would conclude: "No one can rule the world. So stop wasting energy fighting over it. Let people be the way they are and leave it that way. That goes for everyone. All countries, all races, all religions, etc."

Jennifer also believes that we need to protect our children, but without sheltering them. She thinks kids deserve to have experiences that will help define who they are, but with our cautionary oversight. Kind of like how birds train their babies to fly from the nest. She emphasizes that, "I'm not saying leave your three-year-old alone, or drop them off at a sex offenders house, or anything. Yes, I do think children need guidance and protection. Just don't freak out if they fall and scrape their knee! Comfort them; just don't act like they are going to die because of it. It scares the hell out of them!" Basically give their wings room to try to fly, but be there to catch them.

"I think people are teaching their kids to be more close-minded and focusing too much attention on how violent their child's cartoon might be. What I would like to tell them is that is only a cartoon, which we know is fake, and tell your child that! Believe it or not, kids will listen. They need to take a good look at real life where you see these commercials, with people shooting Middle Eastern people, while telling you to join the Army and saying things like 'defeat the enemy' and such. I can't look at my son and say that is fake."

She also wants to share something that she learned the hard way, "Take everything in stride and don't let it stress you out. Just listen to your kids and talk to them." She has observed too many parents treating their children, not like kids, but fashion accessories, which is disheartening. She pleads for parents who had kids for all the not-sure or wrong reasons to please get in touch with yourself as parent, really figure out what you're doing, and why you're doing it, and who you are doing it for—and then build a real connection to your children. She adds it's not too late.

One of her personal struggles has been as a young mother in this society. She has felt stereotyped and looked down upon for being too young and not having enough money. Our culture ignores, yet stigmatizes, moms who aren't the ideal: polished, middle-aged, and wealthy (upper middle class or upper class). This idealized *status-mom* ostracizes most mothers (the mathematical majority), who aren't any of that! The stigma can sometimes be more than she can take, especially when it's been a taxing day. She wishes people weren't so quick to judge her, "This is a twenty-four hour every day job and I think I am doing pretty damn good at it."

Jennifer has always felt a little different than the crowd, and drawn to people who were very strong in their convictions. She saw this frequently demonstrated in subculture circles. Her attraction to the counterculture scene became solidified when she had an identity crisis at the age of thirteen, and stumbled upon the bands that would become her teen favorites: the Circle Jerks, FEAR, Econochrist, Rudimentary Peni, Subhumans, the Exploited and X. She fell in love right then and there.

"I love Oi! and punk rock too! It was there and it rocked and most songs may have only had three chords, but those three chords rocked my face off! Ha-ha. I'm not too sure about what they call 'punk' these days, there are some newer bands I have come across. It's just different; those who were there know what I mean. Back then it was individuality. I try not to discriminate as far as that's concerned though. I don't really like the 'holier than though, I was punk before you were in diapers' attitude.

I think whether you were punk, goth, skinhead, or whatever, you tended to learn more. You had a more open-mind of studying things and learning about things that mainstream people would not normally even think to learn about. It seems now subculture looks are more accepted by the mainstream, even in mainstream fashion. There are people out there that don't have a clue what it's about and just do it for 'trends' or 'fashion'. The people whose hearts are really into it and live the lifestyle, because it is what appeals to them, those are the true people that belong to a subculture or counterculture. How can you call it a subculture when everyone just does it for fashion, you know?"

But I am mainly into rockabilly now. My mom was an Elvis fanatic since before I was born. I used to wear little grass skirts and watch *Elvis: Aloha from Hawaii* at the age of the four, and I went to Graceland at the age of six. So I was bound to become a little rock 'n' roll hillbilly someday. Besides, the music is just rockin'! I love it! Same goes for classic country, western swing, doo-wop, and even psychobilly, just the whole 'billy' genre of music and lifestyle fascinates me."

Jennifer explains what led up to her adolescent punk immersion,

"I have always been different, even before I was into punk rock. I was always the weird kid that got picked on and just didn't quite fit-in. Even after I claimed to be punk, I still got a lot of the same bullshit. Needless to say, I learned how to deal with it and I think it shaped me into a better person. These days I don't really say I am into one thing or another. I have ventured off more into rockabilly and vintage style and living, but I don't ignore my punk rock roots. I might still get 'looks' from people because I may be a little different, but I don't pay much attention anymore. I can't help but be a little different from others. That's just me. I hang out with all types of people from different subcultures, not just one crowd or clique. I think discriminating to one type of genre limits you. There are all kinds of awesome people you could meet."

Jennifer knows a few moms she relates to, and their common ground is that their all young moms. This bonds them despite the varying circumstances that make-up their families, or their differing musical/cultural/political identifications. Most of them face similar obstacles: judgment from society for being 'bad' mothers, i.e., young and single (although, not intentionally either when motherhood happened), trying to find time for themselves, and making ends meet. A more light-hearted struggle they share is ... trying to catch a good show!

"I think single motherhood has affected us subculture moms in ways that, before it seemed so easy to just go where you wanted, when you wanted, and do whatever in the hell you wanted! After becoming a mother, it takes an awful lot of work just to get out for a night or two! I have had conversations with friends of mine with children, and they have the same problem. It just took awhile until we figured out how to deal with having a child and getting to go out. Good shows sometimes come around just once in a blue moon around here, so you just have to prepare ahead of time as opposed to getting up and going at the last minute. The mothers I know wouldn't have it any other way. We all love our kids and get proud when they sing an Adicts song or dance around to The Cramps. Stuff like that brings a smile to all of our faces."

Jennifer feels that subculture moms, from her own personal experience, have a tendency to be more honest with their kids, and also more accepting of them—and that's just a reflection of the life we live and how we see the world, and our role in it. She thinks that is an element that would make motherhood far less stressful for mainstream moms, and would make their kids lives more enjoyable too. She adds:

"It's just different. I think it teaches your child to have more character, and to be who they are, and not to try to impress all of the 'cool kids'. It's not really about what I wear, but my attitude and the way I am. I've been able to take on the worst of things in life without it completely destroying me. It has made me a better and more open-hearted person in the long run. I like to think our lives (as subculture moms) teach our children not to be afraid to learn about new things and find the positive outlook on it. I think we can all learn from each other. I think no one should pressure their children to be something they don't want to be, whether it be a cheerleader or a football player, or take part in subculture/counterculture lifestyle. I have never met or seen a sub-cultural parent try to pressure that lifestyle on their child. It's kind of funny, it seems to me the kids think it is fun, and are more drawn to it without pressure to be that way. I know whatever my son wants to do with his life, I will stand behind him all of the way."

Jennifer cares about Elijah and wants the best for him, and she thinks that most caring moms feel the same way, regardless if they are in a subculture genre or just find life meaningful as 'typical Jane'. We know with socialization that most people accept, and embrace passively, the life they are given and the expectations set for them, *if they want to be accepted and considered normal.* But we also know from mom-media and other non-corporate journalism outlets, there are plenty of mainstream voices that go against the grain to speak up and question what's going on and why. Our job as parents, is to analyze that, and make sure it's up to our standards, and if it's not we can then create deeper meanings and connections with our children, friends, and co-workers. Thus redefining what is acceptable (like mutual respect, allowing others to be themselves safely and free from harm, working together as group, cultivating real ethics and leadership) and what is not acceptable (like rape, exploitation, bullying, discrimination). Most of what is normalized for us, is bad for our kids and our future, like employer exploitation based on 'work ethics', rape culture, big oil/consumer-based lifestyles, greed leaders, society denying legal and equal protection under the law for transgender and homosexual individuals and families, etc.

Although, it may seem we are a dying breed, due to the huge wave of successful big business greed-based politics that drown out our voices, and the retooling of subversive subculture into apolitical/indifferent mainstream fashion culture, were not. We don't buy into it. That's only one side of the story—the one being sold to you. We may have to work around it, negotiate and compromise for our families, while fighting for our voices to be heard, but there is a better way, period, and we have to keep chipping away at it—if we want a righteous world for our kids.

Most of what is normalized for us, is bad for our kids and our future, like employer exploitation based on 'work ethics', rape culture, big oil/consumer-based lifestyles, greed leaders, society denying legal and equal protection under the law for transgender and homosexual individuals and families, etc.

That is what Jennifer, the other Rebel Moms in this book, and I, have been doing in our own little ways, everyday! Engaging, probing, pushing, and challenging those around us, for the good of all of us! While raising our kids in a more holistic, loving, and aware-of-life and our-actions-in-it, environment. Our encounters have led us to other moms, people, and parents, who definitely don't dig what we dig, or vice-versa, but they too are doing things outside the norm and creating more dialogue so that all kids can have a real and tangible future *together*.

Jennifer's plans are to just keep doing what she's doing which is: loving and raising Elijah well, working on her-long term goals, and treating others with the sincere care, interest, and respect that we should accord to one another. She is very excited about her upcoming wedding plans to Adam, and the business dream they are working diligently to make a reality. Other than that, she will continue to adore Elvis and rock it! She closes with, "Regardless, if I've been happy or sad, good or bad, the things that have happened to me has made me into the person I am today, and I am pretty happy with that."

And the Next Momma to be is …

"When I get pregnant I'm going to give birth in Germany or Switzerland. They have great maternity leave policies for parents and great work ethics."

Andi
Pretty Pug Lover
DIY Connoisseur
Quadrilingual
Holistic Medicine Heretic
Hot Homemaker
International Gypsy
Singer and Guitarist/Bassist for
Snap-Her,
The Derita Sisters,
and the Creamers
Leck Kill, Pennsylvania.

Andi is a rad mom-in-the-making who grew up in Argentina and Los Angeles. Her band has toured all over the world, and extensively in Europe. She preferred life as a nomad and as such has lived on three continents. She has countless tales to share and friends all over the globe. She is extremely knowledgeable and opinionated, telling you what she thinks and why. She encourages every woman to get a CUNT pillow from CuntFactory.com—bringing women back-in-touch with their bodies—one musical anthem by her band, and one pillow at-a-time. She also confronts men who think their lack of self-control suffices for raping women, while asserting our rights sexually. She has been on magazine covers internationally, including: *Savage* and *Moloko Plus*. She has recently traded in her dominatrix boots to take up life as an online entrepreneur and homemaker. She loves farmers markets, alternative medicine, classic films, cheesy B-movies, wine, saki, sushi and green tea. She loves her main squeezes: her pugs and her husband. They just relocated to the East Coast to start baby-making.

Check out Andi's favorite reads:

✓ *Women's Bodies Women's Wisdom* **by Christiane Northrup**

✓ *Last Gang in Town: The Story and Myth of the Clash* **by Marcus Gray**

✓ *Der Struwwelpeter* **by Otto Moravec (A very cool children's fable!)**

✓ *There Are No Incurable Diseases* **by Dr. Richard Schulze.**

Oh yeah, don't forget to get your body-loving reading pillow at CuntFactory.com!

She loves books, musing, and music. Her favorite reads are *Women's Bodies Women's Wisdom* by Christiane Northrup, *Last Gang in Town: The Story and Myth of the Clash* by Marcus Gray, *Der Struwwelpeter* by Otto Moravec (A very cool German children's fable!), and *There Are No Incurable Diseases* by Dr. Richard Schulze. Just like her reading, she gets her news reporting from RAI, BBC, as well as Hispanic and Canadian channels, and compares that to what CNN and FOX are reporting, so she can filter out the true story—without commercial, or political, influence and interests being reflected. She is committed to living strongly and passionately with an eye on truth and fun, in tandem. Her personal heroes are her mother, Madalyn Murray O'Hare (An infamous atheist activist whose work resulted in a controversial Supreme Court ruling. She and her family were subsequently butchered in Texas by a convicted felon.), Wendy O. Williams, Janis Martin (Another awesome Rebel Mom in this book!), Josephine Baker, Joan Jett, and Joe Strummer. She also admires Elvis Presley and his motto, *"Being a pioneer is one kind of heroism, but a person who puts someone else's needs ahead of their own is also a real hero."*

★★★★★★★★

Nice Girls Don't Play Rock & Roll

Andi sings in three languages, Spanish, English, and German. Her band Snap-Her's records can be ordered through the website for the label New Red Archives. You can check out awesome classics like *Beer (Don't Touch My Beer!)*, and *Be My Girl* at: Myspace.com/SnapHer.

★★★★★★★★

The music genres she lives for are: tango, flamenco, salsa, swing, surf (including instrumental and zombie), traditional ska, punk rock, and death metal. But her favorite bands are her own. Snap-Her had been her mainstay in life until recently. The band itself dismantled after nine years in 2002. The line-up changed frequently, and Andi played both bass and guitar (as needed) and sung. No matter what the line-up fluctuations were, one thing that was unchanging was the raw punk sound and feel of the late seventies and early eighties. I went from writer/ interviewer to fan mode and shared with her how much I loved Snap-Her, and how many punk girls specifically had, and get to have, so much fun because of their music! I told her some of my road-trip stories, in my early twenties, with my shaved head and teal colored bang's, decked out in purple and black vinyl, singing their songs *Beer (Don't Touch My Beer!)*, *Be My Girl*, and *You're So Lame!* Their album *Queen Bitch of Rock & Roll* is hands-down my favorite with songs like *Nice Girls Don't Play Rock & Roll* and *La Cucaracha.* Andi sings in three languages, Spanish, English, and German. Both records can be ordered through the website for the label New Red Archives. [New Red Archives also put out two of my other favorite bands Reagan Youth and Anti-Flag.]

You can check out Andi's band at: Myspace.com/SnapHer. This is a punk rock band, and they are not politically correct, so if you're easily offended you should skip it—unless you wanna have some crass-ass-fun!

Lyrically, Andi can also be grotesque in such songs as *Golden Cocktail*, *She's a Motorhead*, and *Conformist Cunt*, not to mention the Larry Flynt worthy inserts and PMRC (Parents Music Resource Center) warning label forewarning of content that could be considered objectionable ... [I do appreciate the warning label as a parent; it's a good public compromise to keeping content available and protecting free speech. I think Ice-T would agree.]

Although, political correctness has good intentions, and the PMRC for that matter, we do have to be cautious of letting them evolve to the extent that they control behavior, opinion and speech. If that happens we then are on a slippery slope. The unintended aftermath is censorship and not feeling safe to question what you're being sold as truth. Andi's parents had to flee their home in Argentina when she was a child because of totalitarian dictatorship that started off gradually as popular opinion and propaganda, then absolute control. Andi also has felt the backlash of PC in North America,

> "I am a 'permanent resident alien' in the U.S. Therefore, I do not possess the right to vote. I am originally from Argentina, the land of the tango, soybeans, and Evita. (Also, a lot of beef and leather enthusiasts seem to find Argentina to be THE place to vacation.) I am Hispanic and White (with a hue of olive)—the Census Bureau thinks I am lying. I was annoyed the last time one of their reps came to my door asking for my info. According to them, one can only be Hispanic if their skin is beige or brown (not black, white, olive, or yellow). I ended up verbally abusing him and slamming the door in his face. Also, contrary to popular belief, being married to an American citizen does not automatically make me one by default. I must pay the money to take the American history test and actually pass."

Her parents escaped their country and brutal government when she was only four-years-old.

> "My family moved here due to a lot of political problems in Argentina at that time. My father couldn't even finish his university training because there were riots

on campus. The culture there was people disappeared. The government would round up people who criticized the government and torture them in concentration camps, or dump them into the ocean from airplanes and a lot of innocent people died; very comparable to what happened in WW2 with Hitler."

She cautions us with a favorite quote from a William Shakespeare's play:

"Beware the leader who bangs the drum in order to whip the citizenry into a patriotic fervor, for patriotism is indeed a double-edged sword. It both emboldens the blood, just as it narrows the mind. And when the drums of war have reached a fever pitch and the blood boils with hate and the mind has closed, the leader will have no need in seizing the rights of citizenry. Rather the citizenry, infused with fear, and blinded with patriotism, will offer up all of their rights unto the leader, and gladly so. How do I know? For this is what I have done. And I am Caesar."

They had family at the time living in California, and that is where they had settled. Her parents sought asylum, which was granted, and became U.S. citizens. They left her the choice to make when she became older. They loved their home, their customs, the people and the history, but like all great places that fall under tortuous dictatorship, they could never risk their lives again. California's weather reminded them of home, the weather was perfect, the food wonderful, and there was no snow. If you wanted snow you would just drive up to the mountains, which they did occasionally; Andi recalls being young and sledding with them. She laughs warmly at remembering her dad's pompadour and her mom's mod fashion. After their citizenship was cemented, they tested the waters by relocating to Argentina when Andi was twelve for one year. Her parents wanted her to know her roots,

"In L.A, I never felt safe walking down the street. Buenos Aries though at twelve, when we came back, I felt safe. Buenos Aries was like a safe, beautiful mixture of Paris and Manhattan. In Argentina food is enjoyed much more leisurely. It takes hours to eat and drink, and it is enjoyable. Everyone drinks wine with their meals, even a child has a small glass of wine. It is very relaxed and it's a way to connect to friends and family on a daily basis. Most Argentineans don't go to bed until after midnight, and take naps during the day, and rise early to get fresh bread for breakfast.

It was heaven! This connected and happy living is made possible by six-hour work days and just this is the way of the people. Why live any differently?"

Andi remembers the ease of the city, and the happiness that filled the streets. She knew she would never revoke her citizenship and she wanted more of the world. She has lived and been almost everywhere since then and makes her own rules about life.

"I have lived in four U.S. states, and in three countries on three different continents. Were my relocations military related? No. Insanity related? Yes. In other words, I have no problem with working two jobs for a year, then putting my crap in storage, and going to see the world. I have experienced earthquakes in Argentina, California, Japan, and Mexico. I love the four seasons because the experience of actual weather is an intense feeling that I crave. I study Latin on my own when I have the time, and I am always learning more English, Spanish, Italian and Deutsch. Since I haven't the money to attend school at this time, I am being as studious as possible without the guidance of a strict teacher (which I would prefer). I wasn't designed, or made to be labeled, or deemed to be, or seen, as anything or anyone in particular, I'm a free spirit built with a tender heart, that's human, and tends to break from time-to-time. I'm all for promoting a positive and compassionate lifestyle aided with humor and generosity. I find nothing more satisfying than being filled with ambition, as well as being cultured and educated (not necessarily by means of school).

I enjoy knowing people with an international view of the world. People who are attracted to the idea of traveling to countries where English is not spoken and who are not so rude and arrogant as to presume that the people in said country should speak English; people who have at least bothered to learn the basic language, customs, and geography of where they are traveling. People who understand the logic of 'When in Rome, do as the Romans.' People who enjoy traveling 'outside the plastic bubble', in other words, people who are attracted to traveling and mingling with the locals, or on a low budget, or backpacking style, or to a place where you don't know anyone. In other words, NOT people who travel as part of a tourist group and eat what they would normally eat in their hometown. I enjoy conversing with people who are open-minded and intelligent in general. I'll never limit myself to anything. I'll continue to live and learn throughout this life no matter how long or short it may be. You should too."

Andi has also toured over fifteen countries with Snap-Her. When she encountered other bands, specifically in Germany, England, and Switzerland, they couldn't understand why she would have to come back to the U.S., and get a job to pay the bills. In Germany, she learned that the government partially subsidizes housing and pay for artists and musicians in general, and not just a marginal few. [*I wasn't able to confirm this through research; however I have heard this from other world travelers too. Nonetheless, according to a recent report by Factoidz that cites and compares Quality of Life standards between Europe and the United States, Europeans, currently, got it better overall in terms of happiness, health, lifespan, safety, and the like—indicating there are better ways to construct our values and systems, and spend our money more wisely for the benefit of all versus a few on top of the tax bracket at the expense of everyone else's backs and labor. However, in all fairness pre-WWII the U.S. had absorbed many of Europe's poor, and well, WWII annihilated Europe giving them a chance to rebuild the way they wanted, and Europeans were by then much more sensitive to human sufferings due to the atrocities they just endured. But that doesn't mean we can't or shouldn't re-tool our system to make it more effective and better, nor do we need a wipe-out war to motivate us. Just look north to Canada as a good example.*]

If any of you are wondering how she earned the money needed to travel all across the globe, it wasn't working fast food jobs. She eventually found very lucrative work practicing safe, sane, and consensual bondage and S&M professionally as a dominatrix. Contrary to popular belief, most dominatrixes do not engage in prostitution or sex. They are well-trained and disciplined masters of their submissives, both male and female, who have a need or desire to be punished and controlled. According to Wikipedia, over thirty-nine percent attended graduate school, including Ivy Leagues like Columbia. Typically, pro doms are also very selective about their clients and have a strict adherence to their established rules. However, do your homework very well before trying to engage in this line of work, so that you do not get taken advantage of, or possibly victimized. Seek out an established, well known, and trustworthy dominatrix to mentor you, and/or employ you in their dungeon. If you search online you will find a rich and varied amount of resources to get you *started* in your research, of course that's presuming you have the heart and stomach for this line of work. Andi reminds us that most of us are already ignorantly submissive, and we are exploited by others, including: employers, social intuitions, men, and the like. This is one area as a woman and a worker you can have complete control. Andi retired after thirteen years because,

> "I broke my ankle in 1999 and can no longer wear extreme heels and I am now considered to be 'heavily-tattooed' therefore I am now very unmarketable to any subs or masochists with money. Speaking of money, ever since the Republicunts came back into office after Clinton in 2000, most people just do not have the extra money to see a Pro Domme like they used to."

Andi and her husband currently pay the bills with his full-time work income and from her multiple e-shops online where she sells her collector item gear from Snap-Her, personal punk mementos, and her former work accessories as a dom. She also collects rare and vintage items that she sells.

Andi's childhood and traveling has shaped who she is, and people that she meets are frequently perplexed by the fact they cannot limit her to one role, or one way of being. Some are even shocked to learn that she is now a pretty normal housewife, once they get to know her. She enjoys writing, studying, doing yoga, cooking, making music, and even skating around the house naked while cleaning, which makes it fun and gives her a work-out. (Her husband gets a kick out of it, and it helps with the baby-making work too.) She loves and believes in the "lost art of whole food cooking" from scratch with a focus on quality over quantity, and eating healthy organic foods. She chuckles as she admits she eats "an alarming amount of garlic," she even got fired once when she was younger for reeking of garlic. She enjoys apples daily and doesn't eat the flesh of animals "that have walked or crawled, when they were alive," nor does she use products that have been tested on animals. She is an adamant follower of holistic medicine and refrains from running to the doctor every time she gets ill. She successfully practices home remedies and uses aggressive alternative medicines. She jokes that she gets called a hippie a lot,

"I am a heretic in many ways. I have little faith in orthodox medicine because the medical *industry* is *controlled* by the pharmaceutical companies. They control medical doctors like puppets on strings. I have a much more DIY approach to preventing and healing illness and disease. The only time it makes sense to employ med doctors is for emergency services (an accident) or a birthing. I believe it is optimum to employ a doula, which is what I plan to do, in conjunction with med docs for birth, just in case of a problematic delivery. I am always pleased when getting to know people whom employ DIY or alternative approaches to certain aspects of their lives, but then I am perplexed to find out that they submit themselves to the quackery of orthodox medicine and its doctors."

Andi speaks from direct experience and knowledge. She saw her own mom go through chemotherapy twice for breast cancer, and when Andi found a lump in her own breast, she treated it with a thirty-day holistic detoxification plan and her tumor disappeared.

Andi and her husband share many of the same views on the systems and industries of the world, and both are atheists and music-lovers. They had been dating for fourteen months, when he proposed to her on stage during a Snap-Her show. It was punk rock love. He has always been supportive of her band, and understood her line of work, and is a true life-partner in the most modern, respectful, equitable, and loving way. He is a strong man, and she is a strong woman, and they complement each other. Snap-Her continued for two years after this, and she was ready to move on to something else after dedicating eighteen years to music with Snap-Her, the Derita Sisters, and the Creamers. She wanted to write some books that she had been contemplating. At this time her husband dropped hints he wanted to move out of Los Angeles, and so did she.

They first moved to Rhode Island, and were turned off by the local's snobbishness. They later moved to New Jersey and quickly learned it is very expensive. They tried Pennsylvania, and it felt right, the locals were warm and nice, and it was affordable. They settled into a small town and got comfy. That's when they started talking about starting a family, and agreed that once she became pregnant, they would move to Europe.

Now that they are actively trying to conceive the fears of being a mom are starting to kick in. The fear of giving birth and …

"I don't know what it's going to be like to be a subculture mom, being judged and tattooed. I'm nervous too about our kid being exposed to things in school that I don't want him exposed to. I don't want my kid having religion shoved down his throat, we are both atheists. We want to raise our kid to be an individual and if he has a need or an interest in religion, then we will study each one in the world. Kids shouldn't be forced into a life of religion; it's a big lifestyle, not like choosing a cookie or a candy.

I also worry about the culture here, which is another reason why we want to move to Europe to raise our family. Kids and teenagers are much more respectful of their elders and parents. Here the kids are afraid to be seen with their parents, and there is a lack of respect for elders and parents, and that has a lot to do with the vanity in this culture. As world travelers, we know there are better places with better values to raise our kid and we are going there."

Andi is no doubt going to make an incredible mother, raising her kid affectionately, and with healthy and holistic values, while instilling a sense of questioning politics, government, and culture, to get to the truth of the matter. With her life experience and international mindset she will teach her kid about life in ways that a college classroom never could. And that is cool. She closes with …

"I've always loved music and got into it. I was never one of those who wanted to graduate high school, get married right away, and have kids. I wanted a bohemian life and let the wind take me wherever. I have lived a lot like a gypsy, and have toured in many different countries. I've had the life I wanted, that makes me happy. Now I want to have kids and that will make me happy too."

Afterword

Rebel Moms has been my labor of love for the last eight years. It has been a challenge to execute amongst life's numerous demands and surprises, but also an amazing adventure. I have met so many incredible women, who like me at times felt stuck and silenced, but were damned if they were going to passively accept it. Even though I was, and still am, in transition and have enough full-time jobs on my plate otherwise, I humbly accepted the calling to write this book, asked of me by life and fate, in the late summer of 2003 and did it. After a long, beguiling, and complicated labor, I have given birth to over five-hundred pages, eight chapters, and have written the biographies of over fifty women, from a feminist and alternative parenting perspective. It's out in the world now, to both help and challenge moms and parents, and ultimately it will serve in helping us to raise the kind of world we want our kids in. And so be it.

My afterword is perhaps a bit astray form the norm, but I wanted to share something with you very personal, albeit not profound: I'm a working class writer and I have been to hell and back. That has made me the tenacious, and somewhat difficult (so I have been told) person that I am. A new friend once asked pointedly, over a holiday dinner conversation on music and politics, *"So how did you become so political?"* My reply was equally straightforward, *"Hell and Love."* Hell is what makes us, Love is what saves us. Those who have been there will understand. Hell was followed by exploitation, and partially existed because of. *(Although, my parents and my peers parents, and their choices, bear some responsibility for where we all ended up as little kids and what was going on around us. Those choices also later influenced the bad, bad, bad choices we made as teens, and later young 'adults', at least in my case and most of my friends. It is both generational influence and lack of rearing, as well as environmental and social exploitation.)* There is a reason why Elvis's *In the Ghetto* always makes me tragically weep, Lauren's *Every Ghetto, Every City* reminds me now of some of the good times I had growing up in the hood despite all the hungry summers, violence, fighting, shooting and looting, and Everlast's *What It's Like,* always reminds me to remember where people are at, and what shoes they are walking in, not to mention where I've been. Our neighborhood and home environment caused severe generational damage, and lots of lives were harmed. But there has to be a life-rope somewhere. The key as kids is finding it. The key as adults is putting it out there. Writing and Greek drama was mine (and a whole lot of Madonna love!). So my writings don't stem from a seed planted in college intellectualism, but from the very real personal need of a struggling working class writer, and later a struggling working class mom, and it started with a struggling and starving child, who was saved at a young age by drama and poetry.

Writing this book has taught me how resilient I am, and yes, I am political, ha-ha, as well as the moms in my book that kept getting back up no matter what. If one way did not work, they/we tried another. And that is life, and you have to do it, regardless of what your circumstances were or are. With that said … I must credit the moms and their insights from this book, which has already helped my parenting and life-planning, to a profound extent. I truly feel like I have a wonderful, boisterous, righteous community of awesome Rebel Moms backing me. I hope you feel their support and their cheers, as you turn to them for hope, direction, insight, love, and when needed … a good laugh or a swift kick in the butt! My parenting has blossomed, I've blossomed, and my outlook on love, life, kids, and people has blossomed. My heart is full and I am content.

I lent my professional skill-set of coaching and development to my personal one of writing, to ensure that the Rebel Mom biographies metamorphosed from mere stories to engaging tales of direction, leadership and experience, within the specific role of mentoring, and from the perspective of varying time/cyclical stages of womanhood and motherhood. I hope this personal collection of mentors has inspired you in multiple ways—both seen and yet unseen.

We Rebel Moms aren't so radical, despite what the world or media says, because at the end of the day, were fighting not just for our world, but yours, ours kids and your kids, and frankly there isn't anything fringe, extreme, or radical about that. It should be the norm, and it is problematic if it is not. To help you get the most from Rebel Moms, and for you awesome reading groups out there, I have included an informal impromptu *Circle of Questions* to help you find your own voice and direction, and shape what you take away from this book into a powerful and resourceful tool for change—whatever change you want to make in your life, in the life of your babies, and our world.

Rock 'n' Roll!
Davina Rhine

Circle of Questions

1) Who is your favorite mom from this book? Please list the top three reasons why.
2) What mom did you like least and what made you dislike her so much? What about her, or her story, made you uncomfortable?
3) Of all the self-made careers in the book, such as Rebel Mom Juli's, Nana's, Janis Martin's, Corey Parks's, Hayley's, or Stephanie's—which jobs rocked your world? How did they get from A-to-B-to-C?
4) What is your dream job and what three things can you do today, or initiate now, to start working towards that? Would you use some of the recommended tools by Rebel Mom Suzie? Which ones?
5) What is your long-term strategy to get there—to your dream job? Has Rebel Mom Sarah's step-by-step outline helped you articulate that plan? What was her plan?
6) What do you think about Rebel Mom Sarah Jane's parenting philosophy and social/political stances? Do you think this will provide for a better, healthier environment for her children? Why or why not? How does it compare to yours? What changes would you want to implement in your household for a healthier world, and a healthier child?
7) Did Rebel Mom Carol's combination of stay-at-home mom-work and political activism inspire you to get more involved? What do you want to advocate for most? What is the single most important area to you that is in need of political attention, action and resolution, right now? What is within your means, or circle of influence, that you can start doing today to work towards achieving that change?
8) How would you define your parenting philosophy and how do you model/teach this? What was graphic artist

and political illustrator Kristen's parenting philosophy? Or herbalist Crystal's?

9) Do you think you would be a better mom working outside of the home like Tripper-banned rocker Sharon Needles, yogi Lucid, and insurance underwriter Lindsay? Or a better mom working full-time as a stay-at-home mom like writer and amateur herpetologist Debbey, or retired hairstylist Lola? What are the pros and cons of both? Would being a stay-at-home mom even be an option for you? How can you be the best mom and provider and make the route to get there work for you and your family?
10) What do you think about unschooling (Rebel Mom Lola) or attachment parenting (Rebel Mom Heather)? We see these referenced throughout the book. How does it tie-in to your way? What is your parenting philosophy?
11) Do you think Rebel Mom and political hopeful April's story and insight will better prepare for the teen years of parenting? Do you think she could be the next president? And what are your next-phase-of-life plans when your children are older?
12) Do you think Rebel Mom Beth's positive experience with hypnobirthing will be something you would share to future expectant friends? Or Corey Parks's planned doula delivery?
13) Did Rebel Mom Jenise's value system shed any light on your own? Do you think she has a heart of gold and love? How do you think her inner light, reflects back on the world through her engagement with others, and through her children?
14) Has Rebel Mom Natasha's battle with the military made you think deeper about serving 'God and Country?' How does the military depend on the poor? Why? Wouldn't this be a patriotic duty of all classes? If not, why not? What are your conclusions based on her treatment by the military medical system? Do you think it was sexist?
15) What if you suddenly found yourself disabled, even if short-term, like Rebel Mom Heather—what would be

your action plan for you to survive and thrive even amidst severe poverty? Do you think it's fair or helpful, that our political system attempts to demean and shame her by calling her a welfare mom?

16) What about Ariel Gore, who also was labeled by the Republican Party as a welfare mom, and the enemy of motherhood? Where would the movement, and thus voice, of real motherhood be without her contributions? Do you think her life is an example of where we can invest now as a society, through the means of aid and support to moms, and reap the benefits later? Her books have inspired and helped millions. Do you think the state of California helping her for a few years while she finished school was a good thing or a bad thing? Do you think her writing life and books would have ever existed, and thus helped millions, if they hadn't? Why do you think moms are belittled for needing and getting (some) help, yet corporations aren't ridiculed for the mass welfare they receive in tax money grants, cuts, and freebies? Do you think this could be because they are run by already rich and powerful people? And most homes headed by women are not either rich or powerful? Where should we spend our tax money, in the beginning helping, or at the end treating symptoms? Why isn't there a welfare dad stigma?

17) Rebel Mom Cynthia has clearly broken negative family/generational patterns in her parenting, and has replaced them with positive, constructive, and loving ones. What are your parenting patterns and why?

18) Rebel Mom Katy, ended a non-supportive domestic partnership, even though it meant being a struggling single mom, do you think this provided for a better self-esteem for herself, and for her daughter? What would you do if in her shoes?

19) Rebel Moms Stephanie and Taylore both ended abusive relationships. Do you know anyone being abused? How do you safely intervene? What can we do to raise our boys better, and to respect girls and women? How can

we raise our girls better, and to respect themselves, even when society gives them completely opposite messages? What are the danger signs of being in a physically, or mentally, abusive relationship?

20) How can you as a working mom fulfill your wants and desires to be a stay-at-home mom, while still earning a paycheck? Did Rebel Mom Blaire's story help give you some ideas on how to make work and home co-exist in harmony? To blend them per se?
21) Like many of the moms throughout this book, Rebel Moms Kimberly, Jennifer, and Suzie articulately defined their frustration for the stifling attitudes of bosses, and indifferences towards or exploitations of moms, women, and workers, by their employers. Do you think women are exploited by big business?
22) What about the term *Cervix Industry Worker* that Jennifer coined—how does that make you feel as woman? And do you ever think about the women whose jobs are to help you? Have you ever put yourself in their shoes?
23) As Rebel Moms Kimberly and Suzie wondered, why are so many jobs hostile to the needs of parents and children? Why does the business world ignore the needs of the people that work for them in general? Who benefits? Who is harmed? What are some viable solutions that are a win-win for both? Is sharing really key? As Kimberly suggested, should the needs of employees and the community even be considered by business? Why or why not? What could be the consequences (positive or negative) of indifference, or ignorance, or the initial merging?
24) If faced with the heart-wrenching decision of working to put food on the table, and with no other options, but for your kids to be latch-key, how would that make you feel? Do you think we live in a just world when moms have to make that call all the time? Could some of the child-care solutions devised by Mother Nature, Stacey, Momma Cherry, or Rebel Mom Jenn help you? And if they aren't a financial option, how can you create work

that enables you to be home with your kids when they aren't in school? Or how do we get our economic policy, public policy, and tax system to catch up to the times? So that all kids are safe and taken care of, while their parents are out having to work? We know of other 1st world countries doing it, and doing it very successfully, like France, England and Germany, so why aren't we?

25) Could networking with groups like Rebel Mom Winter's PunkyMoms.com, or Ariel Gore's *HipMama.com*, help you get real world momma answers and find mentors? Have you tried reaching out to social media moms groups for support? What has been your experience?

26) Rebel Mom Dr. Taj Anwar created an amazing activist group, M.O.B.B., to help fulfill the needs of a specific demographic of moms who are typically looked down upon by mainstream charity and activist groups, do you think her model has helped create a voice and a solution for moms-in-need? How would you build on to it or change it to meet the needs of moms in your direct community? What are their needs and struggles? What are yours? How can we work together to help each other?

27) Has the travel stories of Rebel Mom (to be) Andi inspired you to figure out a way to see the world? What are your explorer fantasies? What do you think about her stances on holistic medicine and DIY? Do you look at cancer differently now? How would you live under a tortuous dictatorship? How would you protect your family? Do you think she is going to be an awesome mom? Why or why not?

28) Do you think Rebel Mom Nana's reasons to build a green house in a far away state are well-founded? Do you think global warming will cause California to go under in our lifetime as she fears? What can we do to intervene now to help protect our environment and our future?

29) Rebel Moms Selena and Syren both practice unorthodox (in the classical western sense) religions that are more

connected to the Earth, than traditional Christian male-based dogmas. Do their spiritual beliefs conflict or compliment your own? If so, how? What additional insights were you able to abstract from their articulated belief systems? Did it change any stereotypes you may have held? What was your intellectual and emotional response when you learned that Syren's family specifically keeps their faith and practices on the down-low to avoid discrimination?

30) What is your opinion of Rebel Mom Jenn Bats rejection of a god-concept? Do you feel you have a better understanding of atheism now? Do you think it's scientifically absolute?

31) Did you know any moms, such as Rebel Moms Momma Cherry and Qui Qui, before reading this book that were taking on more traditionally assigned male roles, such as boxing and firefighting, that still largely exclude women? Is there anything you ever wanted to do that you were told because you were a woman or a girl that you couldn't? Or that you weren't strong enough? Do you still have the desire to do this? What steps can you take to make it a reality? What self-sustaining support system can you devise to help you overcome fear, self-doubt, and ridicule?

32) Several of the Rebel Moms were victims of sexual attacks … based on their experiences do you feel we live in a rape-culture, or are women generally respected and protected by society and the legal system? What could you do, based on their stories, to make our environments safer and healthier for women?

33) What about children being exploited or hurt by predators—several moms in the book cited concern and experience with this as both victims and mothers—what contributes to making us and our children vulnerable? Are working class moms and kids more vulnerable, since most working class moms are forced to put work before their kids without adequate or good enough childcare? How can we recognize and prevent, or stop, predators?

Is society part of the problem, or part of the solution, and how?

34) When Rebel Mom Beth's best friend died from a drug overdose, how did it make you feel as a parent? What can we do to better protect our kids from these dangers, without enabling ignorance? Should drug addiction continue to be criminalized? Can we ever live in a world where drugs aren't portrayed or perceived as glamorous, when alcohol, pharmaceuticals, and tobacco are regulated (and promoted) fashion and lifestyle accessories?
35) What about Rebel Mom Kaisea who overcome addiction to alcohol and meth … what empowered her to beat these crippling addictions when so many others painstakingly fail, despite their best intentions?
36) Do you think violence in society will always be pervasive when drug use is criminalized, and have so much black market worth similar to the buying and selling of blood diamonds? Do you think our institutionalized forms of violence, ranging from historical slavery to modern wage indentured servitude, and sexism, to eating animals, encourages this? How can we work for a non-violent or far less violent world? Is greed and privilege the problem? Or lack of moral values? Or human nature? Rebel Mom Jenn Bats thinks it's a combination of all of the above. What do you think?
37) Since we are fighting for a better world, how can we help stop human trafficking? Will addressing the issues under question 36 enable us to solve that problem at the same time? Rebel Mom Natasha thinks so. What would be your strategy to put an end to child exploitation and slavery on an international scale? What about in our own backyard?
38) What do you think happened to the woman that Rebel Mom Pam pierced, who reclaimed her body through symbolic ritual?
39) Does Rebel Mom Stasia's experience as a Suicide Girl and the reason why she choose to model nude as a

pin-up, alter your perceptions of what is considered pornographic? How does it make you feel about your own body? What is your relationship with yourself—do you love yourself, including your flaws? Do you have a good self-esteem? What do you think of the beauty image being sold to us? Do you have a healthy concept of your sexuality? Why or why not? What exactly does healthy self-love mean to you and what are its attributes?

40) Do you think a positive parent's movement could help us provide the guidance needed for young parents to parent differently and better? Does Rebel Mom Kristin's story offer examples of what we could do to help teen moms as well? How can we as a system and a society be there for kids? How can we do a better job by them and for them? What contributes to teen pregnancy? As parents and role-models how can we better help and prepare our teens for their emerging sexuality and hormone flairs? And since most teen moms, started having sex to feel loved, where did we go wrong as parents and as a society—that they felt unloved or unwanted in the first place?

41) When Rebel Mom Dawna's child died, how did that make you feel? Would you be able to find the strength to go on after losing a child? What if she didn't have the responsibility of other children like Janis Martin?

42) When Rebel Mom and demolition queen April faced pregnancy in isolation, did you become upset that she had to go through that alone? Why does social life initially exclude each generation's first round of mothers? Do you think it has to do with the lack of value of motherhood in our cultures and women's work? Or the animosities that our culture implies daughters are suppose to have against their mothers—thus the rejection of the 1st round of new moms per generation, especially by their female peers?

43) Do you think you could ever be as selfless as Rebel Mom Marea? To give your child up for adoption because you couldn't provide the best family environment? Or

do you think it was a selfish act to pursue her dreams? Why or why not? Why aren't women free from judgment and ridicule when we do make the best choices for our reproductive health, or the children we have, even if they are complicated ones? What would you have done in her shoes? Would you have had an abortion instead? Why or why not?

44) In considering all Rebel Moms featured and their stories, how can we determine what good parenting is from bad parenting and what defines that? What if the playing fields aren't all equal? What are your check and balances to ensure your judgment is objective, not emotional, and free from dislikes/likes and/or stereotyping?
45) What takeaways have you gathered from this book and this collection of mentors to enable you to be a better parent and person?
46) Have your perceptions of love and discipline changed at all after reading Rebel Moms?
47) Have your perceptions of other moms, individuals, and/or cultures (including subcultures) that are different from your own been altered at all?
48) What areas in your life do you feel you have a new found need to change or revisit and why?
49) What can you do today to make the world a better place?
50) What about tomorrow? And the day after that?

The Modern Athena

The Modern Athena
is seeing the world through
21st century eyes
She is the cervix worker
The muted maid
The discarded wife
The burned lover
The overworked mother
The denied peace maker and artist

With battle cries she wages her campaign
She feels caged
Stuck in Walmart pin-stripes and promises of 401k's
Six weeks FMLA
Still making much less for doing the same
Family Friendly Work Policies
Just really means, "suck it up"
Take your pump to the bathroom
With your powder and your tampon
Blood and milk mix
Becoming Nuclear

The Modern Athena
views democracy's sexism as a failure
She has been waiting, for progress
for thousands of years
Now she's ready for war
Revenge for the destruction of Themyscira
and everything sacred since

She prepares for battle
Sharpening her swords and her wit
She calls for the New Supper with her Amazons
and her audience is the modern woman
Her agenda is to slaughter
The ass grabbers
The rapists

The bosses who make a woman choose
between work and a needy or sickly child
again and again
The bosses who want you to give
life, liberty, soul, and death
all in return for just a meager paycheck
The earth plunderers
The under-payers
The exploiters
The unfair law-makers
Congress will be burned red
Every man on those seats who have not done
women and children right
will be destroyed and forgotten
Every father/ husband who has not respected
his wife and daughters,
will be blinded
Every tongue that soiled women's name and hindered
humanities progress will be cut out

The Modern Athena won't just be the next president
but rule immortal with the heart of Leonidas and Gorgo,
the mind of Boudicca and her tribes,
the military brilliance of Alexander,
the aim of Artemis,
the intellect of Hypatia

The Modern Athena is many
She will not be subdued, overruled,
or torn apart by men
and their wicked leaders
or built by up material gods
Her temples will no longer contain her

She will take the sons back from the corruption of patriarchy
Giving them birth anew,
fathers like Bachofen and Theon,
mentors like
Mead, Stanton, Goldman, Chicago, Walker, Clinton
with Amazonian mothers and queens from all over the globe

The Modern Athena's eyes are heavy and somber
No more Vietnams
No more African Genocides
No more dowries
No more gang-rapes
No more corporate genocide
No more stoning
No more hungry children
No more neglected children
No more latch-key kids
No more dead-beat-dads
No more oil for water
Cut-throat corn and potatoes

Life is slipping away from women
who have been overruled by their men
and the men of others
Women with no rooms
Women whose voices
have been silenced with violence
Whose daughters and sons have been ignored
The daughters rejected ...
except by property-ownership-marriage
and enslavement motherhood, a mans in house play-bunny
The sons taunted and tormented by ...
fathers, uncles, leaders, teachers, friends
into the macho mold until they too can repeat the patterns of
the past on tomorrows wives, lovers, mothers and daughters

The Modern Athena spits back
She is giving birth to a new Crete,
A new race of women and children,
her afterbirth will give us Atlantis redeemed
Lesbos reborn
She is going to take her battle ax,
And kill Zeus.

Acknowledgements and Permissions

Rebel Moms was such an intense, grueling work-out for me in the areas of women's studies, sociology, alternative parenting, time-management, patience, technical ignorance, and naive bliss ha-ha, I asked for help from everyone I knew! So many friends, family, and strangers have been so helpful and involved with this project from beginning to end, that I don't even know where to start! So, I will simply start from the beginning. I was once had an English professor that rocked and he endured the first early draft of Rebel Moms in 2005. He provided critical feedback on 139 pages at an important fork in the road. His insight helped me better define the contours and shape of the women's voices, and the structure in how you would later meet the moms. A hearty thank you Dr. Edward Garcia! Secondly, was the massive copyline edit and content feedback on the Rebel Moms manuscript in late 2007, then at about 279 pages, by Bill Bolen, who loved grammar, science, and all stuff taboo. I still chuckle, when I remember Bill asking inquisitively, "Just how big do you want this thing to be?" I answered, "As big as it needs to be!" Thanks Bill for all your help! Both of these gentlemen accorded big pushes in the development of the book at crucial stages, and I cannot thank them enough for it. A celebratory copy seems to pale in comparison to the depth of my gratitude. Also, there would be no book without the last-minute copyline edit intervention of Katy Krisak, who gave me a much needed break! (She's also a Rebel Mom and an awesome writer-pro!) So Katy, here's to you lady, a big cheers! And Rebel Mom Pam Spector took the time to read the entire book and fished out all the resources for moms—which is just a cool page or so from now. This was no easy feat with two jobs, and a new, and incredibly cute, baby at home! Pam rules!!! Katherine Hunter, my beautiful guru and life-line to the techy and spiritual world, provided huge insight on all the techy stuff and indie business stuff that I needed to know. She also believed in this project, when frankly my faith, and my faith in myself as a writer, and a mom, waivered. On that note, I want to say thank you to Stacy Phemister (Also, one of my beloved *Ladies of the Night*, and on the *Rebel Moms Street Team*!), Natasha Mulkey (A Rebel Mom in the book and my personal Amazon! I look up to her in so many ways—she doesn't even know! I know if she can do it, I can do it!), Asteria Wofford and Tera Flowers who both have loved me over many years despite my flaws, and encouraged me to keep going, that this is a good thing. Another big thanks to Asteria, and Melissa Beeman for all the babysitting help, which enabled me to not only at work at my paying 'day' job during different times, but to also work on this project by having kiddo sleepovers at your pad! Lisa McKey helped me plenty by encouraging me with her love, warmth, and positive attitude, not to mention providing me with great coffee, chick-flicks, and her company! The same thanks to Mrs. Jenny Blair and Ms. Jenny Cherry whom both threw holy water on me when I absolutely needed it. I love you ladies! Many friends sat in on last minute online editing parties giving feedback and making corrections for numerous stories, all throughout the process. Some serious honorable mentions go to my *Ladies of the Night:* Blaire Byrom (Yep! Another Rebel Mom whose bio is in the book!), Lisa McKey, Jenny Blair, McKenzie Lamm, Adrienne Maresh, Liz Garner (Yes, the one and only Jiz from the raddest band ever Jiz and The Jerk-Off's), Karen Hinebaugh (I still owe you BBQ and margarita time!), Alysia Angel, Raquel 'Rocky' Patterson, Stacey McDaniel and Tricia Wheelis; another wonderful writer, great friend, and mom!

I must thank all the Rebel Moms I recruited, stalked, and nagged (for updates, finishing the interview, pictures, consent forms, etc.) all throughout the process. Thank you for sharing your life's stories with me; being part of this project (I know this was no easy feat with all of our other time-deficit issues. You ladies are the best!), and believing in our vision of the tomorrow we can build by being there for each other today—and sharing the tools of the trade, of being a mom and a woman, a warrior, a survivor, a leader, and a helper. You rock! I reached out to about two-hundred moms. (Including some more you may know like: Lauren Hill, Angelina Jolie, Courtney Love, Erykah

Badu, Madonna, Maya Angelou, Brody from the Distillers, Alice Walker, Naomi Wolf, Sinead O' Connor, Mariska Hargitay [You have to check out Mariska.com by the way, incredible blog and site.] and Hillary Clinton, sadly with no luck, but they are Rebel Moms … whether they know it or not!) I interviewed about a hundred moms or so. Ultimately, for purposes of both space and diversity, I had to narrow the stories down to around fifty mom mentors offering the broadest and most articulated spectrum of experience, for the absolute benefit of any moms reading the book. That was an agonizing selection process, and being a democratic-socialist-idealist of sorts, I often had to get a majority vote on many. With that said, every mom who participated in the project from start-to-end not only contributed, but helped shape the concerns identified, the struggles we are enduring, and how we are working at overcoming them, not only as parents, but as women and as part of the circle of life. There would not be a Rebel Moms book without any of you.

Also, without the cool work of photographers, artists and writers—where would we be in life? I tried to ensure I got all permissions from all parties to use any images, quotes, etc, that complimented the interviews that the moms agreed to. Please know that no intentional overstep was intended. With no further ado, I thank Frank, of FrankBlauPhotography.com for his amazing photo of our favorite roller girl and firefighter, Momma Cherry! Stacey Potter for her great picture of Pam Spector! (You can check out this cool downtown photographer at StaceyPotter.com.) A big thank you to Rich Barker of RichBarker.com and Angie Taksony, both of PunkRockNight.com for use of their awesome and gritty photo of Selena beating the drums! Gleeful thanks goes to Maria Hibbs of Squaresville Studios (.com) for her heart-warming family portrait of Blaire and the kiddos. Another proclamation of gratitude goes to the artist and owner of Firelion Graphix, Juan Leon, who designed the Rebellion Press logos and inadvertently my next tattoo! If you would like to consult him about creative design graphics, or to have him design your next tattoo, feel free to reach out to him at JLeon_Graphix@yahoo.com.

I also must thank Dan Poynter for his helpful guide the *Self Publishing Manual*, which empowered me to revisit a dream I had at eighteen years of age, which was to start my own book press. Thank you for laying out the business and industry mechanics so neatly. Last but not least, there are two brilliant and awe-inspiring books I turned to for strength and ideas in shaping Rebel Moms that are also about cutting-edge changing the-world-as-we-know-it women: *Women of the Beat Generation* by Brenda Knight and *Cinderella's Big Score: Women of the Punk and Indie Underground* by Maria Raha.

Finally, without my family, there would be no book. I love you guys! And to all the cool children and all the awesome Rebel Moms, let's keep rocking!

Xoxo,
Davina Rhine

About the Author

Davina Rhine **spends her days chasing the goddess and dharma, and writing all about it.** She is a socially aware, political activist that lives in Texas with her amazing family. She loves vegetarian BBQs, archaeology, dinosaurs, her upright bass, espresso, mentoring, and aspires to be a professor of women's studies. She has written essays, fiction, poetry, music and book reviews, published by: *Altar Magazine of NYC*, *The Women's Press*, *Women's United Nations Report Network*, the *Feminist Review*, *Mamaphonic*, *Pedestal Magazine*, and the *Poetry Motel*. She has been a featured mom in local mags like *Dallas Child*, and the *Advocate*. Her work was published in the book anthology *If Women Ruled the World* by Inner Ocean Press. Jeffrey Levine of Tupelo Press has called her work, "strong and propulsive." *Rebel Moms* is her first published book, and her next book *The Chronicles of the Pharaoh's Daughter: Ancient Riddles of Love, Loss, and Rebirth* will be released winter of 2011. As a biographer and a rock 'n' roll historian, she is currently researching and writing *The Authorized Biography of Janis Martin: The Female Elvis*. You can check out her musings at RebellionPress.com and on Facebook.

Resources and Cool Stuff mentioned in Rebel Moms!

Books and Magazines:

Adele Faber and Elaine Mazlish's book:
How to Talk so Kids will Listen and Listen so Kids will Talk.
Adrienne Rich's book: *Of Woman Born.*
Alternative Press Magazine (Indie/Undie Music Mag)
Anne Rice's book: *Queen of the Damned.*
Anthony Burgess's book: *A Clockwork Orange.*
Ariel Gore's books: *Bluebird: Women and the New Psychology of Happiness, The Hip Mama Survival Guide* and *Portland Queer: Tales of the Rose City.*
Bitch Magazine
Brenda Knight's book: *Women of the Beat Generation: The Writers, Artists and Muses at the Heart of a Revolution.*
Bust Magazine
Christiane Northrup's book: *Women's Bodies Women's Wisdom.*
Dan Poynter's book: *The Self-Publishing Manual*
Deborah Spungen's book: *And I Don't Want to Live This Life.*
Dick Bolles's book: *What Color is Your Parachute?*
Dr. Richard Schulze's book: *There Are No Incurable Diseases.*
Dr. Ross W. Greene's book: *The Explosive Child.*
Elayne Angel's book: *The Piercing Bible.*
Emma McLaughlin and Nicola Kraus's book: *The Nanny Diaries.*
Gilbert King's book: *Woman, Child for Sale.*
Hip Mama: The Parenting Zine
Herman Hesse's book: *Siddhartha.*
Jack Kerouac's book: *On the Road.*
Jane Nelsen's book: *Positive Discipline.*
J.R.R. Tolkien's book: *The Hobbit.*
Juxtapoz Magazine (The underground art bible!)
Kimberly Wilson's book: *Hip Tranquil Chick.*
Lisa Brown's book: *Baby Make Me a Drink.*
Majjhima Nikaya's book*: Buddha Speaks.*
Marcus Gray's book: *Last Gang in Town: The Story and Myth of the Clash.*
Maria Raha's book: *Cinderella's Big Score: Women of the Punk and Indie Underground.*

Marilyn Sawyer Sommer's book: *Diseases & Disorders: A Nursing Therapeutics Manual.*
Mokolo Plus Magazine
Nicole Hollander's book: *Ma, Can I Be a feminist and Still Like Men? Lyrics from Life.*
Otto Moravec's book: *Der Struwwelpeter.*
Pam England's book: *Birthing from Within.*
Peter Orner's book: *Underground America: Narratives of Undocumented Lives.*
Punk Planet Magazine (now defunct, but cool issues can still be found!)
Shelia Ellison's book: *If Women Ruled the World.*
Starhawk's book: *The Fifth Sacred Thing.*
Stephanie Strowbridge's book's: *Set & Style* and *Grease It Up!*
Tattoo Savage Magazine
Victor Malarek's book: *The Natasha's.*
Wendy Keller's book: *Soaring Solo.*
William Ury's book: *Getting Past No.*
William Ury and Roger Fisher's book: *Getting to Yes.*

Websites and Online Communities:

ADifferentAnglePhotography.com
AliceBag.com/media.html
AmericanHerbalistGuild.com
AntiChips.com
ArielGore.com
Bmezine.com
Burningman.com
CafePress.com
ChildrenoftheNight.org
CoAdobe.org
CuntFactory.com
DadsSandwiches.com
DeliciousOrganics.com
FantaGraphics.com/artist/losbros/losbros.html
(*Love and Rockets* Comic Book)
FoodNotBombs.net
FrankBlauPhotography.com
Frump.com

FtpMovement.com
GreenCleanBook.com
HayleyHara.com
HealingArts.org
HealfromDepression.Blogspot.com
HelpHer.org (Hyperemesis Foundation)
Hildegard-austin.org/grow/the-viriditas-project.html
HipMamaZine.com
HipMama.com
HipTranquilChick.com
HolisticDiva.wordpress.com
IndiaResourceCenter.org
InfoWars.com (Alex Jones's site)
JobHuntersBible.com
KristenFerrell.com
Kristen-McClure-Therapist.com
Lucidawn.com
Lucky-11.com
Mamapalooza.com
Mamaphonic.com
MaryKay.com/PamelaSpector
MicrocosmPublishing.com
Mistletoegroup.com (progressive therapy group)
M.O.B.B. (Mothers of Black/Brown Babies): Mobbb.org
MotherEarthNews.com
Mothering.com
Myspace.com/DynamiteDamesPhotography
Myspace.com/FemaleElvis
Myspace.com/MenstrualTramps
Myspace.com/NeedletotheRecord (cool national DJ competition)
Myspace.com/PlacentaMusic
Myspace.com/SnapHer
Myspace.com/SikLuv
National Domestic Violence Website: TheHotline.org
NewRedArchives.com
PlacentaMusic.com
Permaculture.org
PunkRockNight.com

PunkyMoms.com
RadicalForgiveness.com
Rankinstein.com
ReleasetheBats.com
SarahJaneSemrad.com
SavetheChildren.net
SealPress.com
SilvaPhoto.com
Sisterbrothermgmt.com
SquaresvilleStudios.com
StaceyPorter.com
Store.McSweeneys.net
SuicideGirls.com
666Photography.com
TakeBacktheNight.org (a movement to end violence against women)
The Center for Nonviolent Communication: CNVC.org
TheGreenGuide.org/article/diy/household
ThePathtoAll.com
Trashy.com
USABoxing.org
VDay.org (Eve Ensler's *The Vagina Monologues*)
VerbalAbuse.com
Warrior Mamma's Online Community:
Groups.Myspace.com/NaturalBirth
WarningLabelRecords.com
Wicca.org
WildflowerHerbSchool.com
WomensBoxing.com

Films:

Documentary directed by Anthony Scarpa:
Betty Blowtorch: and Her Amazing True Life Adventures.
[Myspace.com/TheBettyBlowtorchMovie]
Documentary directed by Beth Harrington (released in 2002) featuring Janis Martin: *The Women of Rockabilly: Welcome to the Club.*
[Pbs.org/itvs/WelcometotheClub/]

Documentary directed by Lainy Bagwell and Lacey Leavitt: *Blood on the Flat Track: The Rise of the Rat City Rollergirls.* [RatCityRollergirls.com/news/botft-dvdrelease/]
Documentary directed by Michael Moore: *Sicko.*
Movie directed by Angela Robinson: *Herbie Fully Loaded.*
Movie directed by Blair Hayes: *Bubble Boy.*
Movie directed by Brian Gibson: *What's Love Got to Do with It.*
Movie directed by David Fincher: *Fight Club.*
Movie directed by Frances Lawrence: *Constantine.*
Movie directed by James Bridges: *Urban Cowboy.*
Movies directed by John Waters: *Pink Flamingo* and *Crybaby.*
Movie directed by Joseph Mangine: *Neon Maniacs.*
Movie directed by Julie Taymor: *Frida.*
Movie directed by Martha Coolidge: *Valley Girl.*
Movie directed by Neil Jordan: *Interview with a Vampire: The Vampire Chronicles*; based on Anne Rice's novels.
Movie directed by Ridley Scott: *Blade Runner.*
Movie directed by Scott Ziehl: *Demon Hunter.*
Movie directed by Shari Springer Berman and Robert Pulcini: *The Nanny Diaries.*
Movies directed by Tim Burton: *Edward Scissorhands* & *Beetlejuice.*
Movie directed by Tony Scott: *True Romance.*

Telephone Numbers:

National Domestic Violence Hotline: 1-800-799-SAFE.

Join the Rebel Moms Reader Community:

www.RebellionPress.com

RebelMoms@RebellionPress.com

www.Facebook.com/RebelMoms

Twitter.com/RebellionPress

www.Myspace.com/RebellionPress

Also, check out Rebellion Press.com for exciting updates on Rebel Moms merchandise like: coffee mugs, t-shirts, bumper-stickers, aprons, calendars featuring your beloved kick-ass moms and quotes from the book, and so much more!

To get free merch, including bumper-stickers and pins to sport on your gear, join our street team at: *StreetTeam@RebellionPress.com*, and help spread the word!

Rebellion Press
Books for Rebels with a Cause

Rebellion Press is a simple start-up whose aim is to ensure authentic voices with global engagement on socially aware and challenging topics get aired, printed, and heard … Books for Rebels with a Cause!

If Rebel Moms rocked your world—check out these upcoming titles!

- *The Chronicles of the Pharaoh's Daughter: Ancient Riddles of Love, Loss, and Rebirth*
- *The Modern Pin-up: Rants of a Working Class Feminist*
- *Twenty One & Female: A Riot Grrrl Memoir in Poetry*
- *The Authorized Biography of Janis Martin: The Female Elvis*
- *Healing Poems for Magdalene*

Please feel free to sign up for our quarterly newsletter, get the latest gossip and news at our home page: RebellionPress.com. If you are a mom-in-need and cannot afford a copy of Rebel Moms contact us and we will make sure we help you get one!

If you loved this book and want more visit us at RebellionPress.com. All book orders placed directly through our website, or mail-order form, we will contribute 10% of net sales after expenses to the Salvation Army. Although, we are not associated with the Salvation Army, nor do we endorse their varied religious takes on life, the fact remains that they are single-handedly one of the world's best managed and far-reaching community care groups that help families, veterans, and moms.

Rebellion Press isn't a non-profit because you are then politically castrated, which is counter-productive to our purpose as a meaningful, and open, creative, activist press. In effect, Rebellion Press is a place to re-launch the honest and diverse voices of struggle, hope, and salvation within a progressive long-view global community engagement, free from bottom-line pressures and censorship. And if we can pay our bills at the same time, great!

When you have something to say, and nowhere to say it, rebel!

Place online orders at:
Rebellion Press.com.

E-books: 9.99

For mail orders:
Please send check, money order, or credit card order. No cash please (for your safety!).

Rebel Moms/Paperback
$31.95 x QTY:
____

The Chronicles of the Pharaoh's Daughter/ Paperback
$14.95 x QTY: ____________

MERCHANDISE TOTAL:
____

Shipping & Handling:
4.95 1st item;
Additional items 1.00 each:
____

TOTAL ENCLOSED:
____

ORDER FORM

PO BOX 180622
DALLAS TX 75218
PHONE:
469-955-0694
EMAIL:
REBELLIONPRESS@
REBELLIONPRESS.COM

Charge: Visa/MasterCard/ American Express/Discover
Card#: ________________________________
Expires: ________________________________
Signature: ______________________________
Name: ________________________________
Address: ______________________________
State, City & Zip: __________________________

- **All orders must be accompanied by payment in U.S. funds. Sorry, no CODs.**
- **Make checks payable to Rebellion Press.**
- **Allow four-to-six weeks for delivery.**